REAL WORLD
GLOBALIZATION

THIRTEENTH EDITION

A READER IN ECONOMICS, BUSINESS, AND POLITICS FROM
DOLLARS&SENSE

EDITED BY ARMAGAN GEZICI, ALEJANDRO REUSS, CHRIS STURR,

AND THE *DOLLARS & SENSE* COLLECTIVE

REAL WORLD GLOBALIZATION, 13th edition

ISBN: 978-1-939402-08-0

Articles 1.4, 3.6, 5.5: Copyright © Center for Economic and Policy Research (CEPR). Reprinted with permission.
Article 1.5: Copyright © Political Economy Research Institute (PERI). Reprinted with permission.
Article 2.6: Copyright © Creators Syndicate. Reprinted with permission.

Published by: Economic Affairs Bureau, Inc. d/b/a *Dollars & Sense*

One Milk Street, Boston, MA 02109

617-447-2177; dollars@dollarsandsense.org.

For order information, contact Economic Affairs Bureau or visit: www.dollarsandsense.org.

Real World Globalization is edited by the *Dollars & Sense* Collective, which also publishes *Dollars & Sense* magazine and the books *Real World Macro, Real World Micro, America Beyond Capitalism, Current Economic Issues, The Economic Crisis Reader, The Economics of the Environment, Grassroots Journalism, Introduction to Political Economy, Labor and the Global Economy, Real World Banking and Finance, Real World Latin America, Real World Labor, Striking a Balance: Work, Family, Life, Unlevel Playing Fields: Understanding Wage Inequality and Discrimination,* and *The Wealth Inequality Reader.*

The 2013 *Dollars & Sense* Collective:
Betsy Aron, Arpita Banerjee, Nancy Banks, Ellen Frank, John Miller, Kevin O'Connell, Larry Peterson, Linda Pinkow, Paul Piwko, Smriti Rao, Alejandro Reuss, Dan Schneider, Bryan Snyder, Chris Sturr, and Jeanne Winner.

Editors of this volume: Armagan Gezici, Alejandro Reuss, Chris Sturr

Cover design: Chris Sturr.
Cover photo: Unisphere. Credit: Uri Baruchin, via Wikimedia Commons (commons.wikimedia.org), Creative Commons Attribution 2.0 Generic license.

Production: Alejandro Reuss and Chris Sturr.
Printed in U.S.A.

CONTENTS

Chapter 1

CRITICAL PERSPECTIVES ON GLOBALIZATION

Article 1.1

FREE MARKETS, INTERNATIONAL COMMERCE, AND ECONOMIC DEVELOPMENT

BY ARTHUR MacEWAN
November 2000

The essence of the neo-liberal position on international commerce is the proposition that economic growth will be most rapid when the movement of goods, services, and capital is unimpeded by government regulations. A simple logic lies at the basis of this free trade position. If, for whatever reasons, countries differ in their abilities to produce various goods, then they can all benefit if each specializes in the production of those items it produces most effectively (i.e., at least cost). They can then trade with one another to obtain the entire range of goods they need. In this manner, each country is using its resources to do what it can do best.

As an illustration of this logic, consider two countries, one with an abundance of good farmland and the other with a good supply of energy resources (hydro power, for example). It seems likely that each of these countries will gain from trade if the first specializes in the production of agricultural goods and the latter specializes in the production of manufactures. Moreover, if the governments impose no constraints on international trade, then this specialization is precisely what will occur. Without constraints on trade, people attempting to produce manufactured goods in the country with abundant good farmland will not be able to do so as cheaply as people in the country with a good supply of energy resources—and vice versa for people attempting to produce agricultural goods in the latter country.

The theory appears to run into trouble if one country produces everything more efficiently than the other. Yet the trouble is only apparent, not real. Under these circumstances, all will gain if each country specializes in the production of those goods where it has a *comparative advantage*. For example, let's assume that the country with abundant farmland produces agricultural goods at half what it costs to produce them in the other country. At the same time, this country with abundant farmland has a workforce with great capacity for industrial labor, and it therefore can produce manufactured goods at one-quarter of what it costs to produce them in the other country. Under these circumstances the country's skilled labor force gives it a greater advantage in the production of manufactures than the advantage that its abundant farmland gives it in the production of agricultural goods. Thus it has a *comparative* advantage in the production of manufactures. Similarly, the second country, even though it is less efficient in the production of both categories of goods, has a *comparative* advantage in the production of agricultural goods. To produce manufactures would cost four times as much in this country as in the other, whereas to produce agricultural goods would only cost twice as much. Consequently, both countries can gain if each specializes where it has a comparative advantage, and they then trade to obtain their full set of needs.

The theory of comparative advantage has played an important role in the history of economics, for it has provided an intellectual rationale for free trade policies. An intellectual rationale has been necessary because, whatever the larger efficacy of the policy, free trade is always costly to groups that have prospered under any prior trade restrictions.

Advocates of the neo-liberal position base their policy prescriptions as much on certain myths about history as on the internal coherence of their theory. They argue that their theory is validated by the history of successful economic growth, both in the longer experience of the relatively advanced economies and in the recent experience of successful growth in newly industrialized countries. They cite, in particular, the history of economic development in the United Kingdom, other countries of Western Europe, and the United States, and the more recent experiences of countries in East Asia.

An examination of these experiences, however, quickly demonstrates that the neo-liberal claims are but crude myths, having only a vague connection to reality.

Historical Experience: A Brief Sketch

Virtually all of our experience with economic development suggests that extensive regulation of foreign commerce by a country's government has been an essential foundation for successful economic growth. In the United Kingdom, perhaps the case most frequently cited to demonstrate the success of free trade, textile producers secured protection from import competition at the end of the 17th century, and high tariffs served British manufacturing well through the era of the country's rise to world economic preeminence. At the beginning of the 19th century, the average tariff rate on manufactures was 50%—high by almost any comparative standard. Later in the century, the United Kingdom did eliminate its tariffs on manufactures, but then it had passed the early stage of development and its industry was well established. Moreover, state support for industry in the United Kingdom came through the creation and maintenance of empire.

Tariff protection also played a large role in the emergence of U.S. industry. The textile industry, which was especially important in the country's economic development, got its start when the hostilities leading up to and through the War of 1812 provided implicit protection by limiting international shipping. After the war, the protection became explicit as a tariff was established. According to the World Bank, the average U.S. tariff on manufactures was 40% in 1820. In the last third of the 19th century, with tariff protection well established at an average of around 30% for most of the 1870 to 1910 period, the United States experienced a great industrial expansion. Only after World War II, when U.S. industry's dominant position in the world economy was secure, did a steady and lasting reduction of tariffs take place.

Countries that achieved their developmental advance at a later historical period were generally characterized by a significantly greater role for the state in the regulation of foreign commerce, both with regard to trade and investment. Japan's experience in joining the ranks of advanced capitalist countries provides the prime example and, insofar as any country has broken out of underdevelopment in more recent decades, South Korea would provide the most important case study. In broad terms, the South Korean experience is very similar to that of Japan. From the early 1960s, the South Korean state followed policies of protecting domestic markets, heavily favoring Korean-owned firms, and using state owned industries to develop national production in certain "strategic" sectors.

One of the important aspects of the South Korean experience is that, in protecting and supporting the development of national industry, the government did not by any means encourage Korean firms to abjure exports and follow an "inward looking" policy. On the contrary, the government used a firm's ability to compete in export markets as a measure of whether or not it was succeeding in becoming more efficient. The South Korean experience shows how economic policy can both regulate foreign commerce but at the same time make sure that national firms reap the many advantages associated with international commerce—including, especially, the transfer of knowledge and technology that come with foreign exposure.

Re-examining the Theory

So the neo-liberal theory of international commerce does not sit very well with historical experience, and this lack of congruence between theory and reality suggests that there are some problems with the theory. Indeed, there are several.

Technology in Economic Growth. The theory of free trade is fundamentally flawed because it fails to take account of the ways in which production itself affects technological change. "Learning-by-doing" is a particularly important form of the phenomenon. In a new activity, initial production may be very costly. Yet as time passes and experience accumulates, the people engaged in the activity learn. They change the way they do things, which is to say that they change the technology. Such an activity might never develop were it forced to compete with already established firms in other countries where the learning-by-doing had already taken place. Yet if the activity were protected from foreign competition during an initial phase in which experience could be accumulated, it could develop and become fully competitive.

Yet protection involves costs. Why should society in general bear the costs of protection in order to assure the development of any particular activity? The answer to these questions lies in the concept of *location specific technological externalities*. Different kinds of production activities tend to bring about different kinds of changes in the overall economic environment. In the 18th and 19th century, for example, manufacturing tended to generate new methods of production and a development of skills that had far reaching technological impacts. In the current era, "high tech" production appears to have similar far reaching impacts. Because the gains from these sorts of changes are not confined to the industry or firm where they originate, they are not reflected in the profits of that industry or firm and will not be taken into account as a basis for investment decisions. These positive technological impacts of particular production activity that do not affect the profits and are outside of—or external to—the purview of the people making decisions about that production are "technological externalities." When positive technological externalities exist for a particular activity, then the value of that activity to society will be greater than the private value. Technological externalities are often "location specific," having their greatest impact within relatively close geographic proximity to the site where they are originally generated—or at least having their principal impact within the same national unit.

The U.S. experience with the cotton textile industry, which I have cited above, provides a particularly good example of the generation of location specific technological externalities. The textile industry emerged in the early decades of the 19th century, prospering especially in the Northeastern part of the United States. Mill towns throughout southern New England became centers of growth. Not only did they create a demand for Southern cotton, but they also created a demand for new machinery, maintenance of old machinery, parts, dyes, *skills*, construction materials, construction machinery, *more skills*, equipment to move the raw materials and the products, parts and maintenance for that equipment, *and still more skills*. As centers of economic activity, innovation, and change, mill towns made a contribution to the economic growth of the United States that went far beyond the value of the textiles they produced.

Trade and Employment. The theory of comparative advantage and arguments for free trade rest on the assumption that full employment exists, or at least that the level of employment is independent of the *pattern* of trade and production. In addition, the theory assumes that when patterns of trade and production change, labor will move from one activity to another instantaneously—or at least sufficiently rapidly so as to cause no great welfare loss or disruption of overall demand. In reality, most low income countries are characterized by very high levels of unemployment and under-employment, the pattern of trade and production does affect employment levels (at least in the short run), and labor markets adjust to change relatively slowly.

An illustration of the problems is provided by experience in many low-income countries when trade restrictions on grain imports are lifted. In Mexico, where the internationalization of grain supply was proceeding apace in the 1980s, even before the establishment of the North American Free Trade Agreement (NAFTA), the replacement of peasant grain production by imports has not worked out so favor-ably. In fact, those parts of agriculture that have expanded in recent years—meat production and vegetable exports, for example—and export manufacturing use rel-atively small amounts of labor. Peasants displaced by the import of inexpensive U.S. and Canadian grain, instead of finding employment in these sectors, swell the ranks of the unemployed or underemployed, often in cities. Consequently, instead of labor resources being used more efficiently under the pressure of import competition, labor resources are wasted.

Free Trade and Large Firms. The neo-liberal argument for free trade is based on the assumption that if government did not intervene and regulate international com-merce, then the economy would operate in a competitive manner with advantageous results... International commerce, however, is often dominated by a relatively small number of very large firms that operate in a monopolistic manner. Competition among them exists, and in some cases is very intense. It is, however, monopolistic competition, not simply the price competition that is assumed in the argument for free trade. The patterns of trade and production engaged in by very large firms are determined as part of their complex global strategies—with results that do not nec-essarily coincide with either the price competition model of the free trade argument or the long run development interests of a particular country.

Large firms are sensitive to price considerations, and they are often quick to re-locate production to take advantage of low cost resources. Yet resource costs, the foundation of the theory of comparative advantage, are only one element in the strategies of large, internationally integrated firms. The Japanese automobile companies, for example, established their leading role in the industry through a strategy of developing linkages to suppliers in close physical proximity to the cen-tral plant. Resource costs were secondary to the issue of strategic control, which had important impacts on technological change and the management of inventory. In the international textile industry, flexibility is a paramount concern in the strat-egy of large firms, and issues of market proximity and control over product supply stand along side of resource costs as factors determining the location of production. Similarly, in the semiconductor production of the electronics industry, many firms (particularly U.S. firms) have followed a strategy of vertical integration. When companies produce semiconductors for use in their own final products, their loca-tion decisions tend to be dominated by concerns about control of the technology and production process; concerns about least-cost siting tend to be secondary. In all of these examples, selected from industries that are both highly international in their operations and in which very large companies play central roles, monopolistic firms employ strategies of control that enhance their own long run profits. There is no reason to expect the outcomes to conform to those envisioned in the theoretical arguments for free trade.

Primary Product Problems. When the argument for free trade was developed in the 19th century, it was a rationalization for the particular character of the international division of labor that emerged so clearly at that time. That division of labor placed a few countries of Europe and North America in the position of specializing in the production and export of manufactured goods, while several other countries—many of which are today's low income countries—specialized in the production and export of primary products. Today, although the international division of labor has changed, there are still many low income countries characterized by primary product specialization.

Primary product specialization is problematic, first of all, because the prices of primary products are highly unstable. Primary products are, by definition, the raw materials that enter at an early stage into the production of other goods. Sugar, for example, is used largely in the manufacture of a great variety of sweets, and the cost of sugar plays a small role in affecting the final price of those sweets. Copper finds its demand as an input to houses, automobiles and other machinery. Like sugar, its cost plays a small role in determining the price of the final products of which it is a part. Grains, vanilla, cocoa, cotton, coffee and several other products fit this pattern. Consequently, the demand for such a product is very insensitive to its price (that is, the demand is very price inelastic). When the supply of a primary product increases—for example, because of good weather and a resulting good crop in some region of the world—prices will decline a great deal as producers compete with one another to unload their surpluses on the very limited market. Conversely, with a small decline in the supply—resulting, perhaps, from bad weather and a resulting crop failure—producers will be able to push up the price a great deal. Even when the average price of a primary product is in some sense "reasonable," price fluctuations create severe cyclical problems that, when the product is important, may disrupt the development of an entire national economy.

An additional problem of specialization in primary products is that in general the average prices of primary products are not "reasonable," in the sense that the demand for the products is subject to long-term downward pressure. Consider, for example, the case of foods—sugar, coffee, cocoa—exported from low income countries to the advanced economies of Europe and North America. As income rises in the advanced countries, the demand for food rises less rapidly. Under these circumstances, insofar as countries rely on primary product exports to the advanced countries for their national income, their national income must grow more slowly than income in those advanced countries.

International Commerce, Income Distribution, and Power

The deregulation of international commerce that is envisioned in the neo-liberal model is largely, if not entirely, a deregulation of business. By removing constraints on the operation of business, it necessarily would give more power to the owners of capital. It would allow business to seek out profits with fewer constraints—on the location of production, on its sources of supply, on characteristics of production, and so on. Power is largely a question of options, and by providing more options to the owners of capital, neo-liberal globalization would give them more power. Most clearly, within a deregulated international environment, owners of capital can resist labor's demands by exercising, or threatening to exercise, their option of shifting production to regions of the world where labor costs are lower. This is not only an option of moving from high wage to low wage countries, from Britain to Sri Lanka, for example. Owners of businesses in Sri Lanka may move, or threaten to move, operations to Britain if productivity is sufficiently higher in the latter country. So the power that business gains vis-a-vis labor by the deregulation of international commerce can be important in low wage and high wage countries.

Power in economic life means primarily an ability to shift more and more of the value produced by society into one's own hands. In this way, neo-liberal globalization is a *de facto* formula for shifting income to the owners of capital, that is, for increasing inequality in the distribution of income. ❏

Excerpted from Chapter 2 of Arthur MacEwan's Neo-Liberalism or Democracy? Economic Strategy, Markets, and Alternatives for the 21st Century, *Zed Books and St. Martin's Press, 1999.*

Article 1.2

INEVITABLE, IRRESISTIBLE, AND IRREVERSIBLE?

Questioning the Conventional Wisdom on Globalization

BY ALEJANDRO REUSS
November 2012

Over the last three decades, the world's capitalist economies have become, by almost any measure, more "globalized." And over the same period, battles have erupted all over the world over the direction and pace of economic change: from the protests against water privatization in Bolivia to the fight against new "intellectual property rights" over plant genomes in India; from the Zapatista uprising in Chiapas, Mexico, to the struggles over oil extraction and environmental ruination in Nigeria.

You would think that, in such a contentious environment, the main story told in newspapers and on television—the "first draft of history"—would have been about a raging battleground of conflicting interests and ideas. That was not, however, the main narrative to come from mainstream commentators. *New York Times* columnist and author Thomas Friedman, one of the United States' most prominent globalization advocates in the 1990s, summed up the mainstream message perfectly in his 1999 bestseller *The Lexus and the Olive Tree*:

"I feel about globalization a lot like I feel about the dawn," one of the book's more famous passages began. "[E]ven if I didn't much care for the dawn, there isn't much I could do about it. I didn't start globalization, I can't stop it—except at a huge cost to human development—and I'm not going to waste my time trying."

Globalization advocates embraced this kind of narrative with triumphalist glee, since it placed them on the winning side of history (and cast their opponents, at best, as fools who were "wasting their time" fighting the inevitable). Even globalization critics, though, often glumly accepted the logic that they were struggling against the tide of history—devoted though they might be to keeping it at bay as long as possible.

A decade or so later, how does this story look? Well, it has become harder to convince people around the world that "globalization" was for the best, and it would be "waste of time" to fight about it. Globalization advocates cast the crises that struck individual countries (Mexico, Argentina, Russia, etc.) as being rooted in the particular failings of those nations' policymakers. They even wrote off a crisis encompassing an entire major world region, East Asia, in the late 1990s as revealing the weaknesses of the region's insufficiently "free market" version of capitalism. Today's crisis, however, has engulfed virtually the entire capitalist world economy. The political tide had already turned—at least on a form of globalization that put giant corporations squarely in command—in much of Latin America, and may be turning today in Europe.

Inevitable, irresistible, and irreversible? Not so fast.

Inevitable? Is Globalization the Unavoidable Result of Technological Change?

Politicians, commentators, and members of the public often think of "globalization" as an inevitable and irreversible fact of life. This view is usually based on the assumption that technological changes—like improvements in transportation and communications—are the driving force behind global economic integration, and that technological change is like a powerful river that people can neither stop nor divert.

The increasing global economic integration of recent years, however, has not resulted from technological change alone. It has also required dramatic changes in the economic policies of individual countries, the signing of new economic treaties between countries, and the creation of new international institutions— all issues over which people have fought bitterly. If globalization would have happened in much the same way without these changes, those who fought for them—governments, political parties, and many large corporations—probably would not have bothered.

No matter how low the cost of shipping goods from, say, Mexico to the United States, for example, U.S.-based companies would not have been able to "offshore" production to Mexico (profitably) had there been high tariffs on imports and exports between Mexico and the United States. It is little wonder, then, that large U.S. companies campaigned so strongly for the passage of the North American Free Trade Agreement (NAFTA), bringing down tariffs and other barriers to trade between the two countries.

Restrictions on foreign investment in low-income countries would, likewise, have stood in the way. Governments in lower-income countries—often spurred by international financial institutions—helped promote offshoring by eliminating such restrictions, establishing assurances of equal treatment for foreign companies as for domestic ones, and offering incentives (such as tax breaks) for foreign investment. The rise of offshoring was not some inevitable consequence of technological change. It required changes in public policy. These policy outcomes, in turn, depended on the balance of political power between different social groups.

Irresistible? Does Globalization Spell Doom for Labor Movements Everywhere?

Some critics argue that the new structure of the global economy—especially the ability of large companies to locate operations virtually anywhere in the world— leads to what they call a "race to the bottom." All countries, they say, are dependent on business investment for economic growth, job creation, tax revenue, and so on. Since businesses can locate their operations anywhere, governments are forced to cut taxes on business, offer subsidies, weaken labor and environmental protections, and adopt other "business friendly" policies to attract investment. Since other countries are doing the same thing, they end up leap-frogging each other "down" as they compete for investment—eventually settling at the lowest taxes, the least regulation, and so on.

Meanwhile, workers all over the world find themselves in a similar race to the bottom. If workers in one place will not accept lower pay, cuts to benefits, and worse working conditions, a company can just close its operations there and establish them elsewhere, generally where the wages are much lower. Employers can just abandon areas where unions have been traditionally strong, and set up in places where they are weak or, preferably, nonexistent. This has led some observers to conclude that globalization is turning unions into dinosaurs—if not quite extinct, then well on their way.

To a great extent, the "race to the bottom" story, about both governments and workers, is shared by globalization advocates and critics. The advocates may celebrate these effects, or at least argue that they are inevitable and so there is no point in trying to stop them. The critics, on the other hand, may argue that some aspects of globalization, in its current form, need to be reversed or changed in order to prevent what they see as these destructive effects.

In recent decades, union size and strength have declined not only in the United States, but in most other high-income countries as well. These trends make the view of unions as an endangered species at least superficially plausible. The reasons for union decline, however, are complex, and not due only to globalization.

Global "outsourcing" or "offshoring" of production, certainly, has contributed to the relative decline of manufacturing employment in the United States, as in other high-income capitalist countries, in recent years. This can hardly, however, explain the entire history of U.S. union decline, since the U.S. unionization rate has been heading downhill since the mid 1950s, long before global sourcing became an important factor.

New opportunities for global sourcing have provided employers with a new trump card when workers try to organize unions: the threat to relocate, especially to low-wage countries. Labor researcher Kate Bronfenbrenner has found that, in more than half of all unionization campaigns, employers threatened to close down the plant, in whole or in part. Since the advent of the North American Free Trade Agreement (NAFTA), Bronfenbrenner reports, this has often taken the form of threatening to move production to Mexico. Actual plant closings in response to unionization, she notes, have also become more frequent since NAFTA went into effect.

To a greater or lesser extent, the effects of such threats are probably felt in all high-income countries. Unionization rates, however, have declined in some countries much more than in others. Take, for example, the trajectories of unionization in the United States and its neighbor to the north, Canada (shown in the graph on p. 11). Until the 1960s, the trends in the two countries were similar. Since then, however, the two have diverged. The U.S. unionization rate has traced a long and nearly uninterrupted path of decline for the last half century. Meanwhile, the Canadian rate, which had gone into decline in the 1950s and 1960s, recovered between the 1970s and 1990s. It has declined again since

UNIONIZATION RATES, CANADA AND UNITED STATES, 1920-2009

Source: Kris Warner, "Protecting Fundamental Labor Rights: Lessons from Canada for the United States," Center for Economic and Policy Research (CEPR), August 2012.

then, but remains nearly three times the U.S. rate (about 30%, compared to just over 10% for the United States).

What explains the difference? Is is certainly not that Canada has insulated itself from the global economy. Canada is a member of NAFTA; its economy is highly integrated with that of the United States, both in terms of trade and investment; its imports and exports, as a percentage of GDP, are actually much *larger* than those of the United States. That is, if anything, the Canadian economy is *more* globalized than the U.S. economy.

A recent report from the Center for Economic and Policy Research (CEPR) attributes the much sharper decline of U.S. unions primarily to differences between the two countries' political and legal environments for labor relations. "[E]mployer opposition to unions—together with relatively weak labor law" in the United States compared to Canada, rather than "structural changes to the economy ... related to globalization or technological progress," the report argues, are the main factors.

The report, in particular, focuses on two differences in labor law: In Canada, workers have the right to form a union once most of the workers in a bargaining unit have signed a union card (a system known as "card check unionization"). This prevents employers from fighting unionization—including by firing union supporters or threatening shut downs, as are common in the United States—during a long, drawn-out period before a union election. Second, Canadian law requires, in the event that a union and employer cannot arrive at a first collective bargaining agreement, for the two parties to enter arbitration. As the CEPR report put it, this "ensure[s] that workers who voted to unionize [are] able to negotiate a contract despite continued employer opposition." In the United States, in contrast, employers often stonewall in initial negotiations, and many new unions never actually get a union contract signed.

Finally, the CEPR report notes the possibility that weaknesses of the U.S. labor movement itself—especially the "lack of focus on organizing new members"—accounts for at least part of the divergence. As economic historian Gerald Friedman notes, the labor movements of some countries have been able to make up for declining employment in their traditional strongholds by organizing workers in growing-employment sectors. The U.S. labor movement—mostly, to be sure, due to the hostile environment for new organizing—has not been able to do so.

The Canadian labor movement also differs from its U.S. counterpart in having created an explicitly labor-oriented political party, the New Democratic Party. (Most western European countries also have strong labor, social democratic, or socialist parties with institutional and historical ties to unions.) In many countries, such parties have played an important role in gaining favorable labor legislation, and more generally blunting attacks on labor by employers and governments.

Global economic forces affecting all countries cannot, by themselves, explain the various patterns of union decline across different capitalist countries (or the patterns would be more similar). The differing political environments in different countries likely explain most of the *differences* in the degree of union decline in different high-income countries.

Irreversible? Is Globalization Here to Stay, Whether We Like It or Not?

Laws that have been passed can, in principle, be repealed. Treaties that have been signed can be undone. Countries that have joined international organizations can withdraw from them. The argument that "globalization" is here to stay, if we are to take it seriously, must therfore depend on arguments about the interests and powers of different groups in society. For example, one might argue that elites in many countries benefit from the new global economic order, and that they are powerful enough to keep it in place, whether other people like it or not. Alternately, one might argue that "globalization" benefits a broad majority of people in most countries—and is here to stay because most people want to keep it.

Even these arguments, however, are only of much use in predicting the near future. Institutions that look unshakable can, under changed conditions, be swept away with surprising speed. In the last couple of centuries, many countries have abolished slavery. In many places, colonies have risen up and gained independence from global empires. People have overthrown dictatorships that, almost until the day of reckoning, appeared all-powerful. An earlier wave of economic "globalization," in the early twentieth century, crashed on the rocks of the Great Depression and the Second World War.

Current events today have already resulted in some reversals of the current wave of "globalization," or at least changes in its forms. In the last two decades, governments across Latin America have turned, to varying degrees, away from the neoliberal policies that had dominated the region since the 1980s. The so-called "pink tide" included governments led by self-described socialist or labor parties, as well as some other political currents, in more than a half dozen Latin American nations (including large countries like Argentina, Brazil, and Venezuela). While differing from each other in many ways, most of these parties shared the view that globalization in its current form increases inequalities within countries, causes economic instability, and reinforces the domination of poorer countries by richer ones (and by large international corporations).

None of these countries has cut off all ties with the world economy—for example, by cutting off all imports and exports (a policy known as "autarky") or rejecting all international investment—but they have tried, in various ways, to use government policy to change their relationships with the world economy. For instance, some of the region's resource-rich countries (Venezuela is a major oil exporter; Bolivia, a major producer of natural gas) have instituted government policies to capture more of the revenue from the sale of these resources, and to use these for domestic development projects.

In Europe, the current global economic crisis may also cause some forms of economic integration to unravel. Of the 27 countries in the European Union (EU), 17 have adopted a common currency, the euro. The lower-income, or "peripheral" countries in the "eurozone" have been especially hard-hit by the current global crisis. Meanwhile, the higher-income countries—especially Germany, which has been able to keep its economy growing and unemployment low through increased exports—have balked at measures proposed to boost demand and employment in the EU as a whole. They have insisted that deeply indebted countries, like Greece, impose painful austerity measures (especially make deep cuts in public spending) to reduce their government deficits and external debts—even though these are likely to exacerbate the fall in incomes and the increase in unemployment.

The eurozone's peripheral countries find themselves in a bind of not having their own independent currencies. This means that they cannot unilaterally decide to stimulate their economies by bringing down interest rates, deliberately raise inflation to reduce their real debt burdens, or, in the last resort, print more money to pay debts as they come due (instead of defaulting). Nor can they allow the values of their currencies to fall in relation to those of other countries, like Germany. This would increase the prices of imports from other countries, while making their exports less expensive, and therefore reduce their trade deficits. At this point, is seems possible that one or more countries will abandon the euro. If there is a domino effect—with one exit followed by another, and another—it is unclear whether the monetary union will survive at all.

Globalization and "Anti-Globalization" Movements

From the onset of large protests against the current wave of "free trade" agreements and the rise of new global economic institutions, critics were labeled as "anti-globalization." Many, however, had no objection to international economic relations, in and of themselves, but rather to the specific economic order that has come with "globalization." For this reason, some describe themselves not as "anti-globalization," but as critics of "globalization from above," "corporate globalization," or "globalization dominated by capital"—a form of global integration that favors the interests of large corporations over other values, like decent wages and conditions of work, or protection of the natural environment.

It is not clear what an alternative form of "globalization"—what some activists call "globalization from below"—would look like. Some imagine new international movements of workers (and others), whose interests have been bound together by the new global economic order, to resist the power of capital.

Others suggest new, international systems of regulation and social welfare protection—the same kinds of protections that were once instituted at the national level, and that the new global mobility of capital has undermined. Some advocates of European unification dreamed of what they called "social Europe," with member countries having to adhere to high minimum standards of labor rights, environmental protection, and social-welfare provision. (That vision has not come to pass.)

Still others argue that no humane social order—at least not one that encompasses the majority of the world's people—will be built on the foundation of a capitalist society. While today's anti-capitalist movements may recognize how workers, indigenous people, and the environment have been battered under the current system of global capitalism, that does not mean they aim for a future of self-contained national economies. Indeed, the historical call to arms of the revolutionary socialist movement—*Workers of all lands, unite!*—was nothing if not global. ❏

Sources: Thomas Friedman, *The Lexus and the Olive Tree* (New York: Farrar, Straus and Giroux, 1999); Kris Warner, *Protecting Fundamental Labor Rights: Lessons from Canada for the United States*, Center for Economic and Policy Research (CEPR), August 2012; World Bank, Data, Imports of Goods and Services (% of GDP), Exports of Goods and Services (% of GDP) (data.worldbank. org); Kate Bronfenbrenner, "Final Report: The Effects of Plant Closing or Threat of Plant Closing on the Right of Workers to Organize," International Publications, Paper 1, 1996 (digitalcommons. ilr.cornell.edu/intl/1); Kate Bronfenbrenner, "We'll close! Plant closings, plant-closing threats, union organizing and NAFTA, *Multinational Monitor, 18*(3), pp. 8-14; Gerald Friedman, "Is Labor Dead?" *International Labor and Working Class History*, Vol. 75, Issue 1, Table One: The Decline of the Labor Movement; Peter Cramton, Morley Gunderson, and Joseph Tracy. "Impacts of Strike Replacement Bans in Canada," *Labor Law Journal* 50 (1999) (works.bepress.com/cramton/84); Gerald Friedman, "Greece and the Eurozone Crisis by the Numbers," *Dollars & Sense*, July/August 2012; Jayati Ghosh, "Europe and the Global Crisis," *Dollars & Sense*, November/December 2012; unionization rate series (in graph) calculated from data in W. Craig Riddell, "Unionization in Canada and the United States: A Tale of Two Countries" in David Card and Richard B. Freeman (eds.), Small Differences That Matter: Labor Markets and Income Maintenance in Canada and the United States, University of Chicago Press (1993) (for 1920-1955, nonagricultural workers only); ICTWSS Database, version 3.0. (uva-aias.net/208) (for 1960-2009, all workers).

Article 1.3

THE RISE OF THE GLOBAL BILLIONAIRES

BY ROBIN BROAD AND JOHN CAVANAGH
October 2013

With the help of *Forbes* magazine, we and colleagues at the Institute for Policy Studies have been tracking the world's billionaires and rising inequality the world over for several decades. Just as a drop of water gives us a clue into the chemical composition of the sea, these billionaires offer fascinating clues into the changing face of global power and inequality.

After our initial gawking at the extravagance of this year's list of 1,426, we looked closer. This list reveals the major power shift in the world today: the decline of the West and the rise of the rest. Gone are the days when U.S. billionaires accounted for over 40 percent of the list, with Western Europe and Japan making up most of the rest. Today, the Asia-Pacific region hosts 386 billionaires, 20 more than all of Europe and Russia combined.

In 2013, of the 9 countries that are home to over 30 billionaires each, only three are traditional "developed" countries: the United States, Germany, and the United Kingdom.

Next in line after the United States, with its 442 billionaires today? China, with 122 billionaires (up from zero billionaires in 1995), and third place goes to Russia with 110. China's billionaires have made money from every possible source. Consider the country's richest man, Zong Qinghou, who made his $11.6 billion through his ownership of the country's largest beverage maker. Russia's lengthy billionaire list is led by men who reaped billions from the country's vast oil, gas and mineral wealth with devastating consequences to the environment.

Germany is fourth on the list with 58 billionaires, followed by India (55), Brazil (46), Turkey (43), Hong Kong (39), and the United Kingdom (38). Yes, Turkey has more billionaires than any other country in Europe save Germany.

Moving beyond these top 9 countries, Taiwan has more billionaires than France. Indonesia has more billionaires than Italy or Spain. South Korea now has more billionaires than Japan or Australia.

This surging list of billionaires is tribute to the growing inequality in almost all nations on earth. The richest man in the world, for example, is Carlos Slim of Mexico—with a net worth of $73 billion, comparable to a whopping 6.2% of Mexico's GDP. The world's third richest person is Spain's retail king, Amancio Ortega, who has accumulated a net worth of $57 billion in a country where over a quarter of the people are now unemployed.

U.S. billionaires still dominate. The United States' 442 billionaires represent 31% of the total number. Bill Gates and Warren Buffett remain numbers 2 and 4, and are household names given the combination of their wealth, their philanthropy, and their use of their power and influence to convince other billionaires to increase their own charitable giving.

But, also among the 12 U.S. billionaires in the top 20 richest people in the world are members of two families who have used their vast wealth and concomitant power to corrupt our politics. Charles and David Koch stand at numbers 6 and 7 in the world; they have drawn on a chunk of their combined $68 billion to fund not only candidates of the far right but also political campaigns against environmental and other regulation. So too do four Waltons stand among the top 20; their combined wealth of $107.3 billion has skyrocketed thanks to Walmart's growing profits as the company pressures cities and states to oppose raising wages to livable levels.

How have the numbers changed over the years? Let's travel back to1995, a time of surging wealth amidst the deregulation under the Clinton administration in the United States, and the widespread pressure around the world to deregulate, liberalize, and privatize markets.

In 1995, *Forbes* tallied 376 billionaires in the world. Of these, 129 (or 34%) were from the United States. The fact that the number of U.S. billionaires rose to 442 over the next 18 years while the percentage of U.S. billionaires fell only from 34% to 31% of the global total is testimony to how the deregulatory and tax-cutting atmosphere in the United States under Clinton and Bush proved so favorable to the super-rich.

Notable over these past 18 years is that the so-called developed world has been eclipsed by the so-called developing world. In 1995, the billionaire powerhouses were the United States (129), Germany (47), and Japan (35). These three countries were home to 56% of the world's billionaires. No other country came close, with France, Hong Kong, and Thailand tied in fourth place, with 12 billionaires each. Russia and China didn't have a single billionaire in 1995, although for Russia, *Forbes* admitted that financial disclosure in that country in the years after the Berlin Wall fell was sketchy. And, in 1995, Brazil had only 8 billionaires and India only 2.

Today, these four countries (Russia, China, Brazil, and India) host 333 of the world's 1,426 billionaires—23% of the total. And, Japan's total number of billionaires has actually fallen in the last 18 years, from 35 to 22.

The figures offer a dramatic snapshot of the relative decline of the United States, Europe and Japan in less than two decades and the stunning rise of Brazil, Russia, India, and China, as well as the rest of Asia. And, they remind us that countries where income was relatives equal twenty years ago, like China and Russia, have rushed into the ranks of the unequal. Across the globe, the rapid rise of billionaires in dozens of countries (again, with Japan as the notable exception) is testimony to how the deregulatory climate of these past two decades sped the rise of the super-rich, while corporations kept workers' wages essentially flat.

Suffice it to say: More equal and more healthy societies require a vastly different approach to public policy. As IPS associate fellow Sam Pizzigati has chronicled, fair taxes created a vast middle class in the United States between the 1940s and 1960s. Such fair tax policies are needed today the world over if the gap between the super-haves and the have-nots is to be narrowed rather than widened. ❏

Article 1.4

INEQUALITY: THE SILLY TALES ECONOMISTS LIKE TO TELL

BY DEAN BAKER

October 2012; Al Jazeera English

There is no serious dispute that the United States has seen a massive increase in inequality over the last three decades. However there is a major dispute over the causes of this rise in inequality.

The explanation most popular in elite and policy circles is that the rise in inequality was simply the natural working of the economy. Their story is that the explosion of information technology and globalization have increased demand for highly-skilled workers while sharply reducing the demand for less-educated workers.

While the first part of this story is at best questionable, the second part should invite ridicule and derision. It doesn't pass the laugh test.

As far as the technology story, yes, information technologies have displaced large amounts of less-skilled labor. So did the technologies that preceded them. There are hundreds of books and articles from the 1950s and 1960s that expressed grave concerns that automation would leave much of the workforce unemployed. Is there evidence that the displacement is taking place more rapidly today than in that era? If so, it is not showing up on our productivity data.

More germane to the issue at hand, unlike the earlier wave of technology, computerization offers the potential for displacing vast amounts of highly skilled labor. Legal research that might have previously required a highly skilled lawyer can now be done by an intelligent college grad and a good search engine. Medical diagnosis and the interpretation of test results that may have previously required a physician, and quite possibly a highly paid specialist, can now be done by technical specialists who may not even have a college education.

There is no reason to believe that current technologies are replacing comparatively more less-educated workers than highly educated workers. The fact that lawyers and doctors largely control how their professions are practiced almost certainly has much more to do with the demand for their services.

If the technology explanation for inequality is weak, the globalization part of the story is positively pernicious. The basic story is that globalization has integrated a huge labor force of billions of workers in developing countries into the world economy. These workers are able to fill many of the jobs that used to provide middle class living standards to workers in the United States and will accept a fraction of the wage. This makes many formerly middle class jobs uncompetitive in the world economy given current wages and currency values.

This part of the story is true. The part that our elite leave out is that there are tens of millions of bright and highly educated workers in the developing world who could fill most of the top paying jobs in the US economy: doctors, lawyers, accountants, etc. These workers are also willing to work for a small fraction of the wages of their US counterparts since they come from poor countries with much lower standards of living.

The reason why the manufacturing workers, construction workers, and restaurant workers lose their jobs to low-paid workers from the developing world, and doctors and lawyers don't, is that doctors and lawyers use their political power to limit the extent to which they are exposed to competition from their low-paid counterparts in the developing world. Our trade policy has been explicitly designed to remove barriers that prevent General Electric and other companies from moving their manufacturing operations to Mexico, China or other developing countries. By contrast, many of the barriers that make it difficult for foreign professionals to work in the United States have actually been strengthened in the last two decades.

If economics was an honest profession, economists would focus their efforts on documenting the waste associated with protectionist barriers for professionals. They devoted endless research studies to estimating the cost to consumers of tariffs on products like shoes and tires. It speaks to the incredible corruption of the economics profession that there are not hundreds of studies showing the loss to consumers from the barriers to trade in physicians' services. If trade could bring down the wages of physicians in the United States just to European levels, it would save consumers close to $100 billion a year.

But economists are not rewarded for studying the economy. That is why almost everyone in the profession missed the $8 trillion housing bubble, the collapse of which stands to cost the country more than $7 trillion in lost output according to the Congressional Budget Office (that comes to around $60,000 per household).

Few if any economists lost their 6-figure paychecks for this disastrous mistake. But most economists are not paid for knowing about the economy. They are paid for telling stories that justify giving more money to rich people. Hence we can look forward to many more people telling us that all the money going to the rich was just the natural workings of the economy. When it comes to all the government rules and regulations that shifted income upward, they just don't know what you're talking about. ❏

Article 1.5

FINANCIALIZATION AND THE WORLD ECONOMY
An Interview with Gerald Epstein

October 2005; Political Economy Reserach Institute

Gerald A. Epstein, the co-director of the Political Economy Research Insitute (PERI) at the University of Massachusetts, gave this interview upon the publication of Financialization and the World Economy *(Edward Elgar Publishing, 2005). Economist and then-PERI Research Assistant Adam Hersh conducted the interview. —Eds.*

Adam Hersh: What is "financialization"? What does the term mean and where does it come from?

Gerald Epstein: By "financialization," we mean the increasing importance of financial markets, financial motives, and financial actors in the operations of the economy. This is only one of many different meanings that scholars ascribe to this relatively new term. The origins of the term are obscure, though it is being used with increasing frequency because of its obvious heightened relevance in modern capitalist economies.

AH: What evidence do we see that financialization is increasing? How much is financialization the result of innate market forces versus explicit political or policy choices?

GE: The process of financialization can be seen in a great number of ways: dramatically increased ratios of credit to gross domestic product (GDP) in most developed and semi-industrialized economies; the increased quantity of trading in financial assets such as foreign currency exchange, where trading volumes are now above $1 trillion a day; increased shares of income going to holders of financial assets and those owning financial firms in many developed countries; and the increased importance of financial motives in the governance of non-financial corporations.

   We can't really know definitively how much financialization results, respectively, from organic market processes or politics and policy. Policy definitely has been very permissive of, and indeed, encouraging of financialization. But there are important technological and other structural factors that have encouraged it as well, including the development of communication and computer technology. This is certainly an important question on the agenda for future research.

AH: Why does it matter whether private growth is driven by profits in the financial sector rather than in other sectors of the economy (for example manufacturing, services, etc.)? Isn't economic growth just economic growth?

GE: This is a very important question, and one which is at the center of the controversies over financialization. We find that financialization is associated with substantial economic costs: increased income inequality; increased shares of GDP going to owners of financial assets, who tend to be among the very rich in most countries; and the short-term orientation of financial investors who, through their power over corporate decision making, tend to undermine long term investment that can be so important for healthy economic development, to name a few.

AH: What are some consequences of increasing financialization?

GE: One of the important consequences is the impact of financialization on financial crises in so-called "emerging market" developing countries. In Argentina, Turkey, Brazil and South Korea—among many other countries—financialization contributed to massive dislocations that undermined living standards. Excessive capital inflows and then rapid capital outflows, encouraged by both internal and external financial liberalization, lead to unsustainable debt in some cases, and "sudden stops" of lending that left companies and governments in highly vulnerable positions.

For example, economists James Crotty and Kang-Kook Lee show that South Korea had a huge savings rate, and highly successful industrialization strategy, yet decided to liberalize their financial markets and to make themselves vulnerable to speculative capital flows. (See "The Causes and Consequences of Neoliberal Restructuring in Post-Crisis Korea," *Financialization and the World Economy* (Edward Elgar, 2005).) They then were confronted with a massive crisis and such intrusive structural adjustment demands by the International Monetary Fund (IMF) that even conservative economist and former Reagan economic adviser Martin Feldstein complained. Similarly, financial liberalization in Argentina and Turkey left those governments with insufficient tools to stabilize their economies and financial crises ensued. In the case of Brazil, as shown by economist Nelson Barbosa-Filho, inflows and outflows of international capital, rather than internal decisions about real investment, were the driving forces of the ups and downs of economic growth. (See "International Liquidity and Growth Fluctuations in Brazil," *Financialization and the World Economy*.)

AH: How is the phenomenon of financialization changing how regular people experience the economy? Doesn't it just mean people will have more opportunities to increase their wealth through financial investment?

GE: Yes, to some degree. But at the macro level, because of instabilities and distorted incentives, financialization can undermine the overall growth and development of the economy so that in the end, the real opportunities for investors and workers—except, perhaps for the very wealthiest members of society—are diminished.

AH: What effect—if any—did financialization have for the late 1990s stock market bubble? What about the housing market bubble?

GE: As Robert Parenteau describes, financialization had a huge amount to do with the stock market bubble. (See "The Late 1990s' U.S. Bubble: Financialization in the Extreme," *Financialization and the World Economy*.) The search for financial profits, "short-termism" of investors, abundant access to credit, the distorted information provided by investment houses and brokers—who were sometimes in corrupt relationships with firms—and the desperate need for workers and middle-class citizens to find vehicles for saving because their defined-benefit pension plans from business and government were being eroded. All these factors are really not only affected by financialization but, in fact, constitute financialization as it has evolved in the U.S. economy.

AH: Financial markets play a central economic role in aggregating information and coordinating allocation of resources in the economy. It seems financialization would make this process easier and more efficient, wouldn't it?

GE: Certainly, well-functioning financial markets are crucial to a modern economy. But what economies primarily need are financial institutions that can mobilize long-term, patient capital and allocate it to dynamic and productive sectors of the economy, institutions that can help workers and investors save for important needs, such as education, housing and retirement, and that can diversify risks. Instead, financialization, as it has evolved in the United States, has contributed to short-termism and impatient capital, diversion of resources to speculative investments, and increases in risks for most workers and middle-class investors. The same forces are at work in recent "emerging markets."

AH: Can the costs of financialization be mitigated or avoided? What would it take to achieve this?

GE: This is a very complex question. In some areas our knowledge is still too limited to have many definitive answers. Also, the problems connected with financialization operate at many levels: global, regional, national and local. Global problems probably require global solutions. But for regional and national problems, it is unlikely that a "one-size-fits-all" approach to managing or reversing financialization will work. At the global level—at a minimum—the IMF and other institutions need to stop peddling advice, or (worse) imposing through structural adjustment programs, that developing countries adopt the policies and financial structures that have promoted so much destructive financialization: financial liberalization, the elimination of capital controls, the adoption of inflation targeting by central banks.

More generally, these organizations should allow countries the space to find policy solutions drawn from real success stories and their own institutional conditions for themselves. At the regional and local levels, this policy space must be used to embed financial structures into the industrial, agricultural, and social sectors of the economy to provide long-term capital and widespread financial services. In the developed countries, like the United States, governance of financial and non-financial institutions is a crucial issue. The old financial regulatory system developed under the New Deal has been destroyed, but nothing has been put in its place. There are examples in the book: securities transactions taxes; more regulation of derivatives; capital management policies. But much more is needed. Clearly, there is a pressing need for more research analyzing financialization and developing solutions to the problems financialization creates. ❑

Chapter 2

CORPORATE POWER AND THE GLOBAL ECONOMY

Article 2.1

MONOPOLY CAPITAL AND GLOBAL COMPETITION

BY ARTHUR MacEWAN
September/October 2011

> Dear Dr. Dollar:
> *Is the concept of monopoly capital relevant today, considering such things as global competition?*
> —Paul Tracy, Oceanside, Calif.

In 1960, the largest 100 firms on *Fortune* magazine's "annual ranking of America's largest corporations" accounted for 15% of corporate profits and had revenues that were 24% as large as GDP. By the early 2000s, each of these figures had roughly doubled: the top 100 firms accounted for about 30% of corporate profits and their revenues were over 40% as large as GDP.*

The banking industry is a prime example of what has been going on: In 2007 the top ten banks were holding over 50% of industry assets, compared with about 25% in 1985.

If by "monopoly capital" we mean that a relatively small number of huge firms play a disproportionately large role in our economic lives, then monopoly capital is a relevant concept today, even more so than a few decades ago.

---

* The profits of the top 100 firms (ranked by revenue) were quite low in 2010, back near the same 15% of total profits as in 1960, because of huge losses connected to the financial crisis incurred by some of the largest firms. Fannie Mae, Freddie Mac, and AIG accounted for combined losses of over $100 billion. Also, the revenues of all firms are not the same as GDP; much of the former is sales of intermediate products, but only sales of final products are included in GDP. Thus, the largest firms' revenues, while 40% as large as GDP, do not constitute 40% of GDP.

Global competition has certainly played a role in reshaping aspects of the economy, but it has not altered the importance of very large firms. Even while, for example, Toyota and Honda have gained a substantial share of the U.S. and world auto markets, this does not change the fact that a small number of firms dominate the U.S. and world markets. Moreover, much of the rise in imports, which looks like competition, is not competition for the large U.S. firms themselves. General Motors, for example, has established parts suppliers in Mexico, allowing the company to pay lower wages and hire fewer workers in the states. And Walmart, Target, and other large retailers obtain low-cost goods from subcontractors in China and elsewhere.

Economics textbooks tell us that in markets dominated by a few large firms, prices will be higher than would otherwise be the case. This has generally been true of the auto industry. Also, this appears to be the case in pharmaceuticals, telecommunications, and several other industries.

Walmart and other "big box" stores, however, often do compete by offering very low prices. They are monopsonistic (few buyers) as well as monopolistic (few sellers). They use their power to force down both their payments to suppliers and the wages of their workers. In either case—high prices or low prices—large firms are exercising their market power to shift income to themselves from the rest of us.

Beyond their operation within markets, the very large firms shift income to themselves by shaping markets. Advertising is important in this regard, including, for example, the way pharmaceutical firms effectively create "needs" in pushing their products. Then there is the power of large firms in the political sphere. General Electric, for example, maintains huge legal and lobbying departments that are able to affect and use tax laws to reduce the firm's tax liability to virtually nothing. Or consider the success of the large banks in shaping (or eliminating) financial regulation, or the accomplishments of the huge oil companies and the military contractors that establish government policies, sometimes as direct subsidies, and thus raise their profits. And the list goes on.

None of this is to say that everything was fine in earlier decades when large firms were less dominant. Yet, as monopoly capital has become more entrenched, it has generated increasingly negative outcomes for the rest of us. Most obvious are the stagnant wages and rising income inequality of recent years. The power of the large firms (e.g., Walmart) to hold down wages is an important part of the story. Then there is the current crisis of the U.S. economy—directly a result of the way the very large financial firms were able to shape their industry (deregulation). Large firms in general have been prime movers over recent decades in generating deregulation and the free-market ideology that supports deregulation.

So, yes, monopoly capital is still quite relevant. Globalization does make differences in our lives, but globalization has in large part been constructed under the influence and in the interest of the very large firms. In many ways globalization makes the concept of monopoly capital even more relevant. ❏

Article 2.2

LIBOR LIABILITY

A scandal unfolds that has already affected millions of people.

BY MAX FRAAD WOLFF
July/August 2012

The summer of 2012 is heating up for leading financial firms. HSBC is poised to settle money-laundering charges. JPMorgan is struggling to put billions of bad trade losses behind it. Wells Fargo is settling on mortgage discrimination charges. And now, a growing scandal surrounding leading banks' alleged manipulation of key reference interest rates has claimed large fines, senior executives' careers, and the attention of both regulators and the public.

The London InterBank Offered Rates, known as "Libor," are the interest rates at which banks borrow funds from each other. Each day, the British Bankers' Association (BBA) compiles and reports 150 Libor rates (for ten different currencies and fifteen different "maturities," or borrowing terms) with the business-data provider Thomson Reuters. Libor rates are the most widely cited and influential rates for setting adjustable interest rates on trillions of dollars in loans and derivative contracts.

Since 1986, the BBA has arranged to have between eight and sixteen leading banks report the interest rates at which they can borrow in different currencies. Different committees comprised of multiple leading banks set the rates. The names under investigation read like a roll call of banks that received trillions in assistance from governments during the financial crisis.

Libor rates are set in a self-regulatory process arranged, executed, and policed by private entities (the member banks, the BBA, and Thompson Reuters). Thus, Libor reports are a service by and for financial firms. However, they have impact across the global economy: Libor rates are seen as a measure of bank health and financial-market health, and they affect values and interest rates of hundreds of trillions of dollars worth of financial products and loans—including credit cards, student loans, adjustable-rate mortgage, and small-business loans. When Libor rates rise, individuals, governments, and firms pay more to borrow. When rates fall, they pay less.

Libor rates are created by collecting and averaging individual bank rates from multiple institutions, so each individual bank has only a marginal influence on reported rates. However, investigators have found allegations of traders working to coordinate misreporting and fix interest rates. Emails and calls between traders suggest that some worked to guide reported rates up or down across several years. Although regulators in the United States, the UK, and beyond have long been aware of irregularities in Libor rate reporting, authorities have been slow to take action, and the public is still waiting for details. Reports that regulators encouraged underreporting Libor rates to give an appearance of calm and stability in interbank lending markets during the crisis do not boost public confidence in financial markets.

As of now, authorities in the U.S. and British governments as well as across Asia and Europe are investigating the scandal. Several jurisdictions will bring charges and receive settlements in the many millions of dollars. Barclays has already paid over $450 million and replaced its three most senior executives, and other involved banks are scrambling to reach settlements and avoid serious penalties.

But the Libor scandal is a developing story, with much more still to be told. It appears that separately and together, many of the world's leading banks provided inaccurate and misleading information, possibly in illegal concert, and reported incorrect rates. Sometimes this was done to affect the prices of financial products and make ill-gotten gains. On other occasions, particularly in the depths of the financial crisis in 2008-2009, false rates were reported to hide the high rates and low trust among banks.

Since rates were both under- and over-reported, it's difficult to determine the net effect of misreporting. Because Libor literally sets interest rate benchmarks, we can't be sure what the rates would have been without the tampering. But it's clear that regulators, clients, states, cities, and citizens were misled, affecting millions of people and trillions of dollars.

As clients sue and regulators investigate, investor confidence will continue to suffer. The scandal couldn't have come at a worse time for the global economy. Whatever your views on finance and your interest level in the Libor scandal, if you borrow or invest money, this saga has been a part of your life for at least four years. Libor rate-fixing will be added to the swirl of public anger about mortgage securities, ratings agencies, bad trades, and predatory lending. Accumulating incidents suggest our flawed regulatory framework and dependence on large financial institutions remain painful vulnerabilities in the global economic system. ❑

Article 2.3

SYNERGY IN SECURITY
The Rise of the National Security Complex

BY TOM BARRY
March/April 2010

In his January 17, 1961 farewell address, President Dwight D. Eisenhower cautioned: "In the councils of government, we must guard against the acquisition of unwarranted influence, whether sought or unsought, by the military-industrial complex."

Five decades later, this complex, which Eisenhower defined as the "conjunction of an immense military establishment and a large arms industry," is no longer new. And while Eisenhower's warning is still pertinent, the scale, scope, and substance of the complex have changed in alarming ways. It has morphed into a new type of public-private partnership—one that spans military, intelligence, and homeland-security contracting, and might be better called a "national security complex."

Not counting the supplemental authorizations for the wars in Iraq and Afghanistan, current levels of military spending are, adjusting for inflation, about 45% higher than the military budget when Eisenhower left office. Including the Iraq and Afghanistan war budgets, military spending stands about 30% higher, adjusted for inflation, than any of the post-WWII highpoints—Korea, Vietnam, and the Reagan build-up in the 1980s. Private military contracting, which constituted about half of the Pentagon's spending in the 1960s, currently absorbs about 70% of the Department of Defense (DoD) budget. No longer centered exclusively in the Pentagon, outsourcing to private contractors now extends to all aspects of government. But since 2001, the major surge in federal outsourcing has occurred in the "intelligence community" and in the new Department of Homeland Security (DHS).

Since Sept. 11, 2001, a vastly broadened government-industry complex has emerged—one that brings together all aspects of national security. Several interrelated trends are responsible for its formation and explosive growth: 1) the dramatic growth in government outsourcing since the early 1990s, and particularly since the beginning of the George W. Bush administration, 2) the post-Sept. 11 focus on homeland security, 3) the wars in Iraq and Afghanistan, 4) the Bush-era surge in intelligence budget and intelligence contracts, and 5) the cross-agency focus on information and communications technology.

The term "military-industrial complex" no longer adequately describes the multi-headed monster that has emerged in our times. The industrial (that is, big business) part of the military-industrial complex has become ever more deeply integrated into government—no longer simply providing arms but also increasingly offering their services on the fronts of war and deep inside the halls of government—commissioned to carry out the very missions of the DoD, DHS, and intelligence agencies. In the national security complex, it is ever more difficult to determine what is private sector and what is public sector—and whose interests are being served.

Different Departments, Same Companies

In 2008, the federal government handed out contracts to the private sector totaling $525.5 billion—up from $209 billion in 2000. That's about a quarter of the entire federal budget. The DoD alone accounts for about $390 billion, or nearly three-quarters of total federal contracts.

The living symbol of the new national security complex is Lockheed Martin, whose slogan is "We Never Forget Who We're Working For." That's the U.S. government—sales to which account for more than 80% of the company's revenues, with most of the balance coming from international weapons sales and other security contracts facilitated by Washington. In addition to its sales of military hardware, Lockheed is the government's top provider of IT services and systems integration (see Table 1).

Whether it is military operations, interrogations, intelligence gathering, or homeland security, the country's "national security" apparatus is largely in the same hands. Various components of the U.S. national-security state are divvied up among different federal bureaucracies. But increasingly, the main components are finding a common home within corporate America. Corporations such as Lockheed Martin, Boeing, L-3 Communications, and Northrop Grumman have the entire business—military, intelligence, and "homeland security"—covered.

Lockheed Martin, Northrop Grumman, and Boeing led the top ten military contractors in 2008 (see Table 2).

The 2003 creation of the Department of Homeland Security has helped spawn an explosion of new companies, and new divisions of existing companies, providing "homeland security" products and services. Before President Bush created DHS in

TABLE 1: TOP TEN GOVERNMENT CONTRACTORS, 2008	
Lockheed Martin	$34,785,141,737
Boeing	$23,784,593,887
Northrop Grumman	$18,177,546,625
BAE Systems	$16,137,793,437
General Dynamics	$15,992,669,588
Raytheon	$14,663,608,137
United Technologies	$8,927,106,729
L-3 Communications	$7,597,574,871
KBR	$5,995,025,351
SAIC	$5,945,115,101

Source: USAGovernmentSpending.com

the wake of Sept. 11, the agencies that would be merged into the new department did very little outsourcing. From less than 1% of federal contracts (as a total dollar amount) in 2000, outsourcing by DHS has quadrupled as a portion of federal contracting from 2003 to 2009.

Although DHS contracts with scores of new companies, its top contractors are all leading military contractors that have established "homeland security" divisions and subsidiaries.

The top ten DHS contractors in 2008 were Lockheed Martin, Northrop Grumman, IBM, L-3 Communications, Unisys, SAIC, Boeing, Booz Allen Hamilton, General Electric, and Accenture, all leading military contractors. Other major military contractors among the top 25 DHS contractors include General Dynamics, Fluor, and Computer Sciences Corp (see Table 3).

There is no public list of corporations that contract for U.S. intelligence agencies. But based on company press releases and filings with the Securities and Exchange Commission, Tim Shorrock concludes in his new book *Spies for Hire* that the top five intelligence contractors are probably Lockheed Martin, Northrop Grumman, SAIC, General Dynamics, and L-3 Communications. Other major contractors include Booz Allen Hamilton, CACI International, DRS Technologies, and ManTech International, also leading military contractors.

Within the past eight years—since Sept. 11, 2001—the intelligence budget has soared, rising from an estimated $30 billion in 2000 to an estimated $66.5 billion today. Intelligence agencies have channeled most of the new funding to private contractors, both major companies like CACI and thousands of individual contractors. Private contracts now account for about 70% of the intelligence budget. Intelligence community sources told the *Washington Post* that private contractors constituted

TABLE 2: TOP TEN DoD CONTRACTORS, 2008	
Lockheed Martin	$29,363,894,334
Northrop Grumman	$23,436,442,251
Boeing	$21,838,400,709
BAE Systems	$16,227,370,773
Raytheon	$13,593,610,345
General Dynamics	$13,490,652,077
United Technologies	$8,283,275,612
L-3 Communications	$6,675,712,135
KBR	$5,997,147,425
Navistar Int'l	$4,761,740,206

Source: USAGovernmentSpending.com

"a significant majority" of analysts working at the new National Counterterroism Center, which provides the White House with terrorism intelligence.

The major military contractors are now moving their headquarters from their production centers, often in California and Texas, to the Washington Beltway in pursuit of more intelligence, military, and homeland security contracts. The gleaming Beltway office buildings of the security corporations are now the most visible symbol of this national security complex.

Boots on the Ground, Computers in Cubicles

Another feature of this evolving, ever-expanding complex is that all the U.S. government departments involved in national security—DoD, State Department, DHS, and intelligence—are outsourcing the boots-on-the-ground components of their missions through the use of private security and military provider firms. Companies such as ArmourGroup (which includes Wackhenhut), DynCorp, MPRI, and Xe (formerly Blackwater Worldwide) have injected the private sector directly into the public sector through their work as interrogators, military trainers, prison guards, intelligence agents, and war-fighters.

Five dozen of these security contractors have organized themselves into the International Peace Operations Association (IPOA). After Blackwater came under worldwide scrutiny for its massacre of unarmed Iraqis in central Baghdad on Sept. 17, 2007, the firm left IPOA, whose code of conduct for "peacekeeping" operations it

TABLE 3: TOP TEN HOMELAND SECURITY DEPARTMENT CONTRACTORS, 2008	
Boeing	$591,048,628
IBM	$486,219,723
Accenture Ltd	$392,700,978
General Dynamics	$391,294,040
Integrated Coast Guard Systems (Northrop Grumman/ Lockheed Martin joint venture)	$386,344,211
Unisys	$367,722,670
SAIC	$362,403,533
L-3 Communications	$329,431,785
Lockheed Martin	$294,412,822
Booz Allen Hamilton	$242,899,612

Source: USAGovernmentSpending.com

had flagrantly ignored. Blackwater created a new association of private military contractors called Global Peace and Security Operations—conveniently without any potentially embarrassing code of conduct.

Private contractors are not only on the frontlines of war and clandestine operations, but have also penetrated the national security bureaucracy itself. Reacting to a March 2008 GAO report on conflicts of interest within the Pentagon, Frida Berrigan of the New America Foundation's Arms and Security Initiative observed that alarming numbers of "cubicle mercenaries" are now working within federal bureaucracies as administrators, contract managers, intelligence analysts, and cybersecurity chiefs. No longer does the "large arms industry" that Eisenhower warned about just peddle goods like weapons and missiles, it also sells itself through its services.

Common Dominators of the New Complex: Information and Security

Private contractors are also in control of the core of the complex's information and intelligence systems. Information and communications technology is the fastest-growing sector in government contracting. The DHS's expanding involvement in cybersecurity, information systems, and electronic identification programs, for example, is adding billions of dollars annually to the national security boom.

Lockheed Martin led the ranks of information technology (IT) contractors in 2008, followed by Boeing and Northrop Grumman. Although IT contracts are expanding rapidly, there are few new entrants to the list of top IT providers to the government. Among the top 100 IT contractors, there were just twelve new entrants, as traditional military giants dominated the list (see Table 4).

TABLE 4: TOP TEN FEDERAL IT AND SYSTEMS INTEGRATION CONTRACTORS, 2009	
Lockheed Martin	$14,983,515,367
Boeing	$10,838,231,984
Northrop Grumman	$9,947,316,207
General Dynamics	$ 6,066,178,545
Raytheon	$ 5,942,575,316
KBR	$5,467,721,429
SAIC	$4,811,194,880
L-3 Communications	$4,236,653,555
Computer Sciences	$3,435,767,906
Booz Allen Hamilton	$2,779,421,015

Source: Washington Technology, Eagle Eye Publishers Inc., and Houlihan Lokey

One of the largest sources of federal contracting at DHS has been the EAGLE (Enterprise Acquisition Gateway for Leading Edge Solutions) IT program, which awarded $8.2 billion in contracts in the past three years. Among the leading contractors are CACI, Booz Allen Hamilton, Lockheed Martin, SAIC, Northrop Grumman, General Dynamics, and BAE Systems—all major military contractors. Most of the EAGLE IT bonanza is in the form of "indefinite-delivery, indefinite quantity contracts" that provide generous operating room for IT firms to determine their own solutions to DHS' vast IT and cybersecurity requirements.

The major military corporations have quickly formed new branches to focus on these new opportunities outside of their traditional core contracts with the Pentagon. This year, for example, Northrop Grumman created a new Information Systems division to seek military, homeland security, and intelligence IT contracts. Recognizing the interest in the Obama administration in cyber-security and information war, corporations such as Booz Allen Hamilton and Hewlett-Packard, among others, have created new cybersecurity divisions or subsidiaries. Similarly, the new administration's focus on transnational disease has led military companies such as General Dynamics to acquire medical subsidiaries.

Revolving-Door Security Consultants

Another manifestation of the new national security complex is the rise of a new series of consulting agencies that act as an interface between government and their clients. That's an easy connection for such companies as the Chertoff Group, Ridge Global, and RiceHadley Group, since all their principals recently left government, where they had presided over the unprecedented wave of outsourcing.

Two of these national security agencies are headed by the DHS's first two secretaries, Michael Chertoff and Tom Ridge, while the newest group brings together Condoleezza Rice and Stephen Hadley, who only a year ago were serving as secretary of state and national security adviser, respectively.

When announcing his group's formation, Chertoff boasted, "Our principals have worked closely together for years, as leaders of the Department of Defense, the Department of Homeland Security, the Department of Justice, the National Security Agency and the CIA." Indeed, a leading member of this new group is former CIA director Michael Hayden (2005-2009), who also directed the National Security Agency (1999-2005). Others include former DHS deputy Paul Schneider (who was head of acquisitions for NSA and the U.S. Navy prior to his position at DHS); Admiral Jay Cohen (Ret.), who was DHS director of science and technology and previously the Navy's technology chief; and Charlie Allen, who was the intelligence chief at DHS and, according to Michael Chertoff, "pretty much head of everything you could be for the CIA."

The Chertoff Group has now hooked up with Blue Star Capital, a transatlantic investment company specializing in mergers and acquisitions in the security business. In its announcement of the new partnership, Blue Star emphasized their joint interest in "generating opportunities" across the national security spectrum—"in the homeland security, defense, and intelligence markets."

Chertoff himself applauded the value of the merger: "I believe there are many areas of opportunity within the Homeland Security, Intelligence and Defense sectors where the synergies between Blue Star and the Chertoff Group will provide real value."

Taking Back Security

The "unwarranted influence" that concerned Eisenhower during the Cold War now pervades national politics and is rarely questioned. Nor has there been any evaluation of the achievements of the increasingly privatized national security complex. In his 2010 State of the Union address, President Obama talked about the need for fiscal restraint, but exempted "national security" from the planned spending freeze. Despite manifold evidence of vast waste and scandalous profiteering in the security apparatus—to say nothing of "unnecessary wars"—the president didn't see fit to scale back the security agencies. By failing to do so, he has all but guaranteed that the outsourcing bonanza will continue. With "national security" off limits for budget cuts, Obama signaled that safeguarding the nation against the "unwarranted influence" and "rise of misplaced power" will not be priorities for this administration.

As major corporations such as Lockheed Martin and security consulting agencies such as the Chertoff Group extend their corporate tentacles into the intelligence, military, and homeland security terrains, the greater threat they pose. The corporate penetration of all the government's information-gathering, communications, intelligence, and data systems undermines democratic governance. The new corporate domination of data-mining, communications, and cybersecurity systems—with little or no government oversight —threatens individual liberty and privacy. This also creates a powerful vested interest in a large and growing "national security" apparatus—and one that is deeply integrated with the top echelons of the intelligence agencies, military, and other parts of this secretive state-within-the-state.

In the end, it's not the contractors that are the central problem with the national security complex—it's the outsourcers, that is, the elected politicians and the government administrators they appoint or confirm. The contractors are working to maximize profits, and are answerable mainly to company shareholders. The outsourcers, however, are ultimately answerable, at least in principle, to the public. What is at stake is who really controls public policy—a democratically accountable government, or an unaccountable fusion of governmental and corporate power. ❏

Sources: Center for Defense Information, "Military Budgets 1946-2009,"; Center for Arms Control and NonProliferation, "2008-2009 U.S. Defense Spending Highest Since WWII," Feb. 20, 2008; FedSpending, org, a project of OMB Watch; USASpending.gov; Tim Shorrock, *New Spies for Hire: The Secret World of Intelligence Outsourcing*, 2008; FY2009 Intelligence Budget, GlobalSecurity.org; F.J. Hillhouse, "Outsourcing Intelligence," *The Nation*, July 24, 2007; Walter Pincus, "Lawmakers Want More Data on Contracting Out Intelligence," *Washington Post*, May 7,

2006: David Horowitz, ed., *Corporations and the Cold War*, 1969; GAO, "Defense Contracting: Army Case Study Delineates Concerns with Use of Contractors as Contract Specialists," March 2008; Frida Berrigan, "Military Industrial Complex 2.0," TruthOut, Sept. 14, 2008; "2009 Top 100," Washington Technology; DHS, Enterprise Solutions Office, EAGLE contracts; *Global Homeland Security 2009-2019*, VisionGain, June 23, 2009; Chertoff Group web pages, chertoffgroup.com; Homeland Security & Defense Business Council web pages, homelandcouncil. org; Chalmers Johnson, "Military Industrial Complex: It's Much Later Than You Think," AntiWar. com, July 28, 2008; Allison Stanger, *One Nation Under Contract: The Outsourcing of American Power and the Future of Foreign Policy* (Yale University Press, 2009); Project on Government Oversight (POGO); Deborah Avant, *The Market for Force: The Consequences of Privatizing Security* (Cambridge University Press, 2005); Center for Public Integrity, "Making a Killing: The Business of War," 2002, "The Shadow Pentagon," 2004; Peter Singer, *Corporate Warriors* (Cornell University Press, 2003).

Article 2.4

THE OTHER COLOMBIA
The Economics and Politics of Depropriation

BY PATRICIA M. RODRIGUEZ
November/December 2010

I t has rained for days, and the swampy ocean waters that surround this community of displaced fishermen in northern Colombia rise at their own whim, flooding people's houses and making life even harder than usual. Yet most of the families living in this tiny makeshift encampment in Boca de Aracataca in the Magdalena province of Colombia have gathered under a tarp to eloquently tell a group of activists from Witness for Peace, a Washington-based social justice organization, about their problems. "[The foreign companies] kicked us out of our land. We do not have water, electricity, food, nor any help from the government... we need to be respected, we need to be treated as people, and not as animals," says Alicia Camargo, who has been displaced three times already, once very violently, along with family and neighbors.

As it turns out, the source of the problems in this community—and others nearby—is the presence of multinational corporations. In this particular case, it involves a new port expansion project along the Caribbean coast near the otherwise-idyllic city of Santa Marta. The construction of this mega-port has been funded by foreign coal companies that have operated practically unrestrictedly in Colombia for nearly 15 years. When it is finished in 2013, the port will allow U.S.-based company Drummond and Swiss-based Glencore to ship an extra 30 to 60 million tons of coal per year to global markets, in addition to the nearly 69 million tons they already export. The Colombian government allegedly receives a royalty of 10% of this total export profit, but only a handful of people see this money. A large portion of the money is never transferred to the communities that are most impoverished and environmentally affected by corporate presence. Still, foreign direct investment is embraced wholeheartedly by Colombian elites who equate corporate ventures in the agricultural, mineral, and industrial sectors with growth and prosperity.

It is not uncommon to hear about how corporations bring investment to developing countries and even their "willingness" to address problem areas such as environmental contamination and child labor practices. It is sometimes said that corporations' business practices are completely socially responsible and that corporations give back to the communities in which they operate. The media give much less attention to stories about how corporations destroy local lives, directly and indirectly. Yet it happens, and in some cases it leaves a trail of unimaginable destruction and violence. In this Caribbean region of Colombia, to talk of displacement of communities by corporations does not do justice to the reality; rather, locals speak of depropriation, or the takeover of property and livelihoods with complete impunity.

In this corner of the world, multinational corporations in the coal industry like Drummond and Glencore, and in the banana sector, like Dole and Chiquita Brands (among others), are not just operating on the basis of government-granted licenses to exploit natural resources. Through alliances with authorities, legal and otherwise, these companies have crafted what amounts to an informal ownership of the region. They own a large part of the railroads, highways, ports, and mines, and they have little concern for how communities feel about their presence there.

But what is it about the nature of these enterprises and the context in which they operate that make for such dominance, and what facilitates their exploitation of workers and communities? How have local people resisted these infractions, and to what degree, considering the widespread corruption of their political representatives? To answer both these questions, it helps to understand more about the region. Whether due to its strategic location, its natural resources, or its distance from the centers of power in the capital city, Bogotá, this region is often referred to as "the other Colombia." It is an allusion both to its potential and to its stigma as something of a no man's land.

Free Reign in the "Other Colombia"

Multinational companies began to arrive in the Magdalena and Cesar provinces in large part because the location offers such natural advantages. Surrounded in the east by the Sierra Nevada mountains, several municipalities in Magdalena province have direct access to the rivers that originate in these slopes. This makes the land well suited for banana plantations and other kinds of large-scale agriculture, and therefore for elite and corporate interests. It comes as no surprise that one of the U.S.-based companies with most presence throughout Latin America, the United Fruit Company (UFCO), operated in Magdalena since the beginning of the 20th century. As with its operations elsewhere, UFCO labor practices in Colombia were exploitative and repressive. During a strike by UFCO banana workers on December 6, 1928, in which they asked for better treatment and working conditions, an indefinite number of workers were massacred by company and police security forces in Ciénaga. The Nobel Prize-winning Colombian writer Gabriel García Márquez wrote a fictional account of this massacre in One Hundred Years of Solitude. Though UFCO left the Magdalena region in 1950s and moved to other regions of Colombia, it continued subcontracting with local growers.

In the mid to late 1980s, Chiquita Brands (formerly UFCO) and Dole rediscovered the Zona Bananera, or the Caribbean Banana Zone, at a time when local landowners had already been paying a "security fee" to rebel guerrilla groups that operated from the largely uninhabited Sierra Nevada, like the National Liberation Army (ELN). Noticing the potential for exclusive control of land and/or lucrative contracts with local large-scale banana growers, Chiquita and Dole officials negotiated economic deals with the landowners and security deals with the guerrillas. Their aim was to guarantee the companies' unrestricted access to highways and railroads leading to the coastal ports. In just a few years, however, small private security gangs began brutal confrontations with guerrillas in the mountains and the cities. Aware of their stronger firepower, the companies began to pay these small groups for protection instead of the guerrillas. By the late 1990s, these gang-style private security groups multiplied and fought each other for control of the territory (and for the substantial payments from landowners and multinational companies). A handful of gang leaders emerged victorious, and soon formed more structured paramilitary organizations like the powerful United Self-Defense Forces of Colombia (AUC). AUC and other paramilitary groups are known to have solid ties to drug lords as well as to military and high-level state authorities.

One of the AUC leaders in the Caribbean region is Rodrigo Tovar, popularly known as Jorge 40. He was a former army official and comes from one of a handful of powerful traditional families in the region. In the mid 1990s, Jorge 40 began to work under the command of the Castaño family, who founded the AUC when the patriarch Jesús Castaño was kidnapped and assassinated in the mid 1990s by another guerrilla group, the Revolutionary Armed Forces of Colombia (FARC). To garner control, Jorge 40 was known to carry out "cleansings" of local communities in Magdalena and Cesar provinces, targeting anyone suspected of ties to ELN or FARC. In 2000, after a guerrilla attack on a group of business and mafia leaders in the town of Nueva Venezia, Jorge 40 ordered the massacre of 70 people from this community. According to witnesses, the armed paramilitaries then played soccer with victims' severed heads to show the community that they were in complete control. There are several others like Jorge 40 who have ties to the different landowning families and to different companies.

In 2007, Chiquita Brands admitted in federal court that it paid nearly $2 million to paramilitary death squads over a period of seven years. On its end, Drummond is currently being sued in a United States court under the Alien Tort Claims Act for having contracted paramilitary forces to kill three union leaders. The violence in the region is widespread, and largely tied to corporate interest in acquiring lands and controlling the regions' vast resources. Between 1997 and 2007, 4,000 people died and at least 500 were disappeared. Moreover, during the height of the violence in between 2003 and 2006, 43,300 families from the region suffered forced displacement from their communities.

On their end, the companies suffered no major consequences from the bloodbath, other than occasionally having to rearrange their deals with different paramilitary leaders. As long as they kept scheduled payments, the companies enjoyed complete control over vast lands. By 2002 Chiquita and Dole decided to divvy up the 10,000 hectares of land in the Zona Bananera: the medium-to-large farms that grew bananas for Dole had their main houses painted red and white, and those that grew bananas for Chiquita were painted blue and white. They also happily shared the railroad. On the other hand, small farms that for one or another reason do not have contracts with these companies have hardly survived. Many peasants have agreed to sell their lands, only to lose most of their money to criminal and paramilitary gangs that extorted them shortly after the sale. Others, out of fear, have simply never returned after their violent displacement by paramilitary groups. In the near future, these corporations are likely to continue to buy lands in the region, especially with the impending passage of the free trade agreement (FTA) between the United States and Colombia. While former president Alvaro Uribe championed the push for the FTA deal with the United States, current president Juan Manuel Santos, a former defense minister and a millionaire who has solid ties to many traditional elite Colombian families, is likely to deepen the open-borders approach.

The free reign of foreign coal companies reflects a similar history. The mountainous terrain in neighboring Cesar province contains some of the biggest coal mines in Latin America. Drummond, Prodeco (a subsidiary of Glencore), and now Brazilian-owned Vale, have capitalized on this by buying part of the national railroad company Fenoco, so as to have unrestricted access to the approximately 300 miles of railroad line between the mines and the port of Ciénaga, near Santa Marta. The port installations now cover four kilometers (of a total twelve kilometers) of the coastal shores in Magdalena, but the mega-port currently under construction would extend them by another two kilometers. When the project got under way in 2008, several communities living in the swamps, or ciénaga, near the port were forcibly displaced by armed gunmen, and many ended in the encampment in Boca de Aracataca. The port expansion work has prevented the fishermen from being able to access close-by waters and they now have to fish in far away waters, if their boats are solid enough to make it there.

The damage extends far beyond access. For years, the companies have been dumping millions of tons of coal onto communities where the railroad crosses, and into coastal waters. This is due to negligence, as residuals "accidentally" fall out when the coal is carried uncovered or dumped into the shipping containers. This has resulted in severe erosion and environmental contamination of local flora and fish. As if that did not suffice, Drummond was recently conceded the rights to Rio Toribio, including control over the station that supplies clean water to local communities. According to the fishermen, Drummond uses the water to wet down the coal so that it does not ignite in the containers on the way to global markets. This has generated the contamination of river water with coal dust, and has caused a variety of skin and respiratory diseases among the local population.

State Complicity

This depropriation and destruction occurs under the protective eye of the Colombian state. Though laws exist which delimit any alterations to the agro-ecological balance in much of the coastal area, the government blatantly disregards the laws. In December 2007 the national Ministry of Transportation declared that the entire municipality was a public interest zone for purposes of national development, paving the way for the expansion of the port. Though Drummond and Prodeco appear to have followed all the legal steps to begin the expansion project, the process has certainly faltered in many aspects. According to a report prepared by local community leaders, the companies and municipal authorities did not adequately consult local community groups about worrisome environmental and socio-economic effects. Though the royalties for mining concessions and banana profits by law should remain in the communities for social and infrastructural investment, a majority of this money is simply distributed privately to national and municipal authorities. As a community leader from Ciénaga states, "what we have here is a case of mafia triangulation, with companies, the central government, and local authorities keeping the municipal funds for themselves, and thereby diffusing any responsibility that they should have towards communities."

The foreign companies do as they please, with impunity. When unionized coal workers organize to demand respect for their labor rights, or to ask for appropriate paid sick time for work injuries, the companies fire them. Such is the case of Moisés Padilla, a former Drummond employee who belongs to the Sintraminergética (National Union of Industry and Energy Workers) union. He worked for 50 years as a welder (25 at Drummond), and is now incapacitated due to severe respiratory and heart conditions. The company has successfully resisted any outside intervention, despite legal efforts of the union. In a letter to Moisés Padilla, a company representative stated that it was not company policy to consent to third-party involvement, in this case a committee of independent and state officials that could evaluate his injury claims.

Union workers have less and less job security especially since the company has recently created its own union, Sintradrummond. Although the practice was previously prohibited, a recent judicial decision has opened a loophole for companies to begin organizing their own unions. Anibal Perez, another injured worker from Sintraminergética, affirms that "for us to belong to our union is considered by the state practically a crime...the state does not give us the tools and protections to make our voices heard, and the result is that we have communities full of widows, orphans, and sick workers." The union has had five of its leaders killed since 2001, and several others now live in exile after being threatened by paramilitaries.

The companies are also quick to hold on to the façade of being socially and environmentally responsible. One example: Drummond trains a certain number of people from the community to be mine workers, but rarely hires local trainees. Some think this is because it is cheaper for the company to hire migrants from other regions. Similarly, national companies like Augura (Association of Banana Workers of Colombia) organize some of their own workers in seemingly beneficial cooperatives. Though independent on paper, Augura does business strictly with Dole, and prices are arranged between top level managers from Augura and Dole. So even if cooperative workers would truly get a fair trade price for their bananas, the lack of liberty to make autonomous decisions within the company-run cooperatives is problematic at best.

Not that state intervention would do any good. For one thing, much of the state funding for social programs for local communities is channeled to the companies themselves, such as the Augura-run cooperatives. So while the state has funds that it invests in social programs, these are mostly captured by the companies. Secondly, other state-funded social programs deliver subsidies as if community members were clients. The community at large, whether they belong to the category of low-income families, displaced families, or relatives and victims of violence, barely has access to a program that distributes about $40 every two months; most do not have enough of a connection with municipal authorities to receive even this small benefit. Thirdly, though the laws exist on paper to make the state more responsible and responsive, implementation is a problem. For instance, Colombia has had a Labor Statute since 1991, but the mechanisms for its implementation have not yet been discussed in Congress. Besides, corruption pervades the state. In 2009, a national scandal erupted over a government program aimed at helping struggling farmers, the Agro Ingreso Seguro (AIS) program. The funding (partly from the U.S. Agency for International Development) began in 2006 as part of an effort to ease concern over a potential negative impact of an impending FTA with the United States, but small farmers were not the ones benefiting; the bulk of AIS' $630 million per year was discovered to be going to rich landowners, narco-traffickers, and mobsters.

Organizing an Effective Resistance

Considering the pervasiveness of corporate interests, violence, and state complicity, what can the handful of community leaders, human rights defenders, and union workers do to organize effective resistance? The truth is that they cannot organize freely; their lives are threatened constantly. Despite the threats, is not so hard to understand why those who are still alive publicly denounce the companies, the Colombian government, and the United States for trampling on their dignity. "Our denunciations make us very public personas, and since we do not have money to pay for private security guards, speaking out publicly and internationally ironically gives us some sense of security," says Edgardo Alemán, a local human rights defender.

And so they do challenge, collectively when possible. One of the small victories of the sintramienergética union and other allied groups has been the Collective Labor Agreement signed between the union and Drummond, for the years 2010-2013. Even at quick glance, it is easy to find the voice of the workers, and their concern for community. Article 7 states that when a job opens at Drummond, the company will give preference to skilled members of the local community; upon the death of a worker, the company commits to hiring a family member of the victim. Union leaders concur that the agreement feels more like "our list of demands" than an actual commitment by Drummond representatives. Yet many insist that a more effective interaction between the communities and the companies is the only solution. "We need to guarantee a way to capture the resources, to have a social development policy that favors our communities. If we go through the politicians, we will get nothing," says local activist and economist, Luís Eduardo Rendón.

If the state's lack of responsiveness is any indication, negotiating with the companies might in fact be a viable approach. But the success of that strategy does not depend on the amount of pressure Colombian workers and community leaders exert. In this sense, the context (and place) in which they operate limits their impact. For their voice to mean anything in a system dominated by elite power in Bogotá and abroad, it will take the U.S. government and global citizens en masse to press the companies (American companies!) and the Colombian state to be honest, and to practice their activities legally, with true social responsibility. Perhaps then there can begin to be justice for these communities in the other Colombia. ❏

Sources: Luis E. Barranco, "Como el gobierno nacional convirtió una zona agroecológica en zona de interés público para fines portuarios," *EDUMAG*, Ciénaga, Colombia, 2010; Marcelo Bucheli, *Bananas and Business: The United Fruit Company in Colombia, 1899-2000* (New York University Press, 2005); Peter Chapman, *Bananas: How the United Fruit Company Shaped the World* (Canongate, 2007); Aviva Chomsky, Garry Leech, and Steve Striffler, *Bajo el manto del carbon: Pueblos y multinacionales en las minas de El Cerrejón* (Casa Editorial Pisando Callos, 2007).

Article 2.5

RISKY BUSINESS: DERIVATIVES AND GLOBAL AGRICULTURE

BY SASHA BREGER BUSH
July/August 2013

According to the World Federation of Exchanges, 25 billion derivative contracts were traded on exchanges in 2011, with the number of contracts doubling between 2006 and 2011. Derivatives on commodities like metals and agricultural products are one of the fastest growing segments of the overall derivatives market. Even as overall global derivatives trading fell—by over 15% in 2012—trading in commodity derivatives bucked the trend and continued to rise.

As they grow more popular, agricultural derivatives increasingly factor into a number of important global debates—about the causes of the global food-price crisis, the right policies for agricultural risk management, and the growing power of finance in the global food system. These debates suggest a number of critical questions. How do derivatives work? What explains the growing popularity of agricultural derivatives? What kinds of effects are derivatives having on global agriculture?

On the one hand, proponents of agricultural derivatives argue that these financial instruments are critical tools for managing price volatility and insecurity among farmers, consumers, rural communities, and governments. In fact, it is often suggested that derivatives should substitute for public policies and programs for agricultural risk management, policies that have become less popular with the rise of neoliberalism since the 1970s. On the other hand, growing evidence suggests that agricultural derivatives markets actually make food prices more volatile, increase insecurity among food-system participants, and fail to serve global agriculture's most vulnerable members. Indeed, the major benefits of the growth of derivatives markets appear to be accruing to the financial sector itself, with agriculture, unfortunately, bearing the cost.

How Do They Work?

Derivatives are financial instruments, the values of which are derived (at least in theory) from the value of some kind of "underlier." These underliers can be physical commodities (like coffee, wheat, or copper), currencies, financial assets (like stocks and debt), indexes (like the Dow Jones Industrial Average or the Case-Shiller home-price index), or economic aggregates (like GDP and inflation). Financiers are constantly innovating new derivative products, some of which—like credit default swaps—factored into the recent financial crisis.

Derivatives may be traded on organized exchanges (where products are standardized, prices transparent, and trading more heavily regulated) or they may be traded "over-the-counter" (OTC; where products are customized, prices secret, and trading virtually unregulated). Most of the derivatives implicated in the financial crisis were OTC derivatives. "Forward contracts" are traded OTC, and are customized agreements to buy or sell a specific amount of a good at a specific price, time and place in the future. "Futures contracts" are like forwards, except they are standardized (all contracts have the same terms) and traded en masse on organized exchanges. "Options contracts" are more flexible contracts that give the holder the right, but not the obligation, to buy or sell a good at a specific price, time, and place in the future. "Swaps" are agreements to trade one good or position for another for a set time period (e.g., commodity index swaps are sometimes structured so that buyers trade the rate of return on short-term Treasuries for the rate of return on a specified commodity index).

The late economist Fischer Black, of the MIT Sloan School of Management, argued that "futures markets exist because in some situations they provide an inexpensive way to transfer risk, and because many people both in the business and out like to gamble on commodity prices." Derivatives markets serve two major purposes for traders: hedging and speculation (see sidebar, p. 44). Derivatives markets also produce what Black regarded as an important side effect: a "future price" to guide market participants as they try to navigate the market's uncertain future.

When futures markets were established in the United States in the mid 19th century, they became popular among farmers, merchants, grain elevators, and processors as a way to lock in prices in advance and guarantee a market for purchase or sale. Food processors, for example, have ongoing needs for raw-commodity inputs like wheat. With future prices and supplies uncertain, derivatives trading allows processors to buy the inputs they need many months in advance for a set price, potentially smoothing costs, ensuring continued operations, and permitting easier accounting. The early futures markets were also sites for gambling, much as they are today. But in the late 19th century, unlike today, policymakers considered speculators a danger to the marketplace—by 1900 two bills banning futures and options trading had been considered by the U.S. Congress. (Neither passed, but the seriousness of this debate at such a high level should give the reader pause considering the laissez-faire regulatory approach to derivatives today.) That said, 19th-century futures markets were more of a sideshow; they were not nearly so large, so embedded in the global financial fabric, or so important for food system participants as they are today.

Why So Popular?

Global use of agricultural derivatives has risen enormously over the past thirty years. In the United States, the Department of Agriculture (USDA) includes derivative instruments in its risk management recommendations to farmers. In China, the government sponsors several commodity derivative exchanges. (These have all opened since the 1990s; by 2012, the Dalian Commodity Exchange had become the eleventh-largest derivative exchange in the world, by contract volume.) In India, the government has been gradually loosening restrictions on derivatives trading,

---

Derivatives: Their Role in the Global Economy

Hedging: Hedgers use derivatives markets to compensate for risks that they are already exposed to in the underlying market. A wheat farmer, for example, is exposed to two major risks that could be hedged using derivative instruments—price and weather. By selling her crop forward using a forward contract or a futures contract, or by purchasing a put option, our farmer can lock in a price today for a crop that hasn't yet been harvested. If prices fall by the time the crop is harvested, the trader who bought the future or sold the option will pay the difference between the contract price and the prevailing market price. In this sense, hedgers use derivatives as a form of insurance.

Speculation: Speculators use derivatives to place a bet on the movements of key economic variables (like prices) in order to make a profit. While hedging is designed to reduce risk, speculating increases risk. Speculating on commodity prices is easier with derivatives than it is in the cash market. Cash-market speculation requires one to actually buy and sell a real commodity, and to store it. Derivatives trading, by contrast, allows traders to place bets on prices without owning the real commodity at all. Derivatives also afford traders "leverage"—they can make a big bet while paying a relatively small amount of money up front. The balance is owed upon losing the bet.

Price discovery: Price discovery refers to the end result of derivatives trading—future prices. Derivative markets are also called "futures markets" and "prediction markets" because traders in the markets are making trades on the basis of what they think will happen next in the global economy. When all of these individual opinions are tallied, the "future price" results. In theory, the future price should give a good estimate of market conditions up to a year or two ahead. Future prices can theoretically help observers, farmers for example, decide when and how much to invest in future production, how much of the crop to store for future sale, among other decisions.

---

allowing new exchanges and allowing trading in previously banned instruments (e.g., options). Among the stated goals of the new exchanges is to help food-system actors manage risk.

In places where derivatives are not yet widely used or available, advocates of derivatives as tools for risk management are recommending that new exchanges be established, new users courted, and new products developed. Indeed, because of derivatives' potential risk-reducing role and the central importance of crop prices to the well being of many of the world's poor, some development agencies see derivatives as keys to agricultural development and poverty alleviation. The World Bank, along with the United Nations Conference on Trade and Development (UNCTAD), has been working to integrate derivatives into the toolkits of individual farmers, agricultural cooperatives, food processors and traders, and governments. The Bank has even situated itself as a derivatives dealer, assisting client governments in hedging the risks they incur when borrowing (e.g., interest-rate, exchange-rate, and commodity-price risks). In sub-Saharan Africa and South Asia, a growing horde of social entrepreneurs and non-profits is marketing derivative based micro-insurance to small farmers.

With What Effects?

The growing role of derivatives in agriculture presents at least two interrelated problems. First, derivatives trading is not as easy as advocates imply. For smaller, poorer prospective traders with little previous experience in the markets, it can be especially difficult. For many smaller-scale actors, the contracts traded on most commodity exchanges are too big. As an example, an Ethiopian coffee farmer with a plot of average size and average yields would have grown just over 80 kilos of coffee in 2009. A single coffee 'C' futures contract on the Intercontinental Exchange specifies 17,000 kilos, more than 200 times the farmer's output. Derivatives trading can also be prohibitively costly for smaller traders. Not only must traders pay fees to brokers, clearinghouses, and exchanges, they also must post an "initial margin" prior to trading and maintain this margin level while the trade is open. (Margin accounts serve as collateral, and are used to settle daily gains and losses for traders; a "margin call" can be expensive, and means that traders must replenish the margin account because it has fallen too low.) For Mexican coffee farmers with average revenues, for example, the initial margin required to trade even a single contract is larger than a whole year's revenue from coffee. Yield variability, information costs (successful derivatives trading requires daily access to a variety of data, and the means to process and analyze these data), and knowledge obstacles (the World Bank calls this "technical

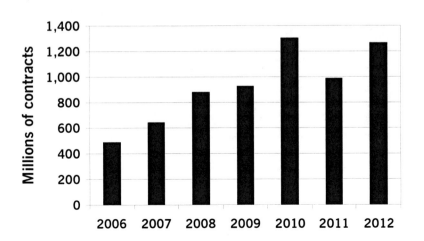

Source: Futures Industry Association (futuresindustry.org).

Derivatives: Why Agriculture?

Price volatility: "[C]ommodity prices are highly volatile in the short term, sometimes varying by as much as 50 per cent in a single year. To make matters worse, price volatility is increasing across a broad range of commodities ," write Brown, Crawford, and Gibson. Volatility is the foundation for the existence of derivatives—if the economy never changed, there would be no risk, nothing to gamble on, and no reason to trade derivatives. As volatility rises, demand for derivative instruments increases by hedgers and speculators alike.

Less public support: Governments historically played a more active role in mitigating price risk in agriculture. In coffee, for example, the 1962 International Coffee Agreement (ICA) restricted world coffee trading via quotas and stabilized prices. Marketing boards, subsidies, and agricultural extension systems were implemented at the national level. The system was dismantled in the 1980s. Coffee prices immediately became more volatile. Derivatives—gaining popularity because of the volatility unleashed by this public retreat—are envisioned by advocates as a substitute for public intervention.

Growing insecurity of farmers and eaters: As markets grow more volatile and governments withdraw assistance, individuals become more insecure. The past three decades have witnessed multiple agricultural-price crises worldwide. These shocks have been disproportionately borne by the food system's poorest members—smallholder farmers and poor urban consumers. In this context, many development agencies argue that derivatives are a force for poverty alleviation, allowing for effective food price risk management without government intervention.

Neoliberal, pro-market ideology and policy: Neoliberal ideology— with its emphasis on free markets, small government, and private property rights—has underpinned global economic policy since the late 1970s and early 1980s. Of course, there are many alternatives available to address problems of volatility, insecurity, hunger and poverty in agriculture, but it is on derivatives markets that many researchers and policymakers focus. Friendly relationships with the financial sector: Many organizations that recommend and facilitate derivative usage in the global food system—like the World Bank and UNCTAD— maintain close ties to the derivatives industry. For example, the World Bank recently partnered with JP Morgan to offer derivatives to clients, while UNCTAD conducts joint research with the Swiss Futures and Options Association to promote derivatives in developing countries.

capacity," referring to the skills required to trade derivatives successfully) can also interrupt or prevent successful market access. While these obstacles exist even for some large, wealthy, and sophisticated agribusinesses, the hurdles are surely higher for the food system's more marginal actors.

Lack of access to derivatives markets, particularly in contexts where there are few other risk management options, reinforces existing inequalities and trends towards consolidation. Food production, retail, trading, and processing are becoming increasingly concentrated on the global stage, with a few firms grabbing hold of ever-larger market shares. In this context, derivatives technologies represent one more advantage that the largest, wealthiest, and most powerful agricultural actors have over everyone else.

In the past century, certain technologies have become integral to commercial success in agriculture. These technologies, accessible only to select actors, increase profits and make firms more competitive, effectively consolidating the marketplace. Firms that cannot adapt are swallowed up. Pasteurization, farm mechanization, and genetic modification are good examples. So are derivatives: accessible only to a particular stratum of the agricultural world (the big, well-funded, and financially sophisticated), derivatives give a competitive advantage to those who can use them and contribute to the marginalization and impoverishment of those who cannot. This problem is more dire now than in the past because other risk management options that used to be available to smaller, poorer actors have disappeared, even as rising volatility has made risk management more important. Public subsidies and price supports, for example, have been eliminated in many countries in the last few decades, with the rise of neoliberalism. Informal insurance mechanisms, based on kinship and community networks, have eroded with urbanization and repeated economic crises.

Second, even when the markets are accessible, there is no guarantee that traders will benefit. Effective hedging requires that future prices be relatively efficient—they need to reliably tell us what will happen next. (Economists refer to this as "predictive efficiency.") Without efficient prices, the insurance a hedger buys in the derivatives market may not cover his or her actual losses in the underlying cash market. (This is called "basis risk.") Unfortunately, there is growing evidence that future prices are rather inefficient, due in part to the behavior of speculators in the marketplace.

Institutional speculators (like investment banks, hedge funds, and pension funds) have taken a growing interest in agricultural derivatives (see Ben Collins, "Hot Commodities, Stuffed Markets, and Empty Bellies," *Dollars & Sense*, May/June 2008), both in the lead-up to the 2008 housing market crash and since. Using derivative instruments called commodity-index swaps, large institutions have been taking "long-only" speculative positions in agricultural derivatives markets. (This means that they only bet prices will rise.) The sheer scale of these positions has pushed future prices higher, irrespective of underlying supply-and demand fundamentals in cash markets: By 2008, speculators outweighed hedgers in global commodity derivatives markets two to one.

To make matters worse, trends in future prices spill over into the underlying cash markets. Some analysts, including economist Jayati Ghosh, argue that speculative commodity-derivative trading caused up to one-fourth of the global increase in food prices from 2007 to 2008. (By 2008, food prices were more than twice as high as they had been between 2002 and 2004.) Food prices reached another peak in 2011, then dipped, and are rising again today, driving continued concern about commodity speculators. Futures prices influence cash prices through at least two channels. First, futures prices guide decisions about food storage, and storage behaviors influence cash prices. Second, futures prices are also increasingly used as "benchmark" prices to guide sales negotiations in cash markets.

Thus, in addition to gambling with the global poor, speculators in these markets are making hedging less viable. A 2008 letter from the Missouri Farm Board to the U.S. Commodity Futures Trading Commission (CFTC) noted, "The lack of convergence between an expiring futures contract and the cash market has … presented major challenges to producers trying to carry out marketing plans involving futures and options contracts." Even as speculators render cash prices more volatile, and effective risk management thus more essential, they are also disabling one of the few risk-management options that remains.

All of this means that we need to seriously rethink how we, as a global community, manage risk in the global food system. Financial firms and agribusiness have been empowered and enriched as derivatives exchanges have proliferated across the globe, providing new opportunities for product innovation, growth and expansion, merger and acquisition, risk reduction, and gambling. But, derivatives market expansion also means that more marginal actors in the global agricultural system face more volatile markets, rising levels of risk and insecurity, more fierce competition, and an even more lopsided global distribution of wealth and power.

Luckily, there are many alternatives that are potentially more equitable and just, and do not require us to let the financial fox into the agricultural hen house. The recent food crisis has reawakened policymakers to the virtues of public agricultural risk management, especially supply-management schemes like those implemented after the Great Depression (see the coffee example above in the sidebar on derivatives' popularity). Enhancing the power of farmers and consumers in the global food system (e.g., through unions) would also be useful in combating price risk—actors who can collectively negotiate prices and longer-term contracts with buyers and suppliers may be less susceptible to short-term price shocks. Support for alternative trading networks that protect the interests of small producers, like the fair-trade certification and labeling scheme set up by Fairtrade International, is a further possibility. Diversification, on the farm and nationally, can reduce the impact of global food-price volatility on local communities. Finally, agricultural price risk is partly a consequence of the fact that we have global markets in food (a recent development, historically speaking). Droughts in Australia would not necessarily impact the price of wheat in New York if New York did not trade wheat with Australia. Rising corn prices in Iowa would not necessarily lead to hunger in Mexico if Mexico grew the corn it needed at home. Indeed, some de-globalization and re-localization in agriculture may also be in order. ❑

Sources : Romain Devai and Gregoire Naacke, "WFE/IOMA Derivatives Market Survey, 2011," World Federation of Exchanges (May 2012); Will Acworth, "FIA Annual Volume Survey," Futures Industry Magazine, March 2013 (FIA volume surveys for 2007-2011 were also consulted); Tickell, Adam, "Dangerous Derivatives," Geoforum 31 (2000); Fischer Black in DeRosa, ed., *Currency Derivatives*, Wiley and Sons (1998); Johnathan Lurie, "Commodities Exchanges, 'Agrarian Power,' and the Antioption Battle," *Agricultural History* (January 1974); Oli Brown, Alec Crawford and Jason Gibson, "Boom or Bust," International Institute for Sustainable Development (2008); Joy Harwood, et al., "Managing Risk in Farming," Agricultural Economic Report No. 774, USDA (March 1999); Sasha Breger Bush, *Derivatives and Development*, New York: Palgrave Macmillan (2012); Ben Collins, "Hot Commodities, Stuffed Markets and Empty Bellies," *Dollars & Sense* (July/August 2008); Michael Masters and Adam White, "Accidental Hunt Brothers" (July 2008); Jayati Ghosh, "The unnatural coupling: Food and global finance" (2009); FAO Food Price Index, June 2013; Susan Newman, "Financialization and Changes in Social Relations Along the Coffee Commodity Chain," *Review of Radical Political Economics* (September 2009); Charles E. Kruse, President of Missouri Farm Board Federation, "Letter to the CFTC" (May 7, 2008); Fairtrade International, fairtrade.net.

Article 2.6

HOW GOLDMAN SACHS CAUSED A GREEK TRAGEDY

BY JIM HIGHTOWER
March 2010

Another Greek-based cargo ship and its crew was recently hijacked by Somalian pirates, costing the Greek owners an undisclosed amount in ransom.

Such ongoing acts of brazen piracy off the coast of Somalia have riveted the establishment media's attention. But the same news hawks have missed (or ignored) a much more brazen, longer-running and far larger robbery in Greece by Gucci-wearing thieves who are more sophisticated than common pirates—but lack a pirate's moral depth.

I refer to—who else?—Wall Street financiers. Specifically, Goldman Sachs.

Goldman, a global financial conglomerate and America's largest banking fiefdom, is notorious in our country for its arrogant, anything-goes corporate ethic that is astonishingly avaricious, even by Wall Street's dissolute standards. The firm is villainous enough that it could be its own reality TV show, perhaps titled, "Bankers Behaving Badly." A few highlights:

- During the past decade, Goldman's wizards were particularly inventive monkey-wrenchers, devising much of the investment gimmickry that enriched crafty Wall Streeters like them, even as it led to the wrecking of our economy.

- In 2006, Goldman's CEO was considered such a whiz that he was elevated to treasury secretary and soon was handed the task of fixing the very economic mess he had helped create. His "fix" was the cockamamie, self-serving, multitrillion-dollar taxpayer bailout that did save Wall Street ... but has left our economy in shambles.

- Rather than apologizing for their failures and using their bailout funds to rush loans to America's credit-starved businesses, Goldman's debauched financiers immediately went back to playing the same old global game of high-risk craps that caused America's crash, this time rolling the dice with the backing of our tax dollars.

- Juiced by an infusion of federal funds, Goldman executives declared a profit this year and promptly lavished more than $16 billion in bonus payments on themselves.

- To keep the fun rolling, Goldman is now lobbying furiously in Washington to kill regulatory and consumer bills that could rein in its destructive greed.

- Moving from mere greed to naked narcissism, Goldman's current CEO, Lloyd Blankfein, has proclaimed that his bonus bonanza is warranted because he is "doing God's work."

Perhaps he was referring to one of the Greek gods. It turns out that, for the past decade, Goldman has also been practicing its ethical flim-flammery in Greece, a nation long mired in a sea of debt.

In 2001, Goldman's financial alchemists formulated a scheme to allow the Greek government to hide the extent of its rising debt from the public and the European Community's budget overseers. Under this diabolical deal, Goldman funneled new capital from super-wealthy investors into the government's coffers.

Fine. Not so fine, though, is that, in exchange, Greek officials secretly agreed that the investors would get 20 years' worth of the annual revenue generated by such public assets as Greece's airports. For its part, Goldman pocketed $300 million in fees paid by the country's unwitting taxpayers.

The financial giant dubbed its airport scheme "Aeolus," after the ancient Greek god of the wind—and, sure enough, any long-term financial benefit for Greece was soon gone with the wind. By hiding the fact that the government's future revenues had been consigned to secret investors, Goldman bankers made the country's balance sheet look much rosier than it was, allowing Greek officials to keep spending like there was no tomorrow.

Last month, however, tomorrow arrived. Greece's crushing debt has exploded into a full-blown crisis, with its leaders disgraced and the country on the precipice of the unthinkable: the default of a sovereign nation.

So, who is getting punished for the finagling of Greek politicos and Goldman profiteers? The people, of course—just like here! Greeks now face deep wage cuts, rising taxes and the elimination of public services just so their government can pay off debts the people didn't even know it had. Meanwhile, Greece's financial conflagration is endangering the stability of Europe's currency and causing financial systems worldwide (including ours) to wobble again. All of this to enrich a handful of global speculators.

Thanks, Goldman Sachs. ❏

By permission of Jim Hightower and Creators Syndicate, Inc.

Chapter 3

INTERNATIONAL TRADE AND INVESTMENT

Article 3.1

THE GOSPEL OF FREE TRADE
The New Evangelists

BY ARTHUR MacEWAN
November 1991, updated July 2009

Free trade! With the zeal of Christian missionaries, for decades the U.S. government has been preaching, advocating, pushing, and coercing around the globe for "free trade."

As the economic crisis emerged in 2007 and 2008 and rapidly became a global crisis, it was apparent that something was very wrong with the way the world economy was organized. Not surprisingly, as unemployment rose sharply in the United States, there were calls for protecting jobs by limiting imports and for the government to "buy American" in its economic stimulus program. Similarly, in many other countries, as unemployment jumped upwards, pressure emerged for protection—and some actual steps were taken. Yet, free trade missionaries did not retreat; they continued to preach the same gospel.

The free-traders were probably correct in claiming that protectionist policies would do more harm than good as a means to stem the rising unemployment generated by the economic crisis. Significant acts of protectionism in one country would lead to retaliation—or at least copying—by other countries, reducing world trade. The resulting loss of jobs from reduced trade would most likely outweigh any gains from protection.

Yet the argument over international economic policies should not be confined simply to what should be done in a crisis. Nor should it simply deal with trade in goods and services. The free-traders have advocated their program as one for long-run economic growth and development, yet the evidence suggests that free trade is not a good economic development strategy. Furthermore, the free-traders preach the virtue of unrestricted global movement of finance as well as of goods and services. As it turns out, the free flow of finance has been a major factor in bringing about and spreading the economic crisis that began to appear in 2007—as well as earlier crises.

The Push

While the U.S. push for free trade goes back several decades, it has become more intense in recent years. In the 1990s, the U.S. government signed on to the North American Free Trade Agreement (NAFTA) and in 2005 established the Central American Free Trade Agreement (CAFTA). Both Republican and Democratic presidents, however, have pushed hard for a *global* free trade agenda. After the demise of the Soviet Union, U.S. advisers prescribed unfettered capitalism for Eastern and Central Europe, and ridiculed as unworkable any move toward a "third way." In low-income countries from Mexico to Malaysia, the prescription has been the same: open markets, deregulate business, don't restrict international investment, and let the free market flourish.

In the push for worldwide free trade, the World Trade Organization (WTO) has been the principal vehicle of change, establishing rules for commerce that assure markets are open and resources are available to those who can pay. And the International Monetary Fund (IMF) and World Bank, which provide loans to many governments, use their financial power to pressure countries around the world to accept the gospel and open their markets. In each of these international organizations, the United States—generally through the U.S. Treasury—plays a dominant role.

Of course, as with any gospel, the preachers often ignore their own sermons. While telling other countries to open their markets, the U.S. government continued, for instance, to limit imports of steel, cotton, sugar, textiles, and many other goods. But publicly at least, free-trade boosters insist that the path to true salvation—or economic expansion, which, in this day and age, seems to be the same thing—lies in opening our market to foreign goods. Get rid of trade barriers at home and abroad, allow business to go where it wants and do what it wants. We will all get rich.

Yet the history of the United States and other rich countries does not fit well with the free-trade gospel. Virtually all advanced capitalist countries found economic success through heavy government regulation of their international commerce, not in free trade. Likewise, a large role for government intervention has characterized those cases of rapid and sustained economic growth in recent decades—for example,

Japan after World War II, South Korea in the 1970s through the 1990s, and China most recently.

Free trade does, however, have its uses. Highly developed nations can use free trade to extend their power and control of the world's wealth, and business can use it as a weapon against labor. Most important, free trade can limit efforts to redistribute income more equally, undermine social programs, and keep people from democratically controlling their economic lives.

A Day in the Park

At the beginning of the 19th century, Lowell, Massachusetts became the premier site of the U.S. textile industry. Today, thanks to the Lowell National Historical Park, you can tour the huge mills, ride through the canals that redirected the Merrimack River's power to those mills, and learn the story of the textile workers, from the Yankee "mill girls" of the 1820s through the various waves of immigrant laborers who poured into the city over the next century.

During a day in the park, visitors get a graphic picture of the importance of 19th-century industry to the economic growth and prosperity of the United States. Lowell and the other mill towns of the era were centers of growth. They not only created a demand for Southern cotton, they also created a demand for new machinery, maintenance of old machinery, parts, dyes, *skills*, construction materials, construction machinery, *more skills*, equipment to move the raw materials and products, parts maintenance for that equipment, *and still more skills*. The mill towns also created markets—concentrated groups of wage earners who needed to buy products to sustain themselves. As centers of economic activity, Lowell and similar mill towns contributed to U.S. economic growth far beyond the value of the textiles they produced.

The U.S. textile industry emerged decades after the industrial revolution had spawned Britain's powerful textile industry. Nonetheless, it survived and prospered. British linens inundated markets throughout the world in the early 19th century, as the British navy nurtured free trade and kept ports open for commerce. In the United States, however, hostilities leading up to the War of 1812 and then a substantial tariff made British textiles relatively expensive. These limitations on trade allowed the Lowell mills to prosper, acting as a catalyst for other industries and helping to create the skilled work force at the center of U.S. economic expansion.

Beyond textiles, however, tariffs did not play a great role in the United States during the early 19th century. Southern planters had considerable power, and while they were willing to make some compromises, they opposed protecting manufacturing in general because that protection forced up the prices of the goods they purchased with their cotton revenues. The Civil War wiped out the planters' power to oppose protectionism, and from the 1860s through World War I, U.S. industry prospered behind considerable tariff barriers.

Different Countries, Similar Experiences

The story of the importance of protectionism in bringing economic growth has been repeated, with local variations, in other advanced capitalist countries. During the late 19th century, Germany entered the major league of international economic powers with substantial protection and government support for its industries. Likewise, in 19th-century France and Italy, national consolidation behind protectionist barriers was a key to economic development.

Britain—which entered the industrial era first—is often touted as the prime example of successful development without tariff protection. Yet, Britain embraced free trade only after its industrial base was well established; as in the U.S., the early and important textile industry was erected on a foundation of protectionism. In addition, Britain built its industry through the British navy and the expansion of empire, hardly prime ingredients in any recipe for free trade.

Japan provides an especially important case of successful government protection and support for industrial development. In the post-World War II era, when the Japanese established the foundations for their economic "miracle," the government rejected free trade and extensive foreign investment and instead promoted its national firms.

In the 1950s, for example, the government protected the country's fledgling auto firms from foreign competition. At first, quotas limited imports to $500,000 (in current dollars) each year; in the 1960s, prohibitively high tariffs replaced the quotas. Furthermore, the Japanese allowed foreign investment only insofar as it contributed to developing domestic industry. The government encouraged Japanese companies to import foreign technology, but required them to produce 90% of parts domestically within five years.

The Japanese also protected their computer industry. In the early 1970s, as the industry was developing, companies and individuals could only purchase a foreign machine if a suitable Japanese model was not available. IBM was allowed to produce within the country, but only when it licensed basic patents to Japanese firms. And IBM computers produced in Japan were treated as foreign-made machines.

In the 20th century, no other country matched Japan's economic success, as it moved in a few decades from a relative low-income country, through the devastation of war, to emerge as one of the world's economic leaders. Yet one looks back in vain to find a role for free trade in this success. The Japanese government provided an effective framework, support, and protection for the country's capitalist development.

Likewise, in many countries that have been late-comers to economic development, capitalism has generated high rates of economic growth where government involvement, and not free trade, played the central role. South Korea is a striking case. "Korea is an example of a country that grew very fast and yet violated the canons of conventional economic wisdom," writes Alice Amsden in *Asia's Next Giant: South Korea and Late Industrialization*, widely acclaimed as perhaps the most important analysis of the South Korean economic success. "In Korea, instead of the market mechanism allocating resources and guiding private entrepreneurship, the government made most of the pivotal investment decisions. Instead of firms operating in a competitive market structure, they each operated with an extraordinary degree of market control, protected from foreign competition."

Free trade, however, has had its impact in South Korea. In the 1990s, South Korea and other East Asian governments came under pressure from the U.S. government and the IMF to open their markets, including their financial markets. When they did so, the results were a veritable disaster. The East Asian financial crisis that began in 1997 was a major setback for the whole region, a major disruption of economic growth. After extremely rapid economic growth for three decades, with output expanding at 7% to 10% a year, South Korea's economy plummeted by 6.3% between 1997 and 1998.

Mexico and Its NAFTA Experience

While free trade in goods and services has its problems, which can be very serious, it is the free movement of capital, the opening of financial markets that has sharp, sudden impacts, sometimes wrecking havoc on national economies. Thus, virtually as soon as Mexico, the United States and Canada formed NAFTA at the beginning of 1994, Mexico was hit with a severe financial crisis. As the economy turned downward at the beginning of that year, capital rapidly left the country, greatly reducing the value of the Mexican peso. With this diminished value of the peso, the cost of servicing international debts and the costs of imports skyrocketed—and the downturn worsened.

Still, during the 1990s, before and after the financial crisis, free-traders extolled short periods of moderate economic growth in Mexico —3% to 4% per year—as evidence of success. Yet, compared to earlier years, Mexico's growth under free trade has been poor. From 1940 to 1990 (including the no-growth decade of the 1980s), when Mexico's market was highly protected and the state actively regulated economic affairs, output grew at an average annual rate of 5%.

Most important, Mexico's experience discredits the notion that free-market policies will improve living conditions for the masses of people in low-income countries. The Mexican government paved the way for free trade policies by reducing or eliminating social welfare programs, and for many Mexican workers wages declined sharply during the free trade era. The number of households living in poverty rose dramatically, with some 75% of Mexico's population below the poverty line at the beginning of the 21st century.

China and Its Impact

Part of Mexico's problem and its economy's relatively weak performance from the 1990s onward has been the full-scale entrance of China into the international economy. While the Mexican authorities thought they saw great possibilities in NAFTA, with the full opening of the U.S. market to goods produced with low-wage Mexican labor, China (and other Asian countries) had even cheaper labor. As China also gained access to the U.S. market, Mexican expectations were dashed.

The Chinese economy has surely gained in terms of economic growth as it has engaged more and more with the world market, and the absolute levels of incomes of millions of people have risen a great deal. However, China's rapid economic growth has come with a high degree of income inequality. Before its era of rapid growth, China was viewed as a country with a relatively equal distribution of income. By the beginning of the new millennium, however, it was much more unequal than any of the other most populace Asian countries (India, Indonesia, Bangladesh, Pakistan), and more in line with the high-inequality countries of Latin America. Furthermore, with the inequality has come a great deal of social conflict. Tens of thousands of "incidents" of conflict involving violence are reported each year, and most recently there have been the major conflicts involving Tibetans and Ouigers.

In any case, the Chinese trade and growth success should not be confused with "free trade." Foundations for China's surge of economic growth were established through state-sponsored infra-structure development and the vast expansion of the country's educational system. Even today, while private business, including foreign business, appears to have been given free rein in China, the government still plays a controlling role—including a central role in affecting foreign economic relations.

A central aspect of the government's role in the county's foreign commerce has been in the realm of finance. As Chinese-produced goods have virtually flooded international markets, the government has controlled the uses of the earnings from these exports. Instead of simply allowing those earnings to be used by Chinese firms and citizens to buy imports, the government has to a large extent held those earnings as reserves. Using those reserves, China's central bank has been the largest purchaser of U.S. government bonds, in effect becoming a major financer of the U.S. government's budget deficit of recent years.

China's reserves have been one large element in creating a giant pool of financial assets in the world economy. This "pool" has also been built up as the doubling of oil prices following the U.S. invasion of Iraq put huge amounts of funds in the pockets of oil-exporting countries and firm and individuals connected to the oil industry. Yet slow growth of the U.S. economy and extremely low interest rates, resulting from the Federal Reserve Bank's efforts to encourage more growth, limited the returns that could be obtained on these funds. One of the consequences—through a complex set of connections—was the development of the U.S. housing bubble, as financial firms, searching for higher returns, pushed funds into more and more risky mortgage loans.

It was not simply free trade and the unrestricted flow of international finance that generated the housing bubble and subsequent crisis in the U.S. economy. However, the generally unstable global economy—both in terms of trade and finance—that has emerged in the free trade era was certainly a factor bringing about the crisis. Moreover, as is widely recognized, it was not only the U.S. economy and

U.S. financial institutions that were affected. The free international flow of finance has meant that banking has become more and more a global industry. So as the U.S. banks got in trouble in 2007 and 2008, their maladies spread to many other parts of the world.

The Uses of Free Trade

While free trade is not the best economic growth or development policy and, especially through the free flow of finance, can precipitate financial crises, the largest and most powerful firms in many countries find it highly profitable. As Britain preached the loudest sermons for free trade in the early 19th century, when its own industry was already firmly established, so the United States—or at least many firms based in the United States—find it a profitable policy at the beginning of the 21st century. The Mexican experience provides an instructive illustration.

For U.S. firms, access to foreign markets is a high priority. Mexico may be relatively poor, but with a population of 105 million it provides a substantial market. Furthermore, Mexican labor is cheap relative to U.S. labor; and using modern production techniques, Mexican workers can be as productive as workers in the United States. For U.S. firms to obtain full access to the Mexican market, the United States has to open its borders to Mexican goods. Also, if U.S. firms are to take full advantage of cheap foreign labor and sell the goods produced abroad to U.S. consumers, the United States has to be open to imports.

On the other side of the border, wealthy Mexicans face a choice between advancing their interests through national development or advancing their interests through ties to U.S. firms and access to U.S. markets. For many years, they chose the former route. This led to some development of the Mexican economy but also—due to corruption and the massive power of the ruling party, the PRI—huge concentrations of wealth in the hands of a few small groups of firms and individuals. Eventually, these groups came into conflict with their own government over regulation and taxation. Having benefited from government largesse, they came to see their fortunes in greater freedom from government control and, particularly, in greater access to foreign markets and partnerships with large foreign companies. National development was a secondary concern when more involvement with international commerce would produce greater riches more quickly.

In addition, the old program of state-led development in Mexico ran into severe problems. These problems came to the surface in the 1980s with the international debt crisis. Owing huge amounts of money to foreign banks, the Mexican government was forced to respond to pressure from the IMF, the U.S. government, and large international banks which sought to deregulate Mexico's trade and investment. That pressure meshed with the pressure from Mexico's own richest elites, and the result was the move toward free trade and a greater opening of the Mexican economy to foreign investment.

Since the early 1990s, these changes for Mexico and the United States (as well as Canada) have been institutionalized in NAFTA. The U.S. government's agenda since then has been to spread free trade policies to all of the Americas through more regional agreements like CAFTA and ultimately through a Free Trade Area of the Americas. On a broader scale, the U.S. government works through the WTO, the IMF, and the World Bank to open markets and gain access to resources beyond the Western Hemisphere. In fact, while markets remain important everywhere, low-wage manufacturing is increasingly concentrated in Asia—especially China— instead of Mexico or Latin America.

The Chinese experience involves many of the same advantages for U.S. business as does the Mexican—a vast market, low wages, and an increasingly productive labor force. However, the Chinese government, although it has liberalized the economy a great deal compared to the pre-1985 era, has not abdicated its major role in the economy. For better (growth) and for worse (inequality and repression), the Chinese government has not embraced free trade.

Who Gains, Who Loses?

Of course, in the United States, Mexico, China and elsewhere, advocates of free trade claim that their policies are in everyone's interest. Free trade, they point out, will mean cheaper products for all. Consumers in the United States, who are mostly workers, will be richer because their wages will buy more. In Mexico and China, on the one hand, and in the United States, on the other hand, they argue that rising trade will create more jobs. If some workers lose their jobs because cheaper imported goods are available, export industries will produce new jobs.

In recent years this argument has taken on a new dimension with the larger entrance of India into the world economy and with the burgeoning there of jobs based in information technology—programming and call centers, for example. This "out-sourcing" of service jobs has received a great deal of attention and concern in the United States. Yet free-traders have defended this development as good for the U.S. economy as well as for the Indian economy.

Such arguments obscure many of the most important issues in the free trade debate. Stated, as they usually are, as universal truths, these arguments are just plain silly. No one, for example, touring the Lowell National Historical Park could seriously argue that people in the United States would have been better off had there been no tariff on textiles. Yes, in 1820, they could have purchased textile goods more cheaply, but in the long run the result would have been less industrial advancement and a less wealthy nation. One could make the same point with the Japanese auto and computer industries, or indeed with numerous other examples from the last two centuries of capitalist development.

In the modern era, even though the United States already has a relatively developed economy with highly skilled workers, a freely open international economy does not serve the interests of most U.S. workers, though it will benefit large firms.

U.S. workers today are in competition with workers around the globe. Many different workers in many different places can produce the same goods and services. Thus, an international economy governed by the free trade agenda will tend to bring down wages for many U.S. workers. This phenomenon has certainly been one of the factors leading to the substantial rise of income inequality in the United States during recent decades.

The problem is not simply that of workers in a few industries—such as auto and steel, or call-centers and computer programming—where import competition is an obvious and immediate issue. A country's openness to the international economy affects the entire structure of earnings in that country. Free trade forces down the general level of wages across the board, even of those workers not directly affected by imports. The simple fact is that when companies can produce the same products in several different places, it is owners who gain because they can move their factories and funds around much more easily than workers can move themselves around. Capital is mobile; labor is much less mobile. Businesses, more than workers, gain from having a larger territory in which to roam.

Control Over Our Economic Lives

But the difficulties with free trade do not end with wages. In both low-income and high-income parts of the world, free trade is a weapon in the hands of business when it opposes any progressive social programs. Efforts to place environmental restrictions on firms are met with the threat of moving production abroad. Higher taxes to improve the schools? Business threatens to go elsewhere. Better health and safety regulations? The same response.

Some might argue that the losses from free trade for people in the United States will be balanced by gains for most people in poor countries—lower wages in the United States, but higher wages in Mexico and China. Free trade, then, would bring about international equality. Not likely. In fact, as pointed out above, free trade reforms in Mexico have helped force down wages and reduce social welfare programs, processes rationalized by efforts to make Mexican goods competitive on international markets. China, while not embracing free trade, has seen its full-scale entrance into global commerce accompanied by increasing inequality.

Gains for Mexican or Chinese workers, like those for U.S. workers, depend on their power in relation to business. Free trade or simply the imperative of international "competitiveness" are just as much weapons in the hands of firms operating in Mexico and China as they are for firms operating in the United States. The great mobility of capital is business's best trump card in dealing with labor and popular demands for social change—in the United States, Mexico, China and elsewhere.

None of this means that people should demand that their economies operate as fortresses, protected from all foreign economic incursions. There are great gains that can be obtained from international economic relations—when a nation manages those relations in the interests of the great majority of the people. Protectionism often simply supports narrow vested interests, corrupt officials, and wealthy industrialists. In rejecting free trade, we should move beyond traditional protectionism.

Yet, at this time, rejecting free trade is an essential first step. Free trade places the cards in the hands of business. More than ever, free trade would subject us to the "bottom line," or at least the bottom line as calculated by those who own and run large companies. ❑

Article 3.2

COMPARATIVE ADVANTAGE

BY RAMAA VASUDEVAN
July/August 2007

Dear Dr. Dollar:

When economists argue that the outsourcing of jobs might be a plus for the U.S. economy, they often mention the idea of comparative advantage. Free trade, they say, would create higher-paying jobs than the ones that would be outsourced. But is it really true that free trade leads to universal benefits?

—*David Goodman, Boston, Mass.*

Y ou're right: The purveyors of the free trade gospel do invoke the doctrine of comparative advantage to dismiss widespread concerns about the export of jobs. Attributed to 19th-century British political-economist David Ricardo, the doctrine says that a nation always stands to gain if it exports the goods it produces *relatively* more cheaply in exchange for goods that it can get *comparatively* more cheaply from abroad. Free trade would lead to each country specializing in the products it can produce at *relatively* lower costs. Such specialization allows both trading partners to gain from trade, the theory goes, even if in one of the countries production of *both* goods costs more in absolute terms.

For instance, suppose that in the United States the cost to produce one car equals the cost to produce 10 bags of cotton, while in the Philippines the cost to produce one car equals the cost to produce 100 bags of cotton. The Philippines would then have a comparative advantage in the production of cotton, producing one bag at a cost equal to the production cost of 1/100 of a car, versus 1/10 of a car in the United States; likewise, the United States would hold a comparative advantage in the production of cars. Whatever the prices of cars and cotton in the global market, the theory goes, the Philippines would be better off producing only cotton and importing all its cars from the United States, and the United States would be better off producing only cars and importing all of its cotton from the Philippines. If the international terms of trade—the relative price—is one car for 50 bags, then the United States will take in 50 bags of cotton for each car it exports, 40 more than the 10 bags it forgoes by putting its productive resources into making the car rather than growing cotton. The Philippines is also better off: it can import a car in exchange for the export of 50 bags of cotton, whereas it would have had to forgo the production of 100 bags of cotton in order to produce that car domestically. If the price of cars goes up in the global marketplace, the Philippines will lose out in relative terms—but will still be better off than if it tried to produce its own cars.

The real world, unfortunately, does not always conform to the assumptions underlying comparative-advantage theory. One assumption is that trade is balanced.

But many countries are running persistent deficits, notably the United States, whose trade deficit is now at nearly 7% of its GDP. A second premise, that there is full employment within the trading nations, is also patently unrealistic. As global trade intensifies, jobs created in the export sector do not necessarily compensate for the jobs lost in the sectors wiped out by foreign competition.

The comparative advantage story faces more direct empirical challenges as well. Nearly 70% of U.S. trade is trade in similar goods, known as *intra-industry trade*: for example, exporting Fords and importing BMWs. And about one third of U.S. trade as of the late 1990s was trade between branches of a single corporation located in different countries (*intra-firm trade*). Comparative advantage cannot explain these patterns.

Comparative advantage is a static concept that identifies immediate gains from trade but is a poor guide to economic development, a process of structural change over time which is by definition dynamic. Thus the comparative advantage tale is particularly pernicious when preached to developing countries, consigning many to "specialize" in agricultural goods or be forced into a race to the bottom where cheap sweatshop labor is their sole source of competitiveness.

The irony, of course, is that none of the rich countries got that way by following the maxim that they now preach. These countries historically relied on tariff walls and other forms of protectionism to build their industrial base. And even now, they continue to protect sectors like agriculture with subsidies. The countries now touted as new models of the benefits of free trade—South Korea and the other "Asian tigers," for instance— actually flouted this economic wisdom, nurturing their technological capabilities in specific manufacturing sectors and taking advantage of their lower wage costs to *gradually* become effective competitors of the United States and Europe in manufacturing.

The fundamental point is this: contrary to the comparative-advantage claim that trade is universally beneficial, nations as a whole do not prosper from free trade. Free trade creates winners and losers, both within and between countries. In today's context it is the global corporate giants that are propelling and profiting from "free trade": not only outsourcing white-collar jobs, but creating global commodity chains linking sweatshop labor in the developing countries of Latin America and Asia (Africa being largely left out of the game aside from the export of natural resources such as oil) with ever-more insecure consumers in the developed world. Promoting "free trade" as a political cause enables this process to continue.

It is a process with real human costs in terms of both wages and work. People in developing countries across the globe continue to face these costs as trade liberalization measures are enforced; and the working class in the United States is also being forced to bear the brunt of the relentless logic of competition. ❏

Sources: Arthur MacEwan, "The Gospel of Free Trade: The New Evangelists," *Dollars & Sense*, July/August 2002; Ha-Joon Chang, *Kicking Away the Ladder: The Real History of Fair Trade*, Foreign Policy in Focus, 2003; Anwar Shaikh, "Globalization and the Myths of Free Trade," in *Globalization and the Myths of Free Trade: History, Theory, and Empirical Evidence*, ed. Anwar Shaikh, Routledge 2007.

Article 3.3

FALSE PROMISES ON TRADE

BY DEAN BAKER AND MARK WEISBROT
November/December 2003; updated, October 2009

Farmers throughout the Third World are suffering not from too much free trade, but from not enough. That's the impression you get from most media coverage of the recent World Trade Organization (WTO) meetings in Cancún. The *New York Times*, *Washington Post*, and other major news outlets devoted huge amounts of space to news pieces and editorials arguing that agricultural subsidies in rich countries are a major cause of poverty in the developing world. If only these subsidies were eliminated, and the doors to imports from developing countries opened, the argument goes, then the playing field would be level and genuinely free trade would work its magic on poverty in the Third World. The media decided that agricultural subsidies were the major theme of the trade talks even if evidence indicated that other issues—for example, patent and copyright protection, rules on investment, or developing countries' right to regulate imports—would have more impact on the well-being of people in those countries.

There is certainly some element of truth in the argument that agricultural subsidies and barriers to imports can hurt farmers in developing countries. There are unquestionably farmers in a number of developing countries who have been undersold and even put out of business by imports whose prices are artificially low thanks to subsidies the rich countries pay their farmers. It is also true that many of these subsidy programs are poorly targeted, benefiting primarily large farmers and often encouraging environmentally harmful farming practices.

However, the media have massively overstated the potential gains that poor countries might get from the elimination of farm subsidies and import barriers. The risk of this exaggeration is that it encourages policy-makers and concerned non-governmental organizations (NGOs) to focus their energies on an issue that is largely peripheral to economic development and to ignore much more important matters.

To put the issue in perspective: the World Bank, one of the most powerful advocates of removing most trade barriers, has estimated the gains from removing all the rich countries' remaining barriers to trade in manufactured and farm products *and* ending agricultural subsidies. The total estimated gain to low- and middle-income countries, when the changes are phased in by 2015, is an extra 0.6% of GDP. In other words, an African country with an annual income of $500 per person would see that figure rise to $503 as a result of removing these barriers and subsidies.

Simplistic Talk on Subsidies

The media often claim that the rich countries give $300 billion annually in agricultural subsidies to their farmers. In fact, this is not the amount of money paid by governments to farmers, which is actually less than $100 billion. The $300 billion figure is an estimate of the excess cost to consumers in rich nations that results from all market barriers in agriculture. Most of this cost is attributable to higher food prices that result from planting restrictions, import tariffs, and quotas.

The distinction is important, because not all of the $300 billion ends up in the pockets of farmers in rich nations. Some of it goes to exporters in developing nations, as when sugar producers in Brazil or Nicaragua are able to sell their sugar in the United States for an amount that is close to three times the world price. The higher price that U.S. consumers pay for this sugar is part of the $300 billion that many accounts mistakenly describe as subsidies to farmers in rich countries.

Another significant misrepresentation is the idea that cheap imports from the rich nations are always bad for developing countries. When subsides from rich countries lower the price of agricultural imports to developing countries, consumers in those countries benefit. This is one reason why a recent World Bank study found that the removal of *all* trade barriers and subsidies in the United States would have no net effect on growth in sub-Saharan Africa.

In addition, removing the rich countries' subsidies or barriers will not level the playing field—since there will still often be large differences in productivity—and thus will not save developing countries from the economic and social upheavals that such "free trade" agreements as the WTO have in store for them. These agreements envision a massive displacement of people employed in agriculture, as farmers in developing countries are pushed out by international competition. It took the United States 100 years, from 1870 to 1970, to reduce agricultural employment from 53% to under 5% of the labor force, and the transition nonetheless caused considerable social unrest. To compress such a process into a period of a few years or even a decade, by removing remaining agricultural trade barriers in poor countries, is a recipe for social explosion.

It is important to realize that in terms of the effect on developing countries, low agricultural prices due to subsidies for rich-country farmers have the exact same impact as low agricultural prices that stem from productivity gains. If the opponents of agricultural subsidies consider the former to be harmful to the developing countries, then they should be equally concerned about the impact of productivity gains in the agricultural sectors of rich countries.

Insofar as cheap food imports might have a negative impact on a developing country's economy, the problem can be easily remedied by an import tariff. In this situation, the developing world would gain the most if those countries that benefit from cheap imported food have access to it, while those that are better served by protecting their domestic agricultural sector are allowed to impose tariffs without fear of retaliation from rich nations. This would make much more sense, and cause much less harm, than simply removing all trade barriers and subsidies on both sides of the North-South economic divide. The concept of a "level playing field" is a false one. Mexican corn farmers, for example, are not going to be able to compete with U.S. agribusiness, subsidies or no subsidies, nor should they have to.

It is of course good that such institutions as the *New York Times* are pointing out the hypocrisy of governments in the United States, Europe, and Japan in insisting that developing countries remove trade barriers and subsidies while keeping some of their own. And the subsidy issue was exploited very skillfully by developing-country governments and NGOs at the recent Cancún talks. The end result—the collapse of the talks—was a great thing for the developing world. So were the ties that were forged among countries such as those in the group of 22, enabling them to stand up to the rich countries. But the WTO remedy of eliminating subsidies and trade barriers across the board will not save developing countries from most of the harm caused by current policies. Just the opposite: the removal of import restrictions in the developing world could wipe out tens of millions of farmers and cause enormous economic damage.

Avoiding the Key Issues

While reducing agricultural protection and subsidies just in the rich countries might in general be a good thing for developing countries, the gross exaggeration of its importance has real consequences, because it can divert attention from issues of far more pressing concern. One such issue is the role that the IMF continues to play as enforcer of a creditors' cartel in the developing world, threatening any country that defies its edicts with a cutoff of access to international credit. One of the most devastated recent victims of the IMF's measures has been Argentina, which saw its economy thrown into a depression after the failure of a decade of neoliberal economic policies. The IMF's harsh treatment of Argentina last year, while it was suffering from the worst depression in its history, is widely viewed in the developing world as a warning to other countries that might deviate from the IMF's recommendations. One result is that Brazil's new president, elected with an overwhelming mandate for change, must struggle to promote growth in the face of 22% interest rates demanded by the IMF's monetary experts.

Similarly, most of sub-Saharan Africa is suffering from an unpayable debt burden. While there has been some limited relief offered in recent years, the remaining debt service burden is still more than the debtor countries in that region spend on health care or education. The list of problems that the current world economic order imposes on developing countries is long: bans on the industrial policies that led to successful development in the West, the imposition of patents on drugs and copyrights on computer software and recorded material, inappropriate macroeconomic policies imposed by the IMF and the World Bank. All of these factors are likely to have far more severe consequences for the development prospects of poor countries than the agricultural policies of rich countries. ❑

Sources: Elena Ianchovichina, Aaditya Mattoo, and Marcelo Olareaga, "Unrestricted Market Access for Sub-Saharan Africa: How much is it worth and who pays" (World Bank, April 2001); Mark Weisbrot and Dean Baker, "The Relative Impact of Trade Liberalization on Developing Countries" (Center for Economic and Policy Research, June 2002).

Update

As of July 2008, the WTO negotiations have failed to reach an agreement, particularly on the issue of farm subsidies. Developing countries, especially India and China, demanded a deeper cut in the farm subsidies provided to U.S. and EU farmers and a much lower threshold for special safeguard mechanism for farmers in the developing countries. Meanwhile, developed countries, especially the United States, were not ready to budge from their position of reducing annual farm subsidies from $18 billion to $14.5 billion. The EU countries spend a total of $280 billion to support domestic farmers, while the official development assistance by the OECD countries to the developing world was $80 billion in 2004).

The IMF and the World Bank pushed the agenda of the structural adjustment program in more than 70 countries. The resulting decline in government spending has forced the farmers of the developing countries to deal with the mounting costs of cultivation. This, coupled with the vagaries of world farm-products prices (thanks to the Northern protectionism) has been driving the farmers in the South to much despair and hopelessness, and in the case of some 190,753 Indian farmers, suicide.

—Arpita Banerjee

Article 3.4

OUTSIZED OFFSHORE OUTSOURCING

The scope of offshore outsourcing gives some economists and the business press the heebie-jeebies.

BY JOHN MILLER
September/October 2007

At a press conference introducing the 2004 *Economic Report of the President*, N. Gregory Mankiw, then head of President Bush's Council of Economic Advisors, assured the press that "Outsourcing is probably a plus for the economy in the long run [and] just a new way of doing international trade."

Mankiw's comments were nothing other than mainstream economics, as even Democratic Party-linked economists confirmed. For instance Janet Yellen, President Clinton's chief economist, told the *Wall Street Journal*, "In the long run, outsourcing is another form of trade that benefits the U.S. economy by giving us cheaper ways to do things." Nonetheless, Mankiw's assurances were met with derision from those uninitiated in the economics profession's free-market ideology. Sen. John Edwards (D-N.C.) asked, "What planet do they live on?" Even Republican House Speaker Dennis Hastert (Ill.) said that Mankiw's theory "fails a basic test of real economics."

Mankiw now jokes that "if the American Economic Association were to give an award for the Most Politically Inept Paraphrasing of Adam Smith, I would be a leading candidate." But he quickly adds, "the recent furor about outsourcing, and my injudiciously worded comments about the benefits of international trade, should not eclipse the basic lessons that economists have understood for more than two centuries."

In fact Adam Smith never said any such thing about international trade. In response to the way Mankiw and other economists distort Smith's writings, economist Michael Meeropol took a close look at what Smith actually said; he found that Smith used his invisible hand argument to favor domestic investment over far-flung, hard-to-supervise foreign investments. Here are Smith's words in his 1776 masterpiece, *The Wealth of Nations*:

> By preferring the support of domestic to that of foreign industry, he [the investor] intends only his own security; and by directing that industry in such a manner as its produce may be of the greatest value, he intends only his own gain, and he is in this, as in many other cases, led by an invisible hand to promote an end, which was no part of his intention.

Outsized offshore outsourcing, the shipping of jobs overseas to take advantage of low wages, has forced some mainstream economists and some elements of the business press to have second thoughts about "free trade." Many are convinced that the painful transition costs that hit before outsourcing produces any ultimate benefits may be the biggest political issue in economics for a generation. And some recognize, as Smith did, that there is no guarantee unfettered international trade will leave the participants better off even in the long run.

Keynes's Revenge

Writing during the Great Depression of the 1930s, John Maynard Keynes, the preeminent economist of the twentieth century, prescribed government spending as a means of compensating for the instability of private investment. The notion of a mixed private/government economy, Keynes's prosthesis for the invisible hand of the market, guided U.S. economic policy from the 1940s through the 1970s.

It is only fitting that Paul Samuelson, the first Nobel Laureate in economics, and whose textbook introduced U.S. readers to Keynes, would be among the first mainstream economist to question whether unfettered international trade, in the context of massive outsourcing, would necessarily leave a developed economy such as that of the United States better off—even in the long run. In an influential 2004 article, Samuelson characterized the common economics wisdom about outsourcing and international trade this way:

> Yes, good jobs may be lost here in the short run. But …the gains of the winners from free trade, properly measured, work out to exceed the losses of the losers. … Never forget to tally the real gains of consumers alongside admitted possible losses of some producers. … The gains of the American winners are big enough to more than compensate the losers.

Samuelson took on this view, arguing that this common wisdom is "dead wrong about [the] *necessary* surplus of winning over losing" [emphasis in the original]. In a rather technical paper, he demonstrated that free trade globalization can sometimes give rise to a situation in which "a productivity gain in one country can benefit that country alone, while permanently hurting the other country by reducing the gains from trade that are possible between the two countries."

Offshored? Outsourced? Confused?

The terms "offshoring" and "outsourcing" are often used interchangeably, but they refer to distinct processes:

Outsourcing—When a company hires another company to carry out a business function that it no longer wants to carry on in-house. The company that is hired may be in the same city or across the globe; it may be a historically independent firm or a spinoff of the first company created specifically to outsource a particular function.

Offshoring or *Offshore Outsourcing*—When a company shifts a portion of its business operation abroad. An offshore operation may be carried out by the same company or, more typically, outsourced to a different one.

Many in the economics profession do admit that it is hard to gauge whether intensified offshoring of U.S. jobs in the context of free-trade globalization will give more in winnings to the winners than it takes in losses from the losers. "Nobody has a clue about what the numbers are," as Robert C. Feenstra, a prominent trade economist, told *BusinessWeek* at the time.

The empirical issues that will determine whether offshore outsourcing ultimately delivers, on balance, more benefits than costs, and to whom those benefits and costs will accrue, are myriad. First, how wide a swath of white-collar workers will see their wages reduced by competition from the cheap, highly skilled workers who are now becoming available around the world? Second, by how much will their wages drop? Third, will the U.S. workers thrown into the global labor pool end up losing more in lower wages than they gain in lower consumer prices? In that case, the benefits of increased trade would go overwhelmingly to employers. But even employers might lose out depending on the answer to a fourth question: Will cheap labor from abroad allow foreign employers to out-compete U.S. employers, driving down the prices of their products and lowering U.S. export earnings? In that case, not only workers, but the corporations that employ them as well, could end up worse off.

Bigger Than A Box

Another mainstream Keynesian economist, Alan Blinder, former Clinton economic advisor and vice-chair of the Federal Reserve Board, doubts that outsourcing will be "immiserating" in the long run and still calls himself "a free-trader down to his toes." But Blinder is convinced that the transition costs will be large, lengthy, and painful before the United States experiences a net gain from outsourcing. Here is why.

First, rapid improvements in information and communications technology have rendered obsolete the traditional notion that manufactured goods, which can generally be boxed and shipped, are tradable, while services, which cannot be boxed, are not. And the workers who perform the services that computers and satellites have now rendered tradable will increasingly be found offshore, especially when they are skilled and will work for lower wages.

Second, another 1.5 billion or so workers—many in China, India, and the former Soviet bloc—are now part of the world economy. While most are low-skilled workers, some are not; and as Blinder says, a small percentage of 1.5 billion is nonetheless "a lot of willing and able people available to do the jobs that technology will move offshore." And as China and India educate more workers, offshoring of high-skill work will accelerate.

Third, the transition will be particularly painful in the United States because the U.S. unemployment insurance program is stingy, at least by first-world standards, and because U.S. workers who lose their jobs often lose their health insurance and pension rights as well.

How large will the transition cost be? "Thirty million to 40 million U.S. jobs are potentially offshorable," according to Blinder's latest estimates. "These include scientists, mathematicians and editors on the high end and telephone operators, clerks and typists on the low end."

Blinder arrived at these figures by creating an index that identifies how easy or hard it will be for a job to be physically or electronically "offshored." He then used the index to assess the Bureau of Labor Statistics' 817 U.S. occupational categories. Not surprisingly, Blinder classifies almost all of the 14.3 million U.S. manufacturing jobs as offshorable. But he also classifies more than twice that many U.S. service sector jobs as offshorable, including most computer industry jobs as well as many others, for instance, the 12,470 U.S. economists and the 23,790 U.S. multimedia artists and animators. In total, Blinder's analysis suggests that 22% to 29% of the jobs held by U.S. workers in 2004 will be potentially offshorable within a decade or two, with nearly 8.2 million jobs in 59 occupations "highly offshorable."

Mankiw dismissed Blinder's estimates of the number of jobs at risk to offshoring as "out of the mainstream." Indeed, Blinder's estimates are considerably larger than earlier ones. But these earlier studies either aim to measure the number of U.S. jobs that will be outsourced (as opposed to the number at risk of being outsourced), look at a shorter period of time, or have shortcomings that suggest they underestimate the number of U.S. jobs threatened by outsourcing.

Global Arbitrage

Low wages are the reason U.S. corporations outsource labor. Computer programmers in the United States make wages nearly *ten times* those of their counterparts in India and the Philippines, for example.

Today, more and more white-collar workers in the United States are finding themselves in direct competition with the low-cost, well-trained, highly educated workers in Bangalore, Shanghai, and Eastern and Central Europe. These workers often use the same capital and technology and are no less productive than the U.S. workers they replace. They just get paid less.

This global labor arbitrage, as Morgan Stanley's chief economist Stephen Roach calls it, has narrowed international wage disparities in manufacturing, and now in services too, by unrelentingly pushing U.S. wages down toward international norms. ("Arbitrage" refers to transactions that yield a profit by taking advantage of a price differential for the same asset in different locations. Here, of course, the "asset" is wage labor of a certain skill level.) A sign of that pressure: about 70% of laid-off workers in the United States earn less three years later than they did at the time of the layoff; on average, those reemployed earn 10% less than they did before.

And it's not only laid-off workers who are hurt. A study conducted by Harvard labor economists Lawrence F. Katz, Richard B. Freeman, and George J. Borjas finds that every other worker with skills similar to those who were displaced also loses out. Every 1% drop in employment due to imports or factories gone abroad shaves 0.5% off the wages of the remaining workers in that occupation, they conclude.

Global labor arbitrage also goes a long way toward explaining the poor quality and low pay of the jobs the U.S. economy has created this decade, according to Roach. By dampening wage increases for an ever wider swath of the U.S. workforce, he argues, outsourcing has helped to drive a wedge between productivity gains and wage gains and to widen inequality in the United States. In the first four years of this decade, nonfarm productivity in the United States has recorded a cumulative increase of 13.3%— more than double the 5.9% rise in real compensation per hour over the same period. ("Compensation" includes wages, which have been stagnant for the average worker, plus employer spending on fringe benefits such as health insurance, which has risen even as, in many instances, the actual benefits have been cut back.) Roach reports that the disconnect between pay and productivity growth during the current economic expansion has been much greater in services than in manufacturing, as that sector weathers the powerful forces of global labor arbitrage for the first time.

Doubts in the Business Press?!

Even in the business press, doubts that offshore outsourcing willy-nilly leads to economic improvement have become more acute. Earlier this summer, a *BusinessWeek* cover story, "The Real Cost of Offshoring," reported that government statistics have underestimated the damage to the U.S. economy from offshore outsourcing. The problem is that since offshoring took off, *import* growth, adjusted for inflation, has been faster than the official numbers show. That means improvements in living standards, as well as corporate profits, depend more on cheap imports, and less on improving domestic productivity, than analysts thought.

Growing angst about outsourcing's costs has also prompted the business press to report favorably on remedies for the dislocation brought on by offshoring that deviate substantially from the non-interventionist, free-market playbook. Even the most unfazed pro-globalization types want to beef up trade adjustment assistance for displaced workers and strengthen the U.S. educational system. But both proposals are inadequate.

More education, the usual U.S. prescription for any economic problem, is off the mark here. Cheaper labor is available abroad up and down the job-skill ladder, so even the most rigorous education is no inoculation against the threat of offshore outsourcing. As Blinder emphasizes, it is the need for face-to-face contact that stops jobs from being shipped overseas, not the level of education necessary to perform them. Twenty years from now, home health aide positions will no doubt be plentiful in the United States; jobs for highly trained IT professionals may be scarce.

Trade adjustment assistance has until now been narrowly targeted at workers hurt by imports. Most new proposals would replace traditional trade adjustment assistance and unemployment insurance with a program for displaced workers that offers wage insurance to ease the pain of taking a lower-paying job and provides for portable health insurance and retraining. The pro-globalization research group McKinsey Global Institute (MGI), for example, claims that for as little as 4% to 5%

of the amount they've saved in lower wages, companies could cover the wage losses of all laid-off workers once they are reemployed, paying them 70% of the wage differential between their old and new jobs (in addition to health care subsidies) for up to two years.

While MGI confidently concludes that this proposal will "go a long way toward relieving the current anxieties," other globalization advocates are not so sure. They recognize that economic anxiety is pervasive and that millions of white-collar workers now fear losing their jobs. Moreover, even if fears of actual job loss are overblown, wage insurance schemes do little to compensate for the downward pressure offshoring is putting on the wages of workers who have not been laid off.

Other mainstream economists and business writers go even further, calling for not only wage insurance but also taxes on the winners from globalization. And globalization has produced big winners: on Wall Street, in the corporate boardroom, and among those workers in high demand in the global economy.

Economist Matthew Slaughter, who recently left President Bush's Council of Economic Advisers, told the *Wall Street Journal*, "Expanding the political support for open borders [for trade] requres making a radical change in fiscal policy." He proposes eliminating the Social Security-Medicare payroll tax on the bottom half of workers—roughly, those earning less than $33,000 a year—and making up the lost revenue by raising the payroll tax on higher earners.

The goal of these economists is to thwart a crippling political backlash against trade. As they see it, "using the tax code to slice the apple more evenly is far more palatable than trying to hold back globalization with policies that risk shrinking the economic apple."

Some even call for extending global labor arbitrage to CEOs. In a June 2006 *New York Times* op-ed, equity analyst Lawrence Orlowski and New York University assistant research director Florian Lengyel argued that offshoring the jobs of U.S. chief executives would reduce costs and release value to shareholders by bringing the compensation of U.S. CEOs (on average 170 times greater than the compensation of average U.S. workers in 2004) in line with CEO compensation in Britain (22 times greater) and in Japan (11 times greater).

Yet others focus on the stunning lack of labor mobility that distinguishes the current era of globalization from earlier ones. Labor markets are becoming increasingly free and flexible under globalization, but labor enjoys no similar freedom of movement. In a completely free market, the foreign workers would come here to do the work that is currently being outsourced. Why aren't more of those workers coming to the United States? Traditional economists Gary Becker and Richard Posner argue the answer is clear: an excessively restrictive immigration policy.

Onshore and Offshore Solidarity

Offshoring is one of the last steps in capitalism's conversion of the "physician, the lawyer, the priest, the poet, the man of science, into its paid wage laborers," as Marx and Engels put it in the *Communist Manifesto* 160 years ago. It has already done much to increase economic insecurity in the workaday world and has become, Blinder suggests, the number one economic issue of our generation.

Offshoring has also underlined the interdependence of workers across the globe. To the extent that corporations now organize their business operations on a global scale, shifting work around the world in search of low wages, labor organizing must also be global in scope if it is to have any hope of building workers' negotiating strength.

Yet today's global labor arbitrage pits workers from different countries against each other as competitors, not allies. Writing about how to improve labor standards, economists Ajit Singh and Ann Zammit of the South Centre, an Indian non-governmental organization, ask the question, "On what could workers of the world unite" today? Their answer is that faster economic growth could indeed be a positive-sum game from which both the global North and the global South could gain. A pick-up in the long-term rate of growth of the world economy would generate higher employment, increasing wages and otherwise improving labor standards in both regions. It should also make offshoring less profitable and less painful.

The concerns of workers across the globe would also be served by curtailing the ability of multinational corporations to move their investment anywhere, which weakens the bargaining power of labor both in advanced countries and in the global South. Workers globally would also benefit if their own ability to move between countries was enhanced. The combination of a new set of rules to limit international capital movements and to expand labor mobility across borders, together with measures to ratchet up economic growth and thus increase worldwide demand for labor, would alter the current process of globalization and harness it to the needs of working people worldwide. ❑

Sources: Alan S. Blinder, "Fear of Offshoring," CEPS Working Paper #119, Dec. 2005; Alan S. Blinder, "How Many U.S. Jobs Might Be Offshorable?" CEPS Working Paper #142, March 2007; N. Gregory Mankiw and P. Swagel, "The Politics and Economics of Offshore Outsourcing," Am. Enterprise Inst. Working Paper #122, 12/7/05; "Offshoring: Is It a Win-Win Game?" McKinsey Global Institute, August 2003; Diane Farrell et al., "The Emerging Global Labor Market, Part 1: The Demand for Talent in Services," McKinsey Global Institute, June 2005; Ashok Bardhan and Cynthia Kroll, "The New Wave of Outsourcing," Research Report #113, Fisher Center for Real Estate and Urban Economics, Univ. of Calif., Berkeley, Fall 2003; Paul A. Samuelson, "Where Ricardo and Mill Rebut and Confirm Arguments of Mainstream Economists Supporting Globalization," *J Econ Perspectives* 18:3, Summer 2004; Alan S. Blinder, "Free Trade's Great, but Offshoring Rattles Me," *Wash. Post*, 5/6/07; Michael Mandel, "The Real Cost of Offshoring," *BusinessWeek*, 6/18/07; Aaron Bernstein, "Shaking Up Trade Theory," *BusinessWeek*, 12/6/04; David Wessel, "The Case for Taxing Globalization's Big Winners," *WSJ*, 6/14/07; Bob Davis, "Some Democratic Economists Echo Mankiw on Outsourcing," *WSJ*; N. Gregory Mankiw, "Outsourcing Redux," gregmankiw.blogspot.com/2006/05/outsourcing-redux; David Wessel and Bob Davis, "Pain From Free Trade Spurs Second Thoughts," *WSJ*, 3/30/07; Ajit Singh and Ann Zammit, "On What Could Workers of the World Unite? Economic Growth and a New Global Economic Order," from *The Global Labour Standards Controversy: Critical Issues For Developing Countries*, South Centre, 2000; Michael Meeropol, "Distorting Adam Smith on Trade," *Challenge*, July/Aug 2004.

Article 3.5

EASTERN EUROPE'S MID-LEVEL MANUFACTURING TRAP

BY CORNEL BAN
December 2012

Perhaps the most powerful economic myth in the European Union's eastern rim has been that massive Foreign Direct Investment (FDI) inflows will not only arrest deindustrialization and consolidate strong export economies integrated into Germany's transnational industrial cluster, but also have a trickle-down effect on research and development and keep at home more value over time. Like all economic myths, when looked at from a certain angle, this expectation had some believable features. Chief amongst these was the region's low cost and vast army of engineers, the wide availability of strong mathematical skills in the skilled labor force, and the extensive network of research institutes left behind by the techno-scientific legacy of state socialism. To wit, Hungary and the Czech Republic have a strong industrial tradition dating back to the early 20th century.

As long as the music kept playing and massive FDI kept flowing in the region, turning East-Central Europe into export powerhouses, there were few incentives for policy elites in those countries to take a second look at the details of the evidence about costs of exclusive reliance on FDI for their development. It took the unprecedented collapse of these inflows after 2008, the collapse of Western European demand after the crisis of the euro, and the resulting fiscal problems experienced by these countries to change the reformers' gazes from starry-eyed to angst-ridden. What has stood out in these expressions of concern has been the realization that this FDI-dependent model had built-in structural weaknesses that made it perform considerably below the potential of, say, many of the up and coming Asian economies.

Most importantly, it became obvious that FDI had only marginal effects on local research and development capacity, the hallmark of sustainable growth. In fact, it became clear that the entire region was stuck in a bad, medium-level manufacturing trap. For all of the region's countries, the FDI story started with investments in basic manufacturing and then it went up the scale of technological sophistication, at different speeds, to the mid-level—and then remained there. At first, it would be textiles, footwear and basic engineering. Then, emboldened by the fact that Cold War propaganda about Eastern Europe's feet-dragging and kleptomaniac labor force was … just propaganda, foreign investors ventured far afield and started investing in car assembly, car parts, and electric and electronic equipment. "We found in Romania an incredibly well-trained corps of engineers and industrial workers, whose skills were not unlike anything you would find in West European countries with strong industrial traditions." This was how it was put to me in 2008 by a Renault executive involved in the manufacturing miracle called Dacia, the Romanian-made car of the Renault group that turned out to be a cash cow for this venerable French industrial firm.

Similar stories came from the Slovakian and Polish car industry or the excellent performance of Hungary-based electronics companies. Indeed, for a while, it seemed like the region would be the next big "tiger," with FDI also triggering the development of R&D capacities in these industrial fields at the domestic level. Yet this has not occurred on a systemic level. In fact, by itself, the FDI did not create more than a gigantic assembly platform of predominantly mid-level manufactured products. This is true whether one refers to the Czech Republic, a country with one of Europe's oldest industrial traditions and one of the most sophisticated export economies of the region, or to Bulgaria, where industrialization did not start until much later. The information technology (IT) sector aside, almost all of innovation was the result of R&D processes taking place in the home base of the foreign investors in question, generally with minimal local content incorporated in them.

What is more, foreign investments in the East European export boom have been carried out using finance provided by the financial institutions of the foreign firms, rather than by the financial sectors of the ex-communist countries. The region was rather special in the world, in that it had converted the bulk of its banks into mere subsidiaries of foreign (mostly western and northern European) banks. But rather than fund domestic industry or some local innovation boom, these banks proved themselves to be much better at funding a consumption bubble. In many cases (Latvia, Hungary, Romania), that helped lead the local economies down on the bleak road of European Union (EU) and International Monetary Fund (IMF) orchestrated bailouts by 2010. When credit rating agencies began to fidget about the high level of foreign ownership in the region's financial sectors, even the most ardent believers in foreign capital as the panacea to the economic challenges of post-communism began to have doubts.

In short, the FDI-driven export miracles of the EU's East European member states have not landed these economies on the high-octane development path of postwar Finland, Austria, and France, or even the recent experiences of Singapore, South Korea, and (to a more limited extent) Brazil. In these countries, the integration into global supply chains involved making an ideal range of domestically designed products compete in world markets against Western household names. But, for that to happen, it is not enough to create the macroeconomic, regulatory, and infrastructure enticement for foreign investors. One also needs intelligent industrial policies, patient public finance, and bold and well-funded public-private partnerships in R&D that will integrate FDI into medium and long-term development targets defined by the government.

Unfortunately, with the possible exception of Slovenia, East European reformers either rejected such policies with anti-government fervor or, following the policy fashions of the day, saw them as items of mothballed policy paradigms. The result is that the industrial future of the region looks more like that of Mexico's *maquiladoras* than that of the Finnish or Korean industrial powerhouses. This makes one wonder whether in fact it's not high time for East European policy elites to develop better critical and independent thinking skills when encountering policy fads. Or, who knows, even read a bit of heterodox development economics, just for fun. For if they don't, their competitors in Asia certainly are. ❑

Article 3.6

U.S.–CHINA TRADE IN A TIME OF ECONOMIC WEAKNESS

BY DEAN BAKER

September 2012; China-U.S. Focus

With China's economy slowing in the second half of 2012 and the U.S. economy still operating far below its full-employment level of output, trade is likely to again be a source of tension between the world's two largest economies. While this might appear to be a zero sum game, where reduced U.S. imports from China save jobs in the U.S. at China's expense, this need not be the case. The key issue will be whether trade between the two countries can be put on a sounder path that will benefit both.

As it stands, China's currency policy effectively subsidizes its exports to the United States. By buying up hundreds of billions of dollars of U.S. government bonds and other dollar-based assets each year, China's central bank has raised the value of the dollar relative to the yuan. This has the effect of reducing the price of imports from China.

This is an effective subsidy from the Chinese government since it is virtually certain that they will end up taking a loss on their dollar assets. The returns are already low measured in dollars; however, since the dollar is virtually certain to fall relative to other currencies once China cuts back the size of its dollar purchases, China will be paid back in dollars that are worth considerably less than the dollars it purchased.

In the short-term, this policy may be an effective way to develop key industries and maintain high rates of employment; it is difficult to see it as an effective long-term strategy. It is hard to imagine that in 20 years China will still be buying up hundreds of billions of dollars of U.S. bonds each year in order to maintain its export market to the United States.

If China's government needs to maintain demand in its economy, it should be much easier to subsidize the demand of its own population. The money that China is likely to lose on its bond holdings could instead be used on domestic stimulus, building up infrastructure, and improving the health care and education systems in China.

To some extent this was the lesson of China's stimulus package in 2009. The country was able to maintain strong growth even as its exports plunged with one of the most aggressive stimulus packages in the world. Of course, the workers and companies who got jobs and profits from the stimulus were not the same ones who were hurt by plunging exports. However, this is a question of transition and adjustment, not one about overall growth. With enough time and the right policies there is no obvious reason that China could not continue and accelerate its evolution toward a more domestically based economy.

If China were to pursue the higher yuan/lower dollar route it would hugely improve the near-term outlook for the U.S. economy. The growth rate of employment and output over the last two years would not return the U.S. economy to full employment until the middle of the next decade, so China's decision to let the yuan rise could prove enormously beneficial. In exchange for this favor, it would be reasonable for China to demand concessions from the United States of equivalent value.

The obvious target would be U.S. patent and copyright protections. The United States government has made stronger enforcement of patents and copyrights on U.S. products a top priority in its trade negotiations with China and other countries. These forms of intellectual property are in fact enormously costly forms of protectionism. They have far more impact on prices to consumers than other forms of protectionism and in the case of patents on prescription drugs, can jeopardize the health and life of millions of patients.

Patents on prescription drugs currently add close to $270 billion a year (1.8% of GDP) to what people in the United States pay for prescription drugs. In addition, because they create an enormous gap between the patent monopoly price and the cost of production, they provide an enormous incentive for rent-seeking by drug companies. It is rare that a month passes without a story of a major drug company misrepresenting the benefits of its drugs, concealing evidence of harmful side effects, or finding some way to pay off doctors or other providers to increase the use of their drugs.

There are similar, if not as harmful, abuses associated with copyright and its enforcement. Requiring consumers to pay large amounts of money for recorded music or movies, which would otherwise be transferred at zero cost, inevitably leads to large amounts of waste, especially from enforcement costs.

Rather than follow the United States blindly down the path of ever stronger patent and copyright laws, China could opt for more efficient mechanisms to support innovation and creative work. Its *quid pro quo* for ending its policy of supporting the dollar could be that it will allow a free market internally in the items where U.S. companies claim patent and copyright protection.

This would be an enormous boon to China's economy and its consumers, with the dividends growing rapidly through time. Imagine that all new drugs could be sold in China for just a few dollars per prescription. Suppose that all recorded music, movies, books, videos and consumer software were available at no cost on the web.

The gains from going this route should compensate China many times over from the transition costs associated with a reduced export market to the United States. In the longer term, as China develops more efficient mechanisms for supporting innovation and creative work, it will likely shoot past the United States and other wealthy countries in these areas.

The key to moving forward is to break with a pattern of development that is now destructive to both countries. This is a path to trade policy that can allow both the United States and China to be big winners. ❑

Chapter 4

INTERNATIONAL FINANCE

Article 4.1

"PRESSURE FROM THE BOND MARKET"

BY ARTHUR MacEWAN
May/June 2010

> Dear Dr. Dollar:
> With the crisis in Greece and other countries, commentators have said that governments are "under pressure from the bond market" or that bond markets will "punish" governments. What does this mean?
> —*Nikolaos Papanikolaou, Queens, N.Y.*

It means that money is power. The people and institutions that buy government bonds have the money. They are "the bond market." By telling governments the conditions under which they will make loans (i.e., buy the governments' bonds), they are able to greatly influence governments' policies.

But let's go back to some basics. When a government spends more than it takes in as taxes, it has to borrow the difference. It borrows by selling bonds, which are promises to pay. So the payments for the bonds are loans.

A government might sell a bond that is a promise to pay $103 a year from the date of sale. If bond buyers are confident that this promise will be kept and if the return they can get on other forms of investments is 3%, they will be willing to pay $100 for the bond. That is, they will be willing to loan the government $100 to be paid back in one year with 3% interest. This investment will then be providing the same return as their other investments.

But what if they are not confident that the promise will be kept? What if the investors ("the bond market") think that the government of Greece, for example, may not be able to make the payments as promised and will default on the bonds? Under these circumstances the investors will not pay $100 for the bonds that return $103 next year. They may be willing to pay only $97.

If the government then does meet its promise, the bond will provide a 6.2% rate of return. But if the "bond market's" fear of default turns out to be correct, then these bonds will have a much lower rate of return—or, in the extreme case, they will be a total loss. The "bond market" is demanding a higher rate of return to compensate for the risk. (The 3% - 6.2% difference was roughly the difference between the return on German and Greek bonds in March, when this column was written. By mid-April Greece was paying 9%.)

However, if the Greek government—or whatever government is seeking the loans—can sell these bonds for only $97, it will have to sell more bonds in order to raise the funds it needs. In a year, the payments (that 6.2%) will place a new, severe burden on the government's budget.

So the investors say, in effect, "If you fix your policies in ways that we think make default less likely, we will buy the bonds at a higher price—not $100, but maybe at $98 or $99." It is not the ultimate purchasers of the bonds who convey this message; it is the underwriters, the large investment banks—Goldman Sachs for example. As underwriters they handle the sale of the bonds for the Greek government (and take hefty fees for this service).

Even if the investment banks were giving good, objective advice, this would be bad enough. However, the nature of their advice—"the pressure from the bond market"—is conditioned by who they are and whom they represent.

Foremost, they push for actions that will reduce the government's budget deficit, even when sensible economic policy would call for a stimulus that would be provided by maintaining or expanding the deficit. Also, investment bankers will not tell governments to raise taxes on the rich or on foreign corporations in order to reduce the deficit. Instead, they tend to advocate cutting social programs and reducing the wages of public-sector workers.

It does not require great insight to see the class bias in these sorts of actions.

Yet the whole problem does not lie with the "pressure from the bond market." The Greek government and other governments have followed policies that make them vulnerable to this sort of pressure. Unwilling or unable to tax the rich, governments borrowed to pay for their operations in good times. Having run budget deficits in good times, these authorities are in a poor position to add more debt when it is most needed—in the current recession in particular. So now, when governments really need to borrow to run deficits, they—and, more important, their people—are at the mercy of the "bond markets."

Popular protests can push back, saving some social programs and forcing governments to place a greater burden on the wealthy. A real solution, however, requires long-term action to shift power, which would change government practices and reduce vulnerability to "the pressure from the bond market." ❑

Article 4.2

WHAT CAUSES EXCHANGE-RATE FLUCTUATIONS?

BY ARTHUR MacEWAN
March/April 2001, updated August 2009

> Dear Dr. Dollar:
> What are the primary forces that cause foreign exchange rates to fluctuate, and what
> are the remedies to these forces?
>
> *—Mario Anthony, West Palm Beach, Fla.*

A foreign exchange rate is the price, in terms of one currency, that is paid for another currency. For example, at the end of December 2000, in terms of the U.S. dollar, the price of a British pound was $1.50, the price of a Japanese yen was 0.9 cents, and the price of a Canadian dollar was 67 cents. Like any other prices, currency prices fluctuate due to a variety of forces that we loosely categorize as "supply and demand." And as with other prices, the forces of "supply and demand" can have severe economic impacts and nasty human consequences.

Two factors, however, make exchange rates especially problematic. One is that they are subject to a high degree of speculation. This is seldom a significant problem for countries with stable economies—the "developed" countries. But for low-income countries, where instability is endemic, small changes in economic conditions can lead speculators to move billions of dollars in the time it takes to press a button, resulting in very large changes in the prices of currencies. This can quickly and greatly magnify small changes in economic conditions. In 1997 in East Asia, this sort of speculation greatly worsened the economic crisis that arose first in Thailand and then in several other countries. The speculators who drive such crises include bankers and the treasurers of multinational firms, as well as individuals and the operatives of investment companies that specialize in profiting off of the international movement of funds.

The second factor making exchange rates especially problematic is that they affect the prices of many other commodities. For a country that imports a great deal, a drop in the price of its currency relative to the currencies of the countries from which it imports means that a host of imported goods—everything from food to machinery—become more costly. When speculators moved funds out of East Asian countries in 1997, the price of foreign exchange (e.g., the price of the dollar in terms of local currencies) rose, imports became extremely expensive (in local currencies), and both living standards and investment fell dramatically. (Strong speculative movement of funds into a country can also create problems—driving up the price of the local currency, thereby hurting demand for the country's exports, and limiting economic growth.)

In the "normal" course of international trade, short-term exchange-rate fluctuations are seldom large. Consider, for example, trade between the United States and Canada. If people in the United States increasingly buy things from Canada—lumber, vacations in the Canadian Rockies, fish, minerals, auto parts—they will need Canadian dollars to do so. Thus these increased purchases of Canadian goods by people in the United States will mean an increased demand for Canadian dollars and a corresponding increased supply of U.S. dollars. If nothing else changes, the price of the Canadian dollar in terms of the U.S. dollar will tend to rise.

A great deal of the demand and supply of international currencies, however, is not for trade but for investment, often speculative investment. With the strong U.S. stock market in the late 1990s, investors in other countries bought a large amount of assets in the United States. To do so, they demanded U.S. dollars and supplied their own currencies. As a result, the price of the dollar in terms of the currencies of other countries rose substantially, by about 25% on average between the middle of 1995 and the end of 2000. One of the results has been to make imports to the U.S. relatively cheap, and this has been a factor holding down inflation in the United States. Also, as the cost of foreign currency dropped, the cost (in terms of dollars) of hiring foreign workers to supply goods also dropped. The result was more severe competition for many U.S. workers (including, for example, people employed in the production of auto parts, glass goods, textiles, and apparel) and, no surprise, their wages suffered.

There is little point in attempts by governments to constrain the "normal" fluctuations in foreign exchange rates that are associated with trade adjustments (as in the U.S.-Canada example above) or those associated with long-run investment movements (as in the case of the United States during the late 1990s). Although these fluctuations can create large problems—like their impact on U.S. wages—it would be very costly and very difficult, if not impossible, to eliminate them. There are other ways to deal with declining wages.

The experience of the East Asian countries in 1997 is another matter. Speculative investment drove huge exchange-rate changes and (along with other factors) severely disrupted these countries' economies. Between mid-1997 and early 1998, for example, the value of the Thai baht lost close to 60% of its value in terms of the U.S. dollar, and the Malaysian ringgit lost close to 50%. Governments can control such speculative swings by a variety of limits on the quick movement of capital into and out of countries. One mechanism would be a tax on short-term investments. Another would be direct limits on movements of funds. These sorts of controls are not easy to implement, but they have worked effectively in many cases—notably in Malaysia following the 1997 crisis.

It has become increasingly clear in recent years that effective development policies in low-income countries cannot be pursued in the absence of some sort of controls on the movement of funds in and out of those countries. Otherwise, any successful program—whatever its particular aims—can be disrupted and destroyed by the actions of international speculators.

Update, August 2009

The years leading into the economic crisis that appeared in 2007 and 2009 illustrate the way a variety of forces affect the value of the dollar relative to other currencies. Between 1995 and the end of the millennium, the value of the dollar relative to other currencies rose by almost 28%. Many factors were involved, but one important force was the demand by foreign interests for dollars to take part in the stock market boom of that period. After the dot-com stock market bubble of the late 1990s burst, however, the value of the dollar did not fall immediately. The value of the dollar was maintained (and even rose a bit through 2001) as the U.S. economy entered into the 2001 recession; with the recession, there was a fall off in demand for imports—which meant a reduction in the supply of dollars.

Then, however, the value of the dollar began to fall. By early 2008, it was back down to its 1995 level, more than 25% below the 2001 peak. Again, several factors account for the fall. In particular, the very large trade deficit (imports greater than exports)—which more than doubled between 2001 and 2006—meant a growing supply of dollars relative to the demand for dollars. This was partly offset by the demand of foreign interests—for example, the central banks of China, Japan and other countries—for U.S. government bonds (which financed the growing federal budget deficit). But low interest rates in the United States kept the demand for U.S. assets from outweighing the huge supply of dollars generated by the trade deficit.

Ironically, from early 2008 through the beginning of 2009, as the U.S. economy plunged, the value of the dollar shot back up—rising by 14% between April 2008 and April 2009. The reason was simple: as the instability of world financial markets became increasingly apparent, there was a rush to security. That is, investors moved their money into U.S. government bonds, widely viewed as the most secure way to hold assets (in spite of the very low interest rates). This meant a strong demand for dollars.

These movements in the value of the dollar over the last two decades tell a story of instability in the world economy and in the economic relation of the United States to other countries. This instability, in turn, can be extremely disruptive for a variety of industries—and for workers in those industries. ❑

Note: In this discussion of recent experience, the value of the dollar is the "trade-weighted value of the dollar"—that is, the average value of the dollar relative to the values of the currencies of U.S. trading partners.

Article 4.3

IS CHINA'S CURRENCY MANIPULATION HURTING THE U.S.?

BY ARTHUR MacEWAN
November/December 2010

> Dear Dr. Dollar:
>
> Is it true that China has been harming the U.S. economy by keeping its currency "undervalued"? Shouldn't the U.S. government do something about this situation?
>
> —*Jenny Boyd, Edmond, W.Va.*

The Chinese government, operating through the Chinese central bank, does keep its currency unit—the yuan—cheap relative to the dollar. This means that goods imported *from* China cost less (in terms of dollars) than they would otherwise, while U.S. exports *to* China cost more (in terms of yuan). So we in the United States buy a lot of Chinese-made goods and the Chinese don't buy much from us. In the 2007 to 2009 period, the United States purchased $253 billion more in goods annually from China than it sold to China.

This looks bad for U.S workers. For example, when money gets spent in the United States, much of it is spent on Chinese-made goods, and fewer jobs are then created in the United States. So the Chinese government's currency policy is at least partly to blame for our employment woes. Reacting to this situation, many people are calling for the U.S. government to do something to get the Chinese government to change its policy.

But things are not so simple.

First of all, there is an additional reason for the low cost of Chinese goods— low Chinese wages. The Chinese government's policy of repressing labor probably accounts for the low cost of Chinese goods at least as much as does its currency policy. Moreover, there is a lot more going on in the global economy. Both currency problems and job losses involve much more than Chinese government actions— though China provides a convenient target for ire.

And the currency story itself is complex. In order to keep the value of its currency low relative to the dollar, the Chinese government increases the supply of yuan, uses these yuan to buy dollars, then uses the dollars to buy U.S. securities, largely government bonds but also private securities. In early 2009, China held $764 billion in U.S. Treasury securities, making it the largest foreign holder of U.S. government debt. By buying U.S. government bonds, the Chinese have been financing the federal deficit. More generally, by supplying funds to the United States, the Chinese government has been keeping interest rates low in this country.

If the Chinese were to act differently, allowing the value of their currency to rise relative to the dollar, both the cost of capital and the prices of the many goods imported from China would rise. The rising cost of capital would probably not be a serious problem, as the Federal Reserve could take counteraction to keep interest rates low. So, an increase in the value of the yuan would net the United States some jobs, but also raise some prices for U.S. consumers.

It is pretty clear that right now what the United States needs is jobs. Moreover, low-cost Chinese goods have contributed to the declining role of manufacturing in the United States, a phenomenon that both weakens important segments of organized labor and threatens to inhibit technological progress, which has often been centered in manufacturing or based on applications in manufacturing (e.g., robotics).

So why doesn't the U.S. government place more pressure on China to raise the value of the yuan? Part of the reason may lie in concern about losing Chinese financing of the U.S. federal deficit. For several years the two governments have been co-dependent: The U.S. government gets financing for its deficits, and the Chinese government gains by maintaining an undervalued currency. Not an easy relationship to change.

Probably more important, however, many large and politically powerful U.S.-based firms depend directly on the low-cost goods imported from China. Walmart and Target, as any shopper knows, are filled with Chinese-made goods. Then there are the less visible products from China, including a power device that goes into the Microsoft Xbox, computer keyboards for Dell, and many other goods for many other U.S. corporations. If the yuan's value rose and these firms had to pay more dollars to buy these items, they could probably not pass all the increase on to consumers and their profits would suffer.

Still, in spite of the interests of these firms, the U.S. government may take some action, either by pressing harder for China to let the value of the yuan rise relative to the dollar or by placing some restrictions on imports from China. But don't expect too big a change. ❏

Article 4.4

W(H)ITHER THE DOLLAR?

The U.S. trade deficit, the global economic crisis, and the dollar's status as the world's reserve currency.

BY KATHERINE SCIACCHITANO
May/June 2010

For more than half a century, the dollar was both a symbol and an instrument of U.S. economic and military power. At the height of the financial crisis in the fall of 2008, the dollar served as a safe haven for investors, and demand for U.S. Treasury bonds ("Treasuries") spiked. More recently, the United States has faced a vacillating dollar, calls to replace the greenback as the global reserve currency, and an international consensus that it should save more and spend less.

At first glance, circumstances seem to give reason for concern. The U.S. budget deficit is over 10% of GDP. China has begun a long-anticipated move away from Treasuries, threatening to make U.S. government borrowing more expensive. And the adoption of austerity measures in Greece—with a budget deficit barely 3% higher than the United States—hovers as a reminder that the bond market can enforce wage cuts and pension freezes on developed as well as developing countries.

These pressures on the dollar and for fiscal cut-backs and austerity come at an awkward time given the level of public outlays required to deal with the crisis and the need to attract international capital to pay for them. But the pressures also highlight the central role of the dollar in the crisis. Understanding that role is critical to grasping the link between the financial recklessness we've been told is to blame for the crisis and the deeper causes of the crisis in the real economy: that link is the outsize U.S. trade deficit.

Trade deficits are a form of debt. For mainstream economists, the cure for the U.S. deficit is thus increased "savings": spend less and the bottom line will improve. But the U.S. trade deficit didn't balloon because U.S. households or the government went on a spending spree. It ballooned because, from the 1980s on, successive U.S. administrations pursued a high-dollar policy that sacrificed U.S. manufacturing for finance, and that combined low-wage, export-led growth in the Global South with low-wage, debt-driven consumption at home. From the late nineties, U.S. dollars that went out to pay for imports increasingly came back not as demand for U.S. goods, but as demand for investments that fueled U.S. housing and stock market bubbles. Understanding the history of how the dollar helped create these imbalances, and how these imbalances in turn led to the housing bubble and sub-prime crash, sheds important light on how labor and the left should respond to pressures for austerity and "saving" as the solution to the crisis.

Gold, Deficits, and Austerity

A good place to start is with the charge that the Federal Reserve triggered the housing bubble by lowering interest rates after the dot-com bubble burst and plunged the country into recession in 2001.

In 2001, manufacturing was too weak to lead a recovery, and the Bush administration was ideologically opposed to fiscal stimulus other than tax cuts for the wealthy. So the real question isn't why the Fed lowered rates; it's why it was able to. In 2000, the U.S. trade deficit stood at 3.7% of GDP. Any other country with this size deficit would have had to tighten its belt and jump-start exports, not embark on stimulating domestic demand that could deepen the deficit even more.

The Fed's ability to lower interest rates despite the U.S. trade deficit stemmed from the dollar's role as the world's currency, which was established during the Bretton Woods negotiations for a new international monetary system at the end of World War II.

A key purpose of an international monetary system—Bretton Woods or any other—is to keep international trade and debt in balance. Trade has to be mutual. One country can't do all the selling while other does all the buying; both must be able to buy and sell. If one or more countries develop trade deficits that persist, they won't be able to continue to import without borrowing and going into debt. At the same time, some other country or countries will have corresponding trade surpluses. The result is a global trade imbalance. To get back "in balance," the deficit country has to import less, export more, or both. The surplus country has to do the reverse.

In practice, economic pressure is stronger on deficit countries to adjust their trade balances by importing less, since it's deficit countries that could run out of money to pay for imports. Importing less can be accomplished with import quotas (which block imports over a set level) or tariffs (which decrease demand for imports by imposing a tax on them). It can also be accomplished with "austerity"—squeezing demand by lowering wages.

Under the gold standard, this squeezing took place automatically. Gold was shipped out of a country to pay for a trade deficit. Since money had to be backed by gold, having less gold meant less money in domestic circulation. So prices and wages fell. Falling wages in turn lowered demand for imports and boosted exports. The deficit was corrected, but at the cost of recession, austerity, and hardship for workers. In other words, the gold standard was deflationary.

Bretton Woods

The gold standard lasted until the Great Depression, and in fact helped to cause it. Beyond the high levels of unemployment, one of the most vivid lessons from the global catastrophe that ensued was the collapse of world trade, as country after country tried to deal with falling exports by limiting imports. After World War II, the industrialized countries wanted an international monetary system that could correct trade imbalances without imposing austerity and risking another depression. This was particularly important given the post-war levels of global debt and deficits, which could have suppressed demand and blocked trade again. Countries pursued these aims at the Bretton Woods negotiations in 1944, in Bretton Woods, New Hampshire.

John Maynard Keynes headed the British delegation. Keynes was already famous for his advocacy of government spending to bolster demand and maintain employment during recessions and depressions. England also owed large war debts to the United States and had suffered from high unemployment for over two decades. Keynes therefore had a keen interest in creating a system that prevented the build-up of global debt and avoided placing the full pressure of correcting trade imbalances on debtor countries.

His proposed solution was an international clearing union—a system of accounts kept in a fictitious unit called the "bancor." Accounts would be tallied each year to see which countries were in deficit and which were in surplus. Countries with trade deficits would have to work to import less and export more. In the meantime, they would have the unconditional right—for a period—to an "overdraft" of bancors, the size of the overdraft to be based on the size of previous surpluses. These overdrafts would both support continued imports of necessities and guarantee uninterrupted global trade. At the same time, countries running trade surpluses would be expected to get back in balance too by importing more, and would be fined if their surpluses persisted.

Keynes was also adamant that capital controls be part of the new system. Capital controls are restrictions on the movement of capital across borders. Keynes wanted countries to be able to resort to macroeconomic tools such as deficit spending, lowering interest rates, and expanding money supplies to bolster employment and wages when needed. He worried that without capital controls, capital flight—investors taking their money and running—could veto economic policies and force countries to raise interest rates, cut spending, and lower wages instead, putting downward pressure on global demand as the gold standard had.

Keynes's system wouldn't have solved the problems of capitalism—in his terms, the problem of insufficient demand, and in Marx's terms the problems of overproduction and under-consumption. But by creating incentives for surplus countries to import more, it would have supported global demand and job growth and made the kind of trade imbalances that exist today—including the U.S. trade deficit—much less likely. It would also have taken the pressure off deficit countries to adopt austerity measures. And it would have prevented surplus countries from using the power of debt to dictate economic policy to deficit countries.

At the end of World War II, the United States was, however, the largest surplus country in the world, and it intended to remain so for the foreseeable future. The New Deal had lowered unemployment during the Depression. But political opposition to deficit spending had prevented full recovery until arms production for the war restored manufacturing. Many feared that without continued large U.S. trade surpluses and expanded export markets, unemployment would return to Depression-era levels.

The United States therefore blocked Keynes' proposal. Capital controls were permitted for the time being, largely because of the danger that capital would flee war-torn Europe. But penalties for surplus countries were abandoned; pressures remained primarily on deficit countries to correct. Instead of an international clearing union with automatic rights to overdrafts, the International Monetary Fund (IMF) was established to make short-term loans to deficit countries. And instead of the neutral bancor, the dollar—backed by the U.S. pledge to redeem dollars with gold at $35 an ounce—would be the world currency.

Limits of the System

The system worked for just over twenty-five years, not because trade was balanced, but because the United States was able and willing to recycle its huge trade surpluses. U.S. military spending stayed high because of the U.S. cold-war role as "global cop." And massive aid was given to Europe to rebuild. Dollars went out as foreign aid and military spending (both closely coordinated). They came back as demand for U.S. goods.

At the same time, memory of the Depression created a kind of Keynesian consensus in the advanced industrial democracies to use fiscal and monetary policy to maintain full employment. Labor movements, strengthened by both the war and the post-war boom, pushed wage settlements and welfare spending higher. Global demand was high.

Two problems doomed the system. First, the IMF retained the power to impose conditions on debtor countries, and the United States retained the power to control the IMF.

Second, the United States stood outside the rules of the game: The larger the world economy grew, the more dollars would be needed in circulation; U.S. trade deficits would eventually have to provide them. Other countries would have to correct their trade deficits by tightening their belts to import less, exporting more by devaluing their currencies to push down prices, or relying on savings from trade surpluses denominated in dollars (known as "reserves") to pay for their excess of imports over exports. But precisely because countries needed dollar reserves to pay for international transactions and to provide cushions against periods of deficits, other countries would need to hold the U.S. dollars they earned by investing them in U.S. assets. This meant that U.S. dollars that went out for imports would come back and be reinvested in the United States. Once there, these dollars could be used to finance continued spending on imports—and a larger U.S. trade deficit. At that point, sustaining world trade would depend not on recycling U.S. surpluses, but on recycling U.S. deficits. The ultimate result would be large, destabilizing global capital flows.

The Crisis of the Seventies

The turning point came in the early 'seventies. Europe and Japan had rebuilt from the war and were now export powers in their own right. The U.S. trade surplus was turning into a deficit. And the global rate of profit in manufacturing was falling. The United States had also embarked on its "War on Poverty" just as it increased spending on its real war in Vietnam, and this "guns and butter" strategy—an attempt to quell domestic opposition from the civil right and anti-war movements while maintaining global military dominance—led to high inflation.

The result was global economic crisis: the purchasing power of the dollar fell, just as more and more dollars were flowing out of the United States and being held by foreigners.

What had kept the United States from overspending up to this point was its Bretton Woods commitment to exchange dollars for gold at the rate of $35 an ounce. Now countries and investors that didn't want to stand by and watch as the purchasing power of their dollar holdings fell—as well as countries that objected to the Vietnam War—held the United States to its pledge.

There wasn't enough gold in Fort Knox. The United States would have to retrench its global military role, reign in domestic spending, or change the rules of the game. It changed the rules of the game. In August 1971, Nixon closed the gold window; the United States would no longer redeem dollars for gold. Countries and individuals would have to hold dollars, or dump them and find another currency that was more certain to hold its value. There was none.

The result was that the dollar remained the global reserve currency. But the world moved from a system where the United States could spend only if could back its spending by gold, to a system where its spending was limited only by the quantity of dollars the rest of the world was willing to hold. The value of the dollar would fluctuate with the level of global demand for U.S. products and investment. The value of other currencies would fluctuate with the dollar.

Trading Manufacturing for Finance

The result of this newfound freedom to spend was a decade of global inflation and crises of the dollar. As inflation grew, each dollar purchased less. As each dollar purchased less, the global demand to hold dollars dropped—and with it the dollar's exchange rate. As the exchange rate fell, imports became even more expensive, and inflation ratcheted up again. The cycle intensified when OPEC—which priced its oil in dollars—raised its prices to compensate for the falling dollar.

Owners of finance capital were unhappy because inflation was eroding the value of dollar assets. Owners of manufacturing capital were unhappy because the global rate of profit in manufacturing was dropping. And both U.S. politicians and elites were unhappy because the falling dollar was eroding U.S. military power by making it more expensive.

The response of the Reagan administration was to unleash neoliberalism on both the national and global levels—the so-called Reagan revolution. On the domestic front, inflation was quelled, and the labor movement was put in its place, with high interest rates and the worst recession since the Depression. Corporate profits were boosted directly through deregulation, privatization, and tax cuts, and indirectly by attacks on unions, unemployment insurance, and social spending.

When it was over, profits were up, inflation and wages were down, and the dollar had changed direction. High interest rates attracted a stream of investment capital into the United States, pushing up demand for the currency, and with it the exchange rate. The inflows paid for the growing trade and budget deficits—Reagan had cut domestic spending, but increased military spending. And they provided abundant capital for finance and overseas investment. But the high dollar also made U.S. exports more expensive for the rest of the world. The United States had effectively traded manufacturing for finance and debt.

Simultaneously, debt was used as a hammer to impose neoliberalism on the Third World. As the price of oil rose in the seventies, OPEC countries deposited their growing trade surpluses—so-called petro-dollars—in U.S. banks, which in turn loaned them to poor countries to pay for the soaring price of oil. Initially set at very low interest rates, loan payments skyrocketed when the United States jacked up its rates to deal with inflation. Third World countries began defaulting, starting with Mexico in 1981. In response, and in exchange for more loans, the U.S.-controlled IMF imposed austerity programs, also known as "structural adjustment programs."

The programs were similar to the policies in the United States, but much more severe, and they operated in reverse. Instead of pushing up exchange rates to attract finance capital as the United States had done, Third World countries were told to devalue their currencies to attract foreign direct investment and export their way out of debt. Capital controls were dismantled to enable transnational corporations to enter and exit at will. Governments were forced to slash spending on social programs and infrastructure to push down wages and demand for imports. Services were privatized to create opportunities for private capital, and finance was deregulated.

Policies dovetailed perfectly. As the high dollar hollowed out U.S. manufacturing, countries in the Global South were turned into low-wage export platforms. As U.S. wages stagnated or fell, imports became cheaper, masking the pain. Meanwhile, the high dollar lowered the cost of overseas production. Interest payments on third world debt—which continued to grow—swelled the already large capital flows into the United States and provided even more funds for overseas investment.

The view from the heights of finance looked promising. But Latin America was entering what became known as "the lost decade." And the United State was shifting from exporting goods to exporting demand, and from recycling its trade surplus to recycling its deficit. The world was becoming dependent on the United States as the "consumer of last resort." The United States was becoming dependent on finance and debt.

Consolidating Neoliberalism

The growth of finance in the eighties magnified its political clout in the nineties. With the bond market threatening to charge higher rates for government debt, Clinton abandoned campaign pledges to invest in U.S. infrastructure, education, and industry. Instead, he balanced the budget; he adopted his own high-dollar policy, based on the theory that global competition would keep imports cheap, inflation low, and the living standard high—regardless of sluggish wage growth; and he continued deregulation of the finance industry—repealing Glass-Steagall and refusing to regulate derivatives. By the end of Clinton's second term, the U.S. trade deficit had hit a record 3.7% of GDP; household debt had soared to nearly 69% of GDP and financial profits had risen to 30% of GDP, almost twice as high as they had been at any time up to the mid 1980s.

Internationally, Clinton consolidated IMF-style structural adjustment policies under the rubric of "the Washington Consensus," initiated a new era of trade agreements modeled on the North American Free Trade Agreement, and led the charge to consolidate the elimination of capital controls.

The elimination of capital controls deepened global economic instability in several ways.

First, eliminating restrictions on capital mobility made it easier for capital to go in search of the lowest wages. This expanded the globalization of production, intensifying downward pressure on wages and global demand.

Second, removing capital controls increased the political power of capital by enabling it to "vote with its feet." This accelerated the deregulation of global finance and—as Keynes predicted—limited countries' abilities to run full-employment policies. Regulation of business was punished, as was deficit spending, regardless of its purpose. Low inflation and deregulation of labor markets—weakening unions and making wages more "flexible"—were rewarded.

Finally, capital mobility fed asset bubbles and increased financial speculation and exchange rate volatility. As speculative capital rushed into countries, exchange rates rose; as it fled, they fell. Speculators began betting more and more on currencies themselves, further magnifying rate swings. Rising exchange rates made exports uncompetitive, hurting employment and wages. Falling exchange rates increased the competitiveness of exports, but made imports and foreign borrowing more expensive, except for the United States, which borrows in its own currency. Countries could try to prevent capital flight by raising interest rates, but only at the cost of dampening growth and lost of jobs. Lacking capital controls, there was little countries could do to prevent excessive inflows and bubbles.

Prelude to a Crash

This increased capital mobility, deregulation, and speculation weakened the real economy, further depressed global demand, and greatly magnified economic instability.

From the eighties onward, international financial crises broke out approximately every five years, in countries ranging from Mexico to the former Soviet Union.

By far the largest crisis prior to the sub-prime meltdown took place in East Asia in the mid-nineties. Speculative capital began flowing into East Asia in the mid nineties. In 1997, the bubble burst. By the summer of 1998, stock markets around the world were crashing from the ripple effects. The IMF stepped in with $40 billion in loans, bailing out investors but imposing harsh conditions on workers and governments. Millions were left unemployed as Asia plunged into depression.

When the dust settled, Asian countries said "never again." Their solution was to build up large dollar reserves—savings cushions—so they would never have to turn to the IMF for another loan. To build up reserves, countries had to run large trade surpluses. This meant selling even more to the United States, the only market in the world able and willing to run ever-larger trade deficits to absorb their exports.

In addition to further weakening U.S. manufacturing, the Asia crisis set the stage for the sub-prime crisis in several ways.

First, as capital initially fled Asia, it sought out the United States as a "safe haven," igniting the U.S. stock market and nascent housing bubbles.

Second, the longer-term recycling of burgeoning Asian surpluses ensured an abundant and ongoing source of capital to finance not only the mounting trade deficit, but also the billowing U.S. consumer debt more generally.

Third, preventing their exchange rates from rising with their trade surpluses and making their exports uncompetitive required Asian central banks to print money, swelling global capital flows even more.

Between 1998 and 2007, when the U.S. housing bubble burst, many policy makers and mainstream economists came to believe this inflow of dollars and debt would never stop. It simply seemed too mutually beneficial to end. By financing the U.S. trade deficit, Asian countries guaranteed U.S. consumers would continue to purchase their goods. The United States in turn got cheap imports, cheap money for consumer finance, and inflated stock and real estate markets that appeared to be self-financing and to compensate for stagnating wages. At the same time, foreign holders of dollars bought increasing quantities of U.S. Treasuries, saving the U.S. government from having to raise interest rates to attract purchasers, and giving the United States cheap financing for its budget deficit as well.

It was this ability to keep interest rates low—in particular, the Fed's ability to lower rates after the stock market bubble collapsed in 2000—that set off the last and most destructive stage of the housing bubble. Lower interest rates simultaneously increased the demand for housing (since lower interest rates made mortgages cheaper) and decreased the returns to foreign holders of U.S. Treasuries. These lower returns forced investors to look for other "safe" investments with higher yields. Investors believed they found what they needed in U.S. mortgage securities.

As Wall Street realized what a lucrative international market they had, the big banks purposefully set out to increase the number of mortgages that could be repackaged and sold to investors by lowering lending standards. They also entered into complicated systems of private bets, known as credit default swaps, to insure against the risk of defaults. These credit default swaps created a chain of debt that exponentially magnified risk. When the bubble finally burst, only massive stimulus spending and infusions of capital by the industrialized countries into their banking systems kept the world from falling into another depression.

Deficit Politics

The political establishment—right and center—is now licking its chops, attacking fiscal deficits as if ending them were a solution to the crisis. The underlying theory harks back to the deflationary operation of the gold standard and the conditions imposed by the IMF: Government spending causes trade deficits and inflation by increasing demand. Cutting spending will cut deficits by diminishing demand.

Like Clinton before him, Obama is now caving in to the bond market, fearful that international lenders will raise interest rates on U.S. borrowing. He has created a bi-partisan debt commission to focus on long-term fiscal balance—read: cutting Social Security and Medicare—and revived "PAYGO," which requires either cuts or increases in revenue to pay for all new outlays, even as unemployment hovers just under 10%.

By acquiescing, the U.S. public is implicitly blaming itself for the crisis and offering to pay for it twice: first with the millions of jobs lost to the recession, and again by weakening the safety net. But the recent growth of the U.S. budget deficit principally reflects the cost of cleaning up the crisis and of the wars in Iraq and Afghanistan. Assumptions of future deficits are rooted in projected health-care costs in the absence of meaningful reform. And the U.S. trade deficit is driven mainly by the continued high dollar.

The economic crisis won't be resolved by increasing personal savings or enforcing fiscal discipline, because its origins aren't greedy consumers or profligate governments. The real origins of the crisis are the neoliberal response to the crisis of the 1970s—the shift from manufacturing to finance in the United States, and the transformation of the Global South into a low-wage export platform for transnational capital to bolster sagging profit rate. The U.S. trade and budget deficits may symbolize this transformation. But the systemic problem is a global economic model that separates consumption from production and that has balanced world demand—not just the U.S. economy—on debt and speculation.

Forging an alternative will be the work of generations. As for the present, premature tightening of fiscal policy as countries try to "exit" from the crisis will simply drain global demand and endanger recovery. Demonizing government spending will erode the social wage and undermine democratic debate about the public investment needed for a transition to an environmentally sustainable global economy.

In the United States, where labor market and financial deregulation have garnered the most attention in popular critiques of neoliberalism, painting a bulls-eye on government spending also obscures the role of the dollar and U.S. policy in the crisis. For several decades after World War II, U.S. workers benefited materially as the special status of the dollar helped expand export markets for U.S. goods. But as other labor movements throughout the world know from bitter experience, it's the dollar as the world's currency, together with U.S. control of the IMF, that ultimately provided leverage for the United States to create the low-wage export model of growth and financial deregulation that has so unbalanced the global economy and hurt "first" and "third" world workers alike.

Looking Ahead

At the end of World War II, John Maynard Keynes proposed an international monetary system with the bancor at its core; the system would have helped balance trade and avoid the debt and deflation inherent in the gold standard that preceded the Great Depression. Instead, Bretton Woods was negotiated, with the dollar as the world's currency. What's left of that system has now come full circle and created the very problems it was intended to avoid: large trade imbalances and deflationary economic conditions.

For the past two and a half decades, the dollar enabled the United States to run increasing trade deficits while systematically draining capital from some of the poorest countries in the world. This money could have been used for development in the Global South, to replace aging infrastructure in the United States, or to prepare for and prevent climate change. Instead, it paid for U.S. military interventions, outsourcing, tax cuts for the wealthy, and massive stock market and housing bubbles.

This mismanagement of the dollar hasn't served the long-term interests of workers the United States any more than it has those in of the developing world. In domestic terms, it has been particularly damaging over the last three decades to U.S. manufacturing, and state budgets and workers are being hit hard by the crisis. Yet even manufacturing workers in the United States cling to the high dollar as if it were a life raft. Many public sector workers advocate cutting back on government spending. And most people in the United States would blame bankers' compensation packages for the sub-prime mess before pointing to the dismantling of capital controls.

After suffering through the worst unemployment since the Depression and paying for the bailout of finance, U.S. unions and the left are right to be angry. On the global scale, there is increased space for activism. Since the summer of 2007, at least 17 countries have imposed or tightened capital controls. Greek workers have been in the streets protesting pension cuts and pay freezes for months now. And a global campaign has been launched for a financial transactions tax that would slow down speculation and provide needed revenue for governments. Together, global labor and the left are actively rethinking and advocating reform of the global financial system, the neoliberal trade agreements, and the role and governance of the International Monetary Fund. And there is increasing discussion of a replacement for the dollar that won't breed deficits, suck capital out of the developing world, impose austerity on deficit countries—or blow bubbles.

All these reforms are critical. All will require more grassroots education. None will come without a struggle. ❑

Sources: C. Fred Bergsten, "The Dollar and the Deficits: How Washington Can Prevent the Next Crisis," Peterson Institute for International Economics, *Foreign Affairs*, Volume 88 No. 6, November 2009; Dean Baker, "The Budget, the Deficit, and the Dollar," Center for Economic Policy and Research, www.cepr.net; Martin Wolf, "Give us fiscal austerity, but not quite yet," *Financial Times* blogs, November 24, 2009; Tom Palley, "Domestic Demand-led Growth: A New Paradigm for Development," paper presented at the Alterantives to Neoliberalism Conference sponsored by the New Rules for Global Finance Coalition, May 21-24, 2002, www. economicswebinstitute.org; Sarah Anderson, "Policy Handcuffs in the Financial Crisis: How U.S. Government And Trade Policy Limit Government Power To Control Capital Flows, " Institute for Policy Studies, February 2009; Susan George, "The World Trade Organisation We Could Have Had," *Le Monde Diplomatique*, January 2007.

Article 4.5

CHINA'S DEVELOPMENT BANKS GO GLOBAL: THE GOOD AND THE BAD

BY KEVIN GALLAGHER
November/December 2013

China is redefining the global development agenda. While the West preaches trade liberalization and financial deregulation, China orchestrates massive infrastructure and industrial policies under regulated trade and financial markets. China transformed its economy and brought more than 600 million people out of poverty. Western policies led to financial crises, slow growth, and relatively less poverty alleviation across the globe.

China is now exporting its model across the world. The China Development Bank (CDB) and the Export-Import Bank of China (EIBC) now provide more financing to developing countries than the World Bank does. What is more, China's finance doesn't come with the harsh conditions—such as trade liberalization and fiscal austerity—that western-backed finance has historically. China's development banks are not only helping to spur infrastructure development across the world, they are also helping China's bottom line as they make a strong profit and often provide opportunities for Chinese firms.

It is well known that China is taking the lead in developing and deploying clean energy technologies, as it has become the world's leading producer of solar panels. China is pumping finance into cleaner energy abroad as well. According to a new study by the World Resources Institute, since 2002 Chinese firms have put an additional $40 billion into solar and wind projects across the globe.

However, China's global stride may be jeopardized unless it begins to incorporate environmental and social safeguards into its overseas operations. In a policy memorandum for the Paulson Institute, I note how there is a growing backlash against China's development banks on these grounds. By remedying these concerns, China can become the global leader in development finance.

There is a growing number of cases where Chinese financial institutions may be losing ground over social and environmental concerns.

One example is CDB's multibillion-dollar China-Burma oil and gas pipeline projects. The Shwe gas project is coordinated by China National Petroleum Corporation, which has contracted out some operations to Sinohydro (the state-owned hydroelectric company). Local civil society organizations have mounted campaigns against land confiscation with limited compensation, loss of livelihoods, the role of Burmese security forces in protecting the project, and environmental degradation (deforestation, river dredging, and chemical pollution).

Another example is the Patuca hydroelectric project in Honduras, supported by EIBC and operated by Sinohydro. Approved by the Honduran government in 2011, one of the projects is said to entail flooding 42 km of rainforest slated to be part of Patuca national park and the TawahkaAsangni biosphere reserve. The project was denounced by local civil society organizations, which cited the shaky foundations of the project's environmental impact assessment. NGOs including International Rivers and The Nature Conservancy have also sought to reevaluate the project. Such campaigns, uniting locally affected communities with globally recognized NGOs that have access to media worldwide, have slowed projects and tainted investors' images.

Extraction from the Belinga iron ore deposit in Gabon was contracted in 2007 between the government in Libreville and the China Machinery Energy Corporation, with financing from EIBC. The project sparked significant local protest over its environmental impact, and, as a result, has been perpetually renegotiated and delayed, and may ultimately be denied.

Environment-related political risk can severely affect the bottom line of the major Chinese development banks to the extent that local skepticism and protests result in delays or even loss of projects. Doing the right thing on the environment and human rights would help maintain China's market access and help mitigate risks to China's development banks.

Adopting established international norms, moreover, may help China's banks to secure markets in more developed countries. Chinese banks clearly seek to further penetrate markets such as the United States and Europe, where even higher environmental and social standards exist. Establishing a track record of good practice in emerging markets and developing countries could help Chinese banks assimilate, adapt, and ultimately incorporate such practices into their daily operations, an experience that could prove essential as they also seek to navigate markets in high-income Organisation for Economic Co-operation and Development (OECD) countries.

For decades, developing countries have pined for a development bank that provides finance for inclusive growth and sustainable development—without the draconian conditions that the IMF and World Bank have often imposed as a condition of their lending. That conditionality, and the egregious environmental record of early World Bank and other international-financial-institution projects, spurred a global backlash against these institutions. If China's development banks can add substantial social and environmental safeguards, they can become a beacon of 21st century development finance. ❏

Article 4.6

BEYOND THE WORLD CREDITORS' CARTEL

BY DARIUSH SOKOLOV
September/October 2009

One group of financiers seems to be doing nicely out of the global recession: the International Monetary Fund and other international financial institutions (IFIs) are enjoying a return to relevance and lining up for increased funding.

The London G20 Summit in April was the IMF's big comeback gig. In 2007 the Fund's loan book was down to just $20 billion; now its capital is set to triple to $750 billion, plus permission to issue $250 billion in "special drawing rights" (the Fund's quasi-currency which allows member countries to borrow from each others' reserves). Since September 2008 a range of East European and ex-Soviet states have taken out new loans. So too have Pakistan, El Salvador, and Iceland—the Fund's first Western European client since Britain in 1976.

The World Bank and regional development banks are also getting in on the party. In Latin America, the World Bank's regional vice president Pamela Cox says she expects lending to triple in 2009 to $14 billion. The Inter-American Development Bank (IDB), the most active IFI in the region, expects to lend $18 billion—its typical loan portfolio is under $8 billion. And the development banks are queuing up behind the IMF with their caps out for capital increases: the Asian Development Bank wants to triple its capital to $165 billion; the IDB is asking for an extra $50 to $80 billion on top of its current $101 billion.

Why now? The IFIs, says Vince McElhinny of the Bank Information Center, a group that monitors them, are opportunists at heart. Just like any private bank or corporation they fight for market share, and as the world economy and global capital markets grow they need to increase their lending apace or lose relevance. The freezing of world capital markets, particularly severe in emerging markets, has created a need which they can seize as opportunity. The Institute of International Finance predicts private net capital flows to emerging markets of $141 billion in 2009, down from $392 billion in 2008, after a record $890 billion in 2007. The IFIs see themselves helping to fill this gap.

But the issues at stake here go beyond the IFIs' own agendas. On the one hand, their revival implies a reassertion of U.S. and global North dominance. They aren't called "Washington-based" just as a matter of real estate: the United States has a 17% voting share on the IMF and World Bank, enough to give it a veto on some major changes; Europe and the United States control the top management positions. On the other hand, the story underscores how parts of the global South are gaining in economic power. In the crises of the 1990s, or so the neoliberal story went, the IMF stepped in to clean up the messes made when fragile Third World economies exploded. This time around things are very different: the mess is in the North, and the likelihood is that the emerging economies of Asia and Latin America will emerge from it stronger and more independent. (It's important to note, though, that large areas in the South, notably Africa, are not part of this story—nor is Eastern Europe.) The so-called BRIC nations in particular (Brazil, Russia, India, China) are getting the bargaining power to back up their claims on the global financial system. Will these claims be met within the existing institutions, or by creating a new financial architecture that bypasses Washington altogether? The future of the IFIs is a key arena in which global rebalancing of economic power is playing out.

New Financial Architecture?

In May 2007 finance ministers from Brazil, Argentina, Venezuela, Bolivia, and Ecuador signed the "Quito Declaration" in the Ecuadorian capital. The plan includes a regional monetary fund and moves toward a South American single currency, but the first step is the creation of the Banco del Sur, a new regional development bank. While the bank's launch is behind schedule, this March its constitution was agreed to, with an initial capitalization of $7 billion. Besides the original five, Paraguay and Uruguay are also members. (Even Colombia had announced its support before its late-2007 row with Venezuela over hostages.)

The aim of Banco del Sur is to replace the Washington-based lenders altogether with institutions run by and for South America. Maria Jose Romero, who researches the IFIs at the Third World Institute in Montevideo, encapsulates this spirit. "In responding to the crisis Latin American countries have two options," she says. "We can return to the old institutions and the failed recipes of the 1990s, or we can move forward with alternatives."

For many Latin American countries a return to the IMF is politically out of the question. According to Mark Weisbrot, co-director of the Center for Economic and Policy Research in Washington, the decline of the IMF started with the Asian financial crisis over a decade ago. After the Fund's failure to act as emergency lender of last resort to Asian banking systems in 1997, those states moved to build up sizeable currency reserves, determined not to be dependent on the Fund again; others followed suit.

This turning away has been more dramatic in Latin America, where IMF policies are blamed for precipitating the 1998 crisis in Argentina which led to the collapse of its banking system and eventually to its 2002 default. Argentina and Bolivia both paid off the last of their debts to the Fund in 2006; in April 2007 Ecuador announced it had paid off its IMF loans and requested the Fund withdraw its country manager; the same month Venezuela announced itself debt-free, and a few weeks later said it would withdraw from fund membership altogether. When Daniel Ortega won the Nicaraguan presidential election in May 2007 he promised the country would be "free from the Fund" within five years.

How has this freedom-from-Washington line held in the current crisis? U.S.-friendly Mexico was the first to sign up for the new Flexible Credit Lines the

IMF is granting without conditions to "pre-approved" governments, followed by Colombia—though neither has yet drawn on them. So far only El Salvador and Costa Rica have taken out new loans. In sharp contrast to Eastern Europe, most Latin American states had healthy reserve cushions coming into the crunch. And with commodity prices now rising again, it may be that the region's anti-IMF resolve is not going to face the test many had anticipated.

As for Banco del Sur, the arrival of crisis no doubt slowed the process: domestic firefighting comes before regional cooperation. But, according to Romero, in the medium term it will help push change: "The crisis has focused attention to the failings of the existing financial system," she says. "It is helping build the impetus for Banco del Sur, as well as for moves to settle bilateral trade in local currencies [rather than dollars], which is the first step towards monetary union, and for broader South-South cooperation initiatives."

To be fair, Banco del Sur may not live up to proponents' hopes. With just $7 billion in capital, the bank won't be in the same league as the Washington-based IFIs. Nor is there any immediate plan to create an emergency monetary fund—an Ecuadorian proposal to that effect has been dropped. And the principle of one country one vote, perhaps the biggest rallying point of all, has been modified: equal votes will apply only on loans under $70 million, above which approval is required from members with two-thirds of the capital contributions.

Finally, there is still no clarity on the focus of lending. Campaigners hope for a true emphasis on poverty reduction and projects to build regional cooperation, and have scored the provision of a socially focused "audit board." But some fear that more conservative members (read: Brazil) could push Banco del Sur toward being just one more development bank.

Across Asia, there are parallel developments. A proposal by Japan to set up an Asian Monetary Fund met the same fate as an earlier Malaysian-backed scheme called the East Asian Economic Caucus—both were dropped after expressions of disapproval from the IMF and U.S. officials. But now the Chiang Mai Initiative, a longstanding plan for a system of swap arrangements between the central banks of the southeast Asian countries plus China, Japan, and South Korea is expected to come on line this year, and the proposed size of the scheme was upped to $120 billion in February. Chiang Mai is linked to the IMF (members need IMF agreements in place to withdraw more than 20% of the total), but some see it leading towards an eventual independent regional fund. For now, though, at least officially, the talk is usually of "complementing," not supplanting, the IMF.

Rise of the BRICs

If the Quito project is the idealistic side of the regionalization movement, the BRIC bloc is global power shift as realpolitik. The BRICs together now account for 22% of world production (by purchasing power parity), up from 16% ten years ago and rising. Even as they move ahead with regional institutions independent of the IFIs, the BRICs are pushing for more power within the Washington- based institutions. Increased say at the IMF is one of the four governments' main demands. In March 2008 China's vote share was raised all the way up to 3.7%— putting the world's most populous country on a par with Belgium plus the Netherlands, combined population 27 million. The BRICs jointly muster a 9.82% quota.

According to Vince McElhinny, the BRICs' contributions to the Fund's current capital boost are aimed at bolstering their demands for more say in IFI governance. When, a week before the BRIC summit, Brazil's President Lula announced a $10 billion contribution, he talked of thereby gaining "moral authority to keep pushing for changes needed at the IMF."

The IMF's desire to placate emerging powers such as the BRICs may explain the makeover it has displayed in its current comeback—dubbed "IMF 2.0" by *Time* magazine. Managing director Dominique Strauss-Kahn has called for the Fund to spend against recession: less structural adjustment, more counter-cyclical stimulus. But the changes may be largely cosmetic. According to a study by the Third World Network, the actual conditions of recent IMF loans to Pakistan, Hungary, Ukraine, and other countries are familiar: the borrowers must reduce their fiscal deficits through public spending cuts, wage freezes, higher fuel tariffs, and interest rate hikes.

What real changes are the BRICs really likely to get? There's plenty of gossip flying around: some are touting Lula as the next World Bank president; perhaps China will get to pick Strauss- Kahn's successor. Mark Weisbrot, however, does not see the U.S. government giving any ground on voting shares. "The U.S. would rather walk away from the IMF than give up control," he says.

Beyond the Cartel

Weisbrot describes the IMF as "the most important instrument of influence the U.S. government has in developing countries—beyond the military, beyond the CIA. Or, at least, that's the role it's played for most of the last 30 years. A good part of that influence has been lost recently; now they're trying to get it back."

The IMF's power has never really been about its own lending, however. Its influence over countries' economic policies is far greater than would be suggested by its share in overall capital flows. The real issue is the Fund's role as "gatekeeper" of a global "creditors' cartel."

Multilateral loans from the World Bank and regional development banks and bilateral loans from the wealthy countries typically come with some form of "cross-conditionality" clause. You only get your loan if you first have an IMF agreement in place; installments only keep flowing so long as you stick to it. Similar conditions can also apply in private capital transactions. For instance, Venezuela's 2007 threat to give up its IMF membership triggered a market sell-off because under covenants written into its sovereign bonds, a break with the Fund would count as a "technical default."

Now, though, recent shifts in Latin America have dealt what Weisbrot says could be "a final blow to the IMF creditors' cartel in middle-income countries."

This is a continental tale, but Argentina is a good place to begin. The country cut itself off from international capital markets with its 2002 default, and is still being chased by "hold-out" bond investors in the New York courts. Yet Argentina grew at almost 9% a year from 2003 through 2007—the country's most rapid growth in 50 years, and some of the fastest growth rates on the continent. This expansion has been funded largely by selling bonds to another emerging regional power, Venezuela. These bond transfers are no subsidies—Argentina pays commercial interest rates— but they do come free of Washington conditions. For Weisbrot, "Venezuela's offers of credit, without policy conditions, to Argentina, Bolivia, Ecuador, Nicaragua, and other countries has changed the equation."

It's true that easy Venezuelan credit dried up early on in the crisis as oil prices plummeted. It's also true that Argentina is now allowing IMF staff in to monitor its economy and taking out new loans from the World Bank and the IDB. But it's telling that Argentina got these loans without any IMF agreement in place: the cartel, at least in its old form, appears to be broken. And then there's the other plank in Argentina's current crisis management strategy: a $10.2 billion swap line direct with China.

In short, the IMF and allied institutions have regained some lost ground in the crisis, but forms of "South-South cooperation" that stand to weaken the Washington-based creditors' cartel have kept on building too.

According to one very plausible interpretation, this crisis has been about the consequences of the rich countries' capital piling into the financial services sphere to compensate for the loss of manufacturing production to the Third World. Control of the world's financial capital flows was one last highly profitable channel where Northern capital still ruled unopposed. Increasingly, though, global- South states and corporations are cutting out the middle man to trade directly with each other. It's against the background of these new possibilities that the next chapter in the story of the IFIs will play out. ❏

Sources: "Special Drawing Rights (SDRs)," IMF fact sheet, Feb. 2009; "IMF 2.0," *Time*, April 20, 2009; Third World Network, "The IMF's Financial Crisis Loans: No change in conditionalities," March 2009; Institute of International Finance, "Capital Flows to Emerging Markets," June 10, 2009; "Latin America in the Midst of the Global Financial Meltdown: A Systemic Proposal," Latin American Shadow Financial Regulatory Committee Statement No. 19, December 2008; Felix Salmon's blog on Ecuador's default, blogs.reuters.com/felix-salmon/; Mark Weisbrot, "Ten Years After: The Lasting Impact of the Asian Financial Crisis," Center for Economic and Policy Research, August 2007; Tadahiro Asami, "Chiang Mai Initiative as the foundation of financial stability in East Asia," ASEAN, March 2005; DominicWilson and Roopa Purushothaman, "DreamingWith BRICs: The Path to 2050," Goldman Sachs Global Economics Paper No. 99, Oct. 2003; Eugenio Diaz-Bonilla, "Argentina's recent growth episode," RGE Monitor, Sept. 18, 2007; Graham Turner, *The Credit Crunch: Housing Bubbles, Globalisation and the Worldwide Economic Crisis*, Pluto Press, 2008.

Article 4.7

BEYOND DEBT AND GROWTH
An Interview with Robert Pollin

July/August 2013

Nothing warms the heart quite like a story of the high and mighty brought low. Harvard economists Carmen Reinhart and Kenneth Rogoff were the high and mighty—prestigious academics whose influential paper on government debt and economic growth was widely cited by policymakers and commentators to justify painful austerity policies. The underdogs who brought them down were three members of the UMass-Amherst economics department: graduate student Thomas Herndon and professors Michael Ash and Robert Pollin. As Dean Baker of the Center for Economic and Policy Research (CEPR) argues, it is no accident that UMass economists were the ones to debunk Reinhart and Rogoff. The department, Baker notes, "stands largely outside the mainstream" of the economics profession and so is "more willing to challenge the received wisdom."

Reinhart and Rogoff had claimed that countries with government-debt-to-GDP ratios of over 90% could expect dramatically lower future economic growth than other countries. But when Herndon attempted to replicate this result for a course in applied econometrics taught by Ash and Pollin, he found that he couldn't. In fact, as the Herndon-Ash-Pollin published paper would report, there was no dramatic growth dropoff above the supposedly critical 90% threshold. The reasons behind the faulty finding? Well, there was the world's most famous spreadsheet error—which has received extraordinary media attention mainly because it is so embarrassing, so all the more delicious given the lofty position of the authors. More importantly, however, was Reinhart and Rogoff's questionable treatment of the data. Most of the difference between their results and Herndon-Ash-Pollin's was due to no mere error, careless or otherwise, but to deliberate (and, in Pollin's view, "indefensible") decisions about how to average the data, how to divide it into different categories, and so on.

Pollin is the co-director of the Political Economy Research Institute (PERI) at UMass-Amherst and is well-known for his work on minimum-wage and living-wage laws as well as the project of building a green economy. Dollars & Sense co-editor Alejandro Reuss sat down with him to talk not only about the Reinhart-Rogoff paper and the Herndon-Ash-Pollin takedown, but also larger issues about the economic crisis and austerity: the role economists have played in abetting austerity, the reasons behind policymakers' determination to impose austerity policies, and the diverging paths before us—the profit-led recovery promised by neoliberal economists versus a wage-led recovery pointing toward a more egalitarian social-democratic system. (Full disclosure: Pollin is a Dollars & Sense Associate, and was Reuss's professor and dissertation advisor at UMass-Amherst.) —Eds.

D&S: While Reinhart and Rogoff's now-famous Excel error got a lot of attention in the media, this was a relatively small factor in the findings they reported. What do you think are the key critiques of the view that high debt-to-GDP ratios doom growth, both in terms of the figures and interpretation?

RP: I recall one commentator said that the Excel coding error was the equivalent of a figure skater who was not doing well, but it wasn't entirely clear until he or she fell. Even though the fall itself wasn't the most significant thing, it dramatized the broader set of problems. I think that's true of the Reinhart-Rogoff paper. The main things that were driving their results were, first, that they excluded data on some countries, which they have continued to defend. Second, and most importantly, was the way that they weighted data. They took each country as a separate observation, no matter how many years the country had a high public-debt-to- GDP ratio. For example, New Zealand had one year, 1951, in which they had a public-debt-to-GDP ratio over 90%. And in that year New Zealand had a depression. GDP growth was negative 7.6%. The UK, by contrast, had 19 years in which the debt-to-GDP ratio was over 90%, and over those 19 years GDP growth averaged 2.5% per year, which is not spectacular, but not terrible. Now, according to the way Reinhart and Rogoff weighted the data, one year in New Zealand was equally weighted with 19 years in the UK, which I find completely indefensible.

D&S: So when you correct for these problems, you end up with a modest—maybe not even statistically significant—negative relationship between the debt-to-GDP ratio and future growth. What are the main arguments about how to interpret this relationship?

RP: Reinhart and Rogoff have been making the defense that even the Herndon-Ash-Pollin results still showed public-debt-to-GDP over 90% being associated with a GDP growth rate of 2.2%. Meanwhile, at less than 90% debt-to-GDP, growth is between 3 and 4%. So they're saying, "Well, we made some mistakes but it's still a 1% difference in growth over time, which matters a lot." And I wouldn't disagree with that observation.

But there are other things in here. First, is it statistically significant? One of the other things we [Herndon-Ash-Pollin] did was to create another public-debt-to-GDP category, 90% to 120%, and then above 120% debt-to-GDP. For the 90-120% category there's no difference in future growth rates [compared to the lower debt-to-GDP category]. So it's only when you go way out, in terms of the debt ratio, that you will observe a drop-off in growth. Second, what happens when you look over time? In their data, for 2000 to 2009, the growth rate for the highest public-debt-to-GDP category was actually a little bit higher than in the lower categories. So what's clear is that there really is no strong association.

In addition, some people have then taken their findings and asked which way causality is running. Is it that when you have a recession, and you're at lower growth, you borrow more? Well, that's certainly part of the story. And Reinhart and Rogoff have now backpedaled on that. But to me, even that is not nearly getting at the heart of the matter. The heart of the matter is that when you're borrowing money you can use it for good things or bad things. You can be doing it in the midst of a recession. If we're going to invest in green technologies to reduce carbon emissions, that's good.

We also need to ask: what is the interest rate at which the government is borrowing? The U.S. government's debt servicing today—how much we have to pay in interest as a share of government expenditures— is actually at a historic low, even though the borrowing has been at a historic high. The answer obviously is because the interest rate is so low. When you're in an economic crisis and you want to stimulate the economy by spending more, does the central bank have the capacity to maintain a low interest rate? In the United States, the answer is yes. In the UK, the answer is yes. Germany, yes. In the rest of Europe, no. If you can borrow at 0%, go for it. If you have to borrow at 9%, that's a completely different world. And the Reinhart-Rogoff framework doesn't answer the question. It doesn't even ask that question.

D&S: Looking at research touted by policymakers to justify austerity policies, which has now been debunked, do you see the researchers putting a "thumb on the scale" to get the results that they wanted? Is that something you want to address, as

---

Who, Me?

Since the publication of the Herndon-Ash-Pollin critique of their research, Reinhart and Rogoff have defended their findings while backing off the strongest interpretations. They claimed in the *New York Times* (April 25, 2013) that, far from arguing simply that high debt causes low growth, their "view has always been that causality runs in both directions, and that there is no rule that applies across all times and places." And they have washed their hands of commentators and politicians who "falsely equated our finding of a negative association between debt and growth with an unambiguous call for austerity."

Judge for yourself, based on Rogoff's words back in 2010:

Indeed, it is folly to ignore the long-term risks of already record peacetime debt accumulation. Even where Greek-style debt crises are unlikely, the burden of debt will ultimately weigh on growth due to inevitable fiscal adjustment. ... [A]n apparently benign market environment can darken quite suddenly as a country approaches its debt ceiling. Even the US is likely to face a relatively sudden fiscal adjustment at some point if it does not put its fiscal house in order.

—Kenneth Rogoff, "No need for a panicked fiscal surge," *Financial Times*, July 20, 2010

—Eds.

opposed to simply getting the data, seeing what's driving the results, and debunking the interpretation when it is not justified?

RP: It's clear that politicians seized on these findings without questioning whether the research was good. That's what you'd expect them to do. Politicians are not researchers. The only research Paul Ryan cited in the 2013 Republican budget was the Reinhart- Rogoff paper. George Osborne, the Chancellor of the Exchequer in the UK—same thing. People at the European Commission—same thing. Now, speaking about Reinhardt and Rogoff themselves, I don't know. In general, it is certainly a tendency that if someone gets a result that they like they may just not push any further. I think that may have happened in their case, without imputing any motives. All I can tell you is that they wrote a paper which does not stand up to scrutiny.

D&S: All this raises the question of why elites in Europe and in the United States have been so determined to follow this austerity course. How much do you see this as being ideologically driven—based on a view of government debt or perhaps government in general being intrinsically bad? And how much should we see this as being in the service of the interests of the dominant class in society? Or should we think of those two things as meshing together?

RP: I think they mesh together. I think part of it comes from our profession, from the world of economics. It's been basically 30 years of pushing neoliberalism. It has become the dominant economic agenda and certainly hegemonic within the profession. When the crisis hit, countries did introduce stimulus policies and one of the criticisms [from economists] was that this is really crude and we don't really know much about multiplier effects and so forth. That's true, and the reason that we have only this crude understanding of how to undertake countercyclical policies is because the mainstream of the profession didn't research this. It was not a question. They spent a generation proving that we didn't need to do these policies—that a market solution is the best. So that's the economics profession and it does filter into the political debates.

But then, beyond that, is the agenda of getting rid of the welfare state and I think a lot of politicians want that to happen. They don't want to have a big public sector. Either they believe that a big public sector is inefficient and that the private sector does things more efficiently, or, whether they believe that or not, they want lower taxes on wealthy people (and wealthy people want lower taxes because that lets them get wealthier). They don't want constraints on their ability to enrich themselves, and they certainly don't want a strong and self-confident working class. They don't want people to have the security of health insurance or pension insurance (i.e., Medicare and Social Security in this country). That's the model of welfare-state capitalism that emerged during the Great Depression and was solidified during the next generation, and these people want to roll it back. The austerity agenda has given them a launching pad to achieve this. I have no idea whether Reinhardt and Rogoff believe this or not, but their research enabled people like Paul Ryan to have the legitimacy of eminent Harvard economists saying we're killing ourselves and we're killing economic growth by borrowing so much money.

D&S: Policymakers in the United States, Europe, and elsewhere, to a great extent, have just tried to "double down" on neoliberal policies. But with the structural problems of neoliberalism, keeping the same structure looks in effect like a way of keeping the same crisis. What do you see as the possible ways out of the impasse, both desirable and undesirable?

RP: I think there are fundamentally only two approaches—basically profit-led models versus wageled models. In the *Financial Times* today [June 10], the well-known columnist Gavyn Davies is saying that the reason the stock market is going up—and it's going up very handsomely—is fundamentally because the current model of capitalism is able to proceed by squeezing workers even harder. The wage share, which had been relatively stable for generations, is going down and the profit share is going up.

Now is that sustainable? Presumably you're going to have a problem of demand at a certain point because if workers don't have enough in their pockets, how are they going to buy the product? One answer is we can export to rising Asian markets and so forth. But the Asian countries themselves are depending on the exact same model. The alternative, which I think makes more sense logically and is also more humane, is to have a more equal distribution of income—a social democratic model of capitalism in which you do have a strong welfare state that acts as a stabilizer to aggregate demand and also enables workers to buy the products that they make. And that's true for China and for the United States.

We have to add into that the issue of environmental sustainability. At the same time that we're building a new growth model it has to be a model in which carbon emissions go down per unit of GDP. I don't think it's that hard to do technically. Whether it happens is another matter. [The 20th-century Polish macroeconomist Michal] Kalecki, of course, recognized this a long time ago, saying you can have a model of capitalism based on repressing workers. (He noted that it's helpful, if you're going to do that, to have a repressive fascist government—not that he was advocating doing that, of course.) After a while, and this was in the *Financial Times* today, workers are going to see that they're not getting any benefit from a recovery, and it's going to create all kinds of political results, and we don't know what they're going to be. But people are going to be pissed off.

D&S: That brings us to a central question, which Kalecki raised, that a social problem may be solved technically and intellectually, but still face barriers of economic and political power. That applies not only to full employment, the issue he was addressing, but also to environmental sustainability and other issues. Can our most serious problems be resolved within the context of capitalism, or do they require a new kind of economy and society, whatever we may call it?

The Legacy of Michal Kalecki

Michal Kalecki (1899-1970) was a Marxist economist, a scholar at Cambridge and Oxford, and an economic advisor to the governments of his native Poland and other countries. His key insights about the causes of the Great Depression preceded Keynes, but he was not widely recognized for these achievements. (Unlike Keynes, he did not publish mainly in English, was not well-known, and was not connected to elite policymaking circles.) Kalecki is perhaps best remembered for his brief article "Political Aspects of Full Employment" (1943), in which he argued that full-employment policies would erode capitalists' power in the workplace and state, and so would be sure to face capitalist opposition. Robert Pollin calls this "probably the most insightful six pages ever written in economics." —Eds.

RP: The challenge that Kalecki introduced points to some version of shared egalitarian capitalism, such as a Nordic model. Whether that model works and how long it works is an open question, and it varies for different countries.

Certainly, when we think about environmental infrastructure investments, collective solutions are workable. We know from Europe that initiatives, which are collectively owned and collectively decided, for building renewable energy systems really do work. In large part, this is because it is the community saying, "We don't mind having wind turbines if it's done right, within our community, and we have a stake in it." If some big corporation were to come and say, "We're wiping out 18 blocks here to put up some turbines and we have a right to do it because we own the property"—it doesn't work. We have public utilities and that works just fine in this country.

Expanding the role of the public sector in my view is totally consistent with what's going to happen in the future. So that starts transcending the primacy of corporate capitalism. But we can't get there in ten years. No matter how much anybody wants it, that's not going to happen. We have a problem of mass unemployment and we have an environmental crisis with climate change, and if we're not going to transcend capitalism in ten years we have to also figure out ways to address the concerns now within the existing political framework. That's not fun. When I deal with mainstream politics in Washington, it's very frustrating, but that's the world we live in.

I think that if we press the limits of the existing system, that helps me to understand how to move forward into something different than the existing structure. My professor Robert Heilbroner, a great professor who had a beautiful way of expressing things, talked about what he called "slightly imaginary Sweden." So it's not the real Sweden but this notion of some kind of egalitarian capitalism. As you press the limits of that model, you can intelligently ask what's wrong with it. If we're pushing the limits and something is holding us back, let's solve that problem. I think that's a good way forward. ❏

Chapter 5

INTERNATIONAL INSTITUTIONS AND TRADE AGREEMENTS

Article 5.1

THE INTERNATIONAL MONETARY FUND AND WORLD BANK

From "The ABCs of the Global Economy"

BY THE *DOLLARS & SENSE* COLLECTIVE
March/April 2000, last revised November 2012

The basic structure of the postwar international capitalist economy was created in 1944, at an international conference in Bretton Woods, New Hampshire. While the Bretton Woods conference included representatives of the U.S. and British governments, the Americans dominated the outcome.

The British delegation (including the legendary economist John Maynard Keynes) argued for an international currency for world trade and debt settlements. The Americans insisted on the U.S. dollar being the de facto world currency (with the dollar's value fixed in terms of gold and the values of other currencies fixed in proportion to the dollar). The British wanted countries that ran trade surpluses and those that ran trade deficits (and became indebted to the "surplus" countries) to share the costs of "adjustment" (bringing the world economy back into balance). The U.S. insisted on a system in which the "deficit" countries would have to do the adjusting, and a central aim would be making sure that the debtors would pay back their creditors at any cost.

Among the institutions coming out of Bretton Woods were the World Bank and the International Monetary Fund (IMF). For this reason, they are sometimes known as the "Bretton Woods twins." Both institutions engage in international lending. The IMF primarily acts as a "lender of last resort" to countries (usually, but not always, lower-income countries) that have become heavily indebted and cannot get loans elsewhere. The World Bank, meanwhile, focuses primarily on longer-term "development" lending.

At both the World Bank and the IMF, the number of votes a country receives is closely proportional to how much capital it contributes to the institution, so the voting power of rich countries like the United States is disproportionate to their numbers. Eleven rich countries, for example, account for more than 50% of the voting power in the IMF Board of Governors. At both institutions, five powerful countries—the United States, the United Kingdom, France, Germany, and Japan— get to appoint their own representatives to the institution's executive board, with 19 other directors elected by the rest of the 180-odd member countries. The president of the World Bank is elected by the Board of Executive Directors, and traditionally nominated by the U.S. representative. The managing director of the IMF is traditionally a European.

The IMF and the World Bank wield power vastly greater than the share of international lending they account for because private lenders follow their lead in deciding which countries are credit-worthy. The institutions have taken advantage of this leverage—and of debt crises in Latin America, Africa, Asia, and even Europe—to push a "free-market" (or "neoliberal") model of economic development.

The IMF

The IMF was a key part, from the very start, of the "debtor pays" system the U.S. government had insisted on at Bretton Woods. When a country fell heavily into debt, and could no longer get enough credit from private sources, the IMF would step in as the "lender of last resort." This made it possible for the debtor to continue to pay its creditors in the short run. The typical IMF adjustment program, however, demanded painful "austerity" or "shock therapy"—elimination of price controls on basic goods (such as food and fuel), cuts in government spending, services, and employment, and "devaluation" of the country's currency. All three of these austerity measures hit workers and poor people the hardest, the first two for fairly obvious reasons. The impact of currency devaluation, however, requires a little more explanation.

Devaluation meant that the currency would buy fewer dollars—and fewer of every other currency "pegged" to the dollar. This made imports to the country more expensive. (Suppose that a country's peso had been pegged at a one-to-one ratio to the dollar. An imported good that cost $10 would cost 10 pesos. If the currency was devalued to a two-to-one ratio to the dollar, an imported good that cost $10 would now cost 20 pesos.) Devaluation also caused domestic prices to rise, since domestic producers faced less import competition. Meanwhile, it made the country's exports less expensive to people in other countries. The idea was that the country would export more, earn more dollars in return, and—this is the key—be able to pay back its debts to U.S. and European banks. In other words, the people of the country (especially workers and the poor) would consume less of what they produced, and send more of it abroad to "service" the country's debt.

For many years, these kinds of measures were the core of IMF "adjustment" plans. Starting in the 1970s, however, the IMF broadened its standard program to include deeper "structural" changes to debtor countries' economies. "Structural adjustment programs" (SAPs) included not only the austerity measures described above, but also the elimination of trade barriers and controls on international investment, the privatization of public enterprises, and the "deregulation" of labor markets (including elimination of minimum wage laws, hours laws, occupational safety and health regulations, and protections for unions). These were the basic ingredients for overturning "regulated" (or "interventionist") forms of capitalism in many lower-income countries, and replacing it with "free-market" (or "neoliberal") capitalism.

Structural adjustment also prepared the ground for the system of globalized production—making it easier for multinational companies to locate operations in affected countries (thanks to the removal of restrictions on foreign investment), employ a relatively cheap and controllable workforce (thanks to the removal of labor regulations), and export the goods back to their home countries or elsewhere in the world (thanks to the elimination of trade barriers). Structural adjustment programs became the lance-point of "free-market" reform, especially in Latin America during the 1980s debt crisis, but also in other low-income regions.

The World Bank

In its early years, just after World War II, the World Bank mostly loaned money to Western European governments to help rebuild their war-ravaged economies. This was an important factor in the postwar reconstruction of the world capitalist economy. European reconstruction bolstered demand for exported goods from the United States, and ultimately promoted the reemergence of Western Europe as a global manufacturing powerhouse.

During the long period (1968-1981) that former U.S. Defense Secretary Robert S. McNamara headed the World Bank, however, the bank turned toward "development" loans to lower-income countries. McNamara brought the same philosophy to development that he had used as a chief architect of the U.S. war against Vietnam: big is good and bigger is better. The World Bank came to favor large, expensive projects regardless of their appropriateness to local conditions, and with little attention to environmental and social impacts. The Bank became especially notorious, for example, for supporting large dam projects that flooded wide areas, deprived others of water, and uprooted the people living in affected regions. The Bank's support for large, capital-intensive "development" projects has also been a disguised way of channeling benefits to large global companies. Many of these projects require inputs—like high-tech machinery—that are not produced in the countries where the projects take place. Instead, they have to be imported, mostly from high-income countries. Such projects may also create long-run dependencies, since the spare parts and technical expertise for proper maintenance may only be available from the companies that produced these inputs in the first place.

While the Bank's main focus is long-term "development" lending, it has also engaged in "structural adjustment" lending. The Bank's structural adjustment policies, much like those from the IMF, have imposed heavy burdens on workers and poor people. In the 1980s and 1990s, during its "structural adjustment era," the Bank went so far as to advocate that governments charge fees even for public primary education. (Predictably, in countries that adopted such policies, many poor families could not afford the fees and school enrollment declined.) The Bank has since then publicly called for the abolition of school fees. Critics argue, however, that the shift is at least partly rhetorical. Katarina Tomasevski, founder of the organization Right to Education, argues that the Bank presents itself as opposing fees, but does not oppose hidden charges, as for textbooks, school uniforms, and other costs of attending school.

The World Bank has also made development loans conditional on the adoption of "free-market" policies, like privatization of public services. Most notoriously, the Bank has pushed for the privatization of water delivery. Where privatization of water or other public services has not been possible, the Bank has urged governments to adopt "cost-recovery" strategies—including raising fees on users. Both privatization and cost-recovery strategies have undermined poor people's access to water and other essentials.

Recent developments

Since the 1990s, opposition to World Bank and IMF policies have shaken the two institutions' power—especially in Latin America, the world region to which "neoliberalism" came first and where it went furthest. This is part of a broader backlash against neoliberal policies, which opponents (especially on the Latin American left) blame for persistent poverty and rising inequality in the region. The last decade or so has seen a so-called "pink tide" in Latin America, with "center-left" parties coming to power in Argentina, Bolivia, Brazil, Chile, Ecuador, and Venezuela. (The center-left has since lost the presidency in Chile.) Different governments have adopted different policies in power, some staying close to the neoliberal path, others veering sharply away from it. Venezuela has, along with several other countries, withdrawn from the World Bank-affiliated International Centre for the Settlement of Investment Disputes (ICSID). Several South American governments, including Argentina, Brazil, and Venezuela, have also jointly formed a new regional lending institution, the Bank of the South, which aims to act as an alternative lender (for both long-term development and short-term "liquidity crises") to the IMF and World Bank.

On the other hand, the IMF has emerged, surprisingly, as a powerful influence in Western Europe. For many years, acute debt crises seemed to be confined to lower-income economies, and most observers did not dream that they could happen in Europe or other high-income regions. (For this reason, the IMF was widely criticized as a hammer that high-income countries used on low-income countries.) During the current economic crisis, however, several Western European countries have fallen deeply into debt. The IMF has stepped in as part of "bailout" programs for Greece, Iceland, and Ireland. True to its origins, it has also pushed for austerity—especially cuts in public spending—in highly indebted countries. Many economists—especially proponents of "Keynesian" views—have argued that weakness in total demand is the main cause of the current economic crisis in Europe and the rest of the world. Under these conditions, they argue, cuts in government spending will only reduce total demand further, and likely cause the crisis to drag on. ❑

Sources: International Monetary Fund, "IMF Members' Quotas and Voting Power, and IMF Board of Governors" (www.imf.org); International Monetary Fund, "IMF Executive Directors and Voting Power" (www.imf.org); World Bank, "Executive Directors and Alternates" (www.worldbank.org); World Bank, "Cost Recovery for Water Supply and Sanitation and Irrigation and Drainage Projects (www.worldbank.org); Zoe Godolphin, "The World Bank as a New Global Education Ministry?" Bretton Woods Project, January 21, 2011 (www.brettonwoodsproject.org); Katerina Tomasevski, "Both Arsonist and Fire Fighter: The World Bank on School Fees," Bretton Woods Project, January 23, 2006 (www.brettonwoodsproject.org); Katerina Tomasevski, "Six Reasons Why the World Bank Should Be Debarred From Education," Bretton Woods Project, September 2, 2006 (www.brettonwoodsproject.org).

Article 5.2

THE WORLD TRADE ORGANIZATION
From "The ABCs of the Global Economy"

BY THE *DOLLARS & SENSE* COLLECTIVE
March/April 2000, last revised November 2012

I f you know one thing about the World Trade Organization (WTO), it is probably that the organization's ministerial meetings have been the target of massive "anti-globalization" protests. The most famous was the "Battle in Seattle." Over 50,000 people went to Seattle in 1999 to say no to the WTO's corporate agenda, successfully shutting down the first day of the ministerial meeting. African, Caribbean, and other least-developed country representatives, in addition, walked out of the meeting. But what is the WTO? Where did it come from? And what does it do?

Where did it come from?

Starting in the 1950s, government officials from around the world began to meet irregularly to hammer out the rules of a global trading system. Known as the General Agreements on Trade and Tariffs (GATT), these negotiations covered, in excruciating detail, such matters as what level of taxation Japan could impose on foreign rice, how many American automobiles Brazil could allow into its market, and how large a subsidy France could give its vineyards. Every clause was carefully crafted, with constant input from business representatives who hoped to profit from expanded international trade.

The GATT process, however, was slow, cumbersome and difficult to monitor. As corporations expanded more rapidly into global markets they pushed governments to create a more powerful and permanent international body that could speed up trade negotiations as well as oversee and enforce provisions of the GATT. The result was the World Trade Organization, formed out of the ashes of GATT in 1995.

Following the shocking demonstrations in Seattle, the WTO held its 2001 ministerial meeting in Doha, Qatar, safe from protest. The WTO initiated a new round of trade talks that it promised would address the needs of developing countries. The Doha Development round, however, continued the WTO's pro-corporate agenda. Two years later "the Group of 20 developing countries" at the Cancún ministerial refused to lower their trade barriers until the United States and EU cleaned up their unfair global agricultural systems. By the summer of 2006, five years after it began, the Doha round had collapsed and the WTO suspended trade negotiations.

What does it do?

The WTO functions as a sort of international court for adjudicating trade disputes. Each of its 153 member countries has one representative, who participates in negotiations over trade rules. The heart of the WTO, however, is not its delegates, but its dispute resolution system. With the establishment of the WTO, corporations now have a place to complain to when they want trade barriers—or domestic regulations that limit their freedom to buy and sell—overturned.

Though corporations have no standing in the WTO—the organization is, officially, open only to its member countries—the numerous advisory bodies that provide technical expertise to delegates are overflowing with corporate representation. The delegates themselves are drawn from trade ministries and confer regularly with the corporate lobbyists and advisors who swarm the streets and offices of Geneva, where the organization is headquartered. As a result, the WTO has become, as an anonymous delegate told the *Financial Times,* "a place where governments can collude against their citizens."

Lori Wallach and Michelle Sforza, in their book *The WTO: Five Years of Reasons to Resist Corporate Globalization*, point out that large corporations are essentially "renting" governments to bring cases before the WTO, and in this way, to win in the WTO battles they have lost in the political arena at home. Large shrimping corporations, for example, got India to dispute the U.S. ban on shrimp catches that were not sea-turtle safe. Once such a case is raised, the resolution process violates most democratic notions of due process and openness. Cases are heard before a tribunal of "trade experts," generally lawyers, who, under WTO rules, are required to make their ruling with a presumption in favor of free trade. The WTO puts the burden squarely on governments to justify any restriction of what it considers the natural order of things. There are no amicus briefs (statements of legal opinion filed with a court by outside parties), no observers, and no public records of the deliberations.

The WTO's rule is not restricted to such matters as tariff barriers. When the organization was formed, environmental and labor groups warned that the WTO would soon be rendering decisions on essential matters of public policy. This has proven absolutely correct. The organization ruled against Europe for banning hormone-treated beef and against Japan for prohibiting pesticide-laden apples. Also WTO rules prohibit selective purchasing laws, even those targeted at human rights abuses. In 1998 the WTO court lodged a complaint against the Massachusetts state law that banned government purchases from Burma in an attempt to punish its brutal dictatorship. Had the WTO's rules been in place at the time at the time of the anti-Apartheid divestment movement, laws barring trade with or investment in South Africa would have violated them as well.

Why should you care?

At stake is a fundamental issue of popular sovereignty—the rights of the people to regulate economic life, whether at the level of the city, state, or nation. The U.S. does not allow businesses operating within its borders to produce goods with child labor, for example, so why should we allow those same businesses—Disney, Gap, or Walmart—to produce their goods with child labor in Haiti and sell the goods here? ❑

Article 5.3

NAFTA AND CAFTA

From "The ABCs of Free-Trade Agreements and Other Regional Economic Blocs"

BY THE *DOLLARS & SENSE* COLLECTIVE
January/February 2001, last revised November 2012

In the early 1990s, as the North American Free Trade Agreement (NAFTA) was under consideration in Canada, Mexico, and the United States, supporters of the pact argued that both business owners and workers in all three countries would gain from the removal of trade and investment barriers. For example, the argument went, U.S. firms that produce more efficiently than their Mexican counterparts would enjoy larger markets, gain more profits, generate more jobs, and pay higher wages. The winners would include information technology firms, biotech firms, larger retailers, and other U.S. corporations that had an advantage because of skilled U.S. labor or because of experience in organization and marketing. On the other hand, Mexican firms that could produce at low cost because of low Mexican wages will be able to expand into the U.S. market. The main examples were assembly plants or *maquiladoras*.

Critics of the agreement, meanwhile, focused on problems resulting from extreme differences among the member countries in living standards, wages, unionization, environmental laws, and social legislation. The options that NAFTA would create for business firms, the critics argued, would put them at a great advantage in their dealings with workers and communities.

As it turned out, NAFTA was approved by the governments of all three countries, and went into effect on January 1, 1994. The agreement eliminated most barriers to trade and investment among the United States, Canada and Mexico. For some categories of goods—certain agricultural goods, for example—NAFTA promised to phase out restrictions on trade over a few years, but most goods and services were to be freely bought and sold across the three countries' borders from the start. Likewise, virtually all investments—financial investments as well as investments in fixed assets such as factories, mines, or farms (foreign direct investment)—were freed from cross-border restrictions.

The agreement, however, made no changes in the restrictions on the movement of labor. Mexican—and, for that matter, Canadian—workers who wish to come to the United States must enter under the limited immigration quotas, or illegally. Thus NAFTA gave new options and direct benefits to those who obtain their income from selling goods and making investments, but the agreement included no parallel provision for those who make their incomes by working.

For example, U.S. unions were weakened because firms could more easily shut down domestic operations and substitute operations in Mexico. With the government suppressing independent unions in Mexico, organization of workers in all three countries was undermined. (Actually, the formal Mexican labor laws are probably as good or better than those in the United States but they are usually not enforced.) While NAFTA may mean more jobs and better pay for computer software engineers in the United States, manufacturing workers in the United States, for example, have seen their wages stagnate or fall. Similarly, the greater freedom of international movement that NAFTA affords to firms has given them greater bargaining power over communities when it comes to environmental regulations. One highly visible result has been severe pollution problems in Mexican *maquiladora* zones along the U.S. border.

An additional and important aspect of NAFTA is that it creates legal mechanisms for firms based in one country to contest legislation in the other countries when it might interfere with their "right" to carry out their business. Thus, U.S. firms operating in Mexico have challenged stricter environmental regulations won by the Mexican environmental movement. In Canada, the government rescinded a public-health law restricting trade in toxic PCBs as the result of a challenge by a U.S. firm; Canada also paid $10 million to the complaining firm, in compensation for "losses" it suffered under the law. These examples illustrate the way in which NAFTA, by giving priority to the "rights" of business, has undermined the ability of governments to regulate the operation of their economies in an independent, democratic manner.

Finally, one of NAFTA's greatest gifts to business was the removal of restrictions on the movement of financial capital. The immediate result for Mexico was the severe financial debacle of 1994. Investment funds moved rapidly into Mexico during the early 1990s, and especially after NAFTA went into effect. Without regulation, these investments were able to abandon Mexico just as rapidly when the speculative "bubble" burst, leading to severe drops in production and employment.

CAFTA: Extending the Free Trade Agenda

After the implementation of NAFTA, it looked like the Americas were on a fast track to a hemisphere-wide free-trade zone. In 1994, then-President Bill Clinton proposed to have the world's largest trading block in place by 2005. Instead, the Free Trade Area of the Americas (FTAA) stalled in its tracks when, in 1997, Congress denied Clinton "fast-track" negotiating authority. President George W. Bush revived the fast-track push in 2001 and succeeded in getting fast-track legislation through both the House of Representatives and the U.S. Senate in 2002. Nonetheless, the entire decade of the 2000s came and went without the FTAA.

The NAFTA model, however, has been extended into Central America and the Caribbean through the Central American Free Trade Agreement (CAFTA). CAFTA is now in effect for trade between the United States and Costa Rica, El Salvador, Guatemala, Honduras, Nicaragua, and the Dominican Republic. Economic size alone assures that U.S. interests dominate the agreement. The combined economic output of the countries in Central America is smaller than the total income of just two U.S.-based agribusiness companies that will benefit from the accord: Cargill and Archer Daniels Midland.

CAFTA, modeled after NAFTA, shares all of its shortcomings and will do as much to hamper sustainable development and no more to further human rights or end labor abuses in Central America than NAFTA did in Mexico. A report from the "Stop CAFTA Coalition" documented the problems evident just one year into the agreement. First, CAFTA did not appear to be creating the promised regional textile complex to offset competition from China. Central American garment exports continued to lose market share to their Asian competitors. In addition, CAFTA contributed to making difficult conditions in the Central American countryside yet worse. U.S. imports of fresh beef, poultry, and dairy products increased dramatically, displacing local producers, and food prices rose. Finally, CAFTA did nothing to improve human rights or extend labor rights in Central America.

And CAFTA poses yet another danger. Rules buried in the technical language of the agreement's investment chapter would make it more difficult for the Central American and Caribbean nations to escape their heavy debt burdens or recover from a debt crisis. ❏

Article 5.4

THE EUROPEAN UNION AND THE EUROZONE
From *"The ABCs of Free-Trade Agreements and Other Regional Economic Blocs"*

BY THE *DOLLARS & SENSE* COLLECTIVE
January/February 2001, last revised November 2012

The European Union (EU) forms the world's largest single market—larger than the United States or even the three NAFTA countries together. From its beginnings in 1951 as the six-member European Coal and Steel Community, the association has grown both geographically (now including 27 countries) and especially in its degree of unity. All national border controls on goods, capital, and people were abolished between member countries in 1993. And seventeen of the EU's members now share a common currency (the euro), collectively forming the "eurozone."

The EU and the "Social Charter": Promises Unkept

At first glance, open trade within the EU seemed to pose less of a threat for wages and labor standards than NAFTA or the WTO. Even the poorer member countries, such as Spain, Portugal, and Greece, were fairly wealthy and had strong unions and decent labor protections. Moreover, most EU countries, including top economic powers like France, Germany, Italy, and the United Kingdom, had strong parties (whether "socialist," social democratic, or labor) with roots in the working-class movement. This relationship had grown increasingly distant over time; still, from the perspective of labor, the EU represented a kind of best-case scenario for freeing trade. The results are, nonetheless, cautionary.

The main thrust of the EU, like other trade organizations, has been trade and investment. Labor standards were never fully integrated into the core agenda of the EU. In 1989, 11 of the then-12 EU countries signed the "Charter of the Fundamental Social Rights of Workers," more widely known as the "Social Charter." (Only the United Kingdom refused to sign.) Though the "Social Charter" did not have any binding mechanism—it is described in public communications as "a political instrument containing 'moral obligations'"—many hoped it would provide the basis for "upward harmonization," that is, pressure on European countries with weaker labor protections to lift their standards to match those of member nations with stronger regulations. The years since the adoption of the "Social Charter" have seen countless meetings, official studies, and exhortations but few appreciable results.

Since trade openness was never directly linked to social and labor standards and the "Social Charter" never mandated concrete actions from corporations, European business leaders have kept "Social Europe" from gaining any momentum simply by ignoring it. Although European anti-discrimination rules have forced countries like Britain to adopt the same retirement age for men and women, and regional funds are dispersed each year to bring up the general living standards of the poorest nations, the social dimension of the EU has never been more than an appendage for buying off opposition. As a result, business moved production, investment, and employment in Europe toward countries with lower standards, such as Ireland and Portugal.

The EU also exemplifies how regional trading blocs indirectly break down trade regulations with countries outside the bloc. Many Europeans may have hoped that the EU would insulate Europe from competition with countries that lacked social, labor, and environmental standards. While the EU has a common external tariff, each member can maintain its own non-tariff trade barriers. EU rules requiring openness between member countries, however, made it easy to circumvent any EU country's national trade restrictions. Up until 1993, member states used to be able to block indirect imports through health and safety codes or border controls, but with the harmonization of these rules across the EU, governments can no longer do so. Since then, companies have simply imported non-EU goods into the EU countries with the most lax trade rules, and then freely transported the goods into the countries with higher standards. (NAFTA similarly makes it possible to circumvent U.S. barriers against the importation of steel from China by sending it indirectly through Mexico.)

EU members that wished to uphold trade barriers against countries with inadequate social, labor, and environmental protections ended up becoming less important trading hubs in the world economy. This has led EU countries to unilaterally abolish restrictions and trade monitoring against non-EU nations. The logic of trade openness seems to be against labor and the environment even when the governments of a trading bloc individually wish to be more protective.

The Eurozone: Caught in a Bind

The process of European economic integration culminated with the establishment of a common currency (the euro) between 1999 and 2002. The creation of the euro seemed to cap the rise of Europe, over many years, from the devastation of the Second World War. Step by step, Western Europe had rebuilt vibrant economies. The largest "core" economy, Germany, had become a global manufacturing power. Even some countries with historically lower incomes, like Ireland, Italy, and Spain, had converged toward the affluence of the core countries. The euro promised to be a major new world currency, ultimately with hundreds of millions of users in one of the world's richest and seemingly most stable regions. Some commentators viewed the euro as a potential rival to the dollar as a key currency in world trade, and as a "reserve" currency (in which individuals, companies, and national banks would hold financial wealth).

Of the 27 European Union (EU) member countries, only 17 have adopted the euro as their currency (joined the "eurozone"). One of the most important EU economies, the United Kingdom, for example, has retained its own national currency (the pound). The countries that did adopt the euro, on the other hand, retired their national currencies. There is no German deutschmark, French franc, or Italian lira anymore. These currencies, and the former national currencies of other eurozone countries, stopped circulating in 2001 or 2002, depending on the country. Bank balances held in these currencies were converted to euros. People holding old bills and coins were also able to exchange them for euros.

The adoption of the euro meant a major change in the control over monetary policy for the eurozone countries. Countries that have their own national currencies generally have a central bank (or "monetary authority") responsible for policies affecting the country's overall money supply and interest rates. In the United States, for example, the Federal Reserve (or "the Fed") is the monetary authority. To "tighten" the money supply, the Fed sells government bonds to "the public" (really, to private banks). It receives money in return, and so reduces the amount of money held by the public. The Fed may do this at the peak of a business-cycle boom, in order to combat or head off inflation. Monetary tightening tends to raise interest rates, pulling back on demand for goods and services. Reduced overall demand, in turn, tends to reduce upward pressure on prices. To "loosen" the money supply, on the other hand, the Fed buys government bonds back from the banks. This puts more money into the banks' hands, which tends to reduce interest rates and stimulate spending. The Fed may do this during a business-cycle downturn or full-blown recession, in order to raise output and employment. As these examples suggest, monetary policy can be an important lever through which governments influence overall demand, output, and employment. Adopting the euro meant giving up control over monetary policy, a step many EU countries, like the UK, were not willing to make.

For eurozone countries, monetary policy is made not by a national central bank, but by the European Central Bank (ECB). ECB policy is made by 23-member "governing council," including the six members of the bank's executive board and the directors of each of the 17 member countries' central banks. The six executive-board members, meanwhile, come from various eurozone countries. (The members in late 2011 are from France, Portugal, Italy, Spain, Germany, and Belgium.) While all countries that have adopted the euro are represented on the governing council, Germany has a much greater influence on European monetary policy than other countries. Germany's is the largest economy in the eurozone. Among other eurozone countries, only France's economy is anywhere near its size. (Italy's economy is less than two-thirds the size of Germany's, in terms of total output; Spain's, less than half; the Netherlands', less than one-fourth.) German policymakers, meanwhile, have historically made very low inflation rates their main priority (to the point of being "inflation-phobic"). In part, this harkens back to a scarring period of "hyperinflation" during the 1920s; in part, to the importance of Germany as a financial center. Even during the current crisis, as economist Paul Krugman puts it, "what we're seeing is an ECB catering to German desires for low inflation, very much at the expense of making the problems of peripheral economies much less tractable."

For countries, like Germany, that have not been hit so hard by the current crisis, the "tight money" policy is less damaging than for the harder-hit countries. With Germany's unemployment rate at 6.5% and the inflation rate at only 2.5%, as of late 2011, an insistence on a tight money policy does reflect an excessive concern with maintaining very low inflation and insufficient concern with stimulating demand and reducing unemployment. If this policy torpedoes the economies of other European countries, meanwhile, it may drag the whole of Europe—including the more stable "core" economies—back into recession.

For the harder-hit countries, the results are disastrous. These countries are mired in a deep economic crisis, in heavy debt, and unable to adopt a traditional "expansionary" monetary policy on their own (since the eurozone monetary policy is set by the ECB). For them, a looser monetary policy could stimulate demand, production, and employment, even without causing much of an increase in inflation. When an economy is producing near its full capacity, increased demand is likely to put upward pressure on prices. (More money "chasing" the same amount of goods can lead to higher inflation.) In Europe today, however, there are vast unused resources—including millions of unemployed workers—so more demand could stimulate the production of more goods, and need not result in rising inflation.

Somewhat higher inflation, moreover, could actually help stimulate the harder-hit European economies. Moderate inflation can stimulate demand, since it gives people an incentive to spend now rather than wait and spend later. It also reduces the real burdens of debt. Countries like Greece, Ireland, Italy, Portugal, and Spain are drowning in debt, both public and private. These debts are generally specified in nominal terms—as a particular number of euros. As the price level increases, however, it reduces the real value of a nominal amount of money. Debts can be paid back in euros that are worth less than when the debt was incurred. As real debt burdens decrease, people feel less anxious about their finances, and may begin to spend more freely. Inflation also redistributes income from creditors, who tend to be wealthier and to save more of their incomes, to debtors, who tend to be less wealth and spend most of theirs. This, too, helps boost demand.

The current crisis has led many commentators to speculate that some heavily indebted countries may decide to abandon the euro. This need not mean that they would repudiate (refuse to pay) their public debt altogether. They could, instead, convert their euro debts to their new national currencies. This would give them more freedom to pursue a higher-inflation policy, which would reduce the real debt burden. (Indeed, independent countries that owe their debt in their own currency need not ever default. A country that controls its own money supply can "print" more money to repay creditors—with the main limit being how the money supply can be expanded without resulting in unacceptably high inflation. Adopting the euro, however, deprived countries in the eurozone of this power.) The current crisis, some economists argue, shows how the euro project was misguided from the start. Paul Krugman, for example, argues that the common currency was mainly driven by a political (not economic) aim—the peaceful unification of a region that had been torn apart by two world wars. It did not make much sense economically, given the real possibility for divergent needs of different national economies. Today, it seems a real possibility that the eurozone, at least, will come apart again. ❑

Sources: Paul Krugman, "European Inflation Targets," *New York Times* blog, January 18, 2011 (krugman.blogs.nytimes.com); European Central Bank, Decision-making, Governing Council (www.ecb.int/); European Central Bank, Decision-making, Executive Board (www.ecb.int/); Federal Statistical Office (Statistisches Bundesamt Deutschland), Federal Republic of Germany, Short-term indicators, Unemployment, Consumer Price Index (www.destatis.de); Paul Krugman, "Can Europe Be Saved?" *New York Times*, January 12, 2011 (nytimes.com).

Article 5.5

THE "TRADE DEAL" SCAM

BY DEAN BAKER
June 2013; Truthout

As part of its overall economic strategy, the Obama administration is rushing full speed ahead with two major trade deals. On the one hand, it has the Trans-Pacific Partnership, which includes Japan and Australia and several other countries in East Asia and Latin America. On the other side, there is an effort to craft a U.S.-EU trade agreement.

There are two key facts people should know about these proposed trade deals. First, they are mostly not about trade. Second, they are not intended to boost the economy in a way that will help most of us. In fact, it is reasonable to say that these deals will likely be bad news for most people in the United States. Most of the people living in our partner countries are likely to be losers too.

On the first point, traditional trade issues, like the reduction of import tariffs and quotas, are a relatively small part of both deals. This is the case because these barriers have already been sharply reduced or even eliminated over the past three decades.

As a result, with a few notable exceptions, there is little room for further reductions in these sorts of barriers. Instead both deals focus on other issues, some of which may reasonably be considered barriers to trade, but many of which are matters of regulation that would ordinarily be left to national, regional, or even local levels of government to set for themselves. One purpose of locking regulatory rules into a trade deal is to push an agenda that favors certain interests (e.g., the large corporations who are at the center of the negotiating process) over the rest of society.

Both of these deals are likely to include restrictions on the sorts of health, safety, and environmental regulations that can be imposed by the countries that are parties to the agreements. While many of the regulations that are currently in place in these areas are far from perfect, there is not an obvious case for having them decided at the international level.

Suppose a country or region decides that the health risks posed by a particular pesticide are too great and therefore bans its use. If the risks are in fact small, then those imposing the ban will be the primary ones who suffer, presumably in the form of less productive agriculture and higher food prices. Is it necessary to have an international agreement to prevent this sort of "mistake"?

As a practical matter, the evidence on such issues will often be ambiguous. For example, does the natural-gas extraction technique of hydraulic fracturing (better known as "fracking") pose a health hazard to the surrounding communities? These agreements could end up taking control of the decision as to whether or not to allow fracking away from the communities who would be most affected.

In addition to limiting local control in many areas, these trade deals will almost certainly include provisions that make for stronger and longer copyright and patent protection, especially on prescription drugs. The latter is coming at the urging of the U.S. pharmaceutical industry, which has been a central player in all the trade agreements negotiated over the last quarter century. This is likely to mean much higher drug prices for our trading partners.

This is, of course, the opposite of free trade. Instead of reducing barriers, the drug companies want to increase them, banning competitors from selling the same drugs. The difference in prices can be quite large. Generic drugs, with few exceptions, are cheap to produce. When drugs sell for hundreds or thousands of dollars per prescription, it is because patent monopolies allow them to be sold for high prices.

If these trade deals result in much higher drug prices for our trading partners, the concern should not just be a moral one about people being unable to afford drugs. The more money people in Vietnam or Malaysia have to pay Pfizer and Merck for their drugs, the less money they will have to spend on other exports from the United States. This means that everyone from manufacturing workers to workers in the tourist sector can expect to see fewer job opportunities because of the copyright and patent protection rules imposed through these trade deals.

To see this point, imagine someone operating a fruit stand in a farmers' market. If the person in the next stall selling meat has a clever way to short-change customers, then his scam will come at least partly at the expense of the fruit stand. The reason is that many potential fruit stand customers will have their wallets drained at the meat stand and won't have any money left to buy fruit.

The drug companies' efforts to get increased patent protection, along with the computer and entertainment industries efforts to get stronger copyright protection, will have the same effect. Insofar as they can force other countries to pay them more in royalties and licensing fees or directly for their products, these countries will have less money to spend on other goods and services produced in the United States. In other words, the short-change artist in the next stall is not our friend and neither are the pharmaceutical, computer, or entertainment industries.

However, these industries all have friends in the Obama administration. As a result, these trade deals are likely to give them the protections they want. The public may not have the power to stop the high-powered lobbyists from getting their way on these trade pacts, but it should at least know what is going on. These trade deals are about pulling more money out of their pockets in order to make the rich even richer. ❑

Article 5.6

STRUCTURAL ADJUSTMENT, HERE AND THERE

BY ARTHUR MacEWAN
November/December 2012

> Dear Dr. Dollar:
> What are the similarities and differences between structural adjustment in the rest of the world/Third World and structural adjustment in the United States? —*Vicki Legion, San Francisco, Calif.*

The similarities are pretty clear. The differences? Not so great.

The term "structural adjustment" came into vogue in the 1980s with the debt crises in many low- and middle-income countries, especially in Latin America. The situation presented two related problems. On the one hand, many countries, devoting large amounts of their resources to paying their debts to globally operating banks, saw their economies spin downward. On the other hand, the banks, most of them based in the United States and western Europe, were on the verge of not getting paid. Horrors!

So in stepped the World Bank and the International Monetary Fund (IMF). They told the governments of the debtor counties, in effect: "We'll loan you money to help meet your debts on the condition that you *adjust the structure* of your economies in ways that we say will get you on a path to economic recovery. Oh, and by the way, the banks must get paid."

Structural adjustment, then, was the particular set of policies that the World Bank and IMF claimed would solve the debtor countries' problems. In a nutshell, these policies required governments to:

- Cut their spending to reduce the budget deficit.
- Restrict the growth of the money supply, curtailing inflation but also bringing higher unemployment.
- Reduce restrictions on foreign investment and imports, providing freer access to multinational firms.
- Sell off government enterprises—i.e., privatize.
- "Rationalize" labor markets—i.e., get rid of protections for workers.
- Cut regulations on business—e.g., environmental regulation.

The slogan supporting all of this was: Reduce the role of the government! In reality, these policies do not so much reduce the role of the government as they shift the government towards supporting business and the well-being of the elites at the expense of lower-income groups.

Familiar? Of course. In the United States, the term "structural adjustment" isn't used, but this is the same set of policies that elite groups here have pushed over the past several decades—and are pushing today as the solution to the country's economic malaise.

Cut the deficit, that's first on the list. And the U.S. government has long taken the lead in establishing agreements that open up the economy to unfettered global trade and investment. The privatization of U.S. education, health care, prisons, and even many aspects of the military has been well underway for years. Hold the line on the minimum wage, and, for god's sake, get rid of the Environmental Protection Agency.

It's not quite that simple of course. In the current U.S. situation, the Federal Reserve has not fully followed the structural adjustment script. (It has taken steps to bring down unemployment that "inflation hawks" opposed.) And for some of the other policies, the process has not been smooth. There is resistance here and there—for example, the Chicago teachers' strike may slow the process of privatizing education in that city, some gains have been made on the minimum wage, and popular concerns about the environment have held back the destruction of environmental regulations. But the drumbeat for structural adjustment in the United States, for leaving things to the market, has not stopped.

In many other countries, structural adjustment has moved more rapidly, partly because of pressure from the Bank and IMF. But don't believe that they imposed these policies without support from elite groups within those countries. The elites were the beneficiaries of many structural adjustment policies. For example, with the privatization of government enterprises, they were able to take control of government assets at fire-sale prices. And "rationalizing" the labor market pushed down wages and shifted the distribution of income and power in favor of business owners. All the while, they could point their fingers at the IMF and the Bank, and say, "They made us do it."

U.S. elites have not had such a convenient scapegoat, and they have not been able to move ahead so rapidly—though the severe crisis of recent years and the slow recovery present a fine opportunity for more structural adjustment at home.

In resisting structural adjustment, people in the United States can learn from what happened during earlier rounds of structural adjustment elsewhere. Destruction of the environment in the Philippines. Devastation of the livelihoods of small farmers in Mexico. Rising inequality in many countries. And, by and large, sluggish economic growth in most structurally adjusted countries.

There have been many popular responses and some popular victories. In Bolivia in 2000, for example, a popular movement reversed the privatization of the water supply, which had been put in the hands of a multinational resource firm. In Ecuador, an indigenous peoples' movement emerged, opposing the depredation of the environment by oil companies and the government's imposition of austerity in 1999 and 2000 (at the behest of the IMF). In Mexico, structural adjustment (along with long-standing grievances) inspired the 1994 Zapatista uprising. Indeed, in many countries of Latin America, the debacles generated by structural adjustment in the 1980s have led to the election of progressive governments.

Good lessons for resistance right here at home. ❏

Article 5.7

DISARMING THE DEBT TRAP

BY ELLEN FRANK
November/December 2000

This article was originally written in 2000, in the immediate wake of the "Jubilee 2000" campaign to cancel the external debts of the world's poorest countries. Author Ellen Frank argues that, admirable though the debt-cancellation campaign was, it would likely fail to keep low-income countries out of debt in the long run unless serious structural reforms were made to the international-payments system. More than ten years later, the international debt picture for developing countries is mixed. Over that period, the ratios of external debt to GDP and external debt payments (or "debt service") to exports are down for most of the world's low-income regions. In part, this is due to debt cancellation, and the fact that debt-cancellation campaigns forced international institutions like the World Bank and International Monetary Fund to accept broader and deeper debt reduction than they had initially planned. Today, however, storm clouds are again visible on the horizon, with debt burdens in some of the world's poorest countries again on the rise. Meanwhile, Frank's proposals have new and unexpected relevance for even high-income world regions, as several countries in Europe face deep debt crises as a result, in large measure, of not being able to repay debt in currencies they control.   —Eds.

Sources: Nick Mead, "A Developing World of Debt," *The Guardian*, May 16, 2012 (guardian. co.uk); World Bank, *Global Development Finance: External Debt of Developing Countries*, 2012 (worldbank.org).

QUESTION: What if the IMF, World Bank and G-7 governments canceled the debts of the poorer countries right now, fully and with no strings attached?

ANSWER: Within five years, most would be up to their necks in debt again. While a Jubilee 2000 debt cancellation would provide short-term relief for heavily indebted countries, the bitter reality of the current global financing system is that poor countries are virtually doomed to be debtors.

When residents of Zambia or Zaire buy maize or medicine in America, they are required to pay in dollars. If they can't earn enough dollars through their own exports, they must borrow them—from the IMF, the World Bank, a Western government agency, or from a commercial lender. But foreign currency loans are problematic for poor countries. If CitiCorp loans funds to a U.S. business, it fully expects that the business will realize a stream of earnings from which the loan can be repaid. When the IMF or World Bank makes foreign currency loans to poor countries—to finance deficits or development projects—no such foreign currency revenue stream is generated and the debt becomes a burdensome obligation that can be met only by abandoning internal development goals in favor of export promotion.

Few poor countries can avoid the occasional trade deficit—of 93 low- and moderate-income countries, only 11 currently have trade surpluses—and most are heavily dependent on imports of food, oil, and manufactured goods. Even the most tightly managed economy is only an earthquake or crop failure away from a foreign currency debt. Once incurred, interest payments and other debt-servicing charges mount quickly. Because few countries can manage payment surpluses large enough to service the debt regularly, servicing charges are rolled over into new loans and the debt balloons. This is why, despite heroic efforts by many indebted less-developed countries (LDCs) to pump up exports and cut imports, the outstanding foreign currency debt of developing countries has more than tripled during the past two decades.

Many poorer nations, hoping to avoid borrowing, have attempted recently to attract foreign investor dollars with the bait of high interest rates or casino-style stock exchanges. But the global debt trap is not so easily eluded. An American financial firm that purchases shares on the Thai stock exchange with baht (the Thai currency) wants, eventually, to distribute gains to shareholders in dollars. Big banks and mutual funds are wary, therefore, of becoming ensnared in minor currencies and, to compensate against potential losses when local currencies are converted back into dollars, they demand sky-high interest rates on LDC bonds. Thailand, Brazil, Indonesia and many other countries recently discovered that speculative financial investors are quick to turn heel and flee, driving interest rates up and exchange rates down, and leaving debtor countries even deeper in the hole.

If plans to revamp the international "financial architecture" are to help anyone but the already rich, they must address these issues. Developing countries need many things from the rest of the world—manufactured goods, skilled advisors, technical know-how—but loans are not among them. A global payments system based on the borrowing and lending of foreign currencies is, for small and poor nations, a life sentence to debtor's prison.

There are alternatives. Rather than scrambling endlessly for the foreign currency they cannot print, do not control, and cannot earn in sufficient amounts through exporting, developing countries could be permitted to pay for foreign goods and services in their own currencies. Americans do this routinely, issuing dollars to cover a trade deficit that will exceed $300 billion this year. Europe, too, finances external deficits with issues of euro-denominated bonds and bank deposits. But private financial firms will generally not hold assets denominated in LDC currencies; when they do hold them, they frequently demand interest rates several times higher than those paid by rich countries. But the governments of the world could jointly agree to hold these minor currencies, even if private investors will not.

The world needs an international central bank, democratically structured and publicly controlled, that would allow countries to settle payment imbalances politically, without relying on loans of foreign currencies. The idea is not new. John Maynard Keynes had something similar in mind in the 1940s, when the International Monetary Fund was established. Cambridge economist Nicholas Kaldor toyed with the idea in the 1960s. Recently, Jane D'Arista of the Financial Markets Center and a number of other international financial specialists have revived this notion, calling for a global settlements bank that could act not as a lender of last resort to international banks (as the IMF does), but as a lender of first resort for payments imbalances between sovereign nations. Such a system would take the problems of debts, deficits, and development out of the marketplace and place them in the international political arena, where questions of fairness and equity could be squarely and openly addressed.

The idea is beguilingly simple, eminently practicable, and easy to implement. It would benefit poor and rich countries alike, since the advanced nations could export far more to developing countries if those countries were able to settle international payments on more advantageous terms. A global settlements bank, however, would dramatically shift the balance of power in the world economy and will be fiercely opposed by those who profit from the international debt trap. If developing countries were not so desperate for dollars, multinational corporations would find them less eager to sell their resources and citizens for a fistful of greenbacks. That nations rich in people and resources, like South Africa, can be deemed bankrupt and forced into debt peonage for lack of foreign exchange is not merely a shame. It is absurd, an unacceptable artifact of a global finance system that enriches the already rich. ❏

Chapter 6

LABOR IN THE GLOBAL ECONOMY

Article 6.1

THE GLOBALIZATION CLOCK

BY THOMAS PALLEY
May/June 2006

Political economy has historically been constructed around the divide between capital and labor, with firms and workers at odds over the division of the economic pie. Within this construct, labor is usually represented as a monolithic interest, yet the reality is that labor has always suffered from internal divisions—by race, by occupational status, and along many other fault lines. Neoliberal globalization has in many ways sharpened these divisions, which helps to explain why corporations have been winning and workers losing.

One of these fault lines divides workers from themselves: since workers are also consumers, they face a divide between the desire for higher wages and the desire for lower prices. Historically, this identity split has been exploited to divide union from nonunion workers, with anti-labor advocates accusing union workers of causing higher prices. Today, globalization is amplifying the divide between people's interests as workers and their interests as consumers through its promise of ever-lower prices.

Consider the debate over Walmart's low-road labor policies. While Walmart's low wages and skimpy benefits have recently faced scrutiny, even some liberal commentators argue that Walmart is actually good for low-wage workers because they gain more as consumers from its "low, low prices" than they lose as workers from its low wages. But this static, snapshot analysis fails to capture the full impact of globalization, past and future.

Globalization affects the economy unevenly, hitting some sectors first and others later. The process can be understood in terms of the hands of a clock. At one o'clock is the apparel sector; at two o'clock, the textile sector; at three, the steel sector; at six, the auto sector. Workers in the apparel sector are the first to have their jobs shifted to lower-wage venues; at the same time, though, all other workers get price reductions. Next, the process picks off textile sector workers at two o'clock. Meanwhile, workers from three o'clock onward get price cuts, as do the apparel workers at one o'clock. Each time the hands of the clock move, the workers taking the hit are isolated. In this fashion, globalization moves around the clock, with labor perennially divided.

Manufacturing was first to experience this process, but technological innovations associated with the Internet are putting service and knowledge workers in the firing line as well. Online business models are making even retail workers vulnerable—consider Amazon.com, for example, which has opened a customer support center and two technology development centers in India. Public-sector wages are also in play, at least indirectly, since falling wages mean falling tax revenues. The problem is that each time the hands on the globalization clock move forward, workers are divided: the majority is made slightly better off while the few are made much worse off.

Globalization also alters the historical divisions within capital, creating a new split between bigger internationalized firms and smaller firms that remain nationally centered. This division has been brought into sharp focus with the debate over the trade deficit and the overvalued dollar. In previous decades, manufacturing as a whole opposed running trade deficits and maintaining an overvalued dollar because of the adverse impact of increased imports. The one major business sector with a different view was retailing, which benefited from cheap imports.

However, the spread of multinational production and outsourcing has divided manufacturing in wealthy countries into two camps. In one camp are larger multinational corporations that have gone global and benefit from cheap imports; in the other are smaller businesses that remain nationally centered in terms of sales, production and input sourcing. Multinational corporations tend to support an overvalued dollar since this makes imports produced in their foreign factories cheaper. Conversely, domestic manufacturers are hurt by an overvalued dollar, which advantages import competition.

This division opens the possibility of a new alliance between labor and those manufacturers and businesses that remain nationally based—potentially a potent one, since there are approximately 7 million enterprises with sales of less than $10 million in the United States, versus only 200,000 with sales greater than $10 million. However, such an alliance will always be unstable as the inherent labor-capital conflict over income distribution can always reassert itself. Indeed, this pattern is already evident in the internal politics of the National Association of Manufacturers (NAM), whose members have been significantly divided regarding the overvalued dollar. As one way to address this division, the group is promoting a domestic "competitiveness" agenda aimed at weakening regulation, reducing corporate legal liability, and lowering employee benefit costs—an agenda designed to appeal to both camps, but at the expense of workers.

Solidarity has always been key to political and economic advance by working families, and it is key to mastering the politics of globalization. Developing a coherent story about the economics of neoliberal globalization around which working families can coalesce is a key ingredient for solidarity. So, too, is understanding how globalization divides labor. These narratives and analyses can help counter deep cultural proclivities to individualism, as well as other historic divides such as racism. However, as if this were not difficult enough, globalization creates additional challenges. National political solutions that worked in the past are not adequate to the task of controlling international competition. That means the solidarity bar is further raised, calling for international solidarity that supports new forms of international economic regulation. ❏

Article 6.2

INTERNATIONAL LABOR STANDARDS

BY ARTHUR MacEWAN
September/October 2008

Dear Dr. Dollar:

U.S. activists have pushed to get foreign trade agreements to include higher labor standards. But then you hear that developing countries don't want that because cheaper labor without a lot of rules and regulations is what's helping them to bring industries in and build their economies. Is there a way to reconcile these views? Or are the activists just blind to the real needs of the countries they supposedly want to help?

—*Philip Bereaud, Swampscott, Mass.*

In 1971, General Emilio Medici, the then-military dictator of Brazil, commented on economic conditions in his country with the infamous line: "The economy is doing fine, but the people aren't."

Like General Medici, the government officials of many low-income countries today see the well-being of their economies in terms of overall output and the profits of firms—those profits that keep bringing in new investment, new industries that "build their economies." It is these officials who typically get to speak for their countries. When someone says that these countries "want" this or that—or "don't want" this or that—it is usually because the countries' officials have expressed this position.

Do we know what the people in these countries want? The people who work in the new, rapidly growing industries, in the mines and fields, and in the small shops and market stalls of low-income countries? Certainly they want better conditions—more to eat, better housing, security for their children, improved health and safety. The officials claim that to obtain these better conditions, they must "build their economies." But just because "the economy is doing fine" does not mean that the people are doing fine.

In fact, in many low-income countries, economic expansion comes along with severe inequality. The people who do the work are not getting a reasonable share of the rising national income (and are sometimes worse off even in absolute terms). Brazil in the early 1970s was a prime example and, in spite of major political change, remains a highly unequal country. Today, in both India and China, as in several other countries, economic growth is coming with increasingly severe inequality.

Workers in these countries struggle to improve their positions. They form—or try to form—independent unions. They demand higher wages and better working conditions. They struggle for political rights. It seems obvious that we should support those struggles, just as we support parallel struggles of workers in our own country. The first principle in supporting workers' struggles, here or anywhere else, is supporting their right to struggle—the right, in particular, to form independent unions without fear of reprisal. Indeed, in the ongoing controversy over the U.S.-Colombia Free Trade Agreement, the assassination of trade union leaders has rightly been a major issue.

Just how we offer our support—in particular, how we incorporate that support into trade agreements—is a complicated question. Pressure from abroad can help, but applying it is a complex process. A ban on goods produced with child labor, for example, could harm the most impoverished families that depend on children's earnings, or could force some children into worse forms of work (e.g., prostitution). On the other hand, using trade agreements to pressure governments to allow unhindered union organizing efforts by workers seems perfectly legitimate. When workers are denied the right to organize, their work is just one step up from slavery. Trade agreements can also be used to support a set of basic health and safety rights for workers. (Indeed, it might be useful if a few countries refused to enter into trade agreements with the United States until we improve workers' basic organizing rights and health and safety conditions in our own country!)

There is no doubt that the pressures that come through trade sanctions (restricting or banning commerce with another country) or simply from denying free access to the U.S. market can do immediate harm to workers and the general populace of low-income countries. Any struggle for change can generate short-run costs, but the long-run gains—even the hope of those gains—can make those costs acceptable. Consider, for example, the Apartheid-era trade sanctions against South Africa. To the extent that those sanctions were effective, some South African workers were deprived of employment. Nonetheless, the sanctions were widely supported by mass organizations in South Africa. Or note that when workers in this country strike or advocate a boycott of their company in an effort to obtain better conditions, they both lose income and run the risk that their employer will close up shop.

Efforts by people in this country to use trade agreements to raise labor standards in other countries should, whenever possible, take their lead from workers in those countries. It is up to them to decide what costs are acceptable. There are times, however, when popular forces are denied even basic rights to struggle. The best thing we can do, then, is to push for those rights—particularly the right to organize independent unions—that help create the opportunity for workers in poor countries to choose what to fight for. ❏

Article 6.3

CAMPUS STRUGGLES AGAINST SWEATSHOPS CONTINUE
Indonesian workers and U.S. students fight back against Adidas.

BY SARAH BLASKEY AND PHIL GASPER
September/October 2012

A bandoning his financially ailing factory in the Tangerang region of Indonesia, owner Jin Woo Kim fled the country for his home, South Korea, in January 2011 without leaving money to pay his workers. The factory, PT Kizone, stayed open for several months and then closed in financial ruin in April, leaving 2,700 workers with no jobs and owed $3.4 million of legally mandated severance pay.

In countries like Indonesia, with no unemployment insurance, severance pay is what keeps workers and their families from literal starvation. "The important thing is to be able to have rice. Maybe we add some chili pepper, some salt, if we can," explained an ex-Kizone worker, Marlina, in a report released by the Worker Rights Consortium (WRC), a U.S.-based labor-rights monitoring group, in May 2012. Marlina, widowed mother of two, worked at PT Kizone for eleven years before the factory closed. She needs the severance payment in order to pay her son's high school registration fee and monthly tuition, and to make important repairs to her house.

When the owner fled, the responsibility for severance payments to PT Kizone workers fell on the companies that sourced from the factory—Adidas, Nike, and the Dallas Cowboys. Within a year, both Nike and the Dallas Cowboys made severance payments that they claim are proportional to the size of their orders from the factory, around $1.5 million total. But Adidas has refused to pay any of the $1.8 million still owed to workers.

Workers in PT Kizone factory mainly produced athletic clothing sold to hundreds of universities throughout the United States. All collegiate licensees like Adidas and Nike sign contracts with the universities that buy their apparel. At least 180 universities around the nation are affiliated with the WRC and have licensing contracts mandating that brands pay "all applicable back wages found due to workers who manufactured the licensed articles." If wages or severance pay are not paid to workers that produce university goods, then the school has the right to terminate the contract.

Using the language in these contracts, activists on these campuses coordinate nationwide divestment campaigns to pressure brands like Adidas to uphold previously unenforceable labor codes of conduct.

Unpaid back wages and benefits are a major problem in the garment industry. Apparel brands rarely own factories. Rather, they contract with independent manufacturers all over the world to produce their wares. When a factory closes for any reason, a brand can simply take its business somewhere else and wash its hands of any responsibilities to the fired workers.

Brands like Nike and Russell have lost millions of dollars when, pressed by United Students Against Sweatshops (USAS), universities haver terminated their contracts. According to the USAS website, campus activism has forced Nike to pay severance and Russell to rehire over 1,000 workers it had laid off, in order to avoid losing more collegiate contracts. Now many college activists have their sights set on Adidas.

At the University of Wisconsin (UW) in Madison, the USAS-affiliated Student Labor Action Coalition (SLAC) and sympathetic faculty are in the middle of a more than year-long campaign to pressure the school to terminate its contract with Adidas in solidarity with the PT Kizone workers.

The chair of UW's Labor Licensing Policy Committee (LLPC) says that Adidas is in violation of the code of conduct for the school's licensees. Even the university's senior counsel, Brian Vaughn, stated publicly at a June LLPC meeting that Adidas is "in breach of the contract based on its failure to adhere to the standards of the labor code." But despite the fact that Vaughn claimed at the time that the University's "two overriding goals are to get money back in the hands of the workers and to maintain the integrity of the labor code," the administration has dragged its feet in responding to Adidas.

Instead of putting the company on notice for potential contract termination and giving it a deadline to meet its obligations as recommended by the LLPC, UW entered into months of fruitless negotiations with Adidas in spring 2012. In July, when these negotiations had led nowhere, UW's interim chancellor David Ward asked a state court to decide whether or not Adidas had violated the contract (despite the senior counsel's earlier public admission that it had). This process will delay a decision for many more months--perhaps years if there are appeals.

Since the Adidas campaign's inception in the fall of 2011, SLAC members have actively opposed the school's cautious approach, calling both the mediation process and the current court action a "stalling tactic" by the UW administration and Adidas to avoid responsibility to the PT Kizone workers. In response, student organizers planned everything from frequent letter deliveries to campus administrators, to petition drives, teach-ins, and even a banner drop from the administration building that over 300 people attended, all in hopes of pressuring the chancellor (who ultimately has the final say in the matter) to cut the contract with Adidas.

While the administration claims that it is moving slowly to avoid being sued by Adidas, it is also getting considerable pressure from its powerful athletics director, Barry Alvarez, to continue its contract with Adidas. As part of the deal, UW's sports programs receive royalties and sports gear worth about $2.5 million every year.

"Just look at the money—what we lose and what it would cost us," Alvarez told the *Wisconsin State Journal*, even though other major brands would certainly jump at the opportunity to replace Adidas. "We have four building projects going on. It could hurt recruiting. There's a trickle-down effect that would be devastating to our whole athletic program."

But Tina Treviño-Murphy, a student activist with SLAC, rejects this logic. "A strong athletics department shouldn't have to be built on a foundation of stolen labor," she told *Dollars & Sense*. "Our department and our students deserve better.".

Adidas is now facing pressure from both campus activists in the United States and the workers in Indonesia--including sit-ins by the latter at the German and British embassies in Jakarta. (Adidas' world headquarters are in Germany, and the company sponsored the recent London Olympics.) This led to a meeting between their union and an Adidas representative, who refused to admit responsibility but instead offered food vouchers to some of the workers. The offer amounted to a tiny fraction of the owed severance and was rejected as insulting by former Kizone workers.

In the face of intransigence from university administrations and multinational companies prepared to shift production quickly from one location to another to stay one step ahead of labor-rights monitors, campus activism to fight sweatshops can seem like a labor of Sisyphus. After more than a decade of organizing, a recent fundraising appeal from USAS noted that "today sweatshop conditions are worse than ever."

Brands threaten to pull out of particular factories if labor costs rise, encouraging a work environment characterized by "forced overtime, physical and sexual harassment, and extreme anti-union intimidation, even death threats," says Natalie Yoon, a USAS member who recently participated in a delegation to factories in Honduras and El Salvador.

According to Snehal Shingavi, a professor at the University of Texas, Austin who was a USAS activist at Berkeley for many years, finding ways to build links with the struggles of the affected workers is key. "What I think would help the campaign the most is if there were actually more sustained and engaged connections between students here and workers who are in factories who are facing these conditions," Shingavi told *Dollars & Sense*. Ultimately, he said, only workers' self-activity can "make the kind of changes that I think we all want, which is an end to exploitative working conditions."

But in the meantime, even small victories are important. Anti-sweatshop activists around the country received a boost in September, when Cornell University President David Skorton announced that his school was ending its licensing contract with Adidas effective October 1, because of the company's failure to pay severance to PT Kizone workers. The announcement followed a sustained campaign by the Sweatfree Cornell Coalition, leading up to a "study in" at the president's office. While the contract itself was small, USAS described the decision as the "first domino," which may lead other campuses to follow suit. Shortly afterwards, Oberlin College in Ohio told Adidas that it would not renew its current four-year contract with the company if the workers in Indonesia are not paid severance.

Perhaps just as significant are the lessons that some activists are drawing from these campaigns. "The people who have a lot of power are going to want to keep that power and the only way to make people give some of that up is if we make them," Treviño-Murphy said. "So it's really pressure from below, grassroots organizing, that makes the difference. We see that every day in SLAC and I think it teaches us to be not just better students but better citizens who will stand up to fight injustice every time." ❑

Sources: Worker Rights Consortium, "Status Update Re: PT Kizone (Indonesia)," May 15, 2012 (workersrights.org); Andy Baggot, "Alvarez Anxiously Awaits Adidas Decision," *Wisconsin State Journal*, July 13, 2012 (host.madison.com); United Students Against Sweatshops (usas.org), PT Kizone update, June 15, 2012 (cleanclothes.org/urgent-actions/kizoneupdate).

Article 6.4

AFTER HORROR, APOLOGETICS

Sweatshop apologists cover for intransigent U.S. retail giants.

BY JOHN MILLER
September/October 2013

> Bangladesh just isn't rich enough to support the sort of worker safety laws that we have ourselves. ...
>
> [S]horter working hours ... , safer workplaces, unemployment protections and the rest ... are the products of wealth. ...
>
> [A]ll of us who would like to see those conditions improve ... should be cheering on the export led growth of that Bangladeshi economy.
>
> —Tim Worstall, "Sadly, Bangladesh Simply Cannot Afford Rich World Safety And Working Standards," *Forbes*, April 28, 2013.

The April 24 collapse of the Rana Plaza building, just outside of Dhaka, Bangladesh's capital city, killed over 1,100 garment workers toiling in the country's growing export sector.

The horrors of the Rana Plaza disaster, the worst ever in the garment industry, sent shockwaves across the globe. In the United States, the largest single destination for clothes made in Bangladesh, newspaper editors called on retailers whose wares are made in the country's export factories to sign the legally binding fire-and-safety accord already negotiated by mostly European major retailers. Even some of the business press chimed in. The editors of *Bloomberg Businessweek* admonished global brand-name retailers that safe factories are "not only right but also smart." But just two U.S. retailers signed on, while most opted to sign a non-legally binding ersatz accord.

The business press, however, also turned their pages over to sweatshop defenders, contrarians who refuse to let the catastrophic loss of life in Bangladesh's export factories shake their faith in neoliberal globalization. Tim Worstall, a fellow at London's free-market Adam Smith Institute, told *Forbes* readers that "Bangladesh simply cannot afford rich world safety and working standards." Economist Benjamin Powell, meanwhile, took the argument that sweatshops "improve the lives of their workers and boost growth" out for a spin on the *Forbes* op-ed pages.

The sweatshop defenders are twisting Bangladesh workers' need for more and better jobs into a case for low wages and bad working conditions. Their misleading arguments, moreover, are no excuse for major U.S. retailers to refuse to sign onto the European-initiated safety agreement, a truly positive development in the fight against sweatshops.

More Jobs, Not More Sweatshops

Bangladesh is "dirt poor," as Worstall puts it. The country is on the United Nations' list of 46 Least Developed Countries. Its gross domestic product (GDP) per capita, the most common measure of economic development, is about one-fiftieth that of the United States.

The garment industry is the leading sector of the Bangladeshi economy, responsible for some 80% of total exports by value. Bangladesh's garment exports tripled between 2005 and 2010, boosting the nation's growth rate. By 2011, Bangladesh was the third-largest exporter of clothes in the world, after China and Italy.

On top of that, the garment industry has provided much-needed jobs. Bangladesh has about 5,000 garment factories that employ 3.6 million workers, the vast majority of them women. Wages for women in the garment industry were 13.7% higher than wages for women with similar years of education and experience in other industries in Bangladesh, according to a 2012 study. And the most common alternative employments for women, such as domestic service and agriculture labor, pay far less than factory jobs.

Still, none of that is a good reason to endorse sweatshops.

While Bangladesh's garment industry boosted economic growth and added to employment, neither its horrific working conditions nor its dismally low wages improved without government intervention.

Rana Plaza was a deathtrap. But it was only the latest tragedy to have struck Bangladeshi workers sewing garments for major U.S. and European retailers. Less than five months earlier, a devastating fire at Tazreen Fashions, a garment factory not far from Rana Plaza, killed 117 workers. In addition to the 1,129 workers killed at Rana Plaza, more than 600 garment workers have died in factory fires in Bangladesh since 2005, according to *Fatal Fashion*, a 2013 report published by SOMO Centre for Research on Multinational Corporations. From 2000 to 2010, wages in the garment industry remained flat, according to a survey conducted by War on Want, a British nonprofit. Even after the minimum wage in the garment industry nearly doubled in 2010, itself part of the fight against sweatshop conditions, wages remained among the lowest in the world. A seamstress in Bangladesh earns less than $50 a month, versus $100 in Vietnam and $235 in China, according to World Bank data. The bottom line, as *Businessweek* puts it, is that "Bangladesh's $18 billion garment industry relies on super-low wages and women desperate for work."

This does not mean that trying to improve these conditions is a futile undertaking. Safer working conditions and higher wages are unlikely to stand in the way of investment in Bangladesh's garment industry and job creation.

Factory costs, including wages, make up only a small portion of the overall cost of most garments. Leading Bangladesh garment makers told *Businessweek* that their total factory costs for a $22 pair of jeans was just 90 cents. That's just 4% of the price paid by consumers. On the other hand, a 2009 study of the sales in a major New York retail store found that the company could use "social labeling" to charge up to

20% more and still expect sales revenues to rise. In other words, doubling the wages paid to Bangladeshi garment workers and at the same time improving working conditions would not have to diminish retailer revenues.

Nor does improving worker safety have to be that expensive. The Worker Rights Consortium, an independent labor-rights monitoring group, estimates that it would cost an average of $600,000 to elevate each of Bangladesh's 5,000 factories to Western safety standards, for a total of $3 billion. If the $3 billion were spread over five years, it would add an average of less than 10 cents to the price paid by retail companies for each of the 7 billion garments that Bangladesh sells each year to Western brands.

How to Stop Sweatshop Abuse

For sweatshop apologists like Worstall and Powell, yet more export-led growth is the key to improving working and safety conditions in Bangladesh. "Economic development, rather than legal mandates," Powell argues, "drives safety improvements." Along the same lines, Worstall claims that rapid economic growth and increasing wealth are what improved working conditions in the United States a century ago and that those same forces, if given a chance, will do the same in Bangladesh.

But their arguments distort the historical record and misrepresent the role of economic development in bringing about social improvement. Working conditions have not improved because of market-led forces alone, but due to economic growth combined with the very kind of social action that sweatshops defenders find objectionable.

U.S. economic history makes that much clear. It was the 1911 Triangle Shirtwaist fire, which cost 146 garment workers their lives, along with the hardships of the Great Depression, that inspired the unionization of garment workers and led to the imposition of government regulations to improve workplace safety. Those reforms, combined with the post-World War II economic boom, nearly eliminated U.S. sweatshops.

Since then, declining economic opportunity, severe cutbacks in inspectors, and declining union representation have paved the way for the return of sweatshops to the United States. This trend further confirms that economic development, by itself, will not eliminate inhuman working conditions.

In contrast, a combination of forces that could eliminate sweatshops is forming in Bangladesh today. Despite the government's record of repressing labor protest and detaining labor leaders, the horror of the Rana Plaza collapse has sparked massive protests and calls for unionization in Bangladesh. In reaction, the government has amended its labor laws to remove some of the obstacles to workers forming unions, although formidible obstacles remain (including the requirement that at least 30% of the workers at an entire company—not at a single workplace as in the United States—be members of a union before the government will grant recognition).

Meanwhile, 80 mostly European retail chains that sell Bangladesh made garments have signed the legally binding Accord on Fire and Building Safety in

Bangladesh. For the first time, apparel manufacturers and retailers will be held accountable for the conditions in the factories that make their clothes. This "joint liability" aspect, a long-held goal of labor-rights advocates, is precisely what makes this international accord so important.

Negotiated with worker-safety groups and labor unions, the five-year accord sets up a governing board with equal numbers of labor and retail representatives, and a chair chosen by the International Labor Organization (ILO). An independent inspector will conduct audits of factory hazards and make the results public. Corrective actions recommended by the inspector will be mandatory and retailers will be forbidden from doing business with noncompliant facilities. Each retailer will contribute to the cost of implementing the accord based on how much they produce in Bangladesh, up to a maximum of $2.5 million over five years to pay for administering the safety plan and pick up the tab for factory repairs and renovations. The accord subjects disputes between retailers and union representatives to arbitration, with decisions enforceable by a court of law in the retailer's home country.

The signatories include Swedish retailer Hennes and Mauritz, which has more of its clothes made in Bangladesh than any other company; Benetton Group S.p.A., the Italian retailer whose order forms were famously found in the rubble of the collapsed Rana Plaza factory; and Canada's Loblow Companies, whose Joe Fresh clothing was also found at Rana Plaza. Together, their clothes are made in over 1,000 of Bangladesh's 5,000 factories.

However, only two U.S. companies, Abercrombie & Fitch and PVH (parent of Tommy Hilfiger and Calvin Klein), have signed the accord. Walmart, The Gap, J.C. Penney, Sears, and the rest of the major U.S. retailers doing business in Bangladesh have refused. The industry trade group, the National Retail Federation, objected to the accord's "one-size-fits-all approach" and its "legally questionable binding arbitration provision" that could bring disputes to court in the highly litigious United States. Several of those retailers cobbled together an alternative agreement signed so far by 17 mostly U.S. retailers.

But their "company-developed and company-controlled" plan, as a coalition of labor-rights groups described it, falls well short of the European-initiated plan. It is not legally binding and lacks labor organization representatives. Moreover, while retailers contribute to the implementation of their safety plan, they will face no binding commitment to pay for improving conditions. An AFL-CIO spokesperson put it most succinctly, "This is a matter of life or death. Quite simply, non-binding is just not good enough." ❏

Sources: Benjamin Powell, "Sweatshops in Bangladesh Improve the Lives of Their Workers, and Boost Growth," *Forbes*, May 2, 2013; Centre for Research on Multinational Corporations (SOMO) and Clean Clothes Campaign, *Fatal Fashion*, March 2013; International Labor Rights Forum, "Accord on Fire and Building and Safety in Bangladesh," May 13, 2012; Michael Hiscox and Nicholas Smyth,"Is There Consumer Demand for Improved Labor Standards: Evidence from Field Experiments in Social Labeling," Department of Government, Harvard University, 2012; Rachel Heath and Mushfiq Mubarak, "Does Demand or Supply Constrain Investments in Education? Evidence from Garment Sector Jobs in Bangladesh," Aug. 15, 2012; Rubana Huq, "The Economics of a $6.75 Shirt," *Wall Street Journal*, May 16, 2003; "Halfhearted Labor Reform in Bangladesh," *New York Times*, July 17, 2013; International Labour Organization, "A Handbook on the Bangladesh Labour Act, 2006"; Renee Dudley, "Bangladesh Fire Safety to Cost Retailers $3 Billion, Group Says," *Bloomberg Businessweek*, Dec. 10, 2012; Mehul Srivastava and Arun Deynath, "Bangladesh's Paradox for Poor Women Workers," *Bloomberg Businessweek*, May 9, 2013; Mehul Srivastava and Sarah Shannon, "Ninety Cents Buys Safety on $22 Jeans in Bangladesh," *Bloomberg Businessweek*, June 6, 2013; "Bloomberg View: How to Fix Bangladesh's Factories," *Bloomberg Businessweek*, May 2, 2013; Steven Greenhouse and Stephanie Clifford, "U.S. Retailers Offer Plan For Safety at Factories," *New York Times*, July 10, 2013; Alliance for Bangladesh Worker Safety, "Alliance of Leading Retailers in North America Join Forces in Comprehensive, Five-Year Commitment to Improve Factory Safety Conditions For Workers in Bangladesh," press release, July 10, 2013.

Article 6.5

NISSAN BURNS MISSISSIPPI
Failure to deliver on $1.3 billion investment galvanizes activists.

BY ROGER BYBEE
September/October 2013

The state of Mississippi, long suffering as the poorest in the nation, has nonetheless just shelled out the largest package of subsidies ever granted to an auto firm. The state has committed an estimated $1.33 billion in public funds to the highly profitable Nissan Motor Company for a $2 billion auto-assembly plant outside Canton, a small hamlet west of Jackson. The eye-popping size of the incentive package for Nissan— revealed in May in a comprehensive study of state and local incentives by the Good Jobs First research group—has accelerated the growth of a vibrant social movement in support of Nissan workers' right to unionize. (The United Auto Workers (UAW) is actively trying to organize the Nissan plant.)

"The $1.3 billion resonates like the Wall St. bailout all over again," says State Rep. Jim Evans (D-70th), who also organizes workers for the AFL-CIO and serves as president of the Mississippi Alliance for Immigrant Rights.

"[H]ere you have the state government turning down billions in federal money for Obamacare to cover 300,000 Mississippians over the next ten years," Evans points out, referring to the decision of Republican governor Phil Bryant and GOP legislators. "But then they have been giving $1.3 billion to Nissan. It's the worst set of decisions imaginable."

The huge giveaway to Nissan, which earned $3.3 billion in profits internationally last year, stands in stark contrast to the state's pervasive poverty. At 21.6%, Mississippi's poverty rate is the highest in the country, more than half again as high as the national average. It also has the lowest median household income of any state—at just under $37,000, only 73% of the U.S. average. Over recent years, Mississippi has witnessed the highest growth in income inequality in the United States. The state faces urgent needs in health, yet devotes the third lowest amount of any state to health care, with predictably negative outcomes on a variety of measures. Mississippi ranks fifth lowest on education spending, and is tied for last in percentage of high-school students who graduate. This juxtaposition of lavish private subsidies and unmet public needs is touching a raw nerve among many Mississippians, especially African-Americans, who make up 37% of state residents and 80% of the Nissan workforce in the state.

While being offered the mammoth giveaway, Nissan has failed to live up to its end of the bargain, which was expected to result in jobs averaging at least $19.70 an hour, according to the Good Jobs First report. According to more recent estimates, 35% to 40% of the 5,600 workers at Canton have been hired through temp agencies at wages of $9.50 to $12 an hour, far below the $22 an hour that permanent Nissan workers typically receive. Nissan's failure to abide by the terms of the incentive deal has condemned some 1,800 Mississippians to poverty-level status despite working 40 or more hours a week.

The absence of a union also prevents Nissan from taking seriously the ideas of workers committed to improving production and safety at the plant, tool-and-die technician Mike Thornberry told *Dollars & Sense*. Thornberry is a member of Nissan Workers Committee for a Fair Election.

Nissan has been waging an all-out war of words against unionism, expressed in captive-audience meetings of workers, incessant anti-union messages on TV monitors throughout the plant, and threats of shutting down the plant in the event that workers unionize. The company has, meanwhile, denied union supporters equal access to their fellow workers to speak with them about unionization. Such company practices have drawn condemnation by activists. "We in the NAACP believe that workers should have a voice in the workplace free of intimidation and retaliation," said the state organization's president, Derrick Johnson, who also is a member of the Mississippi Alliance for Fairness at Nissan (MAFFAN), a group of community leaders who support the Canton workers in their fight to organize.

Contributing to a widely felt sense of second-class treatment is Nissan's decision to exclude Canton workers from the same right to vote for union representation— without heavyhanded management opposition—that it has granted elsewhere around the world. Father Jeremy Tobin, a white Catholic priest and active leader of MAFFAN, pointed out how Nissan has been willing to accept unionization by workers in numerous nations, including Japan, Brazil, South Africa, Mexico, Australia, Russia, Spain, and the United Kingdom. "Why not Mississippi, too?" demands Father Tobin.

In the eyes of some Mississippi activists, Nissan's intransigence against genuinely democratic election procedures in the plant parallels new moves by Republican state officials to impose restrictive "voter ID" laws clearly aimed at suppressing the vote of blacks, Latinos, and college students. "Voting without intimidation in the plant" is a natural extension of the historic fight for full voting rights, says Rep. Evans. Both inside the Nissan plant and across Mississippi, "voter suppression has continued in various forms. That's criminal in a democracy."

The corporation's efforts to crush union organizing have spawned growing support in the plant and increasing activism both in Mississippi and beyond. Much of the activity is driven by MAFFAN, which has catalyzed the efforts of leaders like Rep. Bennie G. Thompson (D-MS), the NAACP's Johnson, Rev. Isiac Jackson, Jr. (president of the General Missionary Baptist State Convention of Mississippi and MAFFAN chairperson), Father Tobin, numerous other clergy, and organizations including the Alliance for Immigrant Rights. MAFFAN has emerged as far more than a "letterhead" organization limited to prominent figures, and has been actively speaking out and organizing across the state, nation, and internationally.

Also active in the movement is the Student Justice Alliance, based at six primarily African-American colleges in the South and seeking to reach more, said Joshua Dedmond, a graduate of Tougaloo College. Dedmond is currently devoting his time to activities with Concerned Students for a Better Nissan, which has begun leafleting Nissan dealerships in Miami, Atlanta, and Washington, D.C.

Another prominent supporter is actor Danny Glover, who grew up in a union household and was an activist in college. Glover has spoken to workers in Canton and elsewhere, addressed college audiences, and led pro-union delegations to auto shows across North America. He also brought MAFFAN leaders to South Africa in May. The South Africa trip was one part of a strategy by union supporters to draw heavily on solidarity among Nissan workers around the world. Among the international voices speaking out for union rights at the Canton plant has been former Brazil President Luiz Inácio "Lula" da Silva, himself a former metalworker and charismatic union leader.

The movement in support of the Nissan workers draws its inspiration from Dr. Martin Luther King, who stressed that civil rights and economic rights are inextricably linked battles for human dignity. The labor and civil rights movements share, in Dr. King's words, "a dream of a land where men will not take necessities from the many to give luxuries to the few."

Sources: Associated Press, "AP analysis: Census Bureau report shows Mississippi education spending at $7,934 per student, among nation's lowest," May 26, 2013; Martin Luther King, Jr., *All Work Has Dignity*, edited and introduced by Michael Honey (Boston: Beacon Press, 2011); Phil Mattera and Kasia Tarczynska, "A Good Deal for Mississippi? A report on Taxpayer Assistance to Nissan in Canton, Mississippi," Good Jobs First, May 2013, updated June 2013 (goodjobsfirst. org); Elizabeth McNichol, Douglas Hall, David Cooper, and Vincent Palacios, "Pulling Apart: A State- By-State Analysis Of Income Trends," Center on Budget and Policy Priorities and Economic Policy Institute, Nov. 15, 2012 (cbpp.org); Bill Fletcher, "Black Students Take on Nissan," *The Progressive*, June 2012 (progressive. org); Danny Glover, "Americans Turn to South Africa for Aid," Huffington Post, June 6, 2013 (huffingtonpost. com); "Mississippi Public Health Data," Trust for American Health (healthyamericans.org).

Article 6.6

ARE LOW WAGES AND JOB LOSS INEVITABLE?

BY ARTHUR MacEWAN
May/June 2011

Dear Dr. Dollar:

The main narrative that I hear in mainstream press is that U.S. workers are being undercut and eventually displaced by global competition. I think this narrative has a tone of inevitability, that low wages and job loss are driven by huge impersonal forces that we can't do much about. Is this right?

—*Vicki Legion, San Francisco, Calif.*

Yes, that is the main narrative. But, no, it's not right.

Globalization, in the sense of increasing international commerce over long distances, has been going on since human beings made their way out of Africa and spread themselves far and wide. Trade between China and the Mediterranean seems to have been taking place at least 3,000 years ago. (We know this through chemical analysis of silk found in the hair of an Egyptian mummy interred around 1000 BCE; the silk was identified as almost certainly from China.) The long history of long-distance commerce does cast an aura of inevitability over globalization.

But the spread of international commerce has not taken shape outside of human control. Globalization takes many forms; its history has variously involved colonial control, spheres of influence, and forms of regulated trade.

The current era of globalization was quite consciously planned by the U.S. government and U.S. business during and after World War II. They saw the United States replacing the British Empire as the dominant power among capitalist countries. But in place of 19th century-style colonial control, they looked to a "free trade" regime to give U.S. firms access to resources and markets around the world. While U.S. business and the U.S. government did not achieve the "free trade" goal immediately, this has been what they have promoted over the last 65 years.

This U.S.-sponsored form of globalization has given great advantage to U.S. business. And it has put many U.S. workers in direct competition with more poorly paid workers elsewhere in the world, who are often denied the right to organize and have little choice but to work long hours in often unsafe conditions. U.S. business can make its profits off these workers elsewhere—often by sub-contracting to local firms. But there is nothing inevitable about this set-up.

Furthermore, there are ways to counter these developments. Just as the current global economic arrangements were created by political decisions, they can be altered by political decisions. Two examples:

- The development of better social programs in the United States would put workers here in a stronger bargaining position, regardless of global competition. With universal health care (a "single-payer" system), for instance, U.S. workers would be in a better position to leave a bad job or turn down a bad offer.

- Rebuilding the labor movement is essential for placing U.S. workers in a stronger bargaining position in relation to their employers. Equally important, stronger unions would give workers more leverage in the political arena, where many decisions about the nature of global commerce are made.

No, we may not be able to create the same labor movement of decades past. However, lest one think that the decline of the labor movement has been itself inevitable in the face of globalization, consider some of the political decisions that have undermined labor's strength:

- The National Labor Relations Board has not done its job. In the '50s, '60s, and early 1970s, fewer than one in ten union elections were marred by illegal firings of union organizers. By the early 1980s, over 30% of union elections involved illegal firings. While the figure declined to 16% by the late 1990s, it was back up to 25% in the early 2000s.

- Or consider the minimum wage. Even with the recent increase of the federal minimum wage to $7.25 per hour, adjusted for inflation it is still below what it was in the 1960s and 1970s.

These are crucial political decisions that have affected organized labor, wage rates, and jobs. But they were not inevitable developments.

It would be folly to think that the changes in the global economy have not affected economic conditions in the United States, including the position of organized labor. But it would also be folly to assume that conditions in the United States are inevitably determined by the global economy. Political action matters.

(Caveat: Advocating a "different shape" for globalization is not a call for protectionism. It is possible to engage in world commerce and protect the interest of U.S. workers without resorting to traditional protectionism. But that is a topic for another day.) ❏

Chapter 7

MIGRATION

Article 7.1

THE NEW POLITICAL ECONOMY OF IMMIGRATION
Since Sept. 11, 2001, immigrants have become America's most wanted.

BY TOM BARRY
January/February 2009

The terrorist attacks of Sept. 11 drastically altered the traditional political economy of immigration. The millions of undocumented immigrants—those who crossed the border illegally or overstayed their visas—who were living and working in the United States were no longer simply regarded as a shadow population or as surplus cheap labor. In the public and policy debate, immigrants were increasingly defined as threats to the nation's security. Categorizing immigrants as national security threats gave the government's flailing immigration law-enforcement and border-control operations a new unifying logic that has propelled the immigrant crackdown forward.

Responsibility for immigration law-enforcement and border control passed from the Justice Department to the new Department of Homeland Security (DHS). In Congress Democrats and Republicans alike readily supported a vast expansion of the country's immigration control apparatus—doubling the number of Border Patrol agents and authorizing a tripling of immigrant prison beds. Today, after the shift in the immigration debate, the $15 billion-plus DHS budget for immigration affairs has fueled an immigrant-crackdown economy that has greatly boosted the already-bloated prison industry. Even now, with the economy imploding, immigrants are currently behind one of the country's most profitable industries: they are the nation's fastest growing sector of the U.S. prison population.

Across the country new prisons are hurriedly being constructed to house the hundreds of thousands of immigrants caught each year. State and local governments are vying with each other to attract new immigrant prisons as the foundation of their rural "economic development" plans.

While DHS is driving immigrants from their jobs and homes, U.S. firms in the business of providing prison beds are raking in record profits from the immigrant crackdown. Although only one piece of the broader story of immigration, it's all a part of the new political economy of immigration.

Dangerous People

In the new national security context, undocumented immigrants are not just out-laws: They are "dangerous people" who threaten the homeland.

The two DHS agencies involved in immigration enforcement—Immigration and Customs Enforcement (ICE) and Customs and Border Protection (CBP)—have seen their funds increased disproportionately over the last several years, doubling in size while total DHS funding has increased by just a third. The funding for these two agencies is set to rise 19.1% in 2009 while the overall DHS budget will increase by only 6.8%. Hunting down immigrants has become a top DHS priority, as DHS says its mission is "to prevent terrorist attacks against the nation and to protect our

---

Detention Profiteers

There may be a new boom in immigrant detention, but captive immigrants as good business is a concept that dates back two decades. Immigrants were the industry's first prisoners.

It all began in 1983 when a klatch of wealthy Tennessee Republicans decided private prisons were just what the country needed to solve the problems of prison riots, overcrowding, and increasing costs. They formed the Corrections Corporation of America (CCA), with the mission to "provide in partnership with government meaning-ful public service," and succeeded in persuading the Reagan administration to help launch prison privatization by having the Immigration and Naturalization Service (INS's legacy agency) issue CCA a contract to keep immigrants locked up in Houston.

Wackenhut Corrections (recently renamed GEO Group), a private security ser-vices firm, branched into the private prison industry when it entered a contract in 1987 to operate an INS immigrant detention center in Colorado.

Using their experience in immigrant detention, CCA and Wackenhut soon began successfully soliciting states and counties to enter into private prison pacts, while win-ning dozens of new contracts with the federal government. However, the initial enthu-siasm of governments at all levels faded with increasing abuse scandals at CCA and Wackenhut prisons, leading some states to cancel contracts and pull prisoners out.

But immigrant detention once again saved the day for CCA, Wackenhut, and other teetering private prison firms. The 1996 immigration law that broadened the guidelines for deporting undocumented and legal immigrants started to kick in, re-sulting in a rising federal demand for more immigrant detention beds that the private prison industry was happy to supply.

nation from dangerous people."

Immigrants caught up in DHS dragnets, worksite enforcement raids, and border patrols were the "metrics of success" that DHS Secretary Michael Chertoff pointed to in his July 18, 2008 congressional testimony. He used the dramatically increased number of immigrant apprehensions and "removals" as metrics to show that DHS is succeeding in its goal to "secure the homeland and protect the American people."

While the increased numbers of immigrants being arrested, imprisoned, and deported certainly demonstrate that DHS is busy, they don't demonstrate that DHS is stopping terrorism. Never in its congressional testimonies or media releases does DHS present evidence that show how the number of immigrants captured improves national security.

A 2007 study by the Transnational Records Access Clearinghouse (TRAC) at Syracuse University found that there has been no increase in terrorism or national security charges against immigrants since 2001. In fact, despite the increased enforcement operations by Homeland Security, more immigrants were charged annually in immigration courts with national security or terrorism-related offenses in a three-year period in the mid-1990s (1994-96) than in a comparable period (2004-06) since Sept. 11. According to the TRAC study, "A decade later, national security charges were brought against 114 individuals, down about a third. Meanwhile for the same period, terrorism charges are down more than three-fourths, to just 12."

Enforcing the "Rule of Law"

Rather than addressing immigration as the complex socioeconomic issue that it is, Homeland Security has reduced immigration policy to a system of crime and punishment. Applying the simplistic law-and-order logic propagated by restrictionists, DHS regards undocumented immigrants not as workers, community members, and parents but as criminals.

Following the lead of the anti-immigration institutes and right-wing think tanks, Chertoff came to Homeland Security with a new interpretation of the department's immigration law enforcement and border control operations: Commitment to a strict enforcement regime to protect the country against foreign terrorists, and to reassert the "rule of law."

In the aftermath of Sept. 11, the restrictionist camp found that their messaging about the "illegality" and "criminality" of undocumented immigrants took on a new resonance. They proceeded to upscale their "what don't you understand about illegal?" message, to a more conceptual framing of undocumented immigration. Undocumented immigrants now represented a threat to the "rule of law" inside a nation that had just come under foreign attack by foreign outlaws.

Their new language about immigration policy started popping up everywhere, from the pronouncements of immigrant-rights groups to the Democratic Party platform. Instead of promising an "earned path to citizenship," as it has in the past, the party stated that undocumented immigrants will be required to "get right with the law."

Looking ahead, Janet Napolitano, President Obama's nominee to replace Chertoff, while no anti-immigration hardliner, still seems poised to adopt the same law-and-order logic. As a lawyer, former federal prosecutor, and a governor who has insisted on more border control and stood behind a tough employer-sanctions law, Napolitano can be expected to follow the lead of Chertoff and the Democratic Party in insisting that current immigration laws be strictly enforced "to reassert the rule of law."

Immigrants Mean Business

Political imperatives—protecting the homeland and enforcing the "rule of law"—have over the past eight years countervailed against the economic forces that have historically led in setting immigration policy. Although the immigrant labor market persists, the increased risks for both employer and worker, along with the recessionary economy, appear to be exercising downward pressure on both supply and demand.

But even in the flagging economy, the immigrant crackdown has invigorated other market forces. Eager to cash in on immigrant detention, private prison firms and local governments are rushing to supply Homeland Security and the Justice Department with the prisons needed to house the hundreds of thousands of immigrants captured by ICE and Border Patrol agents.

In the prison industry, bed is a euphemism for a place behind bars. Even President Bush talked the prison-bed language when discussing immigration policy. When visiting the Rio Grande Valley in south Texas in 2006 to promote the immigrant crackdown, the president said: "Beds are our number one priority."

The number of beds for detained immigrants in DHS centers has increased by more than a third since 2002. There are now 32,000 beds available for the revolving population of immigrants on the path to deportation, and another 1,000 are scheduled to come on line in 2009. This doesn't include beds for immigrants in Homeland Security custody that are provided by county, state, and the federal Bureau of Prisons.

At the insistence of such immigration restrictionists as Rep. Tom Tancredo (R-Colo.), the Intelligence Reform and Terrorism Prevention Act of 2004 contained an authorization for an additional 40,000 beds to accommodate immigrants under U.S. government custody.

At the onset of the immigration crackdown two years ago, ICE dubbed its promise to find a detention center or prison bed for all arrested immigrants "Operation Reservation Guaranteed." The Justice Department has a similar initiative to ensure that the U.S. Marshals Service has beds available for detainees—about 180,000 a year, of whom more than 30% are held on immigration charges.

Most of the prison beds contracted by ICE and DOJ's Office of Federal Detention Trustee are with local governments; ICE has more than 300 intergovernmental agreements with county and city governments to hold immigrants, while DOJ has some 1200 such agreements. In many cases, particularly with contracts for hundreds of prison beds, the local government then subcontracts with a private prison company to operate the facility.

Prison beds translate into per diem payments from the federal government that are well above the hotel room rates in the remote rural communities where most of these immigrant prisons are located. With these per diems running from $70 to $95 for each immigrant imprisoned, local governments and private firms are hurrying to expand existing facilities or to create new ones.

Depending on Immigrants

The uptick in immigrant detention that saved the industry in 2000 turned into a mighty upswing in demand for immigrant prison beds after Sept. 11 and the ensuing immigrant crackdown. The Corrections Corporation of America (CCA) has reported record profits for the last few years, largely on the strength of increasing demand from its ICE and USMS "customers."

Forty percent of total CCA revenue comes from three federal contractors: Bureau of Prisons, U.S. Marshals Service, and ICE. In its 2007 Security and Exchange Commission filing, CCA stated: "We are dependent on government appropriations." CCA Chairman William Andrews warned investors that the company's high returns could be threatened by a change in the policy environment: "The demand for our facilities and services could be adversely affected by the relaxation of enforcement efforts…or through the decriminalization of certain activities that are currently proscribed by our criminal laws."

But to understand just how well the prison business is faring and how immigrants are key to prison profits, you can listen in on the prison firms' quarterly conference call with major Wall Street investment firms of November 2008.

Corrections Corporation of America boasted that it enjoyed a $33.6 million increase in the third quarter over last year, while earnings rose 15% during the same period. Formerly known as Wackenhut, GEO Group, the nation's second largest prison company, saw its earnings jump 29% over 2007. Cornell Companies, another private prison firm that imprisons immigrants, reported a 9% increase in net revenues in the third quarter.

Private prison companies aren't worried that the Democratic Party sweep will mean fewer beds. GEO Group's chairman George Zoley on Nov. 3 assured investors: "These federal initiatives to target, detain and deport criminal aliens throughout the country will continue to drive the need for immigration detention beds over the next several years and these initiatives have been fully funded by Congress on a bipartisan basis."

Addressing investor fears that recent decreases in undocumented immigration inflows might dampen company returns, CCA CEO and board chairman John Ferguson said, "So even though we have seen the border crossings and apprehensions decline in the last couple of years, we are really talking about dealing with a population well north of 12 million illegal immigrants residing in the United States." The CCA chief assured investors that the company's dependence on detained immigrants is not a factor of policy but rather of law enforcement. "The Federal Bureau of Prisons, U.S. Marshals Service, Immigration and Custom Enforcement are carrying out statutory obligations for their responsibility....We should continue to see their utilization of the private sector to meet their statutory obligations and requirements."

The prison executives even intimate that the economic crisis will fatten their business. When asked by an investment company representative about a possible downturn in detained immigrants, James Hyman, president of Cornell Companies, said, "We do not believe we will see a decline in the need for detention beds particularly in an economy with rising unemployment among American workers."

Immigrant Prisons as Economic Development

Hundreds of local governments are also attempting to take advantage of this rising demand for immigrant prison beds by opening their jails to immigrants under ICE and DOJ custody and by building new jails to meet the anticipated increased demand.

Financial considerations weigh heavily for cash-strapped county commissions and sheriff departments. As Sheriff Roger Mulch told Jefferson County (Illinois) commissioners in late February 2008, "ICE, during the last three months, has been hot to do business with us." Each locality negotiates independently with ICE and USMS to set the per diem rates, and as the demand from the feds for local jail beds increases, county sheriff departments are negotiating ever-higher rates.

Along the U.S.-Mexico border, particularly in Texas, prisons are a booming industry. Near the border town of Del Rio, the county's Val Verde Correctional Facility, which is owned and run by GEO Group, had only 180 beds eight years ago. Today, after undergoing its second 600-bed expansion, the maximum-security jail can fit 1,425 prisoners.

In Texas' Willacy County, the county government opened the country's largest immigrant detention center in 2006, and is currently pursuing a federal contract to host one of three new family detention centers for immigrants. County Commissioner Ernie Chapa, explaining how the county government financially depends on jailing immigrants, said: "We would love to have 2,500 [illegal immigrants] but we know that's not going to be . . . If we get 2,200 to 2,300, we'd be very happy."

Joining in the celebration of the opening of the new jail for immigrants, Willacy County Judge Simone Salinas said, "We are proud to have been able to bring on these new detention beds in record time, which will result in improved border security not only for county residents but also our nation."

"You talk about economic development, this is it," Salinas told a reporter, noting the county's initial cut is $2.25 a day per occupied bed.

A year later, a new agreement with ICE for another thousand beds was greeted enthusiastically by some officials in what is one of the poorest counties in the nation. The new county judge Eliseo Barnhart said the expansion of the immigrant detention center run by CCA will "bring jobs that are needed in Willacy County and it means income, which we desperately need."

"It's almost like a futures market. You have private prison companies gambling on expansion of the immigrant detention system, and basically prison speculators who are convincing communities to do this," Bob Libal, director of Grassroots Leadership in Austin and an organizer with South Texans Opposing Private Prisons, told the *Denver Post*. "It's a sick market, but a market nonetheless," Libal said.

New Political Economy of Immigration

What started off as a war against terrorism has devolved into a war against immigrants. The current "enforcement-only" approach to immigration policy has created a morass of new problems, including a host of human rights and financial issues associated with the annual detention and removal of immigrants. The immigrant crackdown has given rise to an unregulated complex of jails, detention centers, and prisons that create profit from the immigrant crackdown.

At the outset of a new administration and new era, the political economy of immigration is decidedly anti-immigrant. Political and economic factors have combined to create a harsh environment for undocumented immigrants, present and future. Immigration reform may not be a top priority, but the Obama administration and new Congress would do well to begin to address the challenge of reshaping the political economy of immigration.

First steps could include a more careful articulation of the intersection of immigration, rule of law, and national security. Napolitano should explain that the real threat to the rule of law is not having an immigration policy that provides a legal pathway to integration for the 11 million immigrants already within the U.S.

What's more, she would do well to disarticulate the links established by the Bush administration between immigrants and terrorists. At the same time, closer links must be made between immigration policy and economic policy, guarding against labor exploitation while considering domestic economic need.

Instead of a policy based on a calm assessment of the costs and benefits of immigrant labor to the U.S. economy, current immigration policy has been hijacked by the politics of fear, resentment, scapegoating, and nativism. The "enforcement only" immigration policy has fostered a national immigrant prison complex that feeds on ever-increasing numbers of arrested immigrants. As County Commissioner Ernie Chapa said, "Any time the numbers are high, it's good for the county because it brings more income." ❏

Sources: "Immigration Enforcement: The Rhetoric, The Reality," TRAC Immigration, 2007; "Corrections Corp. of America Q3 2008 Earnings Call Transcript," Seeking Alpha, November 2008; "The GEO Group, Inc. Q3 2008 (Qtr End 9/28/08) Earnings Call Transcript," Seeking Alpha, November 2008; "Cornell Companies Inc. Q3 2008 Earnings Call Transcript," Seeking Alpha, November 2008; "Mulch: Jail May Soon House Immigrants", Register News February 2008; "Willacy County Goes $50 Million More In Debt to Expand MTC's Tent City," Texas Prison Bid'ness Blog, August 2007; "Federal detention center in Willacy to expand," *The Monitor*, July 2007; "Inmate count continues to climb at detention center," *Brownsville Herald*, April 2008.

Article 7.2

"THEY WORK HERE, THEY LIVE HERE, THEY STAY HERE!"

French immigrants strike for the right to work—and win.

BY MARIE KENNEDY AND CHRIS TILLY

July/August 2007

France has an estimated half-million undocumented immigrants, including many from France's former colonies in Africa. The *sans-papiers* (literally, "without papers"), as the French call them, lead a shadowy existence, much like their U.S. counterparts. And as U.S. immigrants did in 2006 with rousing mass demonstrations, the French undocumented have recently taken a dramatic step out of the shadows. But the *sans-papiers* did it in a particularly French way: hundreds of them occupied their workplaces.

Snowballing Strikes

The snowflake that led to this snowball of sit-in strikes was a November immigration law, sponsored by the arch-conservative government of President Nicolas Sarkozy, that cracked down on family reunification and ramped up expulsions of unauthorized immigrants. The law also added a pro-business provision permitting migration, and even "regularization" of undocumented workers, in occupations facing labor shortages. The French government followed up with a January notice to businesses in labor-starved sectors, opening the door for employers to apply to local authorities for work permits for workers with false papers whom they had "in good faith" hired. However, for low-level jobs, this provision was limited to migrants from new European Union member countries. Africans could only qualify if they were working in highly skilled occupations such as science or engineering—but not surprisingly, most Africans in France are concentrated in low-wage service sector jobs.

At that point, African *sans-papiers* took matters into their own hands. On February 13, Fodie Konté of Mali and eight co-workers at the Grande Armée restaurant in Paris occupied their workplace to demand papers. All nine were members of the Confédération Générale du Travail (CGT), France's largest union federation, and the CGT backed them up. In less than a week, Parisian officials agreed to regularize seven of the nine, with Konté the first to get his papers.

The CGT and *Droits Devant!!* (Rights Ahead!!), an immigrant rights advocacy group, saw an opportunity and gave the snowball a push. They escorted Konté and his co-workers to meetings and rallies with other undocumented CGT workers, where they declared, "We've started it, it's up to you to follow." Small groups began to do just that. Then on April 15, fifteen new workplaces in Paris and the surrounding region sprouted red CGT flags as several hundred "irregular" workers held sit-ins. At France's Labor Day parade on May 1, a contingent of several thousand undocumented, most from West African countries such as Mali, Senegal, and Ivory Coast, were the stars.

But local governments were slow to move on their demands, so with only 70 workers regularized one month into the sit-ins, another 200 *sans-papiers* upped the ante on May 20 by taking over twenty more job sites. Still others have joined the strike since. As of early July, 400 former strikers have received papers (typically one-year permits), and the CGT estimates that 600 are still sitting tight at 41 workplaces.

Restaurants, with their visible locations on main boulevards, are the highest profile strike sites. But strikers are also camping out at businesses in construction, cleaning, security, personal services, and landscaping. Though the movement reportedly includes North Africans, Eastern Europeans, and even Filipinos, its public presence has consisted almost entirely of sub-Saharan Africans, a stunning indication of the degree of racial segregation in immigrant jobs. Strikers are overwhelmingly men, though the female employees of a contract cleaning business, Ma Net, made a splash when they joined the strike on May 26, and groups representing domestics and other women workers began to demonstrate around the same time.

"To Go Around Freely..."

The *sans-papiers* came to France by different means. Some overstayed student or tourist visas. Others paid as much as 7,500 euros ($12,000) to a trafficker to travel to the North African coast, clandestinely cross by boat to Spain, and then find their way to France. Strike leader Konté arrived in Paris, his target, two long years after leaving Mali. A set of false papers for 200 euros, and he was ready to look for work.

But opportunities for the undocumented are, for the most part, limited to jobs with the worst pay and working conditions. The French minimum wage is 8.71 euros an hour (almost $13), but strikers tell of working for 3 euros or even less. "With papers, I would get 1,000 euros a month," Issac, a Malian cleaner for the Quick restaurant chain who has been in France eleven years, told *Dollars & Sense*. "Without papers, I get 300." Even so, he and many others send half their pay home to families who depend on them. Through paycheck withholding, the *sans-papiers* pay taxes and contribute to the French health care and retirement funds. But "if I get sick, I don't have any right to reimbursement," said Camara, a dishwasher from Mali. He told *L'Humanité*, the French Communist Party newspaper, how much he wished "to go around freely." "In the evening I don't go out," he said. "When I leave home in the morning, I don't even know if I will get home that night. I avoid some subway stations" that are closely monitored by the police.

When asked how he would reply to the claim that the undocumented are taking jobs from French workers, Issac replied simply, "We are French workers—just without any rights. Yes, we're citizens, because France owned all of black Africa!"

Business Allies

The surprise allies in this guerrilla struggle for the right to work are many of the employers. When workers seized the Samsic contract cleaning agency in the Paris suburb of Massy, owner Mehdi Daïri first called the police. When they told him there was nothing they could do, he pragmatically decided to apply for permits for his 300-plus employees. "It's in everybody's best interest," he told *Le Monde*, the French daily newspaper. "Their action is legitimate. They've been here for years, working, contributing to the social security system, paying taxes, and we're satisfied with their work." He even has his office staff make coffee for the strikers every morning.

Though some businesses have taken a harder line against the strikers, the major business associations have called for massive regularization of their workforces. According to *L'Humanité*, André Dauguin, president of the hotel operators association, is demanding that 50,000 to 100,000 undocumented workers be given papers. Didier Chenet, president of another association of restaurant and hotel enterprises, declared that with 20,000 jobs going unfilled in these sectors, the *sans-papiers* "are not taking jobs away from other workers."

For the CGT, busy with defensive battles against labor "reforms" such as cutbacks in public employees' pensions, the strike wave represents a step in a new direction. The core of the CGT remains white, native-born French workers. As recently as the 1980s, the Communist Party, to which the CGT was then closely linked, took some controversial anti-immigrant stands. Raymond Chauveau, the general secretary of the CGT's Massy local, acknowledged to *Le Monde* that some union members still have trouble understanding why the organization has taken up this issue. But he added, "Today, these people are recognized for what they are: workers. They are developing class consciousness. Our role as a union is to show that these people are not outside the world of work." While some immigrant rights groups are critical of the CGT for suddenly stepping into the leadership of a fight other groups had been pursuing for years, it is hard to deny the importance of the labor organization's clout.

Half Empty or Half Full?

With only 400 of 1,400 applications for work permits granted four months into the struggle, the CGT is publicly voicing its impatience at the national government's insistence that local authorities make each decision on a case-by-case basis rather than offering broader guidelines. But Chauveau said he is proud that they have compelled the government to accept regularization of Africans in low-end jobs, broadening the opening beyond the intent of the 2007 law. And on its website, the CGT boasted that the *sans-papiers* "have compelled the government to take its first steps back, when that had seemed impossible since the [May 2007] election of Nicolas Sarkozy." Perhaps even more important for the long term is that class consciousness Chauveau mentioned. This is "a struggle that has changed my life," stated Mamadou Dembia Thiam of Senegal, a security guard who won his work authorization in June. "Before the struggle, I was really very timid. I've changed!" Changes like that seem likely to bring a new burst of energy to the struggling French labor movement. ❑

Resources: Confédération Générale du Travail, www.cgt.fr; Droits Devant!!, www.droitsdevant.org.

Article 7.3

MADE IN ARGENTINA

Bolivian Migrant Workers Fight Neoliberal Fashion

BY MARIE TRIGONA

January/February 2007

Dubbed "the Paris of the South," Buenos Aires is known for its European architecture, tango clubs, and *haute couture*. But few people are aware that Argentina's top fashion brands employ tens of thousands of undocumented Bolivian workers in slave-labor conditions. In residential neighborhoods across Buenos Aires, top clothing companies have turned small warehouses or gutted buildings into clandestine sweatshops. Locked in, workers are forced to live and work in cramped quarters with little ventilation and, often, limited access to water and gas. The *Unión de Trabajadores Costureros* (Union of Seamstress Workers—UTC), an assembly of undocumented textile workers, has reported more than 8,000 cases of labor abuses inside the city's nearly 400 clandestine shops in the past year. Around 100,000 undocumented immigrants work in these unsafe plants with an average wage—if they are paid at all—of $100 per month.

According to Olga Cruz, a 29-year-old textile worker, slave-labor conditions in textile factories are systematic. "During a normal workday in a shop you work from 7 a.m. until midnight or 1 a.m. Many times they don't pay the women and they owe them two or three years' pay. For not having our legal documents or not knowing what our rights are in Argentina, we've had to remain silent. You don't have rights to rent a room or to work legally."

Another Bolivian textile worker, Naomi Hernández, traveled to Argentina three years ago in hopes of a well-paying job. "I ended up working in a clandestine sweatshop without knowing the conditions I would have to endure. For two years I worked and slept in a three-square-meter room along with my two children and three sewing machines my boss provided. They would bring us two meals a day. For breakfast a cup of tea with a piece of bread and lunch consisting of a portion of rice, a potato, and an egg. We had to share our two meals with our children because according to my boss, my children didn't have the right to food rations because they aren't workers and don't yield production." She reported the subhuman conditions in her workplace and was subsequently fired.

Diseases like tuberculosis and lung complications are common due to the subhuman working conditions and constant exposure to dust and fibers. Many workers suffer from back injuries and tendonitis from sitting at a sewing machine 12 to 16 hours a day. And there are other hazards. A blaze that killed six people last year brought to light abusive working conditions inside a network of clandestine textile plants in Buenos Aires. The two women and four children who were killed had been locked inside the factory.

The situation of these workers shows that exploitation of migrant labor is not just a first-world/third-world phenomenon. The system of exploitative subcontracting of migrant workers that has arisen in U.S. cities as a result of neoliberal globalization also occurs in the countries of the global south—as does organized resistance to such exploitation.

Survival for Bolivian Workers

Buenos Aires is the number one destination for migrants from Bolivia, Paraguay, and Peru, whose numbers have grown in the past decade because of the declining economic conditions in those countries. More than one million Bolivians have migrated to Argentina since 1999; approximately one-third are undocumented.

Even when Argentina's economy took a nosedive in the 1990s, Bolivians were still driven to migrate there given their homeland's far more bleak economic conditions. Over two-thirds of Bolivians live in poverty, and nearly half subsist on less than a dollar a day. For decades, migration of rural workers (44% of the population) to urban areas kept many families afloat. Now, facing limited employment opportunities and low salaries in Bolivia's cities, many workers have opted to migrate to Argentina or Brazil.

Buenos Aires' clandestine network of sweatshops emerged in the late 1990s, following the influx of inexpensive Asian textile imports. Most of the textile factory owners are Argentine, Korean, or Bolivian. The workers manufacture garments for high-end brands like Lacár, Kosiuko, Adidas, and Montage in what has become a $700 million a year industry.

In many cases workers are lured by radio or newspaper ads in Bolivia promising transportation to Buenos Aires and decent wages plus room and board once they arrive. Truck drivers working for the trafficking rings transport workers in the back of trucks to cross into Argentina illegally.

For undocumented immigrants in Argentina, survival itself is a vicious cycle. The undocumented are especially susceptible to threats of losing their jobs. Workers can't afford to rent a room; even if they could, many residential hotel managers are unwilling to rent rooms to immigrants, especially when they have children.

Finding legal work is almost impossible without a national identity card. For years, Bolivian citizens had reported that Alvaro Gonzalez Quint, the head of Bolivia's consulate in Buenos Aires, would charge immigrants up to $100—equivalent to a textile worker's average monthly pay—to complete paperwork necessary for their documentation. The Argentine League for Human Rights has also brought charges against Gonzalez Quint in federal court, alleging he is tied to the network of smugglers who profit from bringing immigrants into Argentina to work in the sweatshops.

A New Chapter in Argentina's Labor Struggles

Argentina has a notable tradition of labor organizing among immigrants. Since the 19th century, working-class immigrants have fought for basic rights, including

Sundays off, eight-hour workdays, and a minimum wage. The eight-hour workday became law in 1933, but employers have not always complied. Beginning with the 1976-1983 military dictatorship, and continuing through the neoliberal 1990s, many labor laws have been altered to allow flexible labor standards. University of Buenos Aires economist Eduardo Lucita, a member of UDI (Economists from the Left), says that although the law for an eight-hour workday stands, the average workday in Argentina is 10 to 12 hours. "Only half of workers have formal labor contracts; the rest are laboring as subcontracted workers in the unregulated, informal sector. For such workers there are no regulations for production rates and lengths of a workday—much less criteria for salaries." The average salary for Argentines is only around $200 a month, in contrast to the minimum of $600 required to meet the basic needs of a family of four.

Today, the extreme abuses in the new sweatshops have prompted a new generation of immigrant workers to organize.

"We have had to remain silent and accept abuse. I'm tired of taking the blows. We are starting to fight, *compañeros*; thank you for attending the assembly." These are the words of Ana Salazar at an assembly of textile workers that met in Buenos Aires on a Sunday evening last April. The UTC formed out of a neighborhood assembly in the working class neighborhood of Parque Avalleneda. Initially, the assembly was a weekly social event for families on Sundays, the only day textile workers can leave the shop. Families began to gather at the assembly location, situated at the corner of a park. Later, because Argentina's traditional unions refuse to accept undocumented affiliates, the workers expanded their informal assembly into a full-fledged union.

Since the factory fire that killed six on March 30, 2006, the UTC has stepped up actions against the brand-name clothing companies that subcontract with clandestine sweatshops. The group has held a number of *escraches*, or exposure protests, outside fashion makers' offices in Buenos Aires to push the city government to hold inspections inside the companies' textile workshops. Workers from the UTC also presented legal complaints against the top jean manufacturer Kosiuko.

At a recent surprise protest, young women held placards: "I kill myself for your jeans," signed, "a Bolivian textile worker." During the protest, outside Kosiuko's offices in the exclusive Barrio Norte neighborhood, UTC presented an in-depth research report into the brand's labor violations. "The Kosiuko company is concealing slave shops," said Gustavo Vera, member of the La Alemeda popular assembly. "They disclosed false addresses to inspectors and they have other workshops which they are not reporting to the city government." The UTC released a detailed list of the locations of alleged sweatshops. Most of the addresses that the Kosiuko company had provided turned out to be private residences or stores.

To further spotlight large brand names that exploit susceptible undocumented workers, the UTC held a unique fashion show in front of the Buenos Aires city legislature last September. "Welcome to the neoliberal fashion show—Spring Season 2006," announced the host, as spectators cheered—or jeered—the top brands that use slave labor. Models from a local theatre group paraded down a red carpet in brands like Kosiuko, Montagne, Porte Said, and Lacar, while the host shouted out the addresses of the brands' sweatshops and details of subhuman conditions inside shops.

"I repressed all of my rage about my working conditions and violations of my rights. Inside a clandestine workshop you don't have any rights. You don't have dignity," said Naomi Hernández, pedaling away at a sewing machine during the "fashion show."

After the show, Hernández stood up in front of the spectators and choked down tears while giving testimony of her experience as a slave laborer in a sweatshop: "I found out what it is to fight as a human being." She says her life has changed since joining the UTC.

Inspection-Free Garment Shops

To date, the union's campaign has had some successes. In April of 2006, the Buenos Aires city government initiated inspections of sweatshops employing Bolivians and Paraguayans; inspectors shut down at least 100. (Perhaps not surprisingly, Bolivian consul Gonzalez Quint has protested the city government's moves to regulate sweatshops, arguing that the measures discriminate against Bolivian employers who run some of the largest textile shops.) But since then, inspections have been suspended and many clothes manufacturers have simply moved their sweatshops to the suburban industrial belt or to new locations in the city. The UTC has reported that other manufacturers force workers to labor during the night to avoid daytime inspections.

Nestor Escudero, an Argentine who participates in the UTC, says that police, inspectors, and the courts are also responsible for the documented slave-labor conditions inside textile factories. "They bring in illegal immigrants to brutally exploit them. The textile worker is paid 75 cents for a garment that is later sold for $50. This profit is enough to pay bribes and keep this system going."

Since 2003, thousands of reports of slave-labor conditions have piled up in the courts without any resolution. In many cases when workers have presented reports to police of poor treatment, including threats, physical abuse, and forced labor, the police say they can't act because the victims do not have national identity cards.

Seeing their complaints go unheeded is sometimes the least of it. Escudero has confirmed that over a dozen textile workers have received death threats for reporting to media outlets on slave-labor conditions inside the textile plants. Shortly after the UTC went public last spring with hundreds of reports of abuses, over a dozen of the union's representatives were threatened. And in a particularly shocking episode, two men kidnapped the 9-year-old son of José Orellano and Monica Frías, textile workers who had reported slave-labor conditions in their shop. The attackers held the boy at knifepoint and told him to "tell your parents that they should stop messing around with the reports against the sweatshops." The UTC filed criminal charges of abandonment and abuse of power against Argentina's Interior Minister Aníbal Fernández in November for not providing the couple with witness protection.

The Road Ahead

Although the Buenos Aires city government has yet to make much headway in regulating the city's sweatshops, the UTC continues to press for an end to sweatshop slavery, along with mass legalization of immigrants and housing for immigrants living in poverty. Organizing efforts have not been in vain. In an important victory, the city government has opened a number of offices to process immigration documents free of charge for Bolivian and Paraguayan citizens, circumventing the Bolivian Consulate.

The UTC has also proposed that clandestine textile shops be shut down and handed over to the workers to manage them as co-ops and, ultimately, build a cooperative network that can bypass the middlemen and the entire piece-work system. Already, the Alameda assembly has joined with the UTC to form the Alameda Workers' Cooperative as an alternative to sweatshops. Nearly 30 former sweatshop workers work at the cooperative in the same space where the weekly assemblies are held.

Olga Cruz now works with the cooperative sewing garments. She says that although it's a struggle, she now has dignity that she didn't have when she worked in one of the piece-work shops. "We are working as a cooperative, we all make the same wage. In the clandestine shops you are paid per garment: they give you the fabric and you have to hand over the garment fully manufactured. Here we have a line system, which is more advanced and everyone works the same amount."

Fired for reporting on abusive conditions at her sweatshop, Naomi Hernández has also found work at the cooperative. "We are freeing ourselves, that's what I feel. Before I wasn't a free person and didn't have any rights," said Hernández to a crowd of spectators in front of the city legislature. She sent a special message and invitation: "Now we are fighting together with the Alameda cooperative and the UTC. I invite all workers who know their rights are being violated to join the movement against slave labor." ❑

Resources: To contact UTC activists at La Alameda assembly in Parque Avellaneda, email: asambleaparqueavellaneda@hotmail.com. To see videos of recent UTC actions, go to: www. revolutionvideo.org/agoratv/secciones/luchas_obreras/costureros_utc.html; www.revolutionvideo. org/agoratv/secciones/luchas_obreras/escrache_costureros.html.

Article 7.4

THE RIGHT TO STAY HOME

Transnational communities are creating new ways of looking at citizenship and residence that correspond to the realities of migration.

BY DAVID BACON
September/October 2008

For almost half a century, migration has been the main fact of social life in hundreds of indigenous towns spread through the hills of Oaxaca, one of Mexico's poorest states. That's made migrants' rights, and the conditions they face, central concerns for communities like Santiago de Juxtlahuaca. Today the right to travel to seek work is a matter of survival. But this June in Juxtlahuaca, in the heart of Oaxaca's Mixteca region, dozens of farmers left their fields, and weavers their looms, to talk about another right—the right to stay home.

In the town's community center, 200 Mixtec, Zapotec, and Triqui farmers, and a handful of their relatives working in the United States, made impassioned speeches asserting this right at the triannual assembly of the Indigenous Front of Binational Organizations (FIOB). Hot debates ended in numerous votes. The voices of mothers and fathers arguing over the future of their children echoed from the cinderblock walls of the cavernous hall. In Spanish, Mixteco, and Triqui, people repeated one phrase over and over: *el derecho de no migrar*—the right to *not* migrate. Asserting this right challenges not just inequality and exploitation facing migrants, but the very reasons why people have to migrate to begin with. Indigenous communities are pointing to the need for social change.

About 500,000 indigenous people from Oaxaca live in the United States, including 300,000 in California alone, according to Rufino Dominguez, one of FIOB's founders. These men and women come from communities whose economies are totally dependent on migration. The ability to send a son or daughter across the border to the north, to work and send back money, makes the difference between eating chicken or eating salt and tortillas. Migration means not having to manhandle a wooden plough behind an ox, cutting furrows in dry soil for a corn crop that can't be sold for what it cost to plant it. It means that dollars arrive in the mail when kids need shoes to go to school, or when a grandparent needs a doctor.

Seventy-five percent of Oaxaca's 3.4 million residents live in extreme poverty, according to EDUCA, an education and development organization. For more than two decades, under pressure from international lenders, the Mexican government has cut spending intended to raise rural incomes. Prices have risen dramatically since price controls and subsidies were eliminated for necessities like gasoline, electricity, bus fares, tortillas, and milk.

Raquel Cruz Manzano, principal of the Formal Primary School in San Pablo Macuiltianguis, a town in the indigenous Zapotec region, says only 900,000 Oaxacans receive organized health care, and the illiteracy rate is 21.8%. "The educational level in Oaxaca is 5.8 years," Cruz notes, "against a national average of 7.3 years. The average monthly wage for non-governmental employees is less than 2,000 pesos [about $200] per family," the lowest in the nation. "Around 75,000 children have to work in order to survive or to help their families," says Jaime Medina, a reporter for Oaxaca's daily *Noticias*. "A typical teacher earns about 2200 pesos every two weeks [about $220]. From that they have to purchase chalk, pencils and other school supplies for the children." Towns like Juxtlahuaca don't even have waste water treatment. Rural communities rely on the same rivers for drinking water that are also used to carry away sewage.

"There are no jobs here, and NAFTA [the North American Free Trade Agreement] made the price of corn so low that it's not economically possible to plant a crop anymore," Dominguez asserts. "We come to the U.S. to work because we can't get a price for our product at home. There is no alternative." Without large-scale political change, most communities won't have the resources for productive projects and economic development that could provide a decent living.

Citizenship, Political Rights, and Labor Rights

Citizenship is a complex issue in a world in which transnational migrant communities span borders and exist in more than one place simultaneously. Residents of transnational communities don't see themselves simply as victims of an unfair system, but as actors capable of reproducing culture, of providing economic support to families in their towns of origin, and of seeking social justice in the countries to which they've migrated. A sensible immigration policy would recognize and support migrant communities. It would reinforce indigenous culture and language, rather than treating them as a threat. At the same time, it would seek to integrate immigrants into the broader community around them and give them a voice in it, rather than promoting social exclusion, isolation, and segregation. It would protect the rights of immigrants as part of protecting the rights of all working people.

Transnational communities in Mexico are creating new ways of looking at citizenship and residence that correspond more closely to the reality of migration. In 2005 Jesús Martínez, a professor at California State University in Fresno, was elected by residents of the state of Michoacán in Mexico to their state legislature. His mandate was to represent the interests of the state's citizens living in the United States. "In Michoacán, we're trying to carry out reforms that can do justice to the role migrants play in our lives," Martínez said. In 2006 Pepe Jacques Medina, director of the Comité Pro Uno in Los Angeles' San Fernando Valley, was elected to the Federal Chamber of Deputies on the ticket of the left-leaning Party of the Democratic Revolution (PRD) with the same charge. Transnational migrants insist that they have important political and social rights, both in their communities of origin and in their communities abroad.

Because of its indigenous membership, FIOB campaigns for the rights of migrants in the United States who come from those communities. It calls for immigration amnesty and legalization for undocumented migrants. FIOB has also condemned the proposals for guestworker programs. Migrants need the right to work, but "these workers don't have labor rights or benefits," Dominguez charges. "It's like slavery."

At the same time, "we need development that makes migration a choice rather than a necessity—the right to not migrate," explains Gaspar Rivera Salgado, a professor at UCLA. "Both rights are part of the same solution. We have to change the debate from one in which immigration is presented as a problem to a debate over rights. The real problem is exploitation." But the right to stay home, to not migrate, has to mean more than the right to be poor, the right to go hungry and be homeless. Choosing whether to stay home or leave only has meaning if each choice can provide a meaningful future.

In Juxtlahuaca, Rivera Salgado was elected as FIOB's new binational coordinator. His father and mother still live on a ranch half an hour up a dirt road from the main highway, in the tiny town of Santa Cruz Rancho Viejo. There his father

> The two parties that control the Mexican national congress, the Institutional Revolutionary Party (PRI) and the National Action Party (PAN), have taken steps to provide political rights for migrants. But while Mexico's congress voted over a decade ago to enfranchise Mexicans in the United States, it only set up a system to implement that decision in April 2005. They imposed so many obstacles that in the 2006 presidential elections only 40,000 were able to vote, out of a potential electorate of millions.
>
> While it is difficult for Mexicans in the United States to vote in Mexico, they are barred from voting in the United States altogether. But U.S. electoral politics can't remain forever immune from expectations of representation, and they shouldn't. After all, the slogan of the Boston Tea Party was "No taxation without representation"; those who make economic contributions have political rights. That principle requires recognition of the legitimate social status of everyone living in the United States. Legalization isn't just important to migrants—it is a basic step in the preservation and extension of democratic rights for all people. With and without visas, 34 million migrants living in the United States cannot vote to choose the political representatives who decide basic questions about wages and conditions at work, the education of their children, their health care or lack of it, and even whether they can walk the streets without fear of arrest and deportation.
>
> Migrants' disenfranchisement affects U.S. citizens, especially working people. If all the farm workers and their families in California's San Joaquin Valley were able to vote, a wave of living wage ordinances would undoubtedly sweep the state. California's legislature would pass a single-payer health plan to ensure that every resident receives free and adequate health care. If it failed to pass, San Joaquin Valley legislators, currently among the most conservative, would be swept from office.
>
> When those who most need social change and economic justice are excluded

Sidronio planted three hundred avocado trees a few years ago, in the hope that someday their fruit would take the place of the corn and beans that were once his staple crops. He's fortunate—his relatives have water, and a pipe from their spring has kept most of his trees, and those hopes, alive. Fernando, Gaspar's brother, has started growing mushrooms in a FIOB-sponsored project, and even put up a greenhouse for tomatoes. Those projects, they hope, will produce enough money that Fernando won't have to go back to Seattle, where he worked for seven years.

This family perhaps has come close to achieving the *derecho de no migrar*. For the millions of farmers throughout the indigenous countryside, not migrating means doing something like what Gaspar's family has done. But finding the necessary resources, even for a small number of families and communities, presents FIOB with its biggest challenge.

Rivera Salgado says, "we will find the answer to migration in our communities of origin. To make the right to not migrate concrete, we need to organize the forces in our communities, and combine them with the resources and experiences we've accumulated

from the electorate, the range of possible reform is restricted, not only on issues of immigration, but on most economic issues that affect working people. Immigration policy, including political and social rights for immigrants, are integral parts of a broad agenda for change that includes better wages and housing, a national healthcare system, a national jobs program, and the right to organize without fear of being fired. Without expanding the electorate, it will be politically difficult to achieve any of it. By the same token, it's not possible to win major changes in immigration policy apart from a struggle for these other goals.

Anti-immigrant hysteria has always preached that the interests of immigrants and the native born are in conflict, that one group can only gain at the expense of the other. In fact, the opposite is true. To raise wages generally, the low price of immigrant labor has to rise, which means that immigrant workers have to be able to organize effectively. Given half a chance, they will fight for better jobs, wages, schools, and health care, just like anyone else. When they gain political power, the working class communities around them benefit too. Since it's easier for immigrants to organize if they have permanent legal status, a real legalization program would benefit a broad range of working people, far beyond immigrants themselves. On the other hand, when the government and employers use employer sanctions, enforcement, and raids to stop the push for better conditions, organizing is much more difficult, and unions and workers in general suffer the consequences.

The social exclusion and second-class status imposed by guestworker programs only increases migrants' vulnerability. De-linking immigration status and employment is a necessary step to achieving equal rights for migrant workers, who will never have significant power if they have to leave the country when they lose their jobs. Healthy immigrant communities need employed workers, but they also need students, old and young people, caregivers, artists, the disabled, and those who don't have traditional jobs.

in 16 years of cross-border organizing." Over the years FIOB has organized women weavers in Juxtlahuaca, helping them sell their textiles and garments through its chapters in California. It set up a union for rural taxis, both to help farming families get from Juxtlahuaca to the tiny towns in the surrounding hills, and to provide jobs for drivers. Artisan co-ops make traditional products, helped by a cooperative loan fund.

The government does have some money for loans to start similar projects, but it usually goes to officials who often just pocket it. They are supporters of the ruling PRI, which has ruled Oaxaca since it was formed in the 1940s. "Part of our political culture is the use of *regalos*, or government favors, to buy votes," Rivera Salgado explains. "People want *regalos*, and think an organization is strong because of what it can give. It's critical that our members see organization as the answer to problems, not a gift from the government or a political party. FIOB members need political education."

But for the 16 years of its existence, FIOB has been a crucial part of the political opposition to Oaxaca's PRI government. Juan Romualdo Gutierrez Cortéz, a school teacher in Tecomaxtlahuaca, was FIOB's Oaxaca coordinator until he stepped down at the Juxtlahuaca assembly. He is also a leader of Oaxaca's teachers union, Section 22 of the National Education Workers Union, and of the Popular Association of the People of Oaxaca (APPO).

A June 2006 strike by Section 22 sparked a months-long uprising, led by APPO, which sought to remove the state's governor, Ulises Ruíz, and make a basic change in development and economic policy. The uprising was crushed by Federal armed intervention, and dozens of activists were arrested. According to Leoncio Vásquez, an FIOB activist in Fresno, "the lack of human rights itself is a factor contributing to migration from Oaxaca and Mexico, since it closes off our ability to call for any change." This spring teachers again occupied the central plaza, or *zócalo*, of the state capital, protesting the same conditions that sparked the uprising two years ago.

In the late 1990s Gutierrez was elected to the Oaxaca Chamber of Deputies, in an alliance between FIOB and Mexico's left-wing Democratic Revolutionary Party (PRD). Following his term in office, he was imprisoned by Ruíz' predecessor, José Murat, until a binational campaign won his release. His crime, and that of many others filling Oaxaca's jails, was insisting on a new path of economic development that would raise rural living standards and make migration just an option, rather than an indispensable means of survival.

Despite the fact that APPO wasn't successful in getting rid of Ruíz and the PRI, Rivera Salgado believes that "in Mexico we're very close to getting power in our communities on a local and state level." FIOB delegates agreed that the organization would continue its alliance with the PRD. "We know the PRD is caught up in an internal crisis, and there's no real alternative vision on the left," Rivera Salgado says. "But there are no other choices if we want to participate in electoral politics. Migration is part of globalization," he emphasizes, "an aspect of state policies that expel people. Creating an alternative to that requires political power. There's no way to avoid that." ❑

Article 7.5

THE RISE OF MIGRANT WORKER MILITANCY

IMMANUEL NESS

September/October 2006

Testifying before the Senate immigration hearings in early July, Mayor Michael Bloomberg affirmed that undocumented immigrants have become indispensable to the economy of New York City: "Although they broke the law by illegally crossing our borders or overstaying their visas, and our businesses broke the law by employing them, our city's economy would be a shell of itself had they not, and it would collapse if they were deported. The same holds true for the nation." Bloomberg's comment outraged right-wing pundits, but how much more outraged would they be if they knew that immigrant workers, beyond being economically indispensable, are beginning to transform the U.S. labor movement with a bold new militancy?

After years of working in obscurity in the unregulated economy, migrant workers in New York City catapulted themselves to the forefront of labor activism beginning in late 1999 through three separate organizing drives among low-wage workers. Immigrants initiated all three drives: Mexican immigrants organized and struck for improved wages and working conditions at greengroceries; Francophone African delivery workers struck for unpaid wages and respect from labor contractors for leading supermarket chains; and South Asians organized for improved conditions and a union in the for-hire car service industry. (In New York, "car services" are taxis that cannot be hailed on the street, only arranged by phone.) These organizing efforts have persisted, and are part of a growing militancy among migrant workers in New York City and across the United States.

Why would seemingly invisible workers rise up to contest power in their workplaces? Why are vulnerable migrant workers currently more likely to organize than are U.S.-born workers? To answer these questions, we have to look at immigrants' distinct position in the political economy of a globalized New York City and at their specific economic and social niches, ones in which exploitation and isolation nurture class consciousness and militancy.

Labor Migration and Industrial Restructuring

New immigrant workers in the United States, many here illegally, stand at the crossroads of two overwhelming trends. On one hand, industrial restructuring and capital mobility have eroded traditional industries and remade the U.S. political economy in the last 30 years in ways that have led many companies to create millions of low-wage jobs and to seek vulnerable workers to fill them. On the other hand, at the behest of international financial institutions like the International Monetary Fund, and to meet the requirements of free-trade agreements such as NAFTA, governments throughout the global South have adopted neoliberal policies that have restructured their economies, resulting in the displacement of urban workers and rural farmers alike. Many have no choice but to migrate north.

A century ago the United States likewise experienced a large influx of immigrants, many of whom worked in factories for their entire lives. There they formed social networks across ethnic lines and developed a class consciousness that spurred the organizing of unions; they made up the generation of workers whose efforts began with the fight for the eight-hour day around the turn of the last century and culminated in the great organizing victories of the 1930s and 1940s across the entire spectrum of mining and manufacturing industries.

Today's immigrants face an entirely different political-economic landscape. Unlike most of their European counterparts a century ago, immigration restrictions mean that many newcomers to the United States are now here illegally. Workers from Latin America frequently migrate illegally without proper documentation; those from Africa, Asia, and Europe commonly arrive with business, worker, student, or tourist visas, then overstay them.

The urban areas where many immigrants arrive have undergone a 30-year decline in manufacturing jobs. The growing pool of service jobs which have come in their stead tend to be dispersed in small firms throughout the city. The proliferation of geographically dispersed subcontractors who compete on the basis of low wages encourages a process of informalization—a term referring to a redistribution of work from regulated sectors of the economy to new unregulated sectors of the underground or informal economy. As a result, wages and working conditions have fallen, often below government-established norms.

Although informal work is typically associated with the developing world—or Global South—observers are increasingly recognizing the link between the regulated and unregulated sectors in advanced industrial regions. More and more the regulated sector depends on unregulated economic activity through subcontracting and outsourcing of work to firms employing low-wage immigrant labor. Major corporations employ or subcontract to businesses employing migrant workers in what were once established sectors of the economy with decent wages and working conditions.

Informalization requires government regulatory agencies to look the other way. For decades federal and state regulatory bodies have ignored violations of laws governing wages, hours, and workplace safety, leading to illegally low wages and declining workplace health and safety practices. The process of informalization is furthered by the reduction or elimination of protections such as disability insurance, Social Security, health care coverage, unemployment insurance, and workers compensation.

By the 1990s, substandard jobs employing almost exclusively migrant workers had become crucial to key sectors of the national economy. Today, immigrants have gained a major presence as bricklayers, demolition workers, and hazardous waste workers on construction and building rehab sites; as cooks, dishwashers, and busboys in restaurants; and as taxi drivers, domestic workers, and delivery people.

Employers frequently treat these workers as self-employed. They typically have no union protection and little or no job security. With government enforcement shrinking, they lack the protection of minimum-wage laws and they have been excluded from Social Security and unemployment insurance.

These workers are increasingly victimized by employers who force them to accept 19th-century working conditions and sub-minimum wages. Today, New York City, Los Angeles, Miami, Houston, and Boston form a nexus of international labor migration, with constantly churning labor markets. As long as there is a demand for cheap labor, immigrants will continue to enter the United States in large numbers. Like water, capital always flows to the lowest level, a state of symmetry where wages are cheapest.

In turn, the availability of a reserve army of immigrant labor provides an enormous incentive for larger corporations to create and use subcontracting firms. Without this workforce, employers in the regulated economy would have more incentive to invest in labor-saving technology, increase the capital-labor ratio, and seek accommodation with unions.

New unauthorized immigrants residing and working in the United States are ideal workers in the new informalized sectors: Their undocumented legal status makes them more tractable since they constantly fear deportation. Undocumented immigrants are less likely to know about, or demand adherence to, established labor standards, and even low U.S. wages represent an improvement over earnings in their home countries.

Forging Migrant Labor Solidarity

The perception that new immigrants undermine U.S.-born workers by undercutting prevailing wage and work standards cannot be entirely dismissed. The entry of a large number of immigrants into the underground economy unquestionably reduces the labor market leverage of U.S.-born workers. But the story is more complicated. In spite of their vulnerability, migrant workers have demonstrated a willingness and a capacity to organize for improvements in their wages and working conditions; they arguably are responding to tough conditions on the job with greater militancy than U.S.-born workers.

New York City has been the site of a number of instances of immigrant worker organizing. In 1998, Mexicans working in greengroceries embarked on a citywide organizing campaign to improve their conditions of work. Most of the 20,000 greengrocery workers were paid below $3.00 an hour, working on average 72 hours a week. Some did not make enough to pay their living expenses, no less send remittances back home to Mexico. Following a relentless and coordinated four-year organizing campaign among the workers, employers agreed to raise wages above the minimum and improve working conditions. Moreover, the campaign led state Attorney General Eliot Spitzer to establish a Greengrocer Code of Conduct and to strengthen enforcement of labor regulations.

In another display of immigrant worker militancy, beginning in 1999 Francophone African supermarket delivery workers in New York City fought for and won equality with other workers in the same stores. The workers were responsible for bagging groceries and delivering them to affluent customers in Manhattan and throughout the city. As contractors, the delivery workers were paid no wage, instead relying on the goodwill of customers in affluent neighborhoods to pay tips for each delivery.

The workers were employed in supermarkets and drug stores where some others had a union. Without union support themselves, delivery workers staged a significant strike and insurrection that made consumers aware of their appalling conditions of work. In late October, workers went on strike and marched from supermarket to supermarket, demanding living wages and dignity on the job. At the start of their campaign, wages averaged less than $70 a week. In the months following the strike the workers all won recognition from the stores through the United Food and Commercial Workers that had earlier neglected to include them in negotiations with management. The National Employee Law Project, a national worker advocacy organization, filed landmark lawsuits against the supermarkets and delivery companies and won backwage settlements as the courts deemed them to be workers—not independent contractors in business for themselves.

Immigrant workers have organized countless other campaigns, in New York and across the country. How do new immigrants, with weak ties to organized labor and the state, manage to assert their interests? The explanation lies in the character of immigrant work and social life; the constraints immigrant workers face paradoxically encourage them to draw on shared experiences to create solidarity at work and in their communities.

The typical migrant worker can expect to work twelve-hour days, seven days a week. When arriving home, immigrant workers frequently share the same apartments, buildings, and neighborhoods. These employment ghettos typify immigrant communities across the nation. Workers cook for one another, share stories about their oppressively long and hard days, commiserate about their ill treatment at work, and then go to sleep only to start anew the next day.

Migrant women, surrounded by a world of exploitation, typically suffer even more abuse than their male counterparts, suffering from low wages, long hours, and dangerous conditions. Patterns of gender stratification found in the general labor market are even more apparent among migrant women workers. Most jobs in the nonunion economy, such as construction and driving, are stereotypically considered "men's work." Women predominate in the garment industry, as domestic and child care workers, in laundries, hotels, restaurants, and ever more in sex work. A striking example of migrant women's perilous work environment is the massive recruitment of migrant women to clean up the hazardous materials in the rubble left by the collapse of the World Trade Center without proper safety training.

Isolated in their jobs and communities, immigrant workers have few social ties to unions, community groups, and public officials, and few resources to call upon to assist them in transforming their workplaces. Because new immigrants have few social networks outside the workplace, the ties they develop on the job are especially solid and meaningful—and are nurtured every day. The workers' very isolation and status as outsiders, and their concentration into industrial niches by employers who hire on the basis of ethnicity, tend to strengthen old social ties, build new ones, and deepen class solidarity.

Immigrant social networks contribute to workplace militancy. Conversely, activism at work can stimulate new social networks that can expand workers' power. It is through relationships developed on the job and in the community that shared social identities and mutual resentment of the boss evolves into class consciousness and class solidarity: migrant workers begin to form informal organizations, meet with coworkers to respond to poor working conditions, and take action on the shop floor in defiance of employer abuse.

Typically, few workplace hierarchies exist among immigrants, since few reach supervisory positions. As a result, immigrant workers suffer poor treatment equally at the hands of employers. A gathering sense of collective exploitation usually transforms individualistic activities into shared ones. In rare cases where there are immigrant foremen and crew leaders, they may recognize this solidarity and side with the workers rather than with management. One former manager employed for a fast-food sandwich chain in New York City said: "We are hired only to divide the workers but I was really trying to help the workers get better pay and shorter hours."

Migrant workers bring social identities from their home countries, and those identities are shaped through socialization and work in this country. In cities and towns across the United States, segmentation of migrant workers from specific countries reinforces ethnic, national, and religious identities and helps to form other identities that may stimulate solidarity. Before arriving in the United States, Mexican immigrant workers often see themselves as peasants but not initially as "people of color," while Francophone Africans see themselves as Malian or Senegalese ethnics but not necessarily "black." Life and work in New York can encourage them to adopt new identifications, including a new class consciousness that can spur organizing and militancy.

Once triggered, organizing can go from workplace to workplace like wildfire. When workers realize that they can fight and prevail, this creates a sense of invincibility that stimulates militant action that would otherwise be avoided at all costs. This demonstration effect is vitally important, as was the case in the strikes among garment workers and coal miners in the history of the U.S. labor movement.

"Solidarity Forever" vs. "Take This Job and Shove It"

The militancy of many migrant workers contrasts sharply with the passivity of many U.S.-born workers facing the same low wages and poor working conditions. Why do most workers at chain stores and restaurants like Walmart and McDonalds—most of whom were born in the United States—appear so complacent, while new immigrants are often so militant?

Migrants are not inherently more militant or less passive. Instead, the real workplace conditions of migrant workers seem to produce greater militancy on the job. First, collective social isolation engenders strong ties among migrants in low-wage jobs where organizing is frequently the only way to improve conditions. Because migrants work in jobs that are more amenable to organizing, they are highly represented among newly unionized workers. Strong social ties in the workplace drive migrants to form their own embryonic organizations at work and in their communities that are ripe for union representation. Organizing among migrant workers gains the attention of labor unions, which then see a chance to recruit new members and may provide resources to help immigrant workers mobilize at work and join the union.

Employers also play a major role. Firms employing U.S. workers tend to be larger and are often much harder to organize than the small businesses where immigrants work. In 2003, the Merriam-Webster dictionary added the new word McJob, defined as "a low-paying job that requires little skill and provides little opportunity for advancement." The widely accepted coinage reflects the relentless 30-year economic restructuring creating low-end jobs in the retail sector.

Organizing against Home Depot, McDonalds, Taco Bell, or Walmart is completely different from organizing against smaller employers. Walmart uses many of the same tactics against workers that immigrants contend with: failure to pay overtime, stealing time (intentionally paying workers for fewer hours than actually worked), no health care, part-time work, high turnover, and gender division of labor. The difference is that Walmart has far more resources to oppose unionization than do the smaller employers who are frequently subcontractors to larger firms. But Walmart's opposition to labor unions is so forceful that workers choose to leave rather than stay and fight it out. Relentless labor turnover mitigates against the formation of working class consciousness and militancy.

The expanding non-immigrant low-end service sector tends to produce unskilled part-time jobs that do not train workers in skills that keep them in the same sector of the labor market. Because jobs at the low end of the economy require little training, workers frequently move from one industry to the next. One day a U.S.-born worker may work as a sales clerk for Target, the next day as a waiter at Olive Garden. Because they are not stuck in identity-defined niches, U.S. workers change their world by quitting and finding a job elsewhere, giving them less reason to organize and unionize.

The fact that U.S.-born workers have an exit strategy and migrant workers do not is a significant and important difference. Immigrant workers are more prone to take action to change their working conditions because they have far fewer options than U.S.-born workers. Workers employed by companies like Walmart are unable to change their conditions, since they have little power and will be summarily fired for any form of dissent. If workers violate the terms of Walmart's or McDonalds' employee manual by, say, arriving late, and then are summarily fired, no one is likely to fend for them, as is usually the case among many migrant workers. While migrant workers engage in direct action against their employers to obtain higher wages and respect on the job, U.S. workers do not develop the same dense connections in labor market niches that forge solidarity. Employers firing new immigrants may risk demonstrations, picket lines, or even strikes.

Immigrant workers are pushed into low-wage labor market niches as day laborers, food handlers, delivery workers, and nannies; these niches are difficult if not impossible to escape. Yet immigrant workers relegated to dead-end jobs in the lowest echelons of the labor market in food, delivery, and car service work show a greater eagerness to fight it out to improve their wages and conditions than do U.S. workers who can move on to another dead-end job.

The Role of Unions

Today's labor movement is in serious trouble; membership is spiraling downward as employers demand union-free workplaces. Unionized manufacturing and service workers are losing their jobs to low-wage operations abroad. Unions and, more importantly, the U.S. working class, are in dire straits and must find a means to triumph over the neoliberal dogma that dominates the capitalist system.

As organizing campaigns in New York City show, migrant workers are indispensable to the revitalization of the labor movement. As employers turn to migrant labor to fill low-wage jobs, unions must encourage and support organizing drives that emerge from the oppressive conditions of work. As the 1930s workers' movement demonstrates, if conditions improve for immigrants, all workers will prosper. To gain traction, unions must recognize that capital is pitting migrant workers against native-born laborers to lower wages and improve profitability. Although unions have had some success organizing immigrants, most are circling the wagons, disinterested in building a more inclusive mass labor movement. The first step is for unions to go beyond rhetoric and form a broad and inclusive coalition embracing migrant workers. ❑

Article 7.6

Q&A ON IMMIGRATION, WAGES, AND LABOR CONDITIONS

BY ALEJANDRO REUSS

January 2013

Is it true that immigrants take jobs from American workers and, because they are willing to work for less, cause wages to fall?

Immigration critics, in arguing for restrictions on immigration or more aggressive immigration enforcement, have claimed that immigrants "take jobs" away from native-born workers and that immigration is responsible for lower wages and deteriorating working conditions. There are two main ideas underlying these arguments.

First, labor migration to a particular area increases the supply of labor. Increased supply with unchanged demand, in the labor market as in other markets, tends to drive down prices (in the labor market, this means wages). By the same token, increased competition among workers can result in worsened labor conditions, since workers can compete against each other for jobs either by accepting lower wages or worse conditions. These effects of increased labor supply exist even if the new workers are no more willing to accept low wages or unpleasant working conditions than the previously existing labor force.

It is important to keep in mind, however, that inward migration is almost certain to also increase the demand for labor. Migrants coming to an area have to buy goods and services, many of which will be produced within the regional (or at least national) economy. This increased demand for goods and services will, in turn, increase the demand for labor. So the net effect on wages is, contrary to the immigration critics' view, ambiguous.

Second, migrants may be willing to accept lower wages or worse working conditions than longtime residents of a receiving area. One factor in determining the wages or conditions workers are willing to accept is the customary standard of living. Workers who have moved from one place to another, at least initially, may base their wage demands on what they are accustomed to from their home country or region. Workers from a low-income country may be willing to accept lower wages, even after migrating to a high-income country, than longtime residents of the high-income country (giving rise to the view that they "undercut" wages). If workers in the high-income country are unwilling to lower their wage or conditions demands, to match those of newly arrived migrants, they may not be able to find jobs.

On the other hand, workers' wage and conditions demands may change when they migrate from one place to another, especially over the longer term. They may adjust their expectations to match the customary standard of living in their new country or region. So, once again, there is more to the story than the immigration critics suggest.

So what are the arguments on the other side?

Opponents of the view described above—that immigrant workers are responsible for declining wages or worsening labor conditions, and that this justifies immigration restrictions—make several counter-arguments:

First, some argue that immigrants from low-wage countries mainly take jobs that few U.S.-born workers want in the first place. Certainly, there are large concentrations of immigrant workers in occupations such as farm labor and cleaning services, which may fit this description. (See, for example, Esther Cervantes, "Immigrants and the Labor Market," *Dollars & Sense*, March/April 2006.) Immigrant workers, however, are also found in large numbers in some occupations that had been relatively high-wage and sometimes highly unionized in the past, such as construction or taxi driving. (It is still another question whether the entry of immigrants into these occupations is responsible for declining wages and unionization, or whether these changes preceded the entry of immigrants in large numbers.) Finally, it is important to remember that immigrants are found in all sorts of occupations (including relatively high-pay and high-status occupations, such as medicine), not just low-wage and supposedly low-skill occupations.

Second, even if immigration exerts some downward pressure on wages and working conditions, the effect is probably not very large. To begin with, we have to compare the overall scale of immigration to the United States to the overall size of the labor force. In understanding the overall effects of immigration on U.S. labor markets, the number of immigrants compared to U.S. population is more important than just the total number of immigrants. The ratio of immigrants to the total U.S. population today, while fairly high, is not even at its historic peak (which was reached in the early 20th century, on the eve of World War I).

Economists Gianmarco Ottaviano and Giovanni Peri have argued that all but a few U.S. workers benefit from increased immigration ("Rethinking the Effects of Immigration on Wages," Working Paper 12497, National Bureau of Economic Research, August 2006, nber.org). Workers, after all, are also consumers of goods and services produced by other workers. Native-born workers may benefit from lower prices or greater availability of some kinds of goods, thanks to immigration. Meanwhile, if immigrants on average do not have the same types of skills as native-born workers, the two groups may not be in very direct labor-market competition. In fact, the new skills immigrants bring to the economies of receiving areas may make other workers more productive. (In principle, this could lead to higher wages, though workers have, for various reasons, benefited little from the productivity growth in the U.S. economy in the last forty years.) If immigration does exert some downward pressure on wages and working conditions for native workers, Ottaviano and Peri have concluded, most of the impact falls on a relatively small subset (those without a high-school education) of the native-born population.

Third, even if immigration did have negative effects on wages or other labor conditions, this would not by itself justify new immigration restrictions, attempts to expel immigrants, or other policies proposed by immigration "restrictionists." Immigrants are not the only group that adds to the labor supply in the United

States. Every year, millions of high-school and college graduates flood the labor market, looking for jobs. Nobody argues that there should be age restrictions on employment, keeping the new graduates out of the labor market in order to protect wages or conditions for older workers.

Meanwhile, in the United States over the last half century, women have entered the paid labor force—and especially some professional occupations—in much larger numbers. Until not so long ago, people openly made the argument that women should not be allowed to enter the labor force, because they were "taking men's jobs." Today, while there are certainly still opponents of employment opportunities for women, such arguments are seldom made openly (and, when they are, they are met with widespread condemnation). Likewise, arguments for racial discrimination in hiring (to keep people of color from "taking white men's jobs"), common a generation or two ago, are now taboo in U.S. politics. Pro-immigrant groups argue that singling out people for exclusion on the basis of their place of birth is, similarly, discriminatory and wrong—and very often has a strong undertone of racial or ethnic bias.

Finally, if one is really concerned about wages and conditions (especially for low-income workers), there are alternative policies that would be preferable to immigration restrictions. Restrictions on the free movement of people, immigrants' rights advocates argue, are among the most intrusive government interventions in labor markets—suppressing the fundamental right to live and work where one chooses. Minimum wage laws, maximum hours and overtime laws, occupational safety and health regulations, and other well-known labor-market interventions—all aggressively enforced—are a much better way to improve conditions for workers at the "bottom" of the labor market (native-born and immigrant alike).

Well, I've heard people argue that immigration undermines unions. Isn't that true?

Some immigration opponents, especially within the organized labor movement, have argued that immigration undermines unions. (Keep in mind that many opponents of immigration are also opposed to unions, and so are not likely to mention this as an argument against immigration.) Unions are a way that workers mutually agree to not compete against each other (not accept lower wages or worse working conditions). These agreements, however, may not be very effective in raising wages or improving working conditions if there is substantial competition from other workers.

Immigration poses a familiar challenge to the labor movement. Union workers have often faced competition from non-union workers, who are not party to the non-competition agreement that is the basis of unionism. In many cases, non-union workers were not invited to be part of this covenant; in some, they were specifically excluded from it (sometimes on the basis of race, ethnicity, or gender). When faced with such competition, unions have sometimes responded by redoubling their efforts to keep other workers out—not only out of the union but out of the labor market altogether. They have sometimes refused union membership to workers in industries where membership was required for employment, or demanded that employers discriminate in hiring. The alternative is to become more inclusive, to bring more workers into the pact. These two alternatives are present in current debates on immigration. Support for immigration restrictions—as a way to exclude potentially competing workers from the labor market—has a long history in the labor movement. Today, however, U.S. unions are moving toward greater advocacy for immigrants' rights and more attention to unionization campaigns among immigrant workers.

Some commentators (especially those who consider themselves pro-union and pro-immigrant) argue that immigration restrictions, far from protecting unions, actually undermine unions. They emphasize that immigration restrictions do not only affect who can or cannot enter the country, but also the ability of those who are here to stand up for their rights. Immigration restrictions make it harder for immigrant workers, especially undocumented or "guest" workers, to fight for their rights at work or to join unions—since they have every reason to fear that they will be fired or deported if they do. This has been one reason that some unions have opposed guest-worker programs, and favored reforms that would give immigrants greater security (up to and including a "road to citizenship"). With greater security, they argue, immigrants will be in a better position to assert their rights at work—join unions, go on strike, report labor-law violations, and so on.

Over the last 30 years or so, workers in the United States have faced increased employer and government hostility toward unions. Many immigrant workers face the added challenge of insecure status. Some immigrants, however, also bring with them the traditions of labor struggle from their home countries, and have been in the forefront of new struggles here. In recent years, there have been several examples of successful union campaigns in workplaces with large numbers of immigrants (including undocumented immigrants), such as at cleaning companies or in hotels. Immigrant workers have also been prominent in labor organizing outside the traditional union movement (especially in "workers' centers"), campaigning for the enforcement of labor protections for all workers (especially the most vulnerable), and even gaining agreements for better wages and labor conditions from some employers. (See Immanuel Ness, *Immigrants, Unions, and the New U.S. Labor Market* (Temple University Press, 2005).)

Unions focused on industries with large immigrant workforces have been among the most vocal advocates of increased rights and security for immigrants. In part, this has been because union leaders recognized, pragmatically, that they needed to organize immigrant workers if the unions are to thrive (or perhaps even survive) in the current difficult atmosphere. In great measure, though, it has been because immigrant workers have made their own voices heard. ❏

Chapter 8

DEVELOPMENT AND "UNDERDEVELOPMENT"

Article 8.1

HAITI'S FAULT LINES: MADE IN THE U.S.A.

BY MARIE KENNEDY AND CHRIS TILLY
March/April 2010

The mainstream media got half the story right about Haiti. Reporters observed that Haiti's stark poverty intensified the devastation caused by the recent earthquake. True: hillside shantytowns, widespread concrete construction without rebar reinforcement, a grossly inadequate road network, and a healthcare system mainly designed to cater to the small elite all contributed mightily to death and destruction.

But what caused that poverty? U.S. readers and viewers might be forgiven for concluding that some inexplicable curse has handed Haiti corrupt and unstable governments, unproductive agriculture, and widespread illiteracy. Televangelist Pat Robertson simply took this line of "explanation" to its nutty, racist conclusion when he opined that Haitians were paying for a pact with the devil.

But the devil had little to do with Haiti's underdevelopment. Instead, the fingerprints of more mundane actors—France and later the United States—are all over the crime scene. After the slave rebellion of 1791, France wrought massive destruction in attempting to recapture its former colony, then extracted 150 million francs of reparations, only fully paid off in 1947. France's most poisonous legacy may have been the skin-color hierarchy that sparked fratricidal violence and still divides Haiti.

While France accepted Haiti once the government started paying up, the United States, alarmed by the example of a slave republic, refused to recognize Haiti until 1862. That late-arriving recognition kicked off a continuing series of military and political interventions. The U.S. Marines occupied Haiti outright from 1915 to 1934, modernizing the infrastructure but also revising laws to allow foreign ownership, turning over the country's treasury to a New York bank, saddling Haiti with a $40 million debt to the United States, and reinforcing the status gap between mulattos and blacks. American governments backed the brutal, kleptocratic, two-generation Duvalier dictatorship from 1957-86. When populist priest Jean-Bertrand Aristide was elected president in 1990, the Bush I administration winked at the coup that ousted him a year later. Bill Clinton reversed course, ordering an invasion to restore Aristide, but used that intervention to impose the same free-trade "structural adjustment" Bush had sought. Bush II closed the circle by backing rebels who re-overthrew the re-elected Aristide in 2004. No wonder many Haitians are suspicious of the U.S. troops who poured in after the earthquake.

Though coups and invasions grab headlines, U.S. economic interventions have had equally far-reaching effects. U.S. goals for the last 30 years have been to open Haiti to American products, push Haiti's self-sufficient peasants off the land, and redirect the Haitian economy to plantation-grown luxury crops and export assembly, both underpinned by cheap labor. Though Haiti has yet to boost its export capacity, the first two goals have succeeded, shattering Haiti's former productive capacity. In the early 1980s, the U.S. Agency for International Development exterminated Haiti's hardy Creole pigs in the name of preventing a swine flu epidemic, then helpfully offered U.S. pigs that require expensive U.S.-produced feeds and medicines. Cheap American rice imports crippled the country's breadbasket, the Artibonite, so that Haiti, a rice exporter in the 1980s, now imports massive amounts. Former peasants flooded into Port-au-Prince, doubling the population over the last quarter century, building makeshift housing, and setting the stage for the current catastrophe.

In the wake of the disaster, U.S. aid continues to have two-edged effects. Each aid shipment that flies in U.S. rice and flour instead of buying and distributing local rice or cassava continues to undermine agriculture and deepen dependency. Precious trucks and airstrips are used to marshal U.S. troops against overblown "security threats," crowding out humanitarian assistance. The United States and other international donors show signs of once more using aid to leverage a free-trade agenda. If we seek to end Haiti's curse, the first step is to realize that one of the curse's main sources is...us. ❑

Article 8.2

"TIED" FOREIGN AID

BY ARTHUR MacEWAN
January/February 2012

Dear Dr. Dollar:

People complaining about the ungrateful world often talk about the "huge" U.S. foreign aid budget. In fact, isn't U.S. foreign aid relatively small compared to other countries? What's worse, I understand that a lot of economic aid comes with strings attached, requiring that goods and services purchased with the aid be purchased from firms in the aid-giving country. This channels much of the money back out of the recipient country. That sounds nuts! What's going on?
—Katharine Rylaarsdam, Baltimore, Md.

The U.S. government does provide a "huge" amount of development aid, far more than any of the other rich countries. In 2009, the United States provided $29.6 billion, in development aid—Japan was number two, at $16.4 billion.

But wait a minute. What appears huge may not be so huge. The graph below shows the amount of foreign development aid provided by ten high-income countries *and* that amount as a share of the countries' gross domestic products (GDP). Yes, the graph shows that the United States gives far more than any of these other countries. But the graph also shows the United States gives a small amount relative to its GDP. In 2009, U.S. foreign development aid was two-tenths of one percent of the country's GDP. Only Italy gave a lesser amount relative to its GDP

DEVELOPMENT AID, AMOUNT AND PERCENT OF GDP, 2009

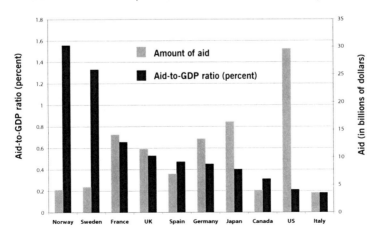

Source: OECD, Official Development Assistance by Donor (stats.oecd.org).

The world's rich countries have long committed to providing 0.7% of GDP to foreign development aid. In 2009, only Norway and Sweden met this goal. The U.S. government did not come close.

Moreover, a large share of U.S. foreign aid is "tied aid"; governments that receive the aid must spend the funds by buying goods and services from U.S. firms. Generally the recipient countries could get more goods and services if they could spend the money without this restriction. So the economic development impact of the aid is less than it appears. Also, whatever the "foreign aid" does for the recipient country, it is a way of channeling money to U.S. firms.

Not only must the recipient country pay more for the goods and services, but the "multiplier impact" is much less. That is, since the money goes to U.S. companies rather than local suppliers, fewer local jobs and salary payments are created; so less is re-spent in the local economy. A 2009 report on aid to Afghanistan by the Peace Dividend Trust notes: "By using Afghan goods and services to carry out development projects in Afghanistan, the international community has the opportunity to spend a development dollar twice. How? Local procurement creates jobs, increases incomes, generates revenue and develops the Afghan marketplace —all of which support economic recovery and stability." Yet most of the aid "for Afghanistan" went to foreign "experts," foreign construction firms, and foreign suppliers of goods.

The U.S. government ties much more of its aid than do most other donor countries. A report by the Organization for Economic Cooperation and Development (OECD) estimated that in the mid-2000s, 54.5% of U.S. aid was tied. Of the 22 donor countries listed in the report (including the United States), the average share of tied aid was only 28.4%. The report notes a "widespread movement to untying [aid], with the exception of the United States."

It is important to recognize that U.S. foreign aid is an instrument of U.S. foreign policy, and is thus highly concentrated in countries where the U.S. government has what it views as "strategic interests." For example, in 2008 almost 16% of U.S. development assistance went to Afghanistan and Iraq, while the top 20 recipient countries received over 50%.

So, yes, the U.S. government provides a "huge" amount of foreign development aid—or not so much. It depends on how you look at things. ❏

Article 8.3

FAMINE MYTHS

Five Misunderstandings Related to the 2011 Hunger Crisis in the Horn of Africa

BY WILLIAM G. MOSELEY

March/April 2012

The 2011 famine in the horn of Africa was one of the worst in recent decades in terms of loss of life and human suffering. While the UN has yet to release an official death toll, the British government estimates that between 50,000 and 100,000 people died, most of them children, between April and September of 2011. While Kenya, Ethiopia, and Djibouti were all badly affected, the famine hit hardest in certain (mainly southern) areas of Somalia. This was the worst humanitarian disaster to strike the country since 1991-1992, with roughly a third of the Somali population displaced for some period of time.

Despite the scholarly and policy community's tremendous advances in understanding famine over the past 40 years, and increasingly sophisticated famine early-warning systems, much of this knowledge and information was seemingly ignored or forgotten in 2011. While the famine had been forecasted nearly nine months in advance, the global community failed to prepare for, and react in a timely manner to, this event. The famine was officially declared in early July of 2011 by the United Nations and recently (February 3, 2012) stated to be officially over. Despite the official end of the famine, 31% of the population (or 2.3 million people) in southern Somalia remains in crisis. Across the region, 9.5 million people continue to need assistance. Millions of Somalis remain in refugee camps in Ethiopia and Kenya.

The famine reached its height in the period from July to September, 2011, with approximately 13 million people at risk of starvation. While this was a regional problem, it was was most acute in southern Somalia because aid to this region was much delayed. Figure 1 provides a picture of food insecurity in the region in the November-December 2011 period (a few months after the peak of the crisis).

The 2011 famine received relatively little attention in the U.S. media and much of the coverage that did occur was biased, ahistorical, or perpetuated long-held misunderstandings about the nature and causes of famine. This article addresses "famine myths"—five key misunderstandings related to the famine in the Horn of Africa.

Myth #1: Drought was the cause of the famine.

While drought certainly contributed to the crisis in the Horn of Africa, there were more fundamental causes at play. Drought is not a new environmental condition for much of Africa, but a recurring one. The Horn of Africa has long experienced erratic rainfall. While climate change may be exacerbating rainfall variability, traditional livelihoods in the region are adapted to deal with situations where rainfall is not dependable.

The dominant livelihood in the Horn of Africa has long been herding, which is well adapted to the semi-arid conditions of the region. Herders traditionally ranged widely across the landscape in search of better pasture, focusing on different areas depending on meteorological conditions.

The approach worked because, unlike fenced in pastures in America, it was incredibly flexible and well adapted to variable rainfall conditions. As farming expanded, including large-scale commercial farms in some instances, the routes of herders became more concentrated, more vulnerable to drought, and more detrimental to the landscape.

Agricultural livelihoods also evolved in problematic ways. In anticipation of poor rainfall years, farming households and communities historically stored surplus crop production in granaries. Sadly this traditional strategy for mitigating the risk of drought was undermined from the colonial period moving forward as

FIGURE 1: FOOD INSECURITY IN THE HORN OF AFRICA REGION, NOVEMBER-DECEMBER 2011.

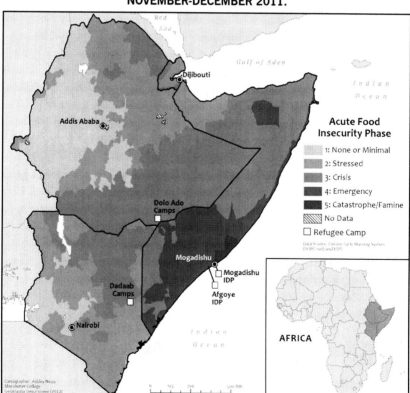

Based on data and assessment by FEWS-Net (a USAID-sponsored program).

Cartography by Ashley Nepp, Macalester College.

households were encouraged (if not coerced by taxation) to grow cash crops for the market and store less excess grain for bad years. This increasing market orientation was also encouraged by development banks, such as the World Bank, International Monetary Fund, and African Development Bank.

The moral of the story is that famine is not a natural consequence of drought (just as death from exposure is not the inherent result of a cold winter), but it is the structure of human society which often determines who is affected and to what degree.

Myth #2: Overpopulation was the cause of the famine.

With nearly 13 million people at risk of starvation last fall in a region whose population doubled in the previous 24 years, one might assume that these two factors were causally related in the Horn of Africa. Ever since the British political economist Thomas Malthus wrote "An Essay on the Principle of Population" in 1798, we have been concerned that human population growth will outstrip available food supply. While the crisis in Somalia, Ethiopia and Kenya appeared to be perfect proof of the Malthusian scenario, we must be careful not to make overly simplistic assumptions.

For starters, the semi-arid zones in the Horn of Africa are relatively lightly populated compared to other regions of the world. For example, the population

---

Land Grabs in Africa

Long term leases of African land for export-oriented food production, or "land grabs," have been on the rise in the past decade. Rather than simply buying food and commodity crops from African farmers, foreign entities increasingly take control of ownership and management of farms on African soil. This trend stems from at least two factors. First, increasingly high global food prices are a problem for many Asian and Middle Eastern countries that depend on food imports. As such, foreign governments and sovereign wealth funds may engage in long-term leases of African land in order to supply their own populations with affordable food. Secondly, high global food prices are also seen as an opportunity for some Western investors who lease African land to produce crops and commodities for profitable global markets.

In the Horn of Africa, Ethiopia (which has historically been one of the world's largest recipients of humanitarian food aid) has made a series of long-term land leases to foreign entities. The World Bank estimates that at least 35 million hectares of land have been leased to 36 different countries, including China, Pakistan, India and Saudi Arabia. Supporters of these leases argue that they provide employment to local people and disseminate modern agricultural approaches. Critics counter that these leases undermine food sovereignty, or people's ability to feed themselves via environmentally sustainable technologies that they control.

density of Somalia is about 13 persons per sq. kilometer, whereas that of the U.S. state of Oklahoma is 21.1. The western half of Oklahoma is also semi-arid, suffered from a serious drought in 2011, and was the poster child for the 1930s Dust Bowl. Furthermore, if we take into account differing levels of consumption, with the average American consuming at least 28 times as much as the average Somali in a normal year, then Oklahoma's population density of 21.1 persons per sq. kilometer equates to that of 591 Somalis.

Despite the fact that Oklahoma's per capita impact on the landscape is over 45 times that of Somalia (when accounting for population density and consumption levels), we don't talk about overpopulation in Oklahoma. This is because, in spite of the drought and the collapse of agriculture, there was no famine in Oklahoma. In contrast, the presence of famine in the Horn of Africa led many to assume that too many people was a key part of the problem.

Why is it that many assume that population growth is the driver of famine? For starters, perhaps we assume that reducing the birthrate, and thereby reducing the number of mouths to feed, is one of the easiest ways to prevent hunger. This is actually a difficult calculation for most families in rural Africa. It's true that many families desire access to modern contraceptives, and filling this unmet need is important. However, for many others, children are crucial sources of farm labor or important wage earners who help sustain the family. Children also act as the old-age social security system for their parents. For these families, having fewer children is not an easy decision. Families in this region will have fewer children when it makes economic sense to do so. As we have seen over time and throughout the world, the average family size shrinks when economies develop and expectations for offspring change.

Second, many tend to focus on the additional resources required to nourish each new person, and often forget the productive capacity of these individuals. Throughout Africa, some of the most productive farmland is in those regions with the highest population densities. In Machakos, Kenya, for example, agricultural production and environmental conservation improved as population densities increased. Furthermore, we have seen agricultural production collapse in some areas where population declined (often due to outmigration) because there was insufficient labor to maintain intensive agricultural production.

Third, we must not forget that much of the region's agricultural production is not consumed locally. From the colonial era moving forward, farmers and herders have been encouraged to become more commercially oriented, producing crops and livestock for the market rather than home consumption. This might have been a reasonable strategy if the prices for exports from the Horn of Africa were high (which they rarely have been) and the cost of food imports low. Also, large land leases (or "land grabs") to foreign governments and corporations in Ethiopia (and to a lesser extent in Kenya and Somalia) have further exacerbated this problem. These farms, designed solely for export production, effectively subsidize the food security of other regions of the world (most notably the Middle East and Asia) at the expense of populations in the Horn of Africa.

Myth #3: Increasing food production through advanced techniques will resolve food insecurity over the long run.

As Sub-Saharan Africa has grappled with high food prices in some regions and famine in others, many experts argue that increasing food production through a program of hybrid seeds and chemical inputs (a so-called "New Green Revolution") is the way to go.

While outsiders benefit from this New Green Revolution strategy (by selling inputs or purchasing surplus crops), it is not clear if the same is true for small farmers and poor households in Sub-Saharan Africa. For most food insecure households on the continent, there are at least two problems with this strategy. First, such an approach to farming is energy intensive because most fertilizers and pesticides are petroleum based. Inducing poor farmers to adopt energy-intensive farming methods is short sighted, if not unethical, if experts know that global energy prices are likely to rise. Second, irrespective of energy prices, the New Green Revolution approach requires farmers to purchase seeds and inputs, which means that it will be inaccessible to the poorest of the poor, i.e., those who are the most likely to suffer from periods of hunger.

If not the New Green Revolution approach, then what? Many forms of bio-intensive agriculture are, in fact, highly productive and much more efficient than those of industrial agriculture. For example, crops grown in intelligent combinations allow one plant to fix nitrogen for another rather than relying solely on increasingly expensive, fossil fuel-based inorganic fertilizers for these plant nutrients. Mixed cropping strategies are also less vulnerable to insect damage and require little to no pesticide use for a reasonable harvest. These techniques have existed for centuries in the African context and could be greatly enhanced by supporting collaboration among local people, African research institutes, and foreign scientists.

Myth #4: U.S. foreign policy in the Horn of Africa was unrelated to the crisis.

Many Americans assume that U.S. foreign policy bears no blame for the food crisis in the Horn and, more specifically, Somalia. This is simply untrue. The weakness of the Somali state was and is related to U.S. policy, which interfered in Somali affairs based on Cold War politics (the case in the 1970s and 80s) or the War on Terror (the case in the 2000s).

During the Cold War, Somalia was a pawn in a U.S.-Soviet chess match in the geopolitically significant Horn of Africa region. In 1974, the U.S. ally Emperor Haile Selassie of Ethiopia was deposed in a revolution. He was eventually replaced by Mengistu Haile Mariam, a socialist. In response, the leader of Ethiopia's bitter rival Somalia, Siad Barre, switched from being pro-Soviet to pro-Western. Somalia was the only country in Africa to switch Cold War allegiances under the same government. The U.S. supported Siad Barre until 1989 (shortly before his demise in

1991). By doing this, the United States played a key role in supporting a long-running dictator and undermined democratic governance.

More recently, the Union of Islamic Courts (UIC) came to power in 2006. The UIC defeated the warlords, restored peace to Mogadishu for the first time in 15 years, and brought most of southern Somalia under its orbit. The United States and its Ethiopian ally claimed that these Islamists were terrorists and a threat to the region. In contrast, the vast majority of Somalis supported the UIC and pleaded with the international community to engage them peacefully. Unfortunately, this peace did not last. The U.S.-supported Ethiopian invasion of Somalia begun in December 2006 and displaced more than a million people and killed close to 15,000 civilians. Those displaced then became a part of last summer and fall's famine victims.

The power vacuum created by the displacement of the more moderate UIC also led to the rise of its more radical military wing, al-Shabaab. Al-Shabaab emerged to engage the Transitional Federal Government (TFG), which was put in place by the international community and composed of the most moderate elements of the UIC (which were more favorable to the United States). The TFG was weak, corrupt, and ineffective, controlling little more than the capital Mogadishu, if that. A low-grade civil war emerged between these two groups in southern Somalia. Indeed, as we repeatedly heard in the media last year, it was al-Shabaab that restricted access to southern Somalia for several months leading up to the crisis and greatly exacerbated the situation in this sub-region. Unfortunately, the history of factors which gave rise to al-Shabaab was never adequately explained to the U.S. public. Until July 2011, the U.S. government forbade American charities from operating in areas controlled by al-Shabaab—which delayed relief efforts in these areas.

Myth #5: An austere response may be best in the long run.

Efforts to raise funds to address the famine in the Horn of Africa were well below those for previous (and recent) humanitarian crises. Why was this? Part of it likely had to do with the economic malaise in the U.S. and Europe. Many Americans suggested that we could not afford to help in this crisis because we had to pay off our own debt. This stinginess may, in part, be related to a general misunderstanding about how much of the U.S. budget goes to foreign assistance. Many Americans assume we spend over 25% of our budget on such assistance when it is actually less than one percent.

Furthermore, contemporary public discourse in America has become more inward-looking and isolationist than in the past. As a result, many Americans have difficulty relating to people beyond their borders. Sadly, it is now much easier to separate ourselves from them, to discount our common humanity, and to essentially suppose that it's okay if they starve. This last point brings us back to Thomas Malthus, who was writing against the poor laws in England in the late 18th century. The poor laws were somewhat analogous to contemporary welfare programs and Malthus argued (rather problematically) that they encouraged the poor to have more children. His essential argument was that starvation is acceptable because it is a natural check to over-population. In other words, support for the poor will only exacerbate the situation. We see this in the way that some conservative commentators reacted to last year's famine.

The reality was that a delayed response to the famine only made the situation worse. Of course, the worst-case scenario is death, but short of death, many households were forced to sell off all of their assets (cattle, farming implements, etc.) in order to survive. This sets up a very difficult recovery scenario because livelihoods are so severely compromised. We know from best practices among famine researchers and relief agencies in that you not only to detect a potential famine early, but to intervene before livelihoods are devastated. This means that households will recover more quickly and be more resilient in the face of future perturbations.

Preventing Famines

While the official famine in the horn of Africa region is over, 9.5 million people continue to need assistance and millions of Somalis remain in refugee camps in Ethiopia and Kenya. While this region of the world will always be drought prone, it needn't be famine prone. The solution lies in rebuilding the Somali state and fostering more robust rural livelihoods in Somalia, western Ethiopia and northern Kenya. The former will likely mean giving the Somali people the space they need to rebuild their own democratic institutions (and not making them needless pawns in the War on Terror). The latter will entail a new approach to agriculture that emphasizes food sovereignty, or locally appropriate food production technologies that are accessible to the poorest of the poor, as well as systems of grain storage at the local level that anticipate bad rainfall years. Finally, the international community should discourage wealthy, yet food-insufficient, countries from preying on poorer countries in Sub Saharan African countries through the practice of land grabs. ❑

Sources: Alex de Waal, *Famine That Kills: Darfur, Sudan*, Oxford University Press, 2005; William G. Moseley, "Why They're Starving: The man-made roots of famine in the Horn of Africa," *The Washington Post*. July 29, 2011; William G. Moseley and B. Ikubolajeh Logan, "Food Security," in B. Wisner, C. Toulmin and R. Chitiga (eds)., *Toward a New Map of Africa*, Earthscan Publications, 2005; Abdi I. Samatar, "Genocidal Politics and the Somali Famine," Aljazeera English, July 30, 2011; Amartya Sen, *Poverty and Famines*, Oxford/Clarendon, 1981; Michael Watts and Hans Bohle, "The space of vulnerability: the causal structure of hunger and famine," *Progress in Human Geography*, 1993.

Article 8.4

MICROCREDIT AND WOMEN'S POVERTY

Granting this year's Nobel Peace Prize to microcredit guru Muhammad Yunus affirms neoliberalism.

BY SUSAN F. FEINER AND DRUCILLA K. BARKER

November/December 2006

The key to understanding why Grameen Bank founder and CEO Muhammad Yunus won the Nobel Peace Prize lies in the current fascination with individualistic myths of wealth and poverty. Many policy-makers believe that poverty is "simply" a problem of individual behavior. By rejecting the notion that poverty has structural causes, they deny the need for collective responses. In fact, according to this tough-love view, broad-based civic commitments to increase employment or provide income supports only make matters worse: helping the poor is pernicious because such aid undermines the incentive for hard work. This ideology is part and parcel of neoliberalism.

For neoliberals the solution to poverty is getting the poor to work harder, get educated, have fewer children, and act more responsibly. Markets reward those who help themselves, and women, who comprise the vast majority of microcredit borrowers, are no exception. Neoliberals champion the Grameen Bank and similar efforts precisely because microcredit programs do not change the structural conditions of globalization—such as loss of land rights, privatization of essential public services, or cutbacks in health and education spending—that reproduce poverty among women in developing nations.

What exactly is microcredit? Yunus, a Bangladeshi banker and economist, pioneered the idea of setting up a bank to make loans to the "poorest of the poor." The term "microcredit" reflects the very small size of the loans, often less than $100. Recognizing that the lack of collateral was often a barrier to borrowing by the poor, Yunus founded the Grameen Bank in the 1970s to make loans in areas of severe rural poverty where there were often no alternatives to what we would call loan sharks.

His solution to these problems was twofold. First, Grameen Bank would hire agents to travel the countryside on a regular schedule, making loans and collecting loan repayments. Second, only women belonging to Grameen's "loan circles" would be eligible for loans. If one woman in a loan circle did not meet her obligations, the others in the circle would either be ineligible for future loans or be held responsible for repayment of her loan. In this way the collective liability of the group served as collateral.

The Grameen Bank toasts its successes: not only do loan repayment rates approach 95%, the poor, empowered by their investments, are not dependent on "handouts." Microcredit advocates see these programs as a solution to poverty because poor women can generate income by using the borrowed funds to start small-scale enterprises, often home-based handicraft production. But these enterprises are almost all in the informal sector, which is fiercely competitive and typically unregulated, in other words, outside the range of any laws that protect workers or ensure their rights. Not surprisingly, women comprise the majority of workers in the informal economy and are heavily represented at the bottom of its already-low income scale.

Women and men have different experiences with work and entrepreneurship because a gender division of labor in most cultures assigns men to paid work outside the home and women to unpaid labor in the home. Consequently, women's paid work is constrained by domestic responsibilities. They either work part time, or they combine paid and unpaid work by working at home. Microcredit encourages women to work at home doing piecework: sewing garments, weaving rugs, assembling toys and electronic components. Home workers—mostly women and children—often work long hours for very poor pay in hazardous conditions, with no legal protections. As progressive journalist Gina Neff has noted, encouraging the growth of the informal sector sounds like advice from one of Dickens' more objectionable characters.

Why then do national governments and international organizations promote microcredit, thereby encouraging women's work in the informal sector? As an anti-poverty program, microcredit fits nicely with the prevailing ideology that defines poverty as an individual problem and that shifts responsibility for addressing it away from government policy-makers and multilateral bank managers onto the backs of poor women.

Microcredit programs do nothing to change the structural conditions that create poverty. But microcredit *has* been a success for the many banks that have adopted it. Of course, lending to the poor has long been a lucrative enterprise. Pawnshops, finance companies, payday loan operations, and loan sharks charge high interest rates precisely because poor people are often desperate for cash and lack access to formal credit networks. According to Sheryl Nance-Nash, a correspondent for Women's eNews, "the interest rates on microfinance vary between 25% to 50%." She notes that these rates "are much lower than informal money lenders, where rates may exceed 10% per month." It is important for the poor to have access to credit on relatively reasonable terms. Still, microcredit lenders are reaping the rewards of extraordinarily high repayment rates on loans that are still at somewhat above-market interest rates.

Anecdotal accounts can easily overstate the concrete gains to borrowers from microcredit. For example, widely cited research by the Canadian International Development Agency (CIDA) reports that "Women in particular face significant barriers to achieving sustained increases in income and improving their status, and require complementary support in other areas, such as training, marketing, literacy, social mobilization, and other financial services (e.g., consumption loans, savings)." The report goes on to conclude that most borrowers realize only very small gains, and that the poorest borrowers benefit the least. CIDA also found little relationship between loan repayment and business success.

However large or small their income gains, poor women are widely believed to find empowerment in access to microcredit loans. According to the World Bank, for instance, microcredit empowers women by giving them more control over household assets and resources, more autonomy and decision-making power, and greater access to participation in public life. This defense of microcredit stands or falls with individual success stories featuring women using their loans to start some sort of small-scale enterprise, perhaps renting a stall in the local market or buying a sewing machine to assemble piece goods. There is no doubt that when they succeed, women and their families are better off than they were before they became micro-debtors.

But the evidence on microcredit and women's empowerment is ambiguous. Access to credit is not the sole determinant of women's power and autonomy. Credit may, for example, increase women's dual burden of market and household labor. It may also increase conflict within the household if men, rather than women, control how loan moneys are used. Moreover, the group pressure over repayment in Grameen's loan circles can just as easily create conflict among women as build solidarity.

Grameen Bank founder Muhammad Yunus won the Nobel Peace Prize because his approach to banking reinforces the neoliberal view that individual behavior is the source of poverty and the neoliberal agenda of restricting state aid to the most vulnerable when and where the need for government assistance is most acute. Progressives working in poor communities around the world disagree. They argue that poverty is structural, so the solutions to poverty must focus not on adjusting the conditions of individuals but on building structures of inclusion. Expanding the state sector to provide the rudiments of a working social infrastructure is, therefore, a far more effective way to help women escape or avoid poverty.

Do the activities of the Grameen Bank and other micro-lenders romanticize individual struggles to escape poverty? Yes. Do these programs help some women "pull themselves up by the bootstraps"? Yes. Will micro-enterprises in the informal sector contribute to ending world poverty? Not a chance. ❑

Sources: Grameen Bank, grameen-info.org; "Informal Economy: Formalizing the Hidden Potential and Raising Standards," ILO Global Employment Forum (Nov. 2001), www-ilo-mirror. cornell.edu/public/english/employment/geforum/informal.htm; Jean L. Pyle, "Sex, Maids, and Export Processing," World Bank, *Engendering Development; Engendering Development Through Gender Equality in Rights, Resources, and Voice* (Oxford University Press, 2001); Naila Kabeer, "Conflicts Over Credit: Re-Evaluating the Empowerment Potential of Loans to Women in Rural Bangladesh," *World Development* 29 (2001); Norman MacIsaac, "The Role of Microcredit in Poverty Reduction and Promoting Gender Equity," South Asia Partnership Canada, Strategic Policy and Planning Division, Asia Branch Canada International Development Agency (June, 1997), www.acdi-cida.gc.ca/index-e.htm.

Article 8.5

MEASURING ECONOMIC DEVELOPMENT
The "Human Development" Approach

BY ALEJANDRO REUSS
April 2012

Some development economists have proposed abandoning per capita GDP, the dominant single-number measure of economic development, in favor of the "human development" approach—which focuses less on changes in average income and more on widespread access to basic goods.

Advocates of this approach to the measurement of development, notably Nobel Prize-winning economist Amartya Sen, aim to focus attention directly on the *ends* (goals) of economic development. Higher incomes, Sen notes, are *means* people use to get the things that they want. The human development approach shifts the focus away from the means and toward ends like a long life, good health, freedom from hunger, the opportunity to get an education, and the ability to take part in community and civic life. Sen has argued that these basic "capabilities" or "freedoms"—the kinds of things almost everyone wants no matter what their goals in life may be—are the highest development priorities and should, therefore, be the primary focus of our development measures.

If a rising average income guaranteed that everyone, or almost everyone, in a society would be better able to reach these goals, we might as well use average income (GDP per capita) to measure development. Increases in GDP per capita, however, do not always deliver longer life, better health, more education, or other basic capabilities to most people In particular, if these income increases go primarily to those who are already better-off (and already enjoy a long life-expectancy, good health, access to education, and so on), they probably will not have much effect on people's access to basic capabilities.

Sen and others have shown that, in "developing" countries, increased average income by itself is not associated with higher life expectancy or better health. In countries where average income was increasing, but public spending on food security, health care, education, and similar programs did not increase along with it, they have found, the increase in average income did not appear to improve access to basic capabilities. If spending on these "public supports" increased, on the other hand, access to basic capabilities tended to improve, whether average income was increasing or not. Sen emphasizes two main lessons based on these observations: 1) A country cannot count on economic growth alone to improve access to basic capabilities. Increased average income appears to deliver "human development" largely by *increasing the wealth a society has available for public supports*, and not in other ways. 2) A country does not have to prioritize economic growth—*does not have to "wait" until it grows richer*—to make basic capabilities like long life, good health, and a decent education available to all.

The Human Development Index (HDI)

The "human development" approach has led to a series of annual reports from the United Nations Development Programme (UNDP) ranking countries according to a "human development index" (HDI). The HDI includes measures of three things: 1) health, measured by average life expectancy, 2) education, measured by average years of schooling and expected years of schooling, and 3) income, measured by GDP per capita. The three categories are then combined, each counting equally, into a single index. The HDI has become the most influential alternative to GDP per capita as a single-number development measure.

Looking at the HDI rankings, many of the results are not surprising. The HDI top 20 is dominated by very high-income countries, including thirteen Western European countries, four "offshoots" of Great Britain (Australia, Canada, New Zealand, and the United States), and two high-income East Asian countries (Japan and South Korea). Most of the next 20 or so are Western or Eastern European, plus a few small oil-rich states in the Middle East. The next 50 or so include most of Latin America and the Caribbean, much of the Middle East, and a good deal of Eastern Europe (including Russia and several former Soviet republics). The next 50 or so are a mix of Latin American, Middle Eastern, South and Southeast Asian, and African

TABLE 1: HDI RANKS COMPARED TO
INCOME-PER-CAPITA RANKS (2010)

Highest HDI ranks compared to income per capita ranks (difference in parentheses)*	Lowest HDI ranks compared to income per capita ranks (difference in parentheses)
New Zealand (+30)	Equatorial Guinea (-78)
Georgia (+26)	Angola (-47)
Tonga (+23)	Kuwait (-42)
Tajikistan (+22)	Botswana (-38)
Madagascar (+22)	South Africa (-37)
Togo (+22)	Qatar (-36)
Fiji (+22)	Brunei (-30)
Ireland (+20)	Gabon (-29)
Iceland (+20)	United Arab Emirates (-28)
Ukraine (+20)	Turkey (-26)

* The numbers in parentheses represent a country's GDP-per-capita rank minus its HDI rank. Remember that in a ranking system, a "higher" (better) rank is indicated by a lower number. If a country is ranked, say, 50th in GDP per capita and 20th in HDI, its number would be 50 – 20 = +30. The positive number indicates that the country had a "higher" HDI rank than GDP per capita rank. If a country is ranked, say, 10th in GDP per capita and 35th in HDI, its number would be 10 – 35 = -25. The negative number indicates that the country had a "lower" HDI rank than GDP per capita rank.

Source: United Nations Development Programme, Indices, Getting and using data, 2010 Report—Table 1: Human Development Index and its components (hdr.undp.org/en/statistics/data/).

countries. The world's poorest continent, Africa, accounts for almost all of the last 30, including the bottom 24.

It is not surprising that higher GDP per capita is associated with a higher HDI score. After all, GDP per capita counts for one third of the HDI score itself. The relationship between the two, however, is not perfect. Some countries have a higher HDI rank than GDP per capita rank. These countries are "over-perform-ing," getting more human development from their incomes, compared to other countries. Meanwhile, some countries have a lower HDI rank than GDP per cap-ita rank. These countries are "under-performing," not getting as much human development from their incomes, compared to other countries. The list of top "over-performing" countries includes three very high-income countries that had still higher HDI ranks (Iceland, Ireland, and New Zealand), three former Soviet republics (Georgia, Tajikistan, and Ukraine), two small South Pacific island nations (Fiji, Togo), and two African countries (Madagascar, Tonga). The list of top "under-performing" countries includes four small oil-rich countries (Brunei, Kuwait, Qatar, and United Arab Emirates) and five African countries (Angola, Botswana, Equatorial Guinea, Gabon, and South Africa).

The UNDP also calculates an inequality-adjusted HDI. Note that, for all the measures included in the HDI, there is inequality within countries. The inequality-adjusted HDI is calculated so that, the greater the inequality for any measure included in the HDI (for health, education, or income), the lower the country's score. Since all countries have some inequality, the inequality-adjusted HDI for any country is always lower than the regular HDI. However, the scores for countries with greater inequality drop more than for those with

TABLE 2: INEQUALITY-ADJUSTED HDI RANKS COMPARED TO UNADJUSTED HDI RANKS

Highest inequality-adjusted HDI ranks compared to unadjusted HDI ranks (difference in parentheses)	Lowest inequality-adjusted HDI ranks compared to unadjusted HDI ranks (difference in parentheses)
Uzbekistan (+17)	Peru (-26)
Mongolia (+16)	Panama (-20)
Moldova (+16)	Colombia (-18)
Kyrgystan (+15)	South Korea (-18)
Maldives (+14)	Bolivia (-17)
Ukraine (+14)	Belize (-16)
Philippines (+11)	Brazil (-15)
Sri Lanka (+11)	Namibia (-15)
Tanzania, Viet Nam, Indonesia, Jamaica, Belarus (+9)	El Salvador (-14)
	Turkmenistan (-12)

Source: United Nations Development Programme, 2010 Report, Table 3: Inequality-adjusted Human Development Index (hdr.undp.org/en/media/HDR_2010_EN_Table3_reprint.pdf).

less inequality. That pushes some countries up in the rankings, when inequality is penalized, and others down. Among the thirteen countries moving up the most, five are former Soviet republics. Among the ten moving down the most, seven are Latin American countries. The United States narrowly misses the list of those moving down the most, with its rank dropping by nine places when inequality is taken into account.

GDP Per Capita and HDI

The relationship between income per capita and the HDI is shown in the "scatterplot" graph below. (Instead of GDP per capita, the graph uses a closely related measure called Gross National Income (GNI) per capita.) Each point represents a country, with its income per capita represented on the horizontal scale and its HDI score represented on the vertical scale. The further to the right a point is, the higher the country's per capita income. The higher up a point is, the higher the country's HDI score. As we can see, the cloud of points forms a curve, rising up as income per capita increases from a very low level, and then flattening out. This means that a change in GDP per capita from a very low level to a moderate level of around $8000 per year is associated with large gains in human development. Above that, we see, the curve flattens out dramatically. A change in income per capita from this moderate level to a high level of around $25,000 is associated with smaller gains in human development. Further increases in income per capita are associated with little or no gain in human development.

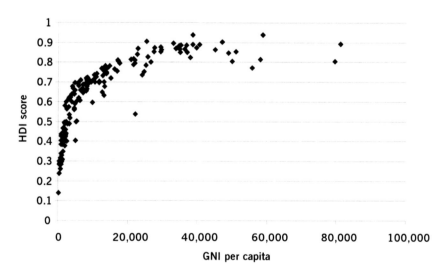

RELATIONSHIP BETWEEN HDI AND INCOME PER CAPITA (2010)

Source: United Nations Development Programme, Indices, 2010 Report - Table 1 Human Development Index and its components (hdr.undp.org/en/statistics/data/).

This relationship suggests two major conclusions, both related to greater economic equality.

First, achieving greater equality in incomes between countries, including by redistributing income from high-income countries to low-income countries, could result in increased human development. Over the highest per capita income range, from about $25,000 on up, increases in income are not associated with higher human development. Decreases in income above this threshold, by the same token, need not mean lower human development. On the other hand, over the lowest income range, below $8000, increases in income are associated with dramatic gains in HDI (largely due to increased public supports). Therefore, the redistribution of incomes from high-income countries to low-income countries could increase human development in the latter a great deal, while not diminishing human development in the former by very much (if at all)—resulting in a net gain in human development.

Second, high-income countries might make greater gains in HDI, as their incomes continued to increase, if a larger share of income went to low-income people or to public supports. Part of the reason that the relationship between per capita income and HDI flattens out at high income levels may be that there are inherent limits to variables like life expectancy (perhaps 90-100 years) or educational attainment (perhaps 20 years). These "saturation" levels, however, have clearly not been reached by all individuals, even in very high-income countries. In the United States, as of 2008, the infant mortality rate for African-Americans was more than double that for whites. The life expectancy at birth for white females was more than three years greater than that of African-American females; for white males, more than five years greater than for African-American males. As of 2010, over 40% of individuals over 25 years old have no education above high school. Over 60% have no degree from a two- or four-year college. It is little wonder that higher income would not bring about greatly increased human development, considering that, over the last 30 years, many public supports have faced sustained attack and most income growth has gone to people already at the top. ❏

Sources: Amartya Sen, *Development as Freedom* (New York: Oxford University Press, 1999); United Nations Development Programme, Indices, Getting and using data, *2010 Human Development Report*, Table 1 Human Development Index and its components (hdr.undp.org/en/statistics/data/); United Nations Development Programme, *2010 Human Development Report*, Table 3: Inequality-adjusted Human Development Index (hdr.undp.org/en/media/HDR_2010_EN_Table3_reprint.pdf); U.S. Census Bureau, *The 2012 Statistical Abstract*, Births, Deaths, Marriages, & Divorces: Life Expectancy, Table 107. Expectation of Life and Expected Deaths by Race, Sex, and Age: 2008; Educational Attainment, Population 25 Years and Over, U.S. Census Bureau, Selected Social Characteristics in the United States, *2010 American Community Survey*, 1-Year Estimates.

Article 8.6

BRAZIL'S BIG PUSH

With a leading government role in industrialization, "neo-developmentalism" represents a sharp break from neoliberalism.

BY JAMES M. CYPHER

March/April 2013

As the undertow of the great financial crash of 2008 sank Brazil's economy in 2009, the Brazilian government quickly responded with a massive, job-creating public-spending program, while facilitating the expansion of consumer credit. Even as the economies of other Latin American nations slowed or declined, Brazil's economy shot ahead, growing at an astonishing 7.5% rate in 2010. Hopes that this miraculous recovery signaled a new era were soon disappointed, as growth slid to less than 3% in 2011 and only about 1% in 2012.

Since Luiz Inácio Lula da Silva's election as president of Brazil in 2002, the Brazilian government has emphasized, above all, "growth with redistribution," including higher minimum wages, pensions for the elderly, and a massive anti-poverty program (*Bolsa Família*). Under Lula, as da Silva is universally known, and his successor, Dilma Rousseff, also of Brazil's Workers' Party, this approach has reduced income inequality and raised over 30 million people above the poverty line. The economic strategy has also increased demand for goods produced in Brazil, creating virtuous circles of increased production, growing employment, and rising wages.

The role of government, however, goes well beyond Keynesian-style policies to promote growth in aggregate demand, full employment, and income redistribution; in fact, it is centered in the *sphere of production* (on supply rather than demand). In contrast to other South American nations that have enjoyed economic growth since 2002, Brazil's "neo-developmentalist" approach has emphasized the role of the government in promoting the country's industrial competitiveness, spearheaded by an active industrial policy and the construction of a national innovation system. Industrial policy entails an activist government and an agile cadre of state functionaries, ideally working constructively with the private sector to identify and incubate new, growth-leading economic sectors. Today, such a policy requires *national* capabilities for scientific research and product-and-process innovation in the favored sectors.

Developmentalist ideas—emphasizing national industrialization, a growing internal market powered by wage gains for the working class and emerging middle class, and often a key role for state-owned enterprises in filling the gaps left by a diffident business class—swept Latin America's policymaking elite back in the 1930s. The results were startling: Annual (inflation-adjusted) per-capita economic growth from 1940-80 *doubled* the level achieved in the 1900-39 period (2.7% vs. 1.3%), and was *more than four times greater* than that achieved in the neoliberal period, 1980-2000, for the six economically largest nations (Argentina, Brazil,

Chile, Colombia, Mexico, and Venezuela). Despite the social gains arising from developmentalist policies, neoliberal economics largely supplanted developmentalism during the 1970s and 1980s. (Neoliberal ideas were notoriously championed by the Latin American economists, trained at the University of Chicago, who became known as the "Chicago boys.") In the 1970s, U.S.-supported military dictatorships overthrew developmentalist regimes in several Southern Cone countries (Argentina, Chile and Uruguay), elevated Chicago-boys-style economists to positions of power, and imposed neoliberal policies. During the 1980s, such policies were pushed on still more countries by the debt crisis and the structural-adjustment programs favored by the International Monetary Fund.

Brazil's current "neo-developmentalist" approach harkens back to the earlier developmentalist approach in various important ways: The state is leading the accumulation project through prodigious catch-up efforts directed at bottlenecks and "choke points" of the Brazilian infrastructure, including railroads, highways, water management, ports, electricity and energy. What is new is the placement of social justice issues on a par with the big-push efforts promoting industrialization and infrastructure. Neo-developmentalism is pushing to even out the distribution of income through large increases in the minimum wage and several comprehensive social programs that protect the poor and the aged (including badly needed support for housing and sanitation), while beginning to target educational reform that will have a dramatic effect on underprivileged youth. Many of the industrialization/infrastructure issues that engrossed the developmentalists remain a central focus of public policy, but now efforts to strengthen the industrial base are complemented by socially driven programs that have the effect of increasing domestic demand and broadening the social base of this demand—hence the idea of *inclusive growth*. Finally, there has been a concerted public-sector effort to foster innovative capacity through expanded national funding for science and engineering.

The Key Role of Petroleum

As Brazil's efforts to implement this neo-developmentalist strategy unfolded, it made major discoveries of offshore oil. This has led to a policy reorientation designed to use petroleum as a major pillar of the industrial strategy. In addition to achieving long-sought energy independence, Brazil anticipates capturing multiple benefits from this effort, including becoming the world leader in "ultra-deep" offshore drilling technologies. Including these offshore efforts, Petrobras, the state-owned oil company, has over 700 projects underway. The government—particularly through the national development bank (Banco Nacional de Desenvolvimento Econômico e Social, or BNDES)—would, once again, play a catalytic role in directing long-term public investment flows to state-owned and public-private enterprises, promoting technological innovation in offshore drilling and production. Since 2007, Brazil has made a massive commitment to developing the oil reserves, a long- term effort with an estimated price tag of $1 trillion. While BNDES is deeply involved, its reach extends far beyond just the petroleum sector. Its annual lending to Brazil's federal, state, and municipal governments (for long-term infrastructure projects) and to state-owned and private Brazilian firms is roughly four times as much as the World Bank's.

Following the insights of Albert Hirschman, an important early developmentalist who acted as an economic advisor to Latin American governments in the 1950s, the state-led effort in the oil sector is designed to exploit forward and backward "linkage" effects, promoting growth in other, related industries. As Hirschman emphasized, investments in one important area can lead to a broad range of mutually supporting economic activities driving the creation of new skills, massive new employment opportunities, improved productivity, and higher wages. Success opens a path for the expansion of education and social programs. In the oil industry today, backward linkages include the vast web of potential suppliers for specialty steel, motors, pumps, ships, drilling platforms, and tools of every size and description. Providing these inputs will stimulate a sweeping revitalization and deepening of the machine-tool sector. Forward linkages constitute the range of activities that spin off from petroleum extraction, producing goods such as fertilizers, plastics, refined petroleum products, and synthetic fibers. The importance of such linkages is well understood by neo-developmentalists, particularly President Rousseff, who was molded by her extensive developmentalist training in economics at two excellent Brazilian public universities.

The state will enable Petrobras to make $224 billion in capital investments during 2011-2015. One result of these massive outlays is that, by 2014, Brazil will have two new petroleum refineries under operation (in the states of Pernambuco and Rio de Janiero), enabling the country to meet its burgeoning need for refined petroleum products. These investments will thereby close a major developmental bottleneck—where Brazil had exported crude while importing high-value-added refined products. Prior to the major oil discoveries, state support and promotion had helped Brazil develop a viable and efficient ethanol industry, a large-scale, innovative strategy to overcome its petroleum resource gap. The current thrust into petroleum is partially based on the developmental legacy of the ethanol industry.

One aspect of Brazil's neo-developmentalist strategy for the oil industry is the ambitious goal of reserving the "supply chain" for Brazilian companies. Unlike Venezuela's efficient national oil company PDVSA—which strives to promote the "democratization of oil resources" by channeling a major portion of its surplus to social programs—Brazil intends to promote national technological capabilities by building a national supplier base. The objective is to have as much as 95% local content in portions of the supply chain by 2017. By mid-2012, Petrobras was already buying nearly 70% of its equipment from Brazilian producers. This approach is designed to internalize, as much as possible, the various positive spinoffs of this massive initiative. Taking into account direct exploration, drilling, and production, transportation and refining, and production of machinery and other inputs, it will encompass an estimated 25% of Brazil's entire economy by 2020. As this industry expands, it will create learning opportunities for both production employees and managers. The development of new homegrown technological capacities, meanwhile, will create increasing returns in a broad range of associated industrial activities, such as shipbuilding, steel fabrication, and machine tools and machinery production.

Macroeconomic Trials and Tribulations

Development economics is concerned with locating and realizing a *long-term, sustainable*, structural transformation of an entire economy. Struggling nations cannot often find the policy space for longterm commitments. In Brazil's case, the major oil discoveries in 2006 were followed by the snowballing effects of the financial panic and global recession. By late 2012, the aftershocks were still convulsing much of Europe, with devastating unemployment levels pushed ever higher by backfiring Chicago-boys-style austerity programs.

Quick, adroit, and massive recession-fighting policies held Brazil's GDP decline in 2009 to less than 1%. As noted earlier, these policies reached their full impact in 2010, allowing the economy to grow dramatically. In part, this was possible because Brazil's dependence on world trade is relatively light—exports were only about 10% of GDP in 2011. (This meant that Brazil was not dragged down by the collapse in export demand, as many other developing countries were.) Furthermore, an increasing portion of Brazil's exports—nearly 20% in late 2012, compared to only 1% in 2000—are sent to China, on which the Great Recession of 2008-2010 scarcely had an impact.

Nonetheless, the fallout from the financial turbulence of the high-income "core" economies has had an impact on Brazil. First, scarred by repeated bouts of hyperinflation, rising above 1,000% per year in 1988-1994, the Brazilian central bank maintained an unnecessarily tight money policy, restricting economic growth. Second, since 2003, a stronger currency (which makes a country's exports more expensive and imports cheaper) has caused imports to boom. During the worst of the current crisis, Brazil had the world's most overvalued currency. Third, households rapidly took on new debt and now repayment problems are rising, making it harder for consumer demand to drive economic growth.

Until recently, Brazil's central bank—functioning independently of the elected government—operated under a monetarist director dedicated solely to defeating phantom inflationary pressures. (Monetarists have been historically known for their single-minded focus on maintaining very low inflation, as opposed to achieving full employment.) Working against the neo-developmentalist strategy, he set interest rates at the highest level in the world. This policy both tended to slow down the economy and to encourage financialization, the diversion of funds away from productive investment and toward speculation and other purely financial activities. Meanwhile, the U.S. Federal Reserve (the "Fed") pushed interest rates nearly down to zero and created massive waves of liquidity, from late 2008 through 2012. With

Brazilian interests rates high and U.S. rates low, hot money (financial investments seeking a big, fast return) sloshed into Brazil. One result was to push up Brazil's exchange rate. Another was to expose Brazil to the risk that the hot funds would quickly exit— creating financial instability and macroeconomic turmoil that could detain, if not derail, Brazil's neo-developmentalist strategy. (See Armagan Gezici, "The Return of Capital Controls," *Dollars & Sense*, January/February 2013.)

Vitally important for the future, investment has been falling as a share of GDP since 2010. In spite of an 83% rise in net foreign direct investment—to a record $68 billion in 2011—total investment (public + private + transnational) was only 18% of GDP in 2012. As foreign money has flowed in, a record number of Brazilian firms— 679 from 2010 through 2012—have been bought out by transnational corporations, fanning fears of denationalization. Transnationals were a major reason for Brazil's negative overall current-account balance, because they returned a record $85 billion of profits reaped from their Brazil operations to their home-office locations in 2011. The high exchange rate (strong *real*) has meant Brazil's manufacturing exports are very expensive, while foreign made, especially Chinese, imports are a bargain. During these years imports of goods and (especially) services soared, with volume growth averaging 15% per year, opening up a rising current-account deficit from 2008 onward, equal to 2.4% of GDP in 2012. (The main component of the current account is the trade balance.) As a result, Brazil has been deindustrializing, contrary to the developmentalist vision.

Only in 2011, when President Rousseff brought in a pragmatic non-monetarist, Alexandre Tombini, to run the central bank, was the "hard money" policy abandoned. The interest rate was cut ten times in a row, to about 7%. By Brazilian standards this is "cheap money," but it remains to be seen whether the ever-hesitant business strata can pivot from trading financial assets to actually building industrial capacity. Since then, the bank has also devised policies to push down the exchange rate, which has declined from about $0.65 to the *real* to less than $0.50 to the *real* in late 2012. This depreciation of the currency will help boost Brazil's exports, but most importantly will reduce imports of consumer goods and give Brazil's broad national manufacturing an opportunity to recover from the import surge.

While a lower exchange rate is important, the new policy to reduce interest rates is much more critical. In 2010-2011, central-bank inflation-adjusted interest rates hovered around 6%. But the new leadership at the central bank—acting in concert for the first time with the state's neo-developmentalist efforts—had forced the interest rate down to only 1.8% by September 2012. The central bank is no longer consistently choking off the forward momentum of the economy and encouraging the diversion of productive investment into the financial sphere. The declines in the exchange rate and interest rates, plus a new surge in government investment, are beginning to reverse over two consecutive years of a consistently declining growth rate. Between September 2011 and September 2012, industrial production grew by over 3%, while the real median household income of the employed increased by more than 4%.

The "Big Push"

Until recently, Brazil had been unable to confront three major barriers: 1) The monetarist doctrine of tight-money and high-interest loans, as practiced by the central bank from 2003 to 2011, 2) a dysfunctional educational system that left Brazilians bereft of adequate knowledge and skills, and 3) a decrepit infrastructure that could not meet the growing demand for transportation, electricity, port facilities, and railways. In addition to reversing the monetarist central-bank policy, the Brazilian government has also taken important steps to address the latter two barriers in the past year.

In what may be the first major step to address the deficiencies in the educational system, President Rousseff announced the "Law of Social Quotas" in August 2012. The law's objective is to change the composition of the student body in the federal university system. By 2016, half the students will enter from the public school system—where poor and working-class students are concentrated. A new admissions policy also aims to change the universities' racial composition, targeting a six-fold increase in enrollment of Afro-Brazilians.

President Rousseff's approach to the pressing issue of infrastructure expansion, meanwhile, is a departure from previous neo-developmentalist initiatives. A February 2012 decision to auction off the operation of three major airports to private companies was followed in August by the major policy innovation of using public-private partnerships to address the infrastructure problem. Under public-private partnerships, firms will commit to invest $66 billion to build over 4,500 miles of new toll roads and over 6,000 miles of railways, supplementing the more than 1% of GDP the federal government allocated to infrastructure in 2011. In addition, further auctions of licenses to form public-private partnerships in port facilities and airports were announced in late 2012 and early 2013. Public-private consortiums in Brazil are not just veiled forms of privatization, as they tend to be in the United States. The state retains broad decision-making powers, including setting relatively low profit rates for the private companies.

According to Robert Devlin and Graciela Moguillansky, who have undertaken a comprehensive study of public-private partnerships in several nations (including Korea, Malaysia, and Singapore), success requires three crucial elements: First, there must be a long-term strategic vision that is shared by society at large. Second, there must be an "understanding" between the public and private sectors—regarding how problems are defined and how they are resolved— that is seen as legitimate by public opinion. Third, state capacity must be sufficient to implement the strategy and to avoid "capture" by the private sector. Brazil's state capacity is considerable— best represented by BNDES and Petrobras—and improving as a result of President Rousseff's relentless efforts to raise professional standards and reduce corruption in the public sector. But, in the case of this infrastructure initiative, the hesitant business sector has answered with resistance and pleas for higher returns (which mean higher user fees) and longer concession contracts than the government had planned. A lack of public-private consensus has slowed this program. At the broader societal level, if sports facilities for the 2014 World Cup and the 2016 Summer Olympics are viewed as crowding out crucial social needs—needs constantly highlighted by the progressive administrations in power since 2002—clashes over policy could escalate. Brazil has broken into new territory with this latest initiative, which will test the strength of the Brazilian state.

Another element of the new strategy will be to lower electricity rates to private firms by 28% in 2013. Meanwhile, in late 2012 railroad freight rates dropped by 25-30%, depending on the nature of the cargo. These measures are designed to lower the so-called "Brazil cost," which, due to infrastructure bottlenecks, has kept the price of producing in Brazil quite high. For example, logistics costs currently absorb 12-15% of GDP, nearly three times the level of the German economy. Thus, policy is shifting from a "demand focus"—transfers to the poor, higher minimum wages, full-employment policies, etc.—to a "supply focus" designed to both promote necessary long-term investment and massively lower costs of production.

Brazil's outsized effort to implement a viable industrial policy and pursue a neo-developmentalist strategy is reminiscent of former Brazilian President Juscelino Kubitschek's massive, and largely successful, drive to accelerate the country's economic growth in the late 1950s and early 1960s. Kubitschek's motto was "fifty years in five." As political scientist Kathryn Sikkink argues, the "Brazilian industrialists saw themselves as protagonists and leaders of the process of industrialization." The interests of the state and the industrialists converged, with the state playing the crucial coordinator role. The always-in-a-hurry Kubitschek set and met ambitious developmental targets in 30 areas, focusing on five key sectors: energy, transportation, agriculture, basic (or "heavy") industries, and technical training. Lacking Kubitschek's high-wire talent to mobilize disparate factions, successor João Goulart was toppled by a U.S.-backed and -funded military coup in 1964, as he sought to address taboo issues such as land reform and the role of (mostly U.S.-based) multinational corporations. Developmentalism continued under nationalist military rule until the neoliberal 1980s, but without any regard for an inclusive social agenda.

Led ably by Lula and Rousseff, Brazil is once again conjuring memories of the Kubitschek era, while breaking the mold in Latin America. ❏

Sources: Pablo Astorga, Ame R. Bergés, and Valpy FitzGerald, "The Standard of Living in Latin America During the Twentieth Century," QEH Working Paper Series—QEHWPS103, Latin American Centre, St. Antony's College, Oxford, 2003; Jeb Blount, "Brazil's onceenvied Energy Matrix a Victim of 'Hubris,'" *Reuters Business and Financial News*, Jan. 7, 2013; Raymond Colitt and Matthew Malinowski, "Brazil to Reduce Power Costs, Pressure Banks to Foster Growth," Bloomberg News, Sept. 6, 2012; Robert Devlin and Graciela Moguillansky, "Aliazas público-privadas como estrategias nacionales de desarrollo a largo plazo," *RevistaCepal*, Vol. 97, April 2009; Economic Commission for Latin America and the Caribbean, *Economic Survey of Latin American and the Caribbean*, 2012; Economic Commission for Latin America and the Caribbean, *Macroeconomic Report on Latin America and the Caribbean*, June 2012; "Briefing: Brazil's oil boom, filling up the future," *The Economist*, Nov. 5, 2011; "The lore of ore," *The Economist*, Oct. 13,

2012; "Brazilian Banks: No more free lunch," *The Economist*, Oct. 20, 2012; "Brazil's economy: Facing Headwinds, Dilma changes course," *The Economist*, Aug. 18, 2012; Albert Hirschman, "A Generalized Linkage Approach to Development, with Special Reference to Staples," *Economic Development and Cultural Change*, Vol. 25, 1977; Joe Leahy, "Brazil's burgeoning appetite for construction," *The Globe and Mail*, Aug. 28, 2012; Carlos Lopes, "Em 2011, foram desnacionalizadas 206 empresas," *Informa CUT*, Jan. 21, 2013; Lecio Morais and Alfredo Saad-Filho, "Da economia política à política econômica: o novo-desenvolvimentismo e o governo Lula," in *Revista de Economia Política*, Vol. 31, No. 4 Oct.-Dec. 2011; PDVSA, "What is Endogenous Development" (pdvsa.com); Simon Romero, "Brazil enacts affirmative action law for universities," *New York Times*, Aug. 31, 2012; Paul Rosenstein-Rodan, "The Theory of the 'Big Push,'" in Gerald Meier, ed., *Leading Issues in Economic Development*, 3rd ed., 1976; Kathryn Sikkink, *Ideas and Institutions: Developmentalism in Brazil and Argentina*, 1991; World Trade Organization, "Country Profile: Brazil," Sept. 2012.

Article 8.7

CHINA AND THE GLOBAL ECONOMY

Why China Must Shift from Export-Led Growth to Domestic Demand-Led Growth

BY THOMAS PALLEY
November/December 2005

Over the last twenty years, China has undergone a massive economic transformation. A generation ago, China's economy was largely agricultural; today, the country is an industrial powerhouse experiencing rapid economic growth. Now, however, many economists question the sustainability of China's development model. Ironically, this debate has been triggered by recent acceleration in China's growth, which exceeded 9% in both 2003 and 2004. Some analysts claim this acceleration is being driven by a private investment bubble and by misdirected state investment, posing the risks of inflation and a hard landing when the bubble pops.

China's development model is indeed unsustainable—but not for the reasons most economists suggest. It is not overinvestment or excessive growth that is the problem. Instead, it is China's impact on the global economy. China's export-led development model threatens to trigger a global recession that will rebound and hit China itself. In short, in the same kind of scenario that Keynes addressed in the 1930s, China has failed to develop the demand side of its economy, and so its massive production growth threatens to swamp a weakening demand picture worldwide, with potentially severe consequences for both China and its customers.

A Brief Review of China's Development Model

Broadly speaking, China's development model aims to reduce the size of the centrally planned economy and increase the size of market-based private-sector activity. The first step in this transition was taken with the historic 1979 reforms of the agricultural sector, which allowed small farmers to produce for the market. Since then, the government has allowed private-sector activity to spread more widely by removing controls on economic activity; at the same time, it is privatizing state-owned enterprises (SOEs) on a limited basis.

This spread of market-centered activity has been accompanied by both external and internal capital accumulation strategies. The external strategy rests on foreign direct investment (FDI) and export-led growth. The internal strategy uses credit creation by state-controlled banks to fund SOEs and infrastructure investment.

Though FDI is small relative to total Chinese fixed asset accumulation, it serves a number of important functions. Construction and operation of foreign-owned plants has created employment. FDI has also brought capital goods and high technology into the country, and the inflow has been financed by foreign multinational companies (MNCs). Industrialization inevitably requires importing capital goods from developed economies. Most poor countries have borrowed to pay for these capital goods, which has constrained their growth and made them vulnerable to ever-fluctuating global currency markets. In China, FDI has been a form of self-financing development that short-circuits these foreign financing problems.

Significantly, FDI has provided a key source of export earnings, since a significant portion of MNC output in China is exported. In 2004, MNCs provided 57% of total exports. These exports earnings have bolstered China's balance of payments and ensured external investor confidence.

Low-wage labor plus the advanced technology and capital that FDI has brought into the country have made China the world's low-cost manufacturing leader. With exports booming, foreign MNCs have been willing to continue building new plants in China. This has given rise to an anomalous situation in which low-income China has been a lender (in the form of its trade surplus) to the high-income United States. Normally, it is expected that high-income households save and lend to low-income households. However, there is a logic to this situation. Exports and a trade surplus (i.e., Chinese savings) are the price that China pays for getting foreign MNCs to invest there. For the Chinese government this is a deal worth striking, since China gains productive capacity, high technology, and jobs. It also gains foreign exchange from the trade surplus, which provides protection against the vagaries of the international economy.

This external capital accumulation strategy has been complemented by an internal strategy predicated on state-directed bank credit expansion. The state-owned banking system has been used to fund large industrial and infrastructure investment projects, as well as to maintain employment in unprofitable SOEs. This has helped support aggregate demand and avoid a precipitous collapse of employment in the SOE sector. With no alternative places to invest their money, Chinese savers have effectively been forced to finance these state investments; the government keeps interest rates low by fiat and thus controls the interest cost of these public investments.

External Contradictions: Limits to Export-Led Growth

Though highly successful to date, China's development strategy is ultimately fundamentally flawed. China has become such a global manufacturing powerhouse that it is now driving the massive U.S. trade deficit and undermining the U.S. manufacturing sector. This threatens the economic health of its major customer. China is putting pressure on the European Union's manufacturing sector, slowing economic growth there as well. The contradiction in China's model, then, is that China's success threatens to undermine the U.S. economy, which has provided the demand that has fueled that success.

China's trade surpluses with the United States have been growing rapidly for several years. In 2004, the United States' bilateral trade deficit with China was $162.0 billion, representing 38.8% of the U.S. trade deficit with all non-OPEC countries. The bilateral China deficit is growing fastest, too: by 30.5% from 2003 to 2004, compared to 16.8% growth in the non-China, non-OPEC trade deficit.

The U.S. trade deficit threatens to become a source of financial instability. More important, the deficit is contributing to the problems in manufacturing that are hindering a robust, investment-led recovery in the United States. There are two ways in which the trade deficit has hindered recovery. First, the deficit drains spending out of the U.S. economy, so that jobs are lost or are created offshore instead of at home. Using a methodology that estimates the labor content embodied in the deficit, economist Robert Scott of the Economic Policy Institute estimates that the U.S. trade deficit with China in 2003 represented 1,339,300 lost job opportunities. Using Scott's job calculations and assuming the composition of trade remained unchanged in 2004, the 2004 trade deficit with China of $162 billion represents 1,808,055 lost job opportunities.

Second, China's policies hurt U.S. investment spending through a range of channels. The draining of demand via the trade deficit creates excess capacity, which reduces demand for new capital. The undervaluation of China's currency makes production in China cheaper, and this encourages firms to both shift existing facilities to China and build new facilities there. Undervaluation also reduces the profitability of U.S. manufacturing and this reduces investment spending.

The U.S. economy is of course a huge economy and these China effects are small in terms of total investment. However, China is likely exerting a chilling effect at the margin of manufacturing investment, and it is at this margin where the recessionary impacts of investment decline have been and continue to be felt.

Together, these employment and investment effects risk tipping the U.S. economy back into recession after what has already been a weak expansion. If this happens, there will be significant adverse consequences for the Chinese economy, and for the global economy as a whole, since the U.S. economy is the main engine of demand growth that has been keeping the world economy flying. (Much is made of China as itself an engine of demand growth, particularly benefiting Japan. China is buying capital goods and production inputs from Japan. However, China's internal demand growth depends on the prosperity generated by exporting to the U.S. economy. In this sense, the U.S. economy is the ultimate source of demand growth; this demand growth is then multiplied in the global economy, where China plays an important role in the multiplier process.)

That's why China must replace its export-led growth strategy with one based on expanding domestic demand. China's people need to have the incomes and the institutions that will enable them to consume a far larger share of what they produce.

For the moment, thanks to continued debt-financed spending by U.S. households, China's adverse impact has not derailed the U.S. economy. China has therefore continued to grow despite the weak U.S. recovery from recession. But there are reasons to believe the U.S. economy is increasingly fragile—a Wile E. Coyote economy running on thinner and thinner air. The recovery has been financed by asset price appreciation, especially in real estate, which has provided collateral for the home-equity loans and other borrowing consumers have used to keep spending. This means the U.S. economy is increasingly burdened by debt which could soon drive the economy into recession. Once in recession, with private sector balance sheets clogged with debt taken on at current low interest rates and not open to refinancing, the U.S. would not have recourse to another recovery based on consumer borrowing and housing price inflation.

Policymakers, including those in China, tend to have a hard time grasping complex scenarios such as this one, where the damage to China is indirect, operating via recession in the United States. Now that it has become a global manufacturing powerhouse, China's export-led manufacturing growth model is exerting huge strains on the global economy. Until now, China has been able to free-ride on global aggregate demand. The strategy worked when Chinese manufacturing was small, but it cannot continue working now that it is so large. The difficulty is to persuade China's policymakers of the need for change now, when the model still seems to be working and the crash has not come.

Developing the Demand Side of the Chinese Economy

In place of export-led growth, China must adopt a model of domestic demand-led growth. Such a model requires developing structures, institutions, and economic relations that generate sustained, stable internal demand growth. This is an enormous task and one that is key to achieving developed-country status, yet it is a task that has received little attention.

Economic theory and policy have traditionally focused on expansion of the supply side in developing countries. This is the core of the export-led growth paradigm, which emphasizes becoming internationally competitive and relying on export markets to provide demand and absorb increases in production. The demand side is generally ignored in the main body of development economics because economists assume that supply generates its own demand, a proposition known as Say's Law.

Nor are traditional Keynesian policies the right answer. Though Keynesian economics does emphasize demand considerations, it operates in the context of mature market economies in which the institutions that generate stable, broad-based demand are well established. For Keynesians, demand shortages can be remedied by policies that stimulate private-sector demand (e.g., lowering interest rates or cutting taxes) or by direct government spending. These policies address temporary failures in an established demand-generation process.

Developing countries, however, face a different problem: they need to build the demand-generation process in the first place. Application of standard Keynesian policies in developing countries tends to create excessive government deficits and promote an oversized government sector. Increased government spending adds to demand but it increases deficits, and it also does little to generate "market" incomes that are the basis of sustainable growth in demand. What is needed is a new analytic approach, one focused on establishing an economic order that ensures income gets into the hands of those who will spend it and encourages production of needed goods that have high domestic employment and expenditure multipliers. This can be termed "structural Keynesianism," in contrast with conventional "demand-side Keynesianism."

In China, then, the challenge is to develop sustainable, growing sources of noninflationary domestic purchasing power. This means attending to both the investment allocation process and the income allocation process. The former is critical to ensure that resources are efficiently allocated, earn an adequate rate of return, and add to needed productive capacity. The latter is critical to ensure that domestic demand grows to absorb increased output. Income must be placed in the hands of Chinese consumers if robust consumer markets are to develop. But this income must be delivered in an efficient, equitable manner that maintains economic incentives.

While banking reform is critical to improving China's capital allocation process, the greater challenge is to develop an appropriate system of household income distribution that supports domestic consumer markets. Investment spending is an important source of demand, but the output generated by investments must find buyers or investment will cease. Likewise, public-sector investment can be an important source of demand, but private-sector income must grow over time or else the government sector will come to dominate, with negative consequences.

With a population of 1.3 billion people, China has an enormous potential domestic market. The challenge is to distribute its rapidly growing income in a decentralized, equitable fashion that leaves work and production incentives intact. The conventional view is that markets automatically take care of the problem by paying workers what they are worth and that all income is spent, thereby generating the demand for output produced. In effect, the problem is assumed away. Indeed, to intervene and raise wages to increase demand would be to cause unemployment by making labor too expensive.

This conventional logic contrasts with Keynesian economics, which identifies the core economic problem as one of ensuring a level of aggregate demand consistent with full utilization of a nation's production capacity. Moreover, the level of aggregate demand is affected by the distribution of income, with worsened income distribution lowering aggregate demand because of the higher propensity to save among higher-income households. From a Keynesian perspective, market forces do not automatically generate an appropriate level of aggregate demand. Demand can be too low because of lack of confidence among economic agents that lowers investment and consumption spending. It can also be too low because the distribution of income is skewed excessively toward upper income groups.

In sum, for neoclassical economists, labor markets set wages such that there is full employment, and income distribution is a by-product that in itself has no effect on employment. For Keynesians, full employment requires an appropriate level of aggregate demand, which is strongly affected by the distribution of income.

The importance of income distribution for demand means that labor markets are of critical significance. Labor markets determine wages, and wages affect income distribution. The problem is that bargaining power can be highly skewed in favor of owners, leading to wages that are too low. This problem is particularly acute in developing countries. Trade unions are a vital mechanism for rectifying imbalances of bargaining power and achieving an appropriate distribution of income. Evidence shows that improved freedom of association in labor markets is associated with improved income distribution and higher wages.

Rather than representing a market distortion, as described in conventional economics, trade unions may correct market failure associated with imbalanced bargaining power. Viewed in this light, trade unions are the market-friendly approach to correcting labor market failure because unions set wages in a decentralized fashion. Though set by collective bargaining, wages can differ across firms with unions in more efficient firms bargaining higher wages than those at less efficient firms. This contrasts with a government-edict approach to wage setting.

This suggests that a key priority for China is to develop democratic trade unions that freely bargain wages. Just as China is reforming its corporate governance and financial system, so too it must embrace labor market reform and allow free democratic trade unions. This is the market-centered way of establishing an income distribution that can support a consumer society. Outside of Western Europe, only the United States, Canada, Japan, South Korea, Australia and New Zealand have successfully made the transformation to mature developed market economies. In all cases this transformation coincided with the development of effective domestic trade unions.

Free trade unions should also be supported by effectively enforced minimum-wage legislation that can also promote demand-led growth. China is a continental economy in which regions differ dramatically by level of development. This suggests the need for a system in which minimum wages are set on a regional basis and take account of regional differences in living costs. Over time, as development spreads and backward regions catch up, these settings can be adjusted with the ultimate goal being a uniform national minimum wage.

Lastly, these wage-targeted labor market reforms should be paired with the development of a social safety net that provides insurance to households. This will increase households' sense of confidence and security; with less need for precautionary saving, households can spend more on consumption.

These reforms raise the issue of wage costs. As long as China follows an export-led growth strategy, production costs will be paramount. This is because export-led growth forces countries to try to ever lower costs to gain international competitive advantage, thereby creating systemic downward pressure on wages.

A domestic demand-led growth paradigm reverses this dynamic. Now, higher wages become a source of demand that strengthens the viability of employment. Capital must still earn an adequate return to pay for itself and entice new investment, but moderately higher wages strengthen the system rather than undercutting it.

Independent democratic trade unions are key to a demand-led growth model, as they are the efficient decentralized way of raising wages. However, independent unions are unacceptable to the current Chinese political leadership. That means China must also solve this political problem as part of moving to a domestic demand-led growth regime. ❏

This article is a shortened and revised version of "External Contradictions of the Chinese Development Model: Export-led Growth and the Dangers of Global Economic Contraction," Journal of Contemporary China, *15:46 (2006).*

Sources: Blecker, R.A. (2000) "The Diminishing Returns to Export-Led Growth," paper prepared for the Council of Foreign Relations Working Group on Development, New York; Palley, T.I. (2003) "Export-led Growth: Is There Any Evidence of Crowding-Out?" in Arestis et al. (eds.), *Globalization, Regionalism, and Economic Activity*, Cheltenham: Edward Elgar; Palley, T.I. (2002) "A New Development Paradigm: Domestic Demand-Led Growth," *Foreign Policy in Focus*, www. fpif.org, also published in After Neoliberalism: Economic Policies That Work for the Poor, Jacobs, Weaver and Baker (eds.), *New Rules for Global Finance*, Washington, D.C., 2002; Palley, T.I. (2005) "Labor Standards, Democracy and Wages: Some Cross-country Evidence," *Journal of International Development* 17:1-16; Hong Kong Trade & Development Council, www.tdctrade. com/main/china.htm.

Article 8.8

COLONIALISM, "UNDERDEVELOPMENT," AND THE INTERNATIONAL DIVISION OF LABOR

BY ALEJANDRO REUSS

November 2012

The creation of large modern empires, in the last 500 years or so, linked together, for the first time, the economies of different continents into a "world economy." Colonial powers like Spain, Portugal, France, and Britain (also Belgium and the Netherlands) conquered territories and peoples in Africa, Asia, and the Americas, creating far-flung global empires. The horrors of colonialism included plunder, slavery, and genocide on an epic scale. The conquest of the Americas resulted in the greatest "demographic catastrophe" (sudden fall in population) in human history. Many indigenous people were killed by violence or the strains of forced labor, many more by the exotic diseases brought in by European colonists (against which the peoples of the Americas had no natural immunity). Europeans kidnapped and enslaved millions of Africans, many of whom died from the horrors of the "middle passage." Those who survived arrived in the Americas in chains, to be exploited on plantations and in mines.

People often think of colonialism as "ancient history." Unlike the United States and much of the rest of the Americas, however, most of the countries of Africa and Asia have gained independence only in recent decades. The Indian subcontinent was a British colony until the late 1940s, ultimately dividing into three independent countries (India, Pakistan, and Bangladesh) in two subsequent partitions. Much of southeast Asia, likewise, did not gain independence until the 1940s or 1950s. For most current African states, meanwhile, independence dates from the 1950s, 1960s, or 1970s.

Colonialism and the International Division of Labor

When we speak of the division of labor within a society, we mean that different people specialize in different kinds of work. The international division of labor, in turn, involves different countries producing different kinds of goods. One country, for example, may be mostly agricultural; another, mostly industrial. Even among agricultural producers, one may produce mostly grains and another mostly fruits and vegetables. Among industrial countries, one may be a major producer of cars or planes, while another may produce clothing.

While the breakdown of total production, among different industries, is often pretty similar for different "developed" economies, it is likely to differ quite a bit between "developed" and "developing" economies. Sometimes, international trade in goods links together countries that produce similar types of goods. A great deal of world trade goes between different "developed" economies, many of which export the same kinds of goods to each other. However, international trade also links together economies that produce different kinds of goods. It is this second kind of linkage that we have in mind when we talk about the "international division of labor."

Colonialism created patterns in the international division of labor that have proved very difficult to escape. Colonial powers were not, by and large, interested in the development of conquered areas for its own sake. Often, the were interested simply in stripping a colony of all the wealth they could as fast as they could. The original Spanish conquerors of the Americas, for example, were interested first and foremost in gold and silver. First they took all the gold and silver ornaments they could lay their hands on. Then they enslaved the indigenous people and forced them to labor in the mines, shipping vast quantities of gold and silver back to Europe. European empires also began to develop agricultural colonies. Colonies in tropical regions, especially, made it possible to produce goods—like sugar, coffee, and tobacco—which were highly prized and not widely available in Europe. In many places, slaves (in the Americas, mainly Africans) did the back-breaking plantation work. Sometimes, colonists simply took the lands of local people, leaving them with little choice but to work for meager wages on the plantations.

As some colonial powers began to industrialize, their colonies took on new significance. First, colonies became sources of materials for industry. Britain's textile industry, for example, began with woolen cloth, but gradually shifted toward cotton. Partly, the cotton came from its former colony, the United States, where it was grown primarily on slave plantations in the South. Increasingly, however, it came from colonies like Egypt and India. Second, colonies became "captive" markets for manufactured exports. Colonial powers restricted their colonies' trade with other

---

Changing Labels: "Underdeveloped" or "Developing"?

What are now termed "less-developed" or "developing" countries were, until recently, often described as "underdeveloped." The use of this term declined for a couple of reasons:

First, it came to be viewed as having pejorative connotations. That is, it took on very negative unspoken meanings, in particular the view that the people of "underdeveloped" countries were to blame for their own plight. It is now widely viewed as offensive to call a country "underdeveloped."

Second, political movements in many of these countries between the 1960s and 1980s took over and transformed the meaning of the word. Their countries, they argued, had not been born "underdeveloped," they had been "underdeveloped" by the colonial powers (or former colonial powers) that dominated the world economy. The shift away from the use of this term was, in part, a way for political and economic elites (both in "developed" and "developing" countries) to silence this argument.

countries, so one country's colony could not trade with another colonial power. (In effect, the imperial powers were practicing their own form of "protectionism," with barriers to trade surrounding the entire empire.) They sometimes even required that trade *between* their colonies go through the "mother" country, where customs duties (taxes) were collected for the imperial coffers.

Partly, colonial powers got the most out of their colonies by restricting the kinds of goods that could be produced there. Some economic historians argue that colonial restrictions, designed to keep India a captive market for the British textile industry, destroyed India's own textile industry. Others emphasize the cheapness of British-made cloth, made using modern water- or coal-powered machinery. Even if the latter is true, however, this does not mean colonialism was blameless. If India had been an independent country, it could have imposed tariffs, in order to protect its "infant" textile manufacturing. But economic policy for India was made in London, and those policies were designed to keep India open to British manufactures. In the end, instead of producing textiles itself, India became a producer of raw material for the British textile industry. This was a pattern that repeated itself across the colonial world, with industrial development stifled and the colonies pushed into "primary goods" production.

Political Independence and Economic "Dependency"

Even after becoming politically independent, many former colonial countries seemed to remain trapped in the colonial-era international division of labor. They had not been able to develop manufacturing industries as colonies, and so they continued to import manufactured goods. To pay for these goods, they continued to export primary products. In many countries, the specialization in a single export good was so extreme that these became known as "monoculture" economies ("mono" = one). In some former colonies, important resources like land and mines remained under the control of foreign companies. In many cases, these were from the former colonial "mother" country. Sometimes, however, a rising new power replaced the old colonial power. After independence from Spain, for example, much of South America became part of Britain's "informal empire." Meanwhile, the United States supplanted Spain and other European colonial countries as the dominant power in Central America and the Caribbean, plus parts of South America.

Critics argued that this situation kept the former colonies poor and "dependent" on the rich industrial countries. (The subordination of the former colonies was so reminiscent of the old patterns of colonialism, that this was often labeled "neo-colonialism" or "imperialism.") The United States' relationship to smaller, poorer, and less powerful countries—especially in its "sphere of influence" of Latin America—exemplified many of the key patterns of post-independence neo-colonialism: Foreign companies extracted vast amounts of wealth, in the form of agricultural goods and minerals, while paying paltry wages to local workers. They employed skilled personnel from their home countries and used imported machinery, so their operations formed economic "enclaves" unconnected to the rest of the country's economy. Finally, they sent the profits back to their home countries, rather than reinvesting them locally, and so did little to spur broader economic development. Critics argued that this system was designed, in the words of Uruguayan author Eduardo Galeano, to bleed wealth out of these countries' "open veins."

Some economists pointed out some major economic disadvantages to specialization in "primary products," which are worth discussing in more detail.

First, economists associated with the United Nations Economic Commission for Latin America (known by its Spanish acronym, CEPAL) observed that the prices of primary products had tended to decline, over time, in relation to the prices of manufactured goods. The lower-income countries, therefore, had to sell larger and larger amounts of the goods they exported (more tons of sugar, coffee, copper, aluminum, or whatever) to afford the same amounts of the goods they imported (cars, televisions, or whatever).

Second, specialization in primary-product exports exposed low-income countries to wild fluctuations of world-market prices for these goods. The world-market price of a cash crop could be very high one year and very low the next. An especially bad year, or a few bad years in a row, might wipe out any savings farmers or farm workers might have from previous good years, and leave them destitute. Ironically, farmers might go hungry, even if the land was fertile and the weather had been good. For most cash crops, including fiber crops (like cotton) and specialized food crops (like coffee and sugar), the farmers could not survive by eating the harvest if world prices were too low. So a move towards cash crops could exacerbate poverty and food insecurity.

The governments of these countries might have found it difficult to challenge this state of affairs, even had they wanted to. Their economies, after all, were heavily dependent on exports to the dominant country (whose government could cut off access to its markets, should it be provoked). In many cases, however, local political elites have enjoyed close political and economic ties to the multinational companies, and little interest in changing anything. As long as they maintained "order," kept workers from organizing unions or demanding higher wages, and protected the multinational companies' investments, they could be sure to keep the favor of the dominant country's government and the multinational companies. In the cases where opposition movements did arise, calling for changes like the redistribution of land ownership or the nationalization of important resources, the dominant power could intervene militarily, if local elites were not up to the task of putting the rebels down.

Changes in the International Division of Labor

For much of the twentieth century, a key dividing line among capitalist economies was between the "industrial" economies of the United States and Western Europe and the "non-industrial" economies of most of Latin America, Africa, and Asia. These two kinds of economies were linked: The high-income industrial economies imported agricultural products and minerals (or "primary products") from the low-income non-industrial economies, and exported manufactured goods (or "secondary products") in return.

In more recent decades, the international division of labor has changed in important ways. First, many formerly "non-industrial" economies have developed substantial manufacturing sectors, often by deliberately promoting manufacturing development through government policies like protective trade barriers, low-interest loans, etc. In some cases, what had been "less developed" economies, such as Japan and South Korea, have become major global industrial producers. Second, foreign investment has created a growing "export platform" manufacturing sector in some countries. Large corporations have increasingly engaged in "offshoring"—locating production facilities outside the countries where they are headquartered and have their traditional base of operations, and exporting the output back to the "home" market or to other countries.

In high-income countries, even as manufacturing employment has declined as a percentage of total employment, other sectors have grown. Over the last few decades, employment in "services" has accounted for an increasing proportion of total employment in high-income countries. When people think of services, they often think of low-wage employment in fast-food restaurants or big-box stores. Services, however, also include education, health care, finance, and other industries which can involve high-skill, and sometimes highly paid, work. All of these services can be "exported"—performed for people who reside in and earn their incomes in other countries—either because they can be done remotely (like most financial services, and some health care and education) or because the recipients travel to the place where providers are located (like students from abroad studying at U.S. universities).

Often, people think the relative decline in manufacturing employment in high-income countries is due only to offshoring—to companies "moving" manufacturing jobs from one country to another. To a great extent, however, the increasing mechanization of production (the substitution of machines for labor) was already driving this process decades before offshoring became a significant factor. As assembly-line employment has declined in high-income countries, fields like product engineering and design have accounted for an increasing proportion of the jobs in the manufacturing sector.

The End of "Underdevelopment"?

Advocates of "globalization" have pointed to the growth of export-oriented manufacturing in some less developed countries as a positive sign. The countries experiencing the least development, they argue, are those that have remained marginal to the new global economy—especially because official corruption, political instability, or government hostility toward foreign investment have made them unattractive locations for offshore production. These countries, the globalization advocates argue, need *more* globalization, not less—and therefore should adopt "neoliberal" policies eliminating barriers to international trade and investment

Critics of the current form of globalization, and of the "offshoring" approach to economic development, on the other hand, point to several less-than-shining realities.

First, it is not always true that the least-developed economies have been relatively untouched by the global economy. In many cases, multinational companies, usually with the connivance of local elites, have seized and extracted valuable resources such as minerals or petroleum, with near-total disregard for the effects on the local population. This process has led to the most extreme patterns of "enclave" development, where the only things developed are the means to get the wealth out of the ground and bound for world markets.

Second, countries aggressively embracing neoliberal economic policies have not always seen a dramatic increase in manufacturing employment. "Free trade agreements" have typically eliminated both barriers to trade and barriers to international investment. The elimination of trade barriers has opened up profitable new markets for multinational companies, while also being an essential ingredient of the offshore-production model. The imports that have flooded in to lower-income countries due to the elimination of tariffs and other barriers, however, have battered domestic industries. As a result, many countries have seen the increase in "offshore" or "export-platform" employment in manufacturing offset by the decimation of domestic manufacturing for the domestic market.

Third, when multinational companies "offshore" manufacturing to lower-income countries, they do not relocate all phases of the manufacturing process. Export-platform production typically involves relatively "low-skill" assembly and finishing work. Meanwhile, functions like engineering, design and styling, marketing, and management largely remain in the company's "home" country. (If you look on the back of an iPhone, for example, you will see that it says, "Designed by Apple in California. Assembled in China.") Countries whose governments simply throw their doors open to multinational corporations—without imposing, for example, "technology transfer" requirements that can help spur domestic technological development—may remain stuck in the assembly-and-finishing phase, much as "less-developed" countries in an earlier era were stuck as primary-product producers.

In the 1950s and 1960s, radical theorists of economic dependency emphasized that "underdevelopment" was not simply an *absence* of development. Indeed, even in that era, there was visible economic development in so-called underdeveloped countries, as there is today in what are now termed "developing" countries. Rather, they argued that we should think of underdevelopment as a *form* of development—of dependent, subordinated, exploited development. Capitalist development, they argued, produced both development (for countries in the wealthy "core") and underdevelopment (in the poorer "periphery"). While offshore production may bring a certain form of industrial development, and may be changing the international division of labor in some ways, it is also reproducing old patterns of subordination. ❏

Chapter 9

NATURAL RESOURCES AND THE ENVIRONMENT

Article 9.1

GENETIC ENGINEERING AND THE PRIVATIZATION OF SEEDS

BY ANURADHA MITTAL AND PETER ROSSET
March/April 2001

In 1998, angry farmers burned Monsanto-owned fields in Karnataka, India, starting a nationwide "Cremate Monsanto" campaign. The campaign demanded that biotech corporations like Monsanto, Novartis, and Pioneer leave the country. Farmers particularly targeted Monsanto because its field trials of the "terminator gene"—designed to prevent plants from producing seeds and so to make farmers buy new seed each year—created the danger of "genetic pollution" that would sterilize other crops in the area. That year, Indian citizens chose Quit India Day (August 9), the anniversary of Mahatma Gandhi's demand that British colonial rulers leave the country, to launch a "Monsanto Quit India" campaign. Ten thousand citizens from across the country sent the Quit India message to Monsanto's Indian headquarters, accusing the company of colonizing the food system.

In recent years, farmers across the world have echoed the Indian farmers' resistance to the biotech giants. In Brazil, the Landless Workers' Movement (MST) has set out to stop Monsanto soybeans. The MST has vowed to destroy any genetically engineered crops planted in the state of Rio Grande do Sul, where the state government has banned such crops. Meanwhile, in September 2000, more than 1,000 local farmers joined a "Long March for Biodiversity" across Thailand. "Rice, corn, and other staple crops, food crops, medicinal plants and all other life forms are significant genetic resources that shape our culture and lifestyle," the farmers declared. "We oppose any plan to transform these into genetically modified organisms."

Industrial Agriculture: From "Green Revoluion" to Biorevolution

For thousands of years, small farmers everywhere have grown food for their local com-munities—planting diverse crops in healthy soil, recycling organic matter, and fol-lowing nature's rainfall patterns. Good farming relied upon the farmer's accumulated knowledge of the local environment. Until the 1950s, most Third World agriculture was done this way.

The "Green Revolution" of the 1960s gradually replaced this kind of farming with monocultures (single-crop production) heavily dependent on chemical fertil-izers, pesticides, and herbicides. The industrialization of agriculture made Third World countries increase exports to First World markets, in order to earn the foreign exchange they needed to pay for agrochemicals and farm machinery manufactured in the global North. Today, as much as 70% of basic grain production in the global South is the product of industrial farming.

The Green Revolution was an attempt by northern countries to export chem-ical- and machine-intensive U.S.-style agriculture to the Third World. After the Cuban revolution, northern policymakers worried that rampant hunger created the basis for "communist" revolution. Since the First World had no intention of redis-tributing the world's wealth, its answer was for First World science to "help" the Third World by giving it the means to produce more food. The Green Revolution was to substitute for the "red."

During the peak Green Revolution years, from 1970 to 1990, world food pro-duction per capita rose by 11%. Yet the number of people living in hunger (averaging less than the minimum daily caloric intake) continued to rise. In the Third World—excluding China—the hungry population increased by more than 11%, from 536 to 597 million. While hunger declined somewhat relative to total Third World popula-tion, the Green Revolution was certainly not the solution for world hunger that its proponents made it out to be.

Not only did the Green Revolution fail to remedy unequal access to food and food-producing resources, it actually contributed to inequality. The costs of improved seeds and fertilizers hit cash-poor small farmers the hardest. Unable to afford the new tech-nology, many farmers lost their land. Over time, the industrialization of agriculture contributed to the replacement of farms with corporations, farmers with machines, mixed crops with monocultures, and local food security with global commerce.

The same companies that promoted chemical-based agriculture are now bring-ing the world genetically engineered food and agriculture. Some of the leading pesticide companies of yesterday have become what today are euphemistically called "life sciences companies"—Aventis, Novartis, Syngenta, Monsanto, Dupont, and others. Through genetic engineering, these companies are now converting seeds into product-delivery systems. The crops produced by Monsanto's Roundup-Ready brand seeds, for example, tolerate only the company's Roundup brand herbicide.

The "life sciences" companies claim that they can solve the environmental prob-lems of agriculture. For example, they promise to create a world free of pesticides by equipping each crop with its own "insecticidal genes." Many distinguished agriculture scientists, corporate bigwigs, and economists are jumping on the "biotechnology" bandwagon. They argue that, in a world where more than 830 million people go to bed hungry, biotechnology provides the only hope of feeding our burgeoning population, especially in the Third World.

In fact, since genetic engineering is based on the same old principles of industrial agriculture—monoculture, technology, and corporate control—it is likely to exacerbate the problems of ecological and social devastation:

- As long as chemical companies dominate the "life sciences" industry, the biotechnology they develop will only reinforce intensive chemical use. Corporations are currently developing plants whose genetic traits can be turned "on" or "off" by applying an external chemical, as well as crops that die if the correct chemical—made by the same company—is not applied.

- The biotechnology industry is releasing hundreds of thousands of genetically engineered organisms into the environment every year. These organisms can reproduce, cross-pollinate, mutate, and migrate. Each release of a genetically engineered organism is a round of ecological Russian roulette. Recently, Aventis' genetically engineered StarLink corn, a variety approved by the U.S. Department of Agriculture only for livestock consumption, entered the food supply by mixing in grain elevators and cross-pollination in the field.

- With the advent of genetic engineering, corporations are using new "intellectual property" rights to stake far-reaching claims of ownership over a vast array of biological resources. By controlling the ownership of seeds, the corporate giants force farmers to pay yearly for seeds they once saved from each harvest to the next planting. By making seed exchanges between farmers illegal, they also limit farmers' capacity to contribute to agricultural biodiversity.

The False Promise of "Golden Rice"

The biotech industry is taking great pains to advertise the humanitarian applications of genetic engineering. "[M]illions of people—many of them children—have lost their sight to vitamin A deficiency," says the Council for Biotechnology Information, an industry-funded public relations group. "But suppose rice consumers could obtain enough vitamin A and iron simply by eating dietary staples that are locally grown? … Biotechnology is already producing some of these innovations." More than $10 million was spent over ten years to engineer vitamin A rice—hailed as the "Golden Rice"—at the Institute of Plant Sciences of the Swiss Federal Institute of Technology in Zurich. It will take millions more and another decade of research and development to produce vitamin A rice varieties that can actually be grown in farmers' fields.

In reality, the selling of vitamin A rice as a miracle cure for blindness depends on blindness to lower-cost and safer alternatives. Meat, liver, chicken, eggs, milk, butter, carrots, pumpkins, mangoes, spinach and other leafy green vegetables, and many other foods contain vitamin A. Women farmers in Bengal, an eastern Indian state, plant more than 100 varieties of green leafy vegetables. The promotion of monoculture and rising herbicide use, however, are destroying such sources of vitamin A. For example, bathua, a very popular leafy vegetable in northern India, has been pushed to extinction in areas of intensive herbicide use.

The long-run solutions to vitamin A deficiency—and other nutritional problems—are increased biodiversity in agriculture and increased food security for poor people. In the meantime, there are better, safer, and more economical short-run measures than genetically engineered foods. UNICEF, for example, gives high-dose vitamin A capsules to poor children twice a year. The cost? Just two cents per pill.

Intellectual Property Rights and Genetic Engineering

In 1998, Monsanto surprised Saskatchewan farmer Percy Schmeiser by suing him for doing what he has always done and, indeed, what farmers have done for millennia— save seeds for the next planting. Schmeiser is one of hundreds of Canadian and U.S. farmers the company has sued for re-using genetically engineered seeds. Monsanto has patented those seeds, and forbids farmers from saving them.

In recent years, Monsanto has spent over $8.5 billion acquiring seed and biotech companies, and DuPont spent over $9.4 billion to acquire Pioneer Hi-Bred, the world's largest seed company. Seed is the most important link in the food chain. Over 1.4 billion people—primarily poor farmers—depend on farm-saved seed for their livelihoods. While the "gene police" have not yet gone after farmers in the Third World, it is probably only a matter of time.

If corporations like Monsanto have their way, genetic technology—like the so-called "terminator" seeds—will soon render the "gene police" redundant. Far from being designed to increase agricultural production, "terminator" technology is meant to prevent unauthorized production—and increase seed-industry profits. Fortunately, worldwide protests, like the "Monsanto Quit India" campaign, forced the company to put this technology on hold. Unfortunately, Monsanto did not pledge to abandon "terminator" seeds permanently, and other companies continue to develop similar systems.

Future Possible

From the United States to India, small-scale ecological agriculture is proving itself a viable alternative to chemical-intensive and bioengineered agriculture. In the United States, the National Research Council found that "alternative farmers often produce high per acre yields with significant reductions in costs per unit of crop harvested," despite the fact that "many federal policies discourage adoption of alternative practices." The Council concluded that "federal commodity programs must be restructured to help farmers realize the full benefits of the productivity gains possible through alternative practices."

Another study, published in the *American Journal of Alternative Agriculture,* found that ecological farms in India were just as productive and profitable as chemical ones. The author concluded that, if adopted on a national scale, ecological farming would have "no negative impact on food security," and would reduce soil erosion and the depletion of soil fertility while greatly lessening dependence on external inputs.

The country where alternative agriculture has been put to its greatest test, however, is Cuba. Before 1989, Cuba had a model Green Revolution-style agricultural economy (an approach the Soviet Union had promoted as much as the United States). Cuban agriculture featured enormous production units, using vast quantities of imported chemicals and machinery to produce export crops, while the country imported over half its food.

Although the Cuban government's commitment to equity and favorable terms of trade offered by Eastern Europe protected Cubans from undernourishment, the collapse of the East bloc in 1989 exposed the vulnerability of this approach. Cuba plunged into its worst food crisis since the revolution. Consumption of calories and protein dropped by perhaps as much as 30%. Nevertheless, today Cubans are eating almost as well as they did before 1989, with much lower imports of food and agrochemicals. What happened?

Cut off from imports of food and agrochemicals, Cuba turned inward to create a more self-reliant agriculture based on higher crop prices to farmers, smaller production units, urban agriculture, and ecological principles. As a result of the trade embargo, food shortages, and the opening of farmers' markets, farmers began to receive much better prices for their products. Given this incentive to produce, they did so, even without Green Revolution-style inputs. The farmers received a huge boost from the reorientation of government education, research, and assistance toward alternative methods, as well as the rediscovery of traditional farming techniques.

While small farmers and cooperatives increased production, large-scale state farms stagnated. In response, the Cuban government parceled out the state farms to their former employees as smaller-scale production units. Finally, the government mobilized support for a growing urban agriculture movement—small-scale organic farming on vacant lots—which, together with the other changes, transformed Cuban cities and urban diets in just a few years.

Will Biotechnology Feed the World?

The biotech industry pretends concern for hungry people in the Third World, holding up greater food production through genetic engineering as the solution to world hunger. If the Green Revolution has taught us one thing, however, it is that increased food production can—and often does—go hand in hand with more hunger, not less. Hunger in the modern world is not caused by a shortage of food, and cannot be eliminated by producing more. Enough food is already available to provide at least 4.3 pounds of food per person a day worldwide. The root of the hunger problem is not inadequate production but unequal access and distribution. This is why the second Green Revolution promised by the "life sciences" companies is no more likely to end hunger than the first.

The United States is the world's largest producer of surplus food. According to the U.S. Department of Agriculture, however, some 36 million of the country's people (including 14 million children) do not have adequate access to food. That's an increase of six million hungry people since the 1996 welfare reform, with its massive cuts in food stamp programs.

Even the world's "hungry countries" have enough food for all their people right now. In fact, about three quarters of the world's malnourished children live in countries with net food surpluses, much of which are being exported. India, for example, ranks among the top Third World agricultural exporters, and yet more than a third of the world's 830 million hungry people live there. Year after year, Indian governments have managed a sizeable food surplus by depriving the poor of their basic human right to food.

The poorest of the poor in the Third World are landless peasants, many of whom became landless because of policies that favor large, wealthy farmers. The high costs of genetically engineered seeds, "technology-use payments," and other inputs that small farmers will have to use under the new biotech agriculture will tighten the squeeze on already poor farmers, deepening rural poverty. If agriculture can play any role in alleviating hunger, it will only be to the extent that we reverse the existing bias toward wealthier and larger farmers, embrace land reform and sustainable agriculture, reduce inequality, and make small farmers the center of an economically vibrant rural economy. ❏

Update

Since this article was written, eight European Union (EU) nations have prohibited genetically modified (GM) cultivation on their territory and banned the import of GM foods from abroad. The prospects of Monsanto, the world's biggest seed producer (and the producer of a variety of GM seeds), meanwhile, have taken a different turn in the United States. On May 13, 2013, the U.S. Supreme Court ruled unanimously that Indiana farmer Vernon Bowman had to pay Monsanto over $80,000 for planting GM soybean seeds that he had culled from seed stock he bought at a grain elevator, rather than from the company itself.

"Farmers who buy Monsanto's patented seeds must generally sign a contract promising not to save seeds from the resulting crop, which means they must buy new seeds every year," the *New York Times* reported. "The seeds are valuable because they are resistant to the herbicide Roundup, itself a Monsanto product." Bowman was ordered to pay Monsanto, however, even though he did not have a contract with the company covering seeds of that type. This ruling is likely to bolster Monsanto's already substantial market power, lead to higher prices for farmers and consumers in the future. —*Armagan Gezici*

Article 9.2

IS THE UNITED STATES A POLLUTION HAVEN?

BY FRANK ACKERMAN
March/April 2003

When this article was originally written, the North American Free Trade Agreement (NAFTA) was nearly a decade old, and many of its main effects were already apparent. One of these was the devastating impact of U.S. corn exports on Mexican small-farmer agriculture. As productive as Mexico's small farmers are, they have been not been able to compete with low-priced corn produced on the United States' gigantic, "super-mechanized" farms using the most petroleum- and chemical-intensive methods. Although some numbers and details have changed since this article was written, more recent findings bear out the continuing heavy toll on Mexican farmers. Researcher Timothy A. Wise points to U.S. agricultural subsidies, permitted under NAFTA, as a cause of U.S. producers' export "dumping" (sales a less than cost of production) in Mexico. This has not only cost Mexican farmers about a billion dollars a year (with the largest impact on corn farmers), but also helped turn Mexico into a large importer of corn. Recent spikes in corn prices, due to the promotion of corn-based ethanol as an alternative motor fuel, have inflicted a heavy blow on low-income Mexicans for whom corn is a staple food. Meanwhile, the environmental impacts of chemical-intensive agriculture in the United States remain serious—with agricultural runoff as a top source of water pollution. —Eds.

Sources: Timothy A. Wise, "Agricultural Dumping Under NAFTA," Woodrow Wilson International Center for Scholars, 2010; Timothy A. Wise, "The Cost to Mexico of U.S. Corn Ethanol Expansion," GDAE Working Paper 12-0, May 2012; Environmental Protection Agency (EPA), Water Quality Assessment and Total Maximum Daily Loads Information (epa.gov/waters/ir/).

Free trade, according to its critics, runs the risk of creating pollution havens— countries where lax environmental standards allow dirty industries to expand. Poor countries are the usual suspects; perhaps poverty drives them to desperate strategies, such as specializing in the most polluting industries.

But could the United States be a pollution haven? A look at agriculture under NAFTA, particularly the trade in corn, suggests that at least one polluting industry is thriving in the United States as a result of free trade.

In narrow economic terms, the United States is winning the corn market. U.S. corn exports to Mexico have doubled since 1994, NAFTA's first year, to more than five million tons annually. Cheap U.S. corn is undermining traditional production in Mexico; prices there have dropped 27% in just a few years, and a quarter of the corn consumed in Mexico is now grown in the United States. But in environmental terms, the U.S. victory comes at a great cost.

While the United States may not have more lax environmental *standards* than Mexico, when it comes to corn U.S. agriculture certainly uses more polluting *methods.* As it is grown in the United States, corn requires significantly more chemicals per acre than wheat or soybeans, the other two leading field crops. Runoff of excess nitrogen fertilizer causes water pollution, and has created a huge "dead zone" in the Gulf of Mexico around the mouth of the Mississippi River. Intensive application of toxic herbicides and insecticides threatens the health of farm workers, farming communities, and consumers. Genetically modified corn, which now accounts for about one-fifth of U.S. production, poses unknown long-term risks to consumers and to ecosystems.

Growing corn in very dry areas, where irrigation is required, causes more environmental problems. The United States also has a higher percentage of irrigated acreage than Mexico. While the traditional Corn Belt enjoys ample rainfall and does not need irrigation, 15% of U.S. corn acreage—almost all of it in Nebraska, Kansas, the Texas panhandle, and eastern Colorado—is now irrigated. These areas draw water from the Ogallala aquifer, a gigantic underground reservoir, much faster than the aquifer naturally refills. If present rates of overuse continue, the Ogallala, which now contains as much fresh water as Lake Huron, will be drained down to unusable levels within a few decades, causing a crisis for the huge areas of the plains states that depend on it for water supplies. Government subsidies, in years past, helped farmers buy the equipment needed to pump water out of the Ogallala, contributing to the impending crisis.

Moreover, the corn borer, a leading insect pest that likes to eat corn plants, flourishes best in dry climates. Thus the "irrigation states," particularly Texas and Colorado, are the hardest hit by corn borers. Corn growers in dry states have the greatest need for insecticides; they also have the greatest motivation to use genetically modified corn, which is designed to repel corn borers.

Sales to Mexico are particularly important to the United States because many countries are refusing to accept genetically modified corn. Europe no longer imports U.S. corn for this reason, and Japan and several East Asian countries may follow suit. Mexico prohibits growing genetically modified corn, but still allows it to be imported; it is one of the largest remaining markets where U.S. exports are not challenged on this issue.

Despite Mexico's ban, genetically modified corn was recently found growing in a remote rural area in the southern state of Oaxaca. As the ancestral home of corn, Mexico possesses a unique and irreplaceable genetic diversity. Although the extent of the problem is still uncertain, the unplanned and uncontrolled spread of artificially engineered plants from the United States could potentially contaminate Mexico's numerous naturally occurring corn varieties.

An even greater threat is the economic impact of cheap U.S. imports on peasant farmers and rural communities. Traditional farming practices, evolved over thousands of years, use combinations of different natural varieties of corn carefully matched to local conditions. Lose these traditions, and we will lose a living reservoir of biodiversity in the country of origin of one of the world's most important food grains.

The United States has won the North American corn market. But the cost looks increasingly unbearable when viewed through the lens of the U.S. environment, or of Mexico's biodiversity. ❑

Article 9.3

CLIMATE ECONOMICS IN FOUR EASY PIECES

Conventional cost-benefit models cannot inform our decisions about how to address the threat of climate change.

FRANK ACKERMAN
November/December 2008

Once upon a time, debates about climate policy were primarily about the science. An inordinate amount of attention was focused on the handful of "climate skeptics" who challenged the scientific understanding of climate change. The influence of the skeptics, however, is rapidly fading; few people were swayed by their arguments, and doubt about the major results of climate science is no longer important in shaping public policy.

As the climate *science* debate is reaching closure, the climate *economics* debate is heating up. The controversial issue now is the fear that overly ambitious climate initiatives could hurt the economy. Mainstream economists emphasizing that fear have, in effect, replaced the climate skeptics as the intellectual enablers of inaction.

For example, William Nordhaus, the U.S. economist best known for his work on climate change, pays lip service to scientists' calls for decisive action. He finds, however, that the "optimal" policy is a very small carbon tax that would reduce greenhouse gas emissions only 25% below "business-as-usual" levels by 2050—that would, in other words, allow emissions to rise well above current levels by mid-century. Richard Tol, a European economist who has written widely on climate change, favors an even smaller carbon tax of just $2 per ton of carbon dioxide. That would amount to all of $0.02 per gallon of gasoline, a microscopic "incentive" for change that consumers would never notice.

There are other voices in the climate economics debate; in particular, the British government's Stern Review offers a different perspective. Economist Nicholas Stern's analysis is much less wrong than the traditional Nordhaus-Tol approach, but even Stern has not challenged the conventional view enough.

What will it take to build a better economics of climate change, one that is consistent with the urgency expressed by the latest climate science? The issues that matter are big, non-technical principles, capable of being expressed in bumper-sticker format. Here are the four bumper stickers for a better climate economics:

- Our grandchildren's lives are important
- We need to buy insurance for the planet
- Climate damages are too valuable to have prices
- Some costs are better than others

1. Our grandchildren's lives are important.

The most widely debated challenge of climate economics is the valuation of the very long run. For ordinary loans and investments, both the costs today and the resulting future benefits typically occur within a single lifetime. In such cases, it makes sense to think in terms of the same person experiencing and comparing the costs and the benefits.

In the case of climate change, the time spans involved are well beyond those encountered in most areas of economics. The most important consequences of today's choices will be felt by generations to come, long after all of us making those choices have passed away. As a result, the costs of reducing emissions today and the benefits in the far future will not be experienced by the same people. The economics of climate change is centrally concerned with our relationship to our descendants whom we will never meet. As a bridge to that unknowable future, consider our grandchildren—the last generation most of us will ever know.

Suppose that you want your grandchildren to receive $100 (in today's dollars, corrected for inflation), 60 years from now. How much would you have to put in a bank account today, to ensure that the $100 will be there 60 years from now? The answer is $55 at 1% interest, or just over $5 at 5%.

In parallel fashion, economists routinely deal with future costs and benefits by "discounting" them, or converting them to "present values"—a process that is simply compound interest in reverse. In the standard jargon, the *present value* of $100, to be received 60 years from now, is $55 at a 1% *discount rate*, or about $5 at a 5% discount rate. As this example shows, a higher discount rate implies a smaller present value.

The central problem of climate economics, in a cost-benefit framework, is deciding how much to spend today on preventing future harms. What should we spend to prevent $100 of climate damages 60 years from now? The standard answer is, no more than the present value of that future loss: $55 at a discount rate of 1%, or $5 at 5%. The higher the discount rate, the less it is "worth" spending today on protecting our grandchildren.

The effect of a change in the discount rate becomes much more pronounced as the time period lengthens. Damages of $1 million occurring 200 years from now have a present value of only about $60 at a 5% discount rate, versus more than $130,000 at a 1% discount rate. The choice of the discount rate is all-important to our stance toward the far future: should we spend as much as $130,000, or as little as $60, to avoid one million dollars of climate damages in the early twenty-third century?

For financial transactions within a single lifetime, it makes sense to use market interest rates as the discount rate. Climate change, however, involves public policy decisions with impacts spanning centuries; there is no market in which public resources are traded from one century to the next. The choice of an intergenerational discount rate is a matter of ethics and policy, not a market-determined result.

Economists commonly identify two separate aspects of long-term discounting, each contributing to the discount rate.

One component of the discount rate is based on the assumption of an upward trend in income and wealth. If future generations will be richer than we are, they will need less help from us, and they will get less benefit from an additional dollar of income than we do. So we can discount benefits that will flow to our wealthier descendants, at a rate based on the expected growth of per capita incomes. Among economists, the income-related motive for discounting may be the least controversial part of the picture.

Setting aside changes in per capita income from one generation to the next, there may still be a reason to discount a sum many years in the future. This component of the discount rate, known as "pure time preference," is the subject of longstanding ethical, philosophical, and economic debate. On the one hand, there are reasons to think that pure time preference is greater than zero: both psychological experiments and common sense suggest that people are impatient, and prefer money now to money later. On the other hand, a pure time preference of zero expresses the equal worth of people of all generations, and the equal importance of reducing climate impacts and other burdens on them (assuming that all generations have equal incomes).

The Stern Review provides an excellent discussion of the debate, explaining Stern's assumption of pure time preference close to zero and an overall discount rate of 1.4%. This discount rate alone is sufficient to explain Stern's support for a substantial program of climate protection: at the higher discount rates used in more traditional analyses, the Stern program would look "inefficient," since the costs would outweigh the present value of the benefits.

2. We need to buy insurance for the planet.

Does climate science predict that things are certain to get worse? Or does it tell us that we are uncertain about what will happen next? Unfortunately, the answer seems to be yes to both questions. For example, the most likely level of sea level rise in this century, according to the latest Intergovernmental Panel on Climate Change reports, is no more than one meter or so—a real threat to low-lying coastal areas and islands that will face increasing storm damages, but survivable, with some adaptation efforts, for most of the world. On the other hand, there is a worst-case risk of an abrupt loss of the Greenland ice sheet, or perhaps of a large portion of the West Antarctic ice sheet. Either one could cause an eventual seven-meter rise in sea level—a catastrophic impact on coastal communities, economic activity, and infrastructure everywhere, and well beyond the range of plausible adaptation efforts in most places.

The evaluation of climate damages thus depends on whether we focus on the most likely outcomes or the credible worst-case risks; the latter, of course, are much larger.

Cost-benefit analysis conventionally rests on average or expected outcomes. But this is not the only way that people make decisions. When faced with uncertain, potentially large risks, people do not normally act on the basis of average outcomes; instead, they typically focus on protection against worst-case scenarios. When you go to the airport, do you leave just enough time for the average traffic delay (so that you would catch your plane, on average, half of the time)? Or do you allow time for some estimate of worst-case traffic jams? Once you get there, of course, you will experience additional delays due to security, which is all about worst cases: your *average* fellow passenger is not a threat to anyone's safety.

The very existence of the insurance industry is evidence of the desire to avoid or control worst-case scenarios. It is impossible for an insurance company to pay out in claims as much as its customers pay in premiums; if it did, there would be no money left to pay the costs of running the company, or the profits received by its owners. People who buy insurance are therefore guaranteed to get back less than they, on average, have paid; they (we) are paying for the security that insurance provides in case the worst should happen. This way of thinking does not apply to every decision: in casino games, people make bets based on averages and probabilities, and no one has any insurance against losing the next round. But life is not a casino, and public policy should not be a gamble.

Should climate policy be based on the most likely outcomes, or on the worst-case risks? Should we be investing in climate protection as if we expect sea level rise of one meter, or as if we are buying insurance to be sure of preventing a seven-meters rise?

In fact, the worst-case climate risks are even more unknown than the individual risks of fire and death that motivate insurance purchases. You do not know whether or not you will have a fire next year or die before the year is over, but you have very good information about the likelihood of these tragic events. So does the insurance industry, which is why they are willing to insure you. In contrast, there is no body of statistical information about the probability of Greenland-sized ice sheets collapsing at various temperatures; it's not an experiment that anyone can perform over and over again.

A recent analysis by Martin Weitzman argues that the probabilities of the worst outcomes are inescapably unknowable—and this deep uncertainty is more important than anything we do know in motivating concern about climate change. There is a technical sense in which the expected value of future climate damages can be infinite because we know so little about the probability of the worst, most damaging possibilities. The practical implication of infinite expected damages is that the most likely outcome is irrelevant; what matters is buying insurance for the planet, i.e., doing our best to understand and prevent the worst-case risks.

3. Climate damages are too valuable to have prices.

To decide whether climate protection is worthwhile, in cost-benefit terms, we would need to know the monetary value of everything important that is being protected. Even if we could price everything affected by climate change, the prices would conceal a critical form of international inequity. The emissions that cause climate change have come predominantly from rich countries, while the damages will be felt first and worst in some of the world's poorest, tropical countries (although no one will be immune from harm for long). There are, however, no meaningful prices for many of the benefits of health and environmental protection. What is the dollar value of a human life saved? How much is it worth to save an endangered species from extinction, or to preserve a unique location or ecosystem? Economists have made up price tags for such priceless values, but the results do not always pass the laugh test.

Is a human life worth $6.1 million, as estimated by the Clinton administration, based on small differences in the wages paid for more and less risky jobs? Or is it worth $3.7 million, as the (second) Bush administration concluded on the basis of questionnaires about people's willingness to pay for reducing small, hypothetical risks? Are lives of people in rich countries worth much more than those in poor countries, as some economists infamously argued in the IPCC's 1995 report? Can the value of an endangered species be determined by survey research on how much people would pay to protect it? If, as one study found, the U.S. population as a whole would pay $18 billion to protect the existence of humpback whales, would it be acceptable for someone to pay $36 billion for the right to hunt and kill the entire species?

The only sensible response to such nonsensical questions is that there are many crucially important values that do not have meaningful prices. This is not a new idea: as the eighteenth-century philosopher Immanuel Kant put it, some things have a price, or relative worth, while other things have a dignity, or inner worth. No price tag does justice to the dignity of human life or the natural world.

Since some of the most important benefits of climate protection are priceless, any monetary value for total benefits will necessarily be incomplete. The corollary is that preventive action may be justified even in the absence of a complete monetary measure of the benefits of doing so.

Average Risks or Worst-Case Scenarios?

You don't have to look far to find situations in which the sensible policy is to address worst-case outcomes rather than average outcomes. The annual number of residential fires in the United States is about 0.4% of the number of housing units. This means that a fire occurs, on average, about once every 250 years in each home—not even close to once per lifetime. By far the most likely number of fires a homeowner will experience next year, or even in a lifetime, is zero. Why don't these statistics inspire you to cancel your fire insurance? Unless you are extremely wealthy, the loss of your home in a fire would be a devastating financial blow; despite the low probability, you cannot afford to take any chances on it.

What are the chances of the ultimate loss? The probability that you will die next year is under 0.1% if you are in your twenties, under 0.2% in your thirties, under 0.4% in your forties. It is not until age 61 that you have as much as a 1% chance of death within the coming year. Yet most U.S. families with dependent children buy life insurance. Without it, the risk to children of losing their parents' income would be too great—even though the parents are, on average, extraordinarily likely to survive.

4. Some costs are better than others.

The language of cost-benefit analysis embodies a clear normative slant: benefits are good, costs are bad. The goal is always to have larger benefits and smaller costs. In some respects, measurement and monetary valuation are easier for costs than for benefits: implementing pollution control measures typically involves changes in such areas as manufacturing, construction, and fuel use, all of which have well-defined prices. Yet conventional economic theory distorts the interpretation of costs in ways that exaggerate the burdens of environmental protection and hide the positive features of some of the "costs."

For instance, empirical studies of energy use and carbon emissions repeatedly find significant opportunities for emissions reduction at zero or negative net cost—the so-called "no regrets" options.

According to a long-standing tradition in economic theory, however, cost-free energy savings are impossible. The textbook theory of competitive markets assumes that every resource is productively employed in its most valuable use—in other words, that every no-regrets option must already have been taken. As the saying goes, there are no free lunches; there cannot be any $20 bills on the sidewalk because someone would have picked them up already. Any new emissions reduction measures, then, must have positive costs. This leads to greater estimates of climate policy costs than the bottom-up studies that reveal extensive opportunities for costless savings.

In the medium term, we will need to move beyond the no-regrets options; how much will it cost to finish the job of climate protection? Again, there are rival interpretations of the costs based on rival assumptions about the economy. The same economic theory that proclaimed the absence of $20 bills on the sidewalk is responsible for the idea that all costs are bad. Since the free market lets everyone spend their money in whatever way they choose, any new cost must represent a loss: it leaves people with less to spend on whatever purchases they had previously selected to maximize their satisfaction in life. Climate damages are one source of loss, and spending on climate protection is another; both reduce the resources available for the desirable things in life.

But are the two kinds of costs really comparable? Is it really a matter of indifference whether we spend $1 billion on bigger and better levees or lose $1 billion to storm damages? In the real-world economy, money spent on building levees creates jobs and incomes. The construction workers buy groceries, clothing, and so on, indirectly creating other jobs. With more people working, tax revenues increase while unemployment compensation payments decrease.

None of this happens if the levees are not built and the storm damages are allowed to occur. The costs of prevention are good costs, with numerous indirect benefits; the costs of climate damages are bad costs, representing pure physical destruction. One worthwhile goal is to keep total costs as low as possible; another is to have as much as possible of good costs rather than bad costs. Think of it as the cholesterol theory of climate costs.

In the long run, the deep reductions in carbon emissions needed for climate stabilization will require new technologies that have not yet been invented, or at best exist only in small, expensive prototypes. How much will it cost to invent, develop, and implement the low-carbon technologies of the future?

Lacking a rigorous theory of innovation, economists modeling climate change have often assumed that new technologies simply appear, making the economy inexorably more efficient over time. A more realistic view observes that the costs of producing a new product typically decline as industry gains more experience with it, in a pattern called "learning by doing" or the "learning curve" effect. Public investment is often necessary to support the innovation process in its early, expensive stages. Wind power is now relatively cheap and competitive, in suitable locations; this is a direct result of decades of public investment in the United States and Europe, starting when wind turbines were still quite expensive. The costs of climate policy, in the long run, will include doing the same for other promising new technologies, investing public resources in jump-starting a set of slightly different industries than we might have chosen in the absence of climate change. If this is a cost, many communities would be better off with more of it.

A widely publicized, conventional economic analysis recommends inaction on climate change, claiming that the costs currently outweigh the benefits for anything more than the smallest steps toward reducing carbon emissions. Put our "four easy pieces" together, and we have the outline of an economics that complements the science of climate change and endorses active, large-scale climate protection.

How realistic is it to expect that the world will shake off its inertia and act boldly and rapidly enough to make a difference? This may be the last generation that will have a real chance at protecting the earth's climate. Projections from the latest IPCC reports, the Stern Review, and other sources suggest that it is still possible to save the planet—if we start at once. ❑

Sources: Frank Ackerman, *Can We Afford the Future? Economics for a Warming World*, Zed Books, 2008; Frank Ackerman, *Poisoned for Pennies: The Economics of Toxics and Precaution*, Island Press, 2008; Frank Ackerman and Lisa Heinzerling, *Priceless: On Knowing the Price of Everything and the Value of Nothing*, The New Press, 2004; J. Creyts, A. Derkach, S. Nyquist, K. Ostrowski and J. Stephenson, *Reducing U.S. Greenhouse Gas Emissions: How Much at What Cost?*, McKinsey & Co., 2007; P.-A. Enkvist, T. Naucler and J. Rosander, "A Cost Curve for Greenhouse Gas Reduction," *The McKinsey Quarterly*, 2007; Immanuel Kant, *Groundwork for the Metaphysics of Morals*, translated by Thomas K. Abbot, with revisions by Lara Denis, Broadview Press, 2005 [1785]; B. Lomborg, *Cool It: The Skeptical Environmentalist's Guide to Global Warming*, Alfred A. Knopf, 2007; W.D. Nordhaus, *A Question of Balance: Economic Modeling of Global Warming*, Yale University Press, 2008; F.P. Ramsey, "A mathematical theory of saving," *The Economic Journal* 138(152): 543-59, 1928; Nicholas Stern et al., *The Stern Review: The Economics of Climate Change*, HM Treasury, 2006; U.S. Census Bureau, "Statistical Abstract of the United States." 127th edition. 2008; M.L. Weitzman, "On Modeling and Interpreting the Economics of Catastrophic Climate Change," December 5, 2007 version, www.economics.harvard.edu/faculty/weitzman/files/modeling.pdf.

Article 9.4

THE COSTS OF EXTREME WEATHER

Climate inaction is expensive—and inequitable.

BY HEIDI GARRETT-PELTIER
November/December 2011

Two thousand eleven has already been a record-setting year. The number of weather disasters in the United States whose costs exceed $1 billion—ten—is the highest ever. August witnessed one of the ten most expensive catastrophes in U.S. history, Tropical Storm Irene. An initial estimate put the damages from Irene at between $7 billion and $13 billion. In this one storm alone, eight million businesses and homes lost power, roads collapsed, buildings flooded, and dozens of people lost their lives. Meanwhile, Texas is experiencing its hottest year in recorded history: millions of acres in the state have burned, over 1,550 homes have been lost to wildfires as of early September, and tens of thousands of people have had to evacuate their homes. The devastation caused by the storms and droughts has left individuals and businesses wondering how they'll recover, and has left cash-strapped towns wondering how they'll pay for road and infrastructure repairs.

Extreme weather events like these are expected to become more frequent and more intense over the next century. That's just one of the impacts of climate change, which, according to the consensus of scientists and research organizations from around the world, is occurring with both natural and human causes, but mainly from the burning of fossil fuels. According to NASA, since 1950 the number of record high-temperature days has been rising while the number of record low-temperature days has been falling. The number of intense rainfall events has also increased in the past six decades. At the same time, droughts and heat waves have also become more frequent, as warmer conditions in drier areas have led to faster evaporation. This is why in the same month we had wildfires in Texas (resulting from more rapid evaporation and drought) and flooding in the Northeast (since warmer air holds more moisture and results in more intense precipitation).

In response to these dramatic weather changes, the courses of action available to us are *mitigation, adaptation,* and *reparation. Mitigation* refers to efforts to prevent or reduce climate change, for example, cutting fossil fuel use by increasing energy efficiency and using more renewable energy. *Adaptation* refers to changing our behaviors, technologies, institutions, and infrastructure to cope with the damages that climate change creates—building levees near flood-prone areas or relocating homes further inland, for example. And as the term implies, *reparation* means repairing or rebuilding the roads, bridges, homes, and communities that are damaged by floods, winds, heat, and other weather-related events.

Of these, mitigation is the one strategy whose costs and benefits can both be shared globally. Moving toward a more sustainable economy less reliant on the burning of fossil fuels for its energy would slow the rise in average global temperatures and make extreme weather events less likely. Mitigation will have the greatest impact with a shared worldwide commitment, but even without binding international agreements, countries can take steps to reduce their use of coal, oil, and natural gas.

According to the Intergovernmental Panel on Climate Change, even the most stringent mitigation efforts cannot prevent further impacts of climate change in the next few decades. We will still need to adapt and repair—all the more in the absence of such efforts. But the costs and burdens of adaptation and reparation are spread unevenly across different populations and in many cases the communities most affected by climate change will be those least able to afford to build retaining walls or relocate to new homes. Farmers who can afford to will change their planting and harvesting techniques and schedules, but others will have unusable land and will be unable to sustain themselves. Roads that are washed away will be more quickly rebuilt in richer towns, while poorer towns will take longer to rebuild if they can at all. The divide between rich and poor will only grow.

Given the high cost of damages we've already faced just this year, mitigation may very well be sound economic planning. But it is also the most humane and equitable approach to solving our climate problem. ❏

Sources: NOAA/NESDIS/NCDC, "Billion Dollar U.S. Weather/Climate Disasters 1980-August 2011"; Michael Cooper, "Hurricane Cost Seen as Ranking Among Top Ten," *New York Times,* August 30, 2011; "Hurricane Irene Damage: Storm Likely Cost $7 Billion to $13 Billion," *International Business Times,* August 29, 2011; Intergovernmental Panel on Climate Change, *Fourth Assessment Report: Climate Change 2007,* Working Group II ch. 19; NASA, "Global Climate Change: Vital Signs of the Planet—Evidence"; U.S. EPA, "Climate Change—Health and Environmental Effects, Extreme Events."

Article 9.5

A NIGHTMARE ON MAPLE STREET
Prime Minister Stephen Harper struggles to slay the specters haunting Canada's oil sands.

BY MAURICE DUFOUR
January/February 2013

Canada now has "one of the most sought-after commodities on the planet," says the *Globe and Mail*. It's a thick, dark fluid on which the Conservative government is betting the country's future.

No, it's not maple syrup, nor is it coffee from Tim Hortons (Canada's answer to Dunkin' Donuts). Rather, the coveted Canadian commodity is crude oil, and exporting increasingly large amounts has become Prime Minister Stephen Harper's top priority. A quarter of Canada's merchandise trade—double the percentage in 2000—is now tied to energy exports, mostly from the oil sands in northern Alberta. Canada's annual production from the oil sands is expected to nearly triple—from just over 400 million barrels in 2006 to nearly 1.2 billion barrels by 2020.

At the current average annual growth rate of 7.1%, the oil sands will account for 80% of total Canadian oil production in 2025 (compared to a little more than half in 2010). "No other country in the world is bringing on [energy] infrastructure projects at the pace and relative scale as Canada," crowed former Conservative environment minister Jim Prentice last year.

The oil sands certainly stand to add dramatically to world oil supply. "Given how significant a portion the oil sands make up of currently accessible reserves," notes AltaCorp Capital, "it is hard to envision any meaningful growth in global oil output without significant development of the oil sands." The International Energy Association (IEA) has also recently predicted that "an energy-thirsty world will need 'every drop' of growing production in Canada's oil sands."

The appeal of Canadian crude, however, is also due in large part to the shrinking number of reserves open to investors. Of the 16% of the world's remaining oil reserves that are not state-owned or controlled, well over half reside in Canada's tar patch.

Canada is a "rare beast" in the world, as the *Wall Street Journal* puts it: "an oil-rich nation where the state [doesn't] confiscate your oil fields." And supermajors, like ExxonMobil, find Alberta's bitumen particularly appealing: oil-sands holdings can be used to inflate reserve numbers, boosting stock prices.

But there's another reason the oil sands have become such a magnet for investors: in 2011 the rate of return on investments was 20 to 30%, compared to 15% two years earlier. The profit-making opportunities have been enhanced as a result of a generous royalty regime, a series of corporate tax cuts, and a recent regulatory overhaul to speed approvals of large energy projects. All of these measures have made Canada among the top five most "economically free" countries in the world—well ahead of the United States—according to Canada's free-market think tank, the Fraser Institute. Envious of Canada's "freedom," the American Institute for Energy Research has advised U.S. politicians to take their cues from "our northern neighbor, [which is] cutting energy taxes/regulation."

Already, over $100 billion has poured into the oil sands over the past decade; another $364 billion is anticipated between 2012 and 2035. Investors far and wide are all hoping to "make hay while the sun shines," as one Canadian energy executive advised not so long ago.

Dusk?

Unfortunately, the sunlight may not be shining for much longer. In fact, the sun may soon be setting on Maple Street, where a series of positively nightmarish scenarios loom on the horizon.

First, foreign money pouring into the oil sector has pushed up the value of the Canadian dollar, with predictably dire consequences for Canada's manufactured exports. That's right: the dreaded Dutch disease (economists' diagnosis when a sharp inflow of foreign capital in the resource sector results in an overvalued currency, rendering exports uncompetitive and hollowing out the manufacturing sector). Canada has all the telltale symptoms: oil has swapped places with cars, and factories are being shuttered in Ontario, Canada's industrial heartland. "For every natural resource job that's been added in Canada since the end of 2007," *Bloomberg* notes, "more than 15 factory jobs have been lost."

A related, albeit less serious, ailment is battered-collective-ego syndrome, the result of our government's shamefully thuggish behavior during international climate summits. The precipitous fall from grace was captured by *Guardian* columnist George Monbiot's caustic comment in Copenhagen: "Until now I believed that the nation which has done most to sabotage a new climate change agreement was the United States. I was wrong. The real villain is Canada."

How bad is our international reputation? Well, since Canada withdrew from Kyoto—the only signatory to have done so—Canadian travelers abroad have been covering the maple leafs on their backpacks with American flags.

Is That a Carbon Bomb in Your Backyard?

Desperate to shed its bad-boy image and restore our national pride, Ottawa has been trying to bury any climate concerns in an avalanche of enthusiasm about the projected windfall. The oil sands, according to industry figures, will contribute $885 billion to the economy over a 20-year period, with $123 billion in royalty and tax revenues for Canada's federal and provincial governments.

But the benefits are not only monetary. The nation's "beating heart," as former Liberal leader Michael Ignatieff called the oil sands, will also supply the lifeblood of national unity, ensure both national and continental energy security, bolster Canada's productivity and competitiveness, sustain our social programs, stimulate innovation, lead the transition to a "green" future, and turn the country into a global energy powerhouse. Oh, and since our crude is more "ethical" than "conflict oil" ("whose revenues fund terrorism" in the Arab world, according to our environment minister), Canadian motorists will get to feel morally smug when they fill up at the pump.

Unfortunately for Ottawa, it's not the image of a "beating heart" that comes to mind when the public thinks of the oil sands. Instead, more and more Canadians are waking up to the realization that they may be sitting on the biggest "carbon bomb" on the continent. "By some calculations," environmental activist Bill McKibben writes, "the tar sands contain the equivalent of about 200 parts per million CO_2—or roughly half the current atmospheric concentration. Put another way, if we burn it, there's no way we can control climate change." Burning the oil sands would be "game over for the planet," adds Jim Hansen, head of the NASA Goddard Institute for Space Studies.

Ottawa's attempts to defuse the carbon bomb with carbon bombast, in short, are not working. The hydrocarbon hubris is only hardening Canada's reputation as an uncaring climate miscreant.

Mermaids, Avatars, and Other Terrorists

Worse yet, the din from anti-oil sands protesters has been getting so loud it's drowning out Ottawa's paeans to pipelines. And recent victories by environmentalists have "embolden[ed] those opposed to ... other new project developments," as Pat Daniel, president and CEO of Enbridge, has reluctantly admitted. This brings us to the most ominous scenario unfolding on Maple Street: the increasing difficulty of getting our crude to market.

This potential horror has officials in Ottawa scurrying for more effective ways to neutralize the fossil foes standing in the way of Canada's energy export markets. All have now agreed to ditch the risible campaign to claim the moral high-octane ground and instead to start playing hardball with anyone who fails to genuflect at the altar of Big Oil.

The new bullying has become so reflexive in Ottawa that when Foreign Affairs and International Trade recently announced it would be looking for martial-arts instructors to train its envoys to handle confrontations in "potentially dangerous situations," some immediately suspected the department had the next climate change talks in mind.

While officials haven't actually begun to engage in fisticuffs with opponents, they have been trying out a few wrestling moves, like the stranglehold. Among the victims are some of Big Oil's most feared adversaries—climate scientists. And the grip has been tightening: scientists working for the federal government can no longer speak freely to the press about their findings, especially those that contradict Ottawa's official oil sands narrative. From wildlife to water quality, any scientific finding implicating the oil sands must first be vetted by members of the prime minister's communications staff, who occasionally relax the chokehold and allow scientists to read carefully scripted media lies, er, "media lines." When the finding is too "controversial," scientists are required to recite the following: "I'm not in a position to answer that question, but I'd be happy to refer you to an appropriate spokesperson."

In the old Soviet Union, we called the practice censorship; in Canada it's called oil sands "messaging." The intent is the same—to prevent the public from getting overly alarmed about, say, the increased levels of cancer-causing contaminants in lakes surrounding the tar patch.

Ottawa has been heavy-handed with other, equally menacing figures, like Daryl Hannah, the star of the 1984 mermaid hit *Splash*, and environmentalist Bill McKibben. Both have been raising awareness of the potential environmental damage caused by the proposed Keystone XL pipeline.

In retaliation, the feds initially considered pulling all of Hannah's films from video stores across Canada (except for *Kill Bill*). But the scheme was unworkable, so they decided instead to create a counterterrorism unit (or so-called "Integrated National Security Enforcement Team") to keep a close eye on environmentalists (now listed alongside white supremacists as threats to national security). Some, apparently, have even proposed waterboarding Hannah if she shows up on this side of the border ... though questions are being raised about the effectiveness of the torture on mermaids.

Joining Hannah in Ottawa's bad books is Hollywood director James Cameron, who was recruited by oil executives as a potential ally. They had hoped a tour of the oil sands would inspire the director to use his cinematographic wizardry to transform toxic-tailings ponds into azure lakes rimmed by verdant fields. Perhaps a sequel to his recent science-fiction blockbuster? To their great disappointment, though, when he visited the future site of *Avatar-sands*, the title that actually came to mind was *Emission Impossible*. Cameron, who had already called the oil sands a "black eye" for Canada, declared himself "appalled" by the "devastation" when he saw it firsthand.

The director is reportedly being fitted for an orange jumpsuit somewhere in the southeastern end of Cuba.

Even the Big Banana Splits

Ottawa is also going after "enemies" in the corporate world: the self-described socially responsible corporations that have been proudly publicizing their efforts to achieve "carbon-neutral" growth or use "low carbon fuels" in their operations. Several are Fortune 500 companies, like Whole Foods Market, Bed Bath and Beyond, Avon, The Gap (including subsidiaries Old Navy and Banana Republic), and Walgreens, all of which have signed on to an anti-oil sands campaign organized by ForestEthics.

To prevent further corporate exposure to "misinformation," Harper has dispatched officials to "engage with" all the Fortune 500 companies. First on the list is Chiquita Brands, which has also snubbed the oil sands. Perhaps impressed by the company's use of paramilitaries to deal with opponents in Colombia (see Patricia

Rodriguez, "The Economics and Politics of Depropriation in the Other Colombia," *Dollars & Sense*, November/December 2010), Canadian officials are thinking of recruiting an elite squad to lean on other companies contemplating a boycott.

Then there are the growing ranks of institutional investors concerned over the long-term performance of companies operating in the oil sands. An international group of 49 ethical funds with investments in Alberta's oil sands has expressed concern that the environmental and social impacts of the oil sands may threaten its "long-term viability as an investment." When told that oil-sands crude had already been certified as "ethical" by Ottawa, the investment managers reportedly guffawed in unison.

The laughter abruptly stopped when they received a visit from a few gentlemen in camouflage fatigues.

Et Tu, Butte?

First there was Butte, Montana, where some of the earliest protests by environmentalists and landowners to stop the Keystone XL pipeline took place. Now there's Mountrail County, in the neighboring state of North Dakota, where extraction from the "Bakken play" oil deposit is centered. It is fast becoming the Canadian oiligarchy's worst nightmare. Currently, 99% of Canada's oil exports are destined for the United States, but our most important trading partner could be self-sufficient in energy by 2035, at least according to projections by the IEA. If trends in the United States continue, with domestic supply "continu[ing] to displace Canadian sources," as the IEA observes, one day our southern neighbor may no longer need Canada's crude. Gasp!

To make matters worse, a Canadian credit-rating agency recently determined that the Bakken play was a better investment than the Alberta oil sands. And Marathon Oil Corp. has publicly mused about pulling out of the oil sands to pursue the higher profits available in North Dakota.

These troubling developments come on the heels of several previous slights: Obama's delay of the Keystone XL, and the introduction of low-carbon fuel standards, now implemented or under consideration in fourteen U.S. states. Lorraine Mitchelmore, Royal Dutch Shell PLC's Canadian president, may have been understating things when she said the U.S. market is "not a given anymore."

Feeling betrayed and driven to despair, Prime Minister Harper has declared it a "national priority to ensure we have the capacity to export our energy products beyond the United States and specifically to Asia." Energy expert Daniel Yergin has also advised Canada to pursue the Asian market more vigorously.

Access to Asia, however, is far from a sure thing. Enbridge's Northern Gateway—the proposed pipeline connecting Alberta to Canada's west coast (where crude will be put on tankers destined for Asia)—is facing fierce resistance. Invigorated by their victory on Keystone, opposition groups are rallying in unprecedented numbers to stop the Northern Gateway pipeline. Adding to Ottawa's woes, aboriginal groups, concerned about treaty violations and potential oil spills on native land, are threatening to hold up current pipeline proposals for years in court battles.

As if these problems aren't bad enough, the existing pipeline network will be bursting at the seams by 2015 unless both the Keystone and Enbridge pipelines are laid, officials warn. Unfortunately, Canada's prison capacity is as inadequate as its pipeline capacity, making it impossible for the government to jail all the eco-terrorists preventing our crude from accessing other markets.

The Great Stick-y Up

Combined with the boom in shale-oil production in North Dakota, the lack of pipeline capacity is depressing the price of Canadian crude (which is confined to "oversupplied markets," according to the *Globe and Mail*). As of mid-December, a barrel of Western Canadian Select fetched only $47.20 (U.S.) a barrel, $40 less than the North American benchmark (West Texas intermediate) and a whopping $62 less than the global benchmark (Brent crude). In fact, oil-sands crude is so far below the market price it is now the cheapest in the world. That's great for our mostly American buyers, but economists are predicting Canada could forego as much as $1.3 trillion of GDP and $276 billion in taxes (from 2011 to 2035) if the current major pipeline expansion projects do not get built.

Two solutions have been floated to deal with the sleep-depriving scenarios unfolding in Canada. The first is a precision missile strike on oil facilities in North Dakota, which would eliminate the competition responsible for the oil glut and bolster prices for our crude. Why else, many have been wondering, has Ottawa been celebrating the war of 1812 (when we repelled an American invasion) and shopping around for a new fleet of stealth-fighter aircraft, if not to mobilize the nation and prepare for an attack?

Luckily for North Dakota, the plan has been scrapped, since we can't afford the planes. Besides, someone reminded Prime Minister Harper that the American military has undergone several upgrades since 1812. In any case, alienating one's largest trading partner is not considered sound economics.

The second solution is a trade embargo that would remove an essential Canadian import from American pantries. Remember our other dark, viscous export, maple syrup? Well Americans probably don't know it, but Canada is home to the "global strategic maple syrup reserve," which regulates the supply of about 70% of the world's maple syrup. The United States is the largest buyer.

Americans may also not know that the embargo is already being put into effect. It started a few months ago when newspapers around the world, including the *New York Times*, reported the heist of six million pounds of Canadian maple syrup. What the papers didn't report, though, was that the perpetrators have connections to the prime minister, who has concocted an elaborate maple-syrup-for-oil plot with extortionate intent. His plan is to take enough syrup off the market long enough to push prices sky high. This will drive American pancake eaters IHOP-ping mad and force the nation to accede to his key demand: buy our sticky bitumen at top-dollar prices if you want to buy our sticky syrup at market rates, too. And no waffling on it!

Sadly, the attempt at sweet revenge is expected to be shelved in the coming days: in his haste to hoard the syrup, the prime plotter forgot about that notorious sanction buster, Aunt Jemima. So only a sap would take his threat seriously.

Unless Schemin' Stephen comes up with a better plan very soon, the oil peddlers on Maple Street can expect many more sleepless nights. ❏

Sources: Tim Kiladze, "Why Canada's Oil Sands are So Highly Coveted," *Globe and Mail*, Sept. 26, 2012; "Oilsands Production Expected to Keep Growing," *Oilsands Review*, Jan. 2013; David Collyer, "Market Access will Remain a Driving Issue in 2013," *Oilweek*, Jan. 2013; Javier Blas, "Canada's Oil Now the Cheapest in the World," *Financial Times*, December 14, 2012; Paul Wells and Tamsin McMahon, "Oil Power," *Maclean's*, April 2, 2012, p.17; Shawn McCarthy, "World Needs Oil Sands Crude, IEA Economist Says," *Globe and Mail*, Nov. 26, 2012; Guy Chazan, "Oil Sands Are Shifting in Alberta," Wall Street Journal, Feb. 5, 2008; Steve Coll, *Private Empire: ExxonMobil and American Power* (New York: Penguin, 2012), 55-56; Tim Kiladze, "The Game Has Changed for Investors in Oil Sands," *Globe and Mail*, April 2, 2011; American Institute for Energy Research, "Our Northern Neighbor Moves to Cut Energy Taxes/Regulation to Boost Its Economy, But Not the U.S.," May 29, 2012 (instituteforenergyresearch.org); "Massive Oilsands Investments Will Benefit More Than Alberta," *Oilsands Review*, Jan. 2013; Rita Trichur, "Indian Firms Explore the Possibilities of Canadian Energy," *Globe and Mail*, Sept. 27, 2012; Mike De Souza, "Majority of Oil Sands Ownership and Profits are Foreign, Says Analysis," *National Post*, May 10, 2012; Clifford Krauss and Eric Lipton, "After the Boom in Natural Gas," *New York Times*, Oct. 20, 2012; Jeffrey Simpson, "Oil Sands Vision, Red Herrings and a Sea of Platitudes," *Globe and Mail*, Sept. 20, 2006; George Monbiot, "Canada's Image Lies in Tatters. It is Now to Climate What Japan is to Whaling," *Guardian*, Nov. 20, 2009; Steven Chase, "Peter Kent's Green Agenda: Clean up Oil Sands' Dirty Reputation," *Globe and Mail*, Jan. 6, 2011; Bill McKibben, "Barack Obama, the Carbon President," *Guardian*, June 3, 2011; James Hansen, "Game Over for the Climate," *New York Times*, May 9, 2012; Michael McCullough, "Oilsands in Canada: No Apologies," *Canadian Business*, Feb. 14, 2012; "Chuck Norris diplomacy? Foreign affairs Plans to Teach Diplomats Martial Arts," *Canadian Press*, Jan. 5, 2013; Ian Austen, "Oil Sands Industry in Canada Tied to Higher Carcinogen Level," *New York Times*, Jan. 7, 2013; Mike De Souza, "Harper Deploys Diplomats to Counter U.S. Climate Change Campaign," *National Post*, July 12, 2012; Bob Weber, "Group of 49 Ethical Funds Call for Greener Oilsands," *National Post*, Oct. 22, 2012; Geoffrey Vanderburg, "Looking Back," *Oilweek*, Jan. 2013; Paul Vieira, "Bakken Vs. Oil Sands? DBRS Sees More Value in North Dakota," *Wall Street Journal*, Dec. 13, 2012; Nathan Vanderklippe, "In U.S. Energy Renaissance, Flares of Fear for Alberta's Oil Patch," *Globe and Mail*, Nov. 17, 2012; Nathan Vanderklippe, "Federal Documents Spark Outcry by Oil Sands Critics," *Globe and Mail*, Jan. 26, 2012; Yadullah Hussain, "Canada's Place in New World Order," *National Post*, Dec. 10, 2012; Nathan VanderKlippe, "Opposition to Trans Mountain Pipeline nearing Northern Gateway Levels," *Globe and Mail*, Sept. 18, 2012; Shawn McCarthy and Nathan Vanderklippe, "Ottawa Failing to Consult First Nations on Pipelines, Former Tory Cabinet Minister Says," *Globe and Mail*, Sept. 27, 2012; Javier Blas, "Canada's Oil Now the Cheapest in the World," *Financial Times*, Dec. 14, 2012; Madhavi Acharya-Tom Yew, "Pipeline Expansion Should be 'a National Priority' for Canada: TD Economics," *Toronto Star*, Dec. 17, 2012.

Article 9.6

IS IT OIL?

BY ARTHUR MacEWAN
May/June 2003

Foreword, October 2013

The long U.S. military engagement in Iraq is over. There were no weapons of mass destruction, so the U.S. government shifted its rationale for the invasion to "regime change" and the establishment of a democratic Iraq. While regime change was accomplished, virtually no one would claim that a meaningful democracy was left in place as U.S. troops departed. Untold numbers of Iraqis died—estimates range from 100,000 upwards to one-million—and over 4,000 U.S. deaths were recorded.

From the perspective of U.S. and other internationally operating major oil companies, however, the U.S. invasion was a success—at least a partial success. ExxonMobil, Shell, BP, Haliburton and others are back in Iraq. Having secured contracts to extract the county's low-cost oil, they are expanding their operations in the country—and expanding their profits from those operations. Iraq's oil production in 2011 stood at 2,798 thousand barrels a day (bpd), surpassing output in all previous years except for the 2,832 bpd in 1989.

However, the western firms—the "majors" that have dominated the international oil industry for decades—have not obtained all they had hoped for when the invasion began a decade ago. Some U.S. firms—Chevron and ConocoPhillips—have failed to get contacts that they sought.

Most important, the major oil companies have had to share the lucrative Iraqi contacts with newer players in the global industry. Firms from China especially, but also from Russia, Norway, and elsewhere are getting in on the action. In 2013 China is the largest customer for Iraqi oil, buying nearly half of the country's production. Also, Chinese companies are increasingly making inroads into production by accepting less favorable terms—both lower profit rates and more restrictions—than U.S. firms. Apparently, Chinese firms, largely under the control of the Chinese government, are more concerned with securing sources of supply than with profits.

Substantial opposition to the foreign oil companies has developed in Iraq, including actions by unions and popular demonstrations. This opposition has had an impact in spite of its repression by the Iraqi government.

The Iraqi parliament has never enacted the Iraq Oil Law, a law which would secure the full opening of the country's oil reserves to the major firms and which the U.S. government continues to push.

Iraq events of the decade since this article was originally written have verified the importance of the interests of U.S.-based firms—and especially of the oil companies— in affecting the course of the U.S. government's global policies. At the same time, those

events have demonstrated the limits of U.S. power. Neither the government, with all its
military might, nor the firms can shape the world's economy exactly as they wish. There
are, it turns out, people involved, and they don't always cooperate.
—*Arthur MacEwan*

Before U.S. forces invaded Iraq, the United Nations inspection team that had been
searching the country for weapons of mass destruction was unable to find either
such weapons or a capacity to produce them in the near future. As of mid-April,
while the U.S. military is apparently wrapping up its invasion, it too has not found
the alleged weapons. The U.S. government continues to claim that weapons of mass
destruction exist in Iraq but provides scant evidence to substantiate its claim.

While weapons of mass destruction are hard to find in Iraq, there is one thing
that is relatively easy to find: oil. Lots of oil. With 112.5 billion barrels of proven
reserves, Iraq has greater stores of oil than any country except Saudi Arabia. This
combination—lots of oil and no weapons of mass destruction—begs the question:
Is it oil and not weapons of mass destruction that motivates the U.S. government's
aggressive policy towards Iraq?

The U.S. "Need" for Oil?

Much of the discussion of the United States, oil, and Iraq focuses on the U.S. economy's overall dependence on oil. We are a country highly dependent on oil, consuming far more than we produce. We have a small share, about 3%, of the world's total
proven oil reserves. By depleting our reserves at a much higher rate than most other
countries, the United States accounts for about 10% of world production. But, by
importing from the rest of the world, we can consume oil at a still higher rate: U.S. oil
consumption is over 25% of the world's total. (See the accompanying figures for these
and related data.) Thus, the United States relies on the rest of the world's oil in order
to keep its economy running—or at least running in its present oil-dependent form.
Moreover, for the United States to operate as it does and maintain current standards
of living, we need access to oil at low prices. Otherwise we would have to turn over a
large share of U.S. GDP as payment to those who supply us with oil.

Iraq could present the United States with supply problems. With a hostile government in Baghdad, the likelihood that the United States would be subject to some
sort of boycott as in the early 1970s is greater than otherwise. Likewise, a government in Baghdad that does not cooperate with Washington could be a catalyst to a
reinvigoration of the Organization of Petroleum Exporting Countries (OPEC) and
the result could be higher oil prices.

Such threats, however, while real, are not as great as they might first appear.
Boycotts are hard to maintain. The sellers of oil need to sell as much as the buyers need to buy; oil exporters depend on the U.S. market, just as U.S. consumers
depend on those exporters. (An illustration of this mutual dependence is provided
by the continuing oil trade between Iraq and the United States in recent years.

YEARS OF RESERVES AT CURRENT ANNUAL PRODUCTION RATES*

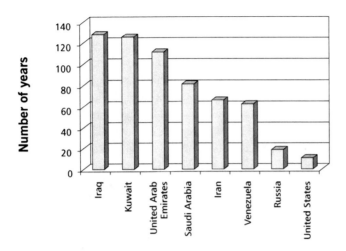

*The number of years it would take to use up existing reserves at current production rate. Past experience, however, suggests that more reserves will be found. In the 1980s, the world's proven reserves expanded by 47%, even as the consumption continued apace. With a more rapid rate of economic growth in the 1990s, and thus with the more rapid rate of oil consumption, the world's reserves rose by almost 5%.

Source: BP Statistical Review of World Energy 2002 <www.bp.com/centres/energy2002>

During 2001, while the two countries were in a virtual state of war, the United States bought 284 million barrels of oil from Iraq, about 7% of U.S. imports and almost a third of Iraq's exports.) Also, U.S. oil imports come from diverse sources, with less than half from OPEC countries and less than one-quarter from Persian Gulf nations.

Most important, ever since the initial surge of OPEC in the 1970s, the organization has followed a policy of price restraint. While price restraint may in part be a strategy of political cooperation, resulting from the close U.S.-Saudi relationship in particular, it is also a policy adopted because high prices are counter-productive for OPEC itself; high prices lead consumers to switch sources of supply and conserve energy, undercutting the longer term profits for the oil suppliers. Furthermore, a sudden rise in prices can lead to general economic disruption, which is no more desirable for the oil exporters than for the oil importers. To be sure, the United States would prefer to have cooperative governments in oil producing countries, but the specter of another boycott as in the 1970s or somewhat higher prices for oil hardly provides a rationale, let alone a justification, for war.

The Profits Problem

There is, however, also the importance of oil in the profits of large U.S. firms: the oil companies themselves (with ExxonMobil at the head of the list) but also the numerous drilling, shipping, refining, and marketing firms that make up the rest of the oil industry. Perhaps the most famous of this latter group, because former CEO Dick Cheney is now vice president, is the Halliburton Company, which supplies a wide range of equipment and engineering services to the industry. Even while many governments—Saudi Arabia, Kuwait, and Venezuela, for example—have taken ownership of their countries' oil reserves, these companies have been able to maintain their profits because of their decisive roles at each stage in the long sequence from exploration through drilling to refining and marketing. Ultimately, however, as with any resource-based industry, the monopolistic position—and thus the large profits—of the firms that dominate the oil industry depends on their access to the supply of the resource. Their access, in turn, depends on the relations they are able to establish with the governments of oil-producing countries.

From the perspective of the major U.S. oil companies, a hostile Iraqi government presents a clear set of problems. To begin with, there is the obvious: because Iraq has a lot of oil, access to that oil would represent an important profit-making opportunity. What's more, Iraqi oil can be easily extracted and thus produced at very low cost. With all oil selling at the same price on the world market, Iraqi oil thus presents opportunities for especially large profits per unit of production. According to the *Guardian* newspaper (London), Iraqi oil could cost as little as 97 cents a barrel to produce, compared to the UK's North Sea oil produced at $3 to $4 per barrel. As one oil executive told the *Guardian* last November, "Ninety cents a barrel for oil that sells for $30—that's the kind of business anyone would want to be in. A 97% profit margin—you can live with that." The *Guardian* continues: "The stakes are high. Iraq could be producing 8 million barrels a day within the decade. The math is impressive—8 million times 365 at $30 per barrel or $87.5 billion a year. Any share would be worth fighting for." The question for the oil companies is: what share will they be able to claim and what share will be claimed by the Iraqi government? The split

OIL CONSUMPTION 2001

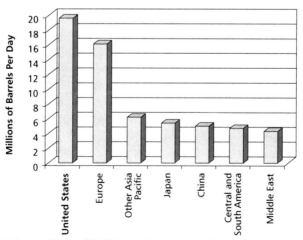

Source: BP Statistical Review of World Energy 2002 (www.bp.com/centres/energy2002

would undoubtedly be more favorable for the oil companies with a compliant U.S.-installed government in Baghdad.

Furthermore, the conflict is not simply one between the private oil companies and the government of Iraq. The U.S.-based firms and their British (and British-Dutch) allies are vying with French, Russian, and Chinese firms for access to Iraqi oil. During recent years, firms from these other nations signed oil exploration and development contracts with the Hussein government in Iraq, and, if there were no "regime change," they would preempt the operations of the U.S. and British firms in that country. If, however, the U.S. government succeeds in replacing the government of Saddam Hussein with its preferred allies in the Iraqi opposition, the outlook will change dramatically. According to Ahmed Chalabi, head of the Iraqi National Congress and a figure in the Iraqi opposition who seems to be currently favored by Washington, "The future democratic government in Iraq will be grateful to the United States for helping the Iraqi people liberate themselves and getting rid of Saddam.... American companies, we expect, will play an important and leading role in the future oil situation." (In recent years, U.S. firms have not been fully frozen out of the oil business in Iraq. For example, according to a June 2001 report in the *Washington Post*, while Vice President Cheney was CEO at Halliburton Company during the late 1990s, the firm operated through subsidiaries to sell some $73 million of oil production equipment and spare parts to Iraq.)

The rivalry with French, Russian and Chinese oil companies is in part driven by the direct prize of the profits to be obtained from Iraqi operations. In addition, in order to maintain their dominant positions in the world oil industry, it is important for the U.S. and British-based firms to deprive their rivals of the growth potential that access to Iraq would afford. In any monopolistic industry, leading firms need to deny their potential competitors market position and control of

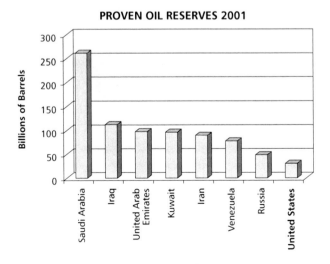

PROVEN OIL RESERVES 2001

Source: BP Statistical Review of World Energy 2002 (www.bp.com/centres/energy2002

new sources of supply; otherwise, those competitors will be in a better position to challenge the leaders. The British *Guardian* reports that the Hussein government is "believed to have offered the French company TotalFinaElf exclusive rights to the largest of Iraq's oil fields, the Majoon, which would more than double the company's entire output at a single stroke." Such a development would catapult TotalFinaElf from the second ranks into the first ranks of the major oil firms. The basic structure of the world oil industry would not change, but the sharing of power and profits among the leaders would be altered. Thus for ExxonMobil, Chevron, Shell and the other traditional "majors" in the industry, access to Iraq is a defensive as well as an offensive goal. ("Regime change" in Iraq will not necessarily provide the legal basis for cancellation of contracts signed between the Hussein regime and various oil companies. International law would not allow a new regime simply to turn things over to the U.S. oil companies. "Should 'regime change' happen, one thing is guaranteed," according to the *Guardian*, "shortly afterwards there will be the mother of all legal battles.")

Oil companies are big and powerful. The biggest, ExxonMobil, had 2002 profits of $15 billion, more than any other corporation, in the United States or in the world. Chevron-Texaco came in with $3.3 billion in 2002 profits, and Phillips-Tosco garnered $1.7 billion. British Petroleum-Amoco-Arco pulled in $8 billion, while Royal Dutch/Shell Group registered almost $11 billion. Firms of this magnitude have a large role affecting the policies of their governments, and, for that matter, the governments of many other countries.

With the ascendancy of the Bush-Cheney team to the White House in 2000, perhaps the relationship between oil and the government became more personal, but it was not new. Big oil has been important in shaping U.S. foreign policy since the end of the 19th century (to say nothing of its role in shaping other policy realms, particularly environmental regulation). From 1914, when the Marines landed at Mexico's Tampico Bay to protect U.S. oil interests, to the CIA-engineered overthrow of the Mosadegh government in Iran in 1953, to the close relationship with the oppressive Saudi monarchy through the past 70 years, oil and the interests of the oil companies have been central factors in U.S. foreign policy. Iraq today is one more chapter in a long story.

The Larger Issue

Yet in Iraq today, as in many other instances of the U.S. government's international actions, oil is not the whole story. The international policies of the U.S. government are certainly shaped in significant part by the interests of U.S.-based firms, but not only the oil companies. ExxonMobil may have had the largest 2002 profits, but there are many additional large U.S. firms with international interests: Citbank and the other huge financial firms; IBM, Microsoft, and other information technology companies; General Motors and Ford; Merck, Pfizer and the other pharmaceutical corporations; large retailers like MacDonald's and Walmart (and many more) depend on access to foreign markets and foreign sources of supply for large shares of their sales and profits.

The U.S. government (like other governments) has long defined its role in international affairs as protecting the interests of its nationals, and by far the largest interests of U.S. nationals abroad are the interests of these large U.S. companies. The day-to-day activities of U.S. embassies and consular offices around the world are dominated by efforts to further the interests of particular U.S. firms—for example, helping the firms establish local markets, negotiate a country's regulations, or develop relations with local businesses. When the issue is large, such as when governments in low-income countries have attempted to assure the availability of HIV-AIDS drugs in spite of patents held by U.S. firms, Washington steps directly into the fray. On the broadest level, the U.S. government tries to shape the rules and institutions of the world economy in ways that work well for U.S. firms. These rules are summed up under the heading of "free trade," which in practice means free access of U.S. firms to the markets and resources of the rest of the world.

In normal times, Washington uses diplomacy and institutions like the International Monetary Fund, the World Bank, and the World Trade Organization to shape the rules of the world economy. But times are not always "normal." When governments have attempted to remove their economies from the open system and break with the "rules of the game," the U.S. government has responded with overt or covert military interventions. Latin America has had a long history of such interventions, where Guatemala (1954), Cuba (1961), Chile (1973) and Nicaragua (1980s) provide fairly recent examples. The Middle East also provides several illustrations of this approach to foreign affairs, with U.S. interventions in Iran (1953), Lebanon (1958), Libya (1981), and now Iraq. These interventions are generally presented as efforts to preserve freedom and democracy, but, if freedom and democracy were actually the goals of U.S. interventions the record would be very different; both the Saudi monarchy and the Shah of Iran, in an earlier era, would then have been high on the U.S. hit list. (Also, as with maintaining the source of supply of oil, the U.S. government did not intervene in Guatemala in 1954 to maintain our supply of bananas; the profits of the United Fruit Company, however, did provide a powerful causal factor.)

The rhetorical rationale of U.S. foreign policy has seen many alterations and adjustments over the last century: at the end of the 19th century, U.S. officials spoke of the need to spread Christianity; Woodrow Wilson defined the mission as keeping the world safe for democracy; for most of the latter half of the 20th century, the fight against Communism was the paramount rationale; for a fleeting moment during the Carter administration, the protection of human rights entered the government's vocabulary; in recent years we have seen the war against drugs; and now we have the current administration's war against terrorism.

What distinguishes the current administration in Washington is neither its approach toward foreign affairs and U.S. business interests in general nor its policy in the Middle East and oil interests in particular. Even its rhetoric builds on well established traditions, albeit with new twists. What does distinguish the Bush administration is the clarity and aggressiveness with which it has put forth its goal of maintaining U.S. domination internationally. The "Bush Doctrine" that the administration has articulated claims legitimacy for pre-emptive action against those who might threaten U.S. interests, and it is clear from the statement of that doctrine in last September's issuance of *The National Security Strategy of the United States of America* that "U.S. interests" includes economic interests.

The economic story is never the whole story, and oil is never the whole economic story. In the particular application of U.S. power, numerous strategic and political considerations come into play. With the application of the Bush Doctrine in the case of Iraq, the especially heinous character of the Hussein regime is certainly a factor, as is the regime's history of conflict with other nations of the region (at times with U.S. support) and its apparent efforts at developing nuclear, chemical, and biological weapons; certainly the weakness of the Iraqi military also affects the U.S. government's willingness to go to war. Yet, as September's *Security Strategy* document makes clear, the U.S. government is concerned with domination and a major factor driving that goal of domination is economic. In the Middle East, Iraq and elsewhere, oil—or, more precisely, the profit from oil— looms large in the picture. ❏

An earlier version of this article was prepared for the newsletter of the Joiner Center for War and Social Consequences at the University of Massachusetts-Boston. This article was originally prepared largely before the start of the war on Iraq.

Chapter 10

GLOBAL ECONOMIC CRISIS

Article 10.1

PUTTING THE "GLOBAL" IN THE GLOBAL ECONOMIC CRISIS

BY SMRITI RAO

November/December 2009; updated, October 2013

There is no question that the current economic crisis originated in the developed world, and primarily in the United States. Much of the analysis of the crisis has thus focused on institutional failures within the United States and there is, rightly, tremendous concern about high rates of unemployment and underemployment within the country. But after three decades of globalization, what happens in the United States does not stay in the United States and the actions of traders in New York City will mean hunger for children in Nairobi. We now know what crisis looks like in the age of globalization and it is not pretty.

The recent economic crisis of 2007-09 was uniquely a child of the neoliberal global order. For developing countries the key elements of neoliberalism have consisted of trade liberalization and an emphasis on export growth; reductions in government spending on subsidies and public sector wages; a greater reliance on the market for determining the price of everything from the currency exchange rate to water from the tap and, last but not least, economy-wide privatization and deregulation. In each case, the aim was also to promote cross-border flows of good, services and capital—although not quite as much of people.

Despite *New York Times* columnist Thomas Friedman's assertions of a "flat" world, this age of globalization did not in fact eliminate global inequality. Indeed if we exclude China and India, inter-country inequality actually increased during this period. These asymmetries in economic and political power across countries were in turn reflected in the asymmetrical flows of resources globally. The globalization of the last 30 years was predicated upon the extraction by the developed world of the natural resources, cheap labor and, in particular, capital of the developing world, via financial markets that siphoned the world's savings for U.S. middle-class consumption. What could be more ironic than the billions of dollars in capital flowing every year from developing countries with unfunded domestic development projects to developed countries, which then failed to meet even their minimum obligations with respect to foreign aid? Africa, for example, has actually been a net creditor to the United States for some time, suggesting that the underlying dynamic of the world economy today is not that different from age-old colonialism.

These "reverse flows" are partly the result of developing-country attempts to ward off balance-of-payment crises by holding large foreign exchange reserves. Within the United States, this capital helped sustain indebted households, corporations, and governments, exacerbating the debt bubble of the 2000s. Meanwhile, the global "race to the bottom" among developing-county exporters ensured that the prices of most manufactured goods and services remained low, taking the threat of inflation off the table and enabling the U.S. Federal Reserve to keep interest rates low and facilitate the housing bubble. Once the debt bubble finally burst, it was no surprise that the crisis was transmitted back to the global South at record speed.

The Extent of the Impact

We currently have consistent cross-country macroeconomic data from 2008 to 2011 that allow us to estimate the relative slowdown in real GDP growth by country, when compared to average GDP growth in the preceding three years (2005-2007). Data are available for 178 developed and developing countries.

Overall, GDP growth for these 178 countries fell by 1.4 percentage points in 2008 and 5.7 percentage points in 2009, compared to the average for 2005-2007. Despite some recovery in 2010 and 2011, the average growth rate over 2010-11 was still 2 percentage points below the 2005-07 average. The average growth rate for 2010-11 was significantly correlated with the average for 2008-09, suggesting that countries that suffered the largest economic slowdowns in 2008-09 were not able to significantly reverse that trend in 2010-11. According to the International Labor Organization, global unemployment jumped by 10.7 million in 2008 alone.

The initial impact in 2008 and 2009 was greatest in Eastern Europe and Central Asia. For 2008-09, seven of the top ten countries by steepest relative declines in real GDP were from the Eastern Europe/Central Asia region (Table 1). Joined by Ireland, this is a list of global high-fliers—countries that had very high rates of growth, as well as countries that globalized rapidly and enthusiastically in the last decade and a half. Antigua and Angola were also very dependent on the global economy, relying heavily on tourism and commodity exports of oil and diamonds respectively, until the crisis intervened. This pattern of globalizers being most affected by the crisis is no accident. Even allowing for the recovery in 2010-11, if we rank these 178 countries by relative declines in GDP growth over the entire 2008-11 period, as well by their pre-crisis exports as a percentage of GDP (average from 2005-07), we find a correlation between the two. The top 50 countries in terms of export shares of GDP actually saw larger relative declines in GDP than those ranked lower (Table 2). It turns out that each of the three primary channels through which the crisis was transmitted from the United States to other countries was

TABLE 1: STEEPEST DECLINES IN ECONOMIC GROWTH

Top ten countries by decline real GDP growth, 2008-9 average vs. 2005-07 average.		
	Country	Change in 2008-9 real GDP growth compared to 2005-07 (percentage points)
1	Latvia	-21.4
2	Estonia	-17.7
3	Armenia	-17.3
4	Azerbaijan	-16.0
5	Lithuania	-14.2
6	Antigua/Barbuda	-12.8
7	Ukraine	-12.2
8	Angola	-11.7
9	Georgia	-11.2
10	Ireland	-9.8

Source: Author's calculations based on data from World Economic Outlook(WEO) Database, April 2013.

TABLE 2: EXPORTS AND FOREIGN INVESTMENT

Change in 2008-11 real GDP growth vs. 2005-07 average (percentage points) for countries ranked by:		
	Export share of GDP	FDI share of GDP
Average, top 50 countries	-3.7	-3.3
Average, countries 51-100	-2.3	-3.0
Average, remaining countries	-2.1	-2.1
Total number of countries	167	171

Source: Author's calculations based on data from WEO Database, April 2013 and the De Facto Classification of Exchange Rate Regimes and Monetary Policy Frameworks as of April 31, 2008. IMF.

a direct outcome of the policies countries were urged and sometimes coerced into adopting, with assurances that this particular form of globalization was the best way to build a healthy and prosperous economy (see Figure 1, p. 262).

Transmission Channels of the Crisis

Lowered exports and remittances. The recession in the United States and Europe hit exports from the developing world hard. Globally, trade in goods and services did rise by 3% in 2008, but that was compared to increases of 10% and 7% in the previous two years. Within the United States, the world's most important importer, imports dropped by an unprecedented 30% between 2008 and 2009. For countries ranging from Pakistan to Cameroon, this meant lower foreign exchange earnings and employment and a slowdown in economic growth.

Meanwhile, for many developing countries, the emphasis on export promotion resulted in the increasing export of people, rather than goods and services. Remittance flows from temporary and permanent migrants accounted for 25% of net inflows of private capital to the global South in 2007. These flows were also affected by the crisis, although they proved more resilient than other sources of private capital.

Migrant workers in construction, in particular, found that they were no longer able to find work and send money back home, and countries in Latin America saw sharp declines in remittance inflows. However, as Indian economist Jayati Ghosh points out, women migrants working as maids, nurses, and nannies in the West were not hit as hard by the recession. This meant that remittance flows to countries with primarily female migrants, such as Sri Lanka and the Phillipines, were not as badly affected. The Middle Eastern countries that were important host countries for many Asian migrants were also relatively shielded from the crisis. Interestingly, the number of migrants even in hard-hit countries did not decrease, with most migrants choosing to wait out the crisis. As a result, for the developing world as a whole, remittances actually rose in 2008. Given that other private capital flows declined sharply post-crisis, remittances accounted for 46% of net private capital inflows to the developing world in 2008.

Given that remittances were, on average, more stable than other sources of foreign exchange earnings, the ranking of countries by relative GDP decline do not correlate quite as clearly with the ranking of countries by share of remittances in GDP (Table 2).

Outflows of portfolio capital. In the boom years up to 2007, developing countries were encouraged to liberalize their financial sectors. This meant removing regulatory barriers to the inflow (and outflow) of foreign investors and their money. While some foreign investors did put money into buying actual physical assets in the developing world, a substantial portion of foreign capital came in the form of portfolio capital—short-term investments in stock and real estate markets. This money is called "hot money" for a reason—it tends to be incredibly mobile, and its mobility has been enhanced by the systematic dismantling of various government restrictions (capital controls) that prevented this money from both entering and leaving countries at the speed it can today.

FIGURE 1: THE CRISIS AND IMF POLICIES: MAKING THE LINKS

Lowered exports, remittances ("openness") +

Outflows of portfolio capital ("openness" + no capital controls) =

Depreciating currencies (floating exchange rates) ⇨

Worsening current account balances/debt burdens +

Falling flows of FDI and development aid +

"Inflation targeting" and "fiscal restraint"

After early 2008, around the time of the collapse of the U.S. investment bank and brokerage, various global financial powerhouses began pulling their money out of developing-country markets. The pace of the pullout only accelerated after the crash in September of that year. One consequence for developing countries was a fall in stock-market indices that, in turn, depressed growth. Another was that as these foreign investors converted their krona, rupees, or rubles into dollars in order to leave, the value of the local currency got pushed down.

The IMF has long touted the virtues of allowing freely floating exchange rates, where market forces determine the value of the currency. In the aftermath of the financial crisis, however, this meant a sharp depreciation in the value of local currencies relative to the dollar. This, in turn, meant that every gallon of oil priced in dollars would require that many more rupees to buy. Similarly, any dollar-denominated debt a country held became harder to repay. The dollar cost of imports and debt servicing went up, just as exports and remittances—the ability to earn those dollars—were falling.

Once again, Table 3 (p. 264) tells us that countries with "floating" exchange rates (i.e., market determined exchange rates) were harder hit post-recession.

Falling flows of FDI and development aid. Meanwhile, one other source of foreign exchange, foreign investment in actual physical assets such as factories, known as foreign direct investment (FDI), has been stagnant as companies across the world shelved expansion plans. The signs of vulnerability are evident in the fact that countries most dependent upon FDI inflows (as a percentage of GDP) between 2005 and 2007 also suffered greater relative GDP declines over the period 2008-11 (Table 2).

Developed countries have also cut back on foreign-aid budgets, citing the cost of domestic stimulus programs and reduced tax revenues. The countries impacted are among the poorest in the world. Given that this long period of economic stagnation means that developing-country governments have lost domestic tax and other revenues, falling aid flows hurt even more. The importance of continued aid flows can be seen in the fact that higher levels of aid per capita from 2005 to 2007 were actually negatively associated with relative GDP decline in 2008 (Table 2). This may be partly due to the fact that these countries already had low or negative rates of GDP growth, so that 2008 declines were smaller relative to that baseline. Nevertheless, aid flows appear to have protected the most vulnerable countries from even greater economic disaster. In fact, highly indebted poor countries (HIPCs) actually saw an increase of one percentage point in GDP growth rates in 2008 when compared to the 2005-07 average.

Conclusions

The simultaneous transmission of the crisis through these three channels left developing countries reeling. What made the situation even worse is that, unlike developed countries, developing countries were not able to afford generous stimulus packages (China is an important exception). Meanwhile, the IMF and its allies, rather than supporting developing-country governments in their quest to stimulate domestic demand and investment, hindered the process by insisting on the same old policy mix of deficit

TABLE 3: EXCHANGE RATE AND FISCAL POLICY

Average change in 2008-11 real GDP growth vs. 2005-07 average (percentage points) for country groupings:			
Exchange Rate Policy		**Fiscal Policy**	
Countries with fixed exchange rate	-2.6	Countries with no inflation targeting	-2.6
Countries with managed float or other mixed policy	-2.7	Countries with inflation targeting	-3.3
Countries with freely floating exchange rate	-2.9		
Total number of countries	**178**		**178**

Source: Author's calculations based on data from WEO Database, April 2013 and the De Facto Classification of Exchange Rate Regimes and Monetary Policy Frameworks as of April 31, 2008. IMF.

reductions and interest-rate hikes. The European Union provides an illustration of how ruinous this policy mix can be in the developed world; meanwhile, in the developing world, countries that followed IMF advice and adopted "inflation targeting" before the crisis actually suffered greater relative GDP declines once the crisis hit (Table 3).

The tragedy of course is that—while the crumbling remnants of the welfare state do protect citizens of the developed world from the very worst effects of the crisis—developing countries have been urged for two decades to abandon the food and fuel subsidies and public-sector provision of essential services that are the only things that come close to resembling a floor for living standards. They were told they didn't need that safety net, that it only got in the way, and then of course, they were free to fall.

It is worth recalling that the end of the previous "age of globalization," signaled by the Great Depression, led to a renewed role for the public sector the world over and an attempt to achieve growth alongside self-reliance. Led by Latin America, developing countries attempted to prioritize building a domestic producer and consumer base. In the long run, perhaps this crisis will result in a similar rethinking of the currently dominant model of development. In the short run, however, the world seems ready to stand by and watch while the poor and vulnerable in developing countries, truly innocent bystanders, suffer. ❑

Sources: Dilip Ratha, Sanket Mohapatra, and Ani Silwal, "Migration and Development Brief 10," Migration and Remittances Team, Development Prospects Group, World Bank, July 13, 2009; Atish R. Ghosh et al. 2009, "Coping with the Crisis: Policy Options for Emerging Market Countries," IMF Staff Position Note, SPN/09/08, April 23, 2009; World Bank, "Swimming Against the Tide: How Developing Countries Are Coping with the Global Crisis," Background Paper prepared by World Bank Staff for the G20 Finance Ministers and Central Bank Governors Meeting, Horsham, United Kingdom on March 13-14, 2009; Jayati Ghosh, "Current Global Financial Crisis: Curse or Blessing in Disguise for Developing Countries?" Presentation prepared for the IWG-GEM Workshop, Levy Economics Institute, New York, June 29-July 10, 2009.

Article 10.2

(ECONOMIC) FREEDOM'S JUST ANOTHER WORD FOR...CRISIS-PRONE

BY JOHN MILLER
September/October 2009

In "Capitalism in Crisis," his May op-ed in the *Wall Street Journal*, U.S. Court of Appeals judge and archconservative legal scholar Richard Posner argued that "a capitalist economy, while immensely dynamic and productive, is not inherently stable." Posner, the long-time cheerleader for deregulation added, quite sensibly, "we may need more regulation of banking to reduce its inherent riskiness."

That may seem like a no-brainer to you and me, right there in the middle of the road with yellow lines and dead armadillos, as Jim Hightower is fond of saying. But *Journal* readers were having none of it. They wrote in to set Judge Posner straight. "It is not free markets that fail, but government-controlled ones," protested one reader.

And why wouldn't they protest? The *Journal* has repeatedly told readers that "economic freedom" is "the real key to development." And each January for 15 years now the *Journal* tries to elevate that claim to a scientific truth by publishing a summary of the Heritage Foundation Index of Economic Freedom, which they assure readers proves the veracity of the claim. But in the hands of the editors of the *Wall Street Journal* and the researchers from the Heritage Foundation, Washington's foremost right-wing think tank, the Index of Economic Freedom is a barometer of corporate and entrepreneurial freedom from accountability rather than a guide to which countries are giving people more control over their economic lives and over the institutions that govern them.

This January was no different. "The 2009 Index provides strong evidence that the countries that maintain the freest economies do the best job promoting prosperity for all citizens," proclaimed this year's editorial, "Freedom is Still the Winning Formula." But with economies across the globe in recession, the virtues of free markets are a harder sell this year. That is not lost on *Wall Street Journal* editor Paul Gigot, who wrote the foreword to this year's report. Gigot allows that, "ostensibly free-market policymakers in the U.S. lost their monetary policy discipline, and we are now paying a terrible price." Still Gigot maintains that, "the *Index of Economic Freedom* exists to chronicle how steep that price will be and to point the way back to policy wisdom."

What the Heritage report fails to mention is this: while the global economy is in recession, many of the star performers in the Economic Freedom Index are tanking. Fully one half of the ten hardest-hit economies in the world are among the 30 "free" and "mostly free" economies at the top of the Economic Freedom Index rankings of 179 countries.

Here's the damage, according to the IMF. Singapore, the Southeast Asian trading center and perennial number two in the Index, will suffer a 10.0% drop in output this year. Slotting in at number 4, Ireland, the so-called Celtic tiger, has seen its rapid export-led growth give way to an 8.0% drop in output. Number 13 and number 30, the foreign-direct-investment-favored Baltic states, Estonia and Lithuania, will each endure a 10.0% loss of output this year. Finally, the economy of Iceland, the loosely regulated European banking center that sits at number 14 on the Index, will contract 10.6% in 2009.

As a group, the Index's 30 most "free" economies will contract 4.1% in 2009. All of the other groups in the Index ("moderately free," "mostly unfree," and "repressed" economies) will muddle through 2009 with a much smaller loss of output or with moderate growth. The 67 "mostly unfree" countries in the Index will post the fastest growth rate for the year, 2.3%.

So it seems that if the Index of Economic Freedom can be trusted, then Judge Posner was not so far off the mark when he described capitalism as dynamic but "not inherently stable." That wouldn't be so bad, one *Journal* reader pointed out in a letter: "Economic recessions are the cost we pay for our economic freedom and economic prosperity is the benefit. We've had many more years of the latter than the former."

Not to Be Trusted

But the Index of Economic Freedom cannot and should not be trusted. How free or unfree an economy is according to the Index seems to have little do with how quickly it grows. For instance, economist Jeffery Sachs found "no correlation" between a country's ranking in the Index and its per capita growth rates from 1995 to 2003. Also, in this year's report North America is the "freest" of its six regions of the world, but logged the slowest average rate over the last five years, 2.7% per annum. The Asia-Pacific region, which is "less free" than every other region except Sub-Saharan Africa according to the Index, posted the fastest average growth over the last five years, 7.8% per annum. That region includes several of fastest growing of the world's economies, India, China, and Vietnam, which ranked 123, 132, and 145 respectively in the Index and were classified as "mostly unfree." And there are

ECONOMIC FREEDOM AND ECONOMIC GROWTH IN 2009	
Degree of Economic Freedom	IMF Projected Growth Rate for 2009
"Free" (7 Countries)	-4.54%
"Mostly Free" (23 Counties)	-3.99%
"Moderately Free" (53 Countries)	-0.92%
"Mostly Unfree" (67 Countries)	+2.31%
"Repressed" (69 Counties)	+1.65%

Sources: International Monetary Fund, *World Economic Outlook,: Crisis and Recovery*, April 2009, Tables A1, A2, A3; Terry Miller and Kim R. Holmes, eds., *2009 Index of Economic Freedom*, heritage.org/Index/, Executive Summary.

plenty of relatively slow growers among the countries high up in the Index, including Switzerland (which ranks ninth).

The Heritage Foundation folks who edited the Index objected to Sachs' criticisms, pointing out that they claimed "a close relationship" between *changes* in economic freedom, not the *level* of economic freedom, and growth. But even that claim is fraught with problems. Statistically it doesn't hold up. Economic journalist Doug Henwood found that improvements in the Index and GDP growth from 1997 to 2003 could explain no more than 10% of GDP growth. In addition, even a tight correlation would not resolve the problem that many of the fastest growing economies are "mostly unfree" according to the Index.

But even more fundamental flaws with the Index render any claim about the relationship between prosperity and economic freedom, as measured by the Heritage Foundation, questionable. Consider just two of the ten components the Economic Freedom Index uses to rank countries: fiscal freedom and government size.

Fiscal freedom (what we might call the "hell-if-I'm-going-to-pay-for-government" index) relies on the top income tax and corporate income tax brackets as two of its three measures of the tax burden. These are decidedly flawed measures even if all that concerned you was the tax burden of the rich and owners of corporations (or the super-rich). Besides ignoring the burden of other taxes, singling out these two top tax rates don't get at effective corporate and income tax rates, or how much of a taxpayer's total income goes to paying these taxes. For example, on paper U.S. corporate tax rates are higher than those in Europe. But nearly one half of U.S. corporate profits go untaxed. The effective rate of taxation on U.S. corporate profits currently stands at 15%, far below the top corporate tax rate of 35%. And relative to GDP, U.S. corporate income taxes are no more than half those of other OECD countries.

Even their third measure of fiscal freedom, government tax revenues relative to GDP, bears little relationship to economic growth. After an exhaustive review, economist Joel Selmrod, former member of the Reagan Treasury Department, concludes that the literature reveals "no consensus" about the relationship between the level of taxation and economic growth.

The Index's treatment of government size, which relies exclusively on the level of government spending relative to GDP, is just as flawed as the fiscal freedom index. First, "richer countries do not tax and spend less" than poorer countries, reports economist Peter Lindhert. Beyond that, this measure does not take into account how the government uses its money. Social spending programs—public education, child-care and parental support, and public health programs—can make people more productive and promote economic growth. That lesson is not lost on Hong Kong and Singapore, number one and number two in the index. They both provide universal access to health care, despite the small size of their governments.

The size-of-government index also misses the mark because it fails to account for industrial policy. This is a serious mistake, because it overestimates the degree to which some of the fastest growing economies of the last few decades, such as Taiwan and South Korea, relied on the market and underestimates the positive role that government played in directing economic development in those countries by guiding investment and protecting infant industries.

This flaw is thrown into sharp relief by the recent report of the World Bank's Commission on Growth and Development. That group studied 13 economies that grew at least 7% a year for at least 25 years since 1950. Three of the Index's "free" and "mostly free" countries made the list (Singapore, Hong Kong, and Japan) but so did three of the index's "mostly unfree" countries (China, Brazil, and Indonesia). While these rapid growers were all export-oriented, their governments "were not free-market purists," according the Commission's report. "They tried a variety of policies to help diversify exports or sustain competitiveness. These included industrial policies to promote new investments."

Still More

Beyond all that, the Index says nothing about political freedom. Consider once again the two city-states, Hong Kong and Singapore, which top their list of free countries. Both are only "partially free" according to Freedom House, which the editors have called "the Michelin Guide to democracy's development." Hong Kong is still without direct elections for it legislatures or its chief executive and a proposed internal security laws threaten press and academic freedom as well as political dissent. In Singapore, freedom of the press and rights to demonstrate are limited, films, TV and the like are censored, and preventive detention is legal.

So it seems that the Index of Economic Freedom in practice tells us little about the cost of abandoning free market policies and offers little proof that government intervention into the economy would either retard economic growth or contract political freedom. In actuality, this rather objective-looking index is a slip-shod measure that would seem to have no other purpose than to sell the neoliberal policies that brought on the current crisis, and to stand in the way of policies that might correct the crisis. ❑

Sources: "Capitalism in Crisis," by Richard A Posner, *Wall Street Journal*, 5/07/09; "Letters: Recessions are the Price We Pay for Economic Freedom," *Wall Street Journal*, 5/19/09/; "Freedom is Still the Winning Formula," by Terry Miller, *Wall Street Journal*, 1/13/09 ; "The Real Key to Development," by Mary Anastasia O'Grady, *Wall Street Journal*, 1/15/08; Terry Miller and Kim R. Holmes, eds., *2009 Index of Economic Freedom*, heritage.org/Index/; Freedom House, "Freedom in the World 2009 Survey," freedomhouse.org; Joel Selmrod and Jon Bakija, *Taxing Ourselves: A Citizen's Guide to the Debate over Taxes*, MIT Press, 2008; International Monetary Fund, *World Economic Outlook,: Crisis and Recovery*, April 2009; Peter H. Lindert, *Growing Public*, Cambridge University Press, 2004; Doug Henwood, "*Laissez-faire* Olympics: An LBO Special Report," leftbusinessobserver.com, March 26, 2005; Jeffrey Sachs, *The End of Poverty: Economic Possibilities for Our Time*, Penguin, 2005.

Article 10.3

THE GIANT POOL OF MONEY

BY ARTHUR MacEWAN
September/October 2009

Dear Dr. Dollar:

On May 9, the public radio program This American Life broadcast an explanation of the housing crisis with the title: "The Giant Pool of Money." With too much money looking for investment opportunities, lots of bad investments were made—including the bad loans to home buyers. But where did this "giant pool of money" come from? Was this really a source of the home mortgage crisis?

—Gail Radford, Buffalo, N.Y.

The show was both entertaining and interesting. A good show, but maybe a bit more explanation will be useful.

There was indeed a "giant pool of money" that was an important part of the story of the home mortgage crisis—well, not "money" as we usually think of it, but financial assets, which I'll get to in a moment. And that pool of money is an important link in the larger economic crisis story.

The giant pool of money was the build-up of financial assets—U.S. Treasury bonds, for example, and other assets that pay a fixed income. According to the program, the amount of these assets had grown from roughly $36 trillion in 2000 to $70 trillion in 2008. That's $70 *trillion*, with a T, which is a lot of money, roughly the same as total world output in 2008.

These financial assets built up for a number of reasons. One was the doubling of oil prices (after adjusting for inflation) between 2000 and 2007, largely due to the U.S. invasion of Iraq. This put a lot of money in the hands of governments in oil-producing countries and private individuals connected to the oil industry.

A second factor was the large build up of reserves (i.e., the excess of receipts from exports over payments for imports) by several low-income countries, most notably China. One reason some countries operated in this manner was simply to keep the cost of their currency low in terms of U.S. dollars, thus maintaining demand for their exports. (Using their own currencies to buy dollars, they were increasing both the supply of their currencies and the demand for dollars; this pushed the price of their currencies down and of dollars up.) But another reason was to protect themselves from the sort of problems they had faced in the early 1980s, when world recession cut their export earnings and left them unable to meet their import costs and pay their debts—thus the debt crisis of that era.

This build-up of dollar reserves by governments (actually, central banks) of other countries was also a result of the budgetary deficits of the Bush administration.

Spending more than it was taking in as taxes (after the big tax cuts for the wealthy and with the heavy war spending), the Bush administration needed to borrow. Foreign governments, by buying the U.S. securities, were providing the loans.

Still a third factor explaining the giant pool of financial assets was the high level of inequality within the United States and elsewhere in the global economy. Since 1993, half of all income gains in the United States have gone to the highest-income 1% of households. While the very rich spend a good share of their money on mansions, fancy cars, and other luxuries, there was plenty more money for them to put into investments—the stock market but also fixed-income securities (i.e., bonds).

So there is the giant pool of money or, again, of financial assets.

The financial assets became a problem for two connected reasons. First, in the recovery following the 2001 recession, economic growth was very slow; there were thus very limited real investment opportunities. Between 2001 and 2007, private fixed investment (adjusted for inflation) grew by only 11%, whereas in the same number of years following the recession of the early 1990s, investment grew by 59%.

Second, in an effort to stimulate more growth, the Federal Reserve kept interest rates very low. But the low interest rates meant low returns on financial assets—U.S. government bonds in particular, but financial assets in general. So the holders of financial assets went searching for new investment opportunities, which, as the radio program explained, meant pushing money into high-risk mortgages. The rest, as they say, is history.

So the giant pool of money was the link that tied high inequality, the war, and rising financial imbalances in the world economy (caused in large part by the U.S. government's budgetary policies) to the housing crisis and thus to the more general financial crisis.

Again, check out the *This American Life* episode for the details of how this "link" operated. It's quite a story! ❏

Article 10.4

IN CHINA, CHANGE—AND UNCERTAINTY—ARE IN THE AIR

BY SARA HSU

September 2013

Concerns over China's economy are all over the news—stories like "Feeling the Heat from China's Slowdown," "China's Economic Hard Landing," and "China's Slowdown Digs a Hole for U.S. Industrials" are now everywhere. One of the most pressing questions is: Will China face a massive slowdown in economic growth? Here, we explain why this is such a concern and consider what possibilities exist for continued growth.

First, a primer on growth and the way it is tabulated: Growth simply refers to the change in GDP, usually from one year to the next. GDP is calculated any of three different ways—the income approach (how much individuals and entities earn in a period), the expenditure approach (how much is spent in a period), or the production approach (how much value is added during the production process). If we focus on a single approach—say, the expenditure approach—we can look at the individual components to determine how China can improve its GDP—and therefore growth—outlook.

Expenditures include spending on consumption (C), fixed investment (I), government spending (G), and net exports (exports (X) minus imports (M)), that is:

$$Y = C + I + G + (X - M)$$

Until the global economic crisis hit in 2008, China had performed well in terms of net exports and consumption, producing a prodigious amount of goods for itself and the rest of the world. After the crisis hit, China bolstered its level of GDP growth even in the face of slowing export demand from abroad by increasing government stimulus. Over this period, too, fixed investment in real estate and manufacturing continued to rise.

As government stimulus declines (with new stimulus limited in size), fixed investment faces a likely slowdown, and export demand struggles to regain its pre-crisis level, China faces a rush to "rebalance."

The new administration was to focus on building domestic consumption within a period of five to ten years—now the pressure is on to make it appear immediately. This is a nearly impossible task. With fewer jobs being created and no additional ongoing sources of income for citizens, consumption is doomed to slow in the short run. This would increase unemployment and poverty, and reduce Chinese trade demand from the rest of the world. Global growth would fall.

The current experiment with boosting on pushing up domestic consumption is China's urbanization policy that has moved rural residents to urban areas, with a small chunk of cash (not enough to cover housing costs) and no jobs in place. The process has started in Shaanxi Province and will likely be announced formally in the October Third Plenary Meeting of the Central Committee of the Chinese Communist Party. Domestic consumption has (surprise!) not been boosted by the urbanization process since residents lack a steady source of income.

So what can be done? There are two sources of growth that may "save" China from a woeful pace of growth. The first is further government stimulus. The government has committed to some stimulus to shore up the economy to make up for a shortfall in GDP. Further stimulus will bolster this commitment and keep the economy going. The second is a rebound in export demand. If Europe can pull out of its ongoing crisis and increase its demand for Chinese products, all may not be lost. This would be the easiest way to support China's flagging economy until the administration is able to restructure China's economy toward domestic consumption. Restructuring, after all, takes time, and time, if it can be bought, will be worth every penny.In the meantime, some analysts believe that a sudden contraction in GDP may be in the works. Although Premier Li's government is not expected to allow for a "hard landing," its dedication to restructuring will usher the Chinese economy into new territory. Change—and uncertainty—are in the air as we anxiously await the formalized plans. ❑

Article 10.5

GREECE AND THE EUROZONE CRISIS BY THE NUMBERS

BY GERALD FRIEDMAN
July/August 2012

With its surging debt and sinking economy, Greece has been held up as the poster-child for the need for fiscal discipline and austerity. Instead, it should be seen as a case study in the danger of neoliberal financial integration. Greece's economic problems stem from its joining the eurozone, a single-currency region where monetary policy is managed by a largely independent European Central Bank (ECB). The ECB is based in Frankfurt, Germany, and is committed to maintaining stable prices without regard for levels of unemployment or economic growth. Within the eurozone, Greek industry has been unable to compete with its German competitors. If Greece had retained an independent currency, it could have maintained balanced trade and supported domestic industries and employment by devaluing its currency. Membership in the European Union and the eurozone, though, prevents Greece from adjusting its currency value or otherwise imposing trade restraints, even in the face of a rising tide of German imports which have devastated much of Greek industry.

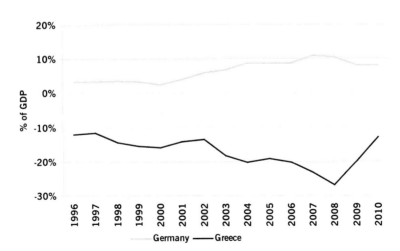

ANNUAL TRADE BALANCE, PERCENTAGE OF GDP, GERMANY AND GREECE, 1996-2010

Greece's trade deficits were financed by borrowing, including deposits in Greek banks from Germany and other northern European countries. When the financial crisis began in 2008, however, these countries sought to pull their deposits out of

Greek banks and reduce their lending. If Greece had an independent central bank, as it did before joining the euro, that bank would provide liquidity to replace these financial flows and thus guarantee the stability of the Greek banking system. But Greece gave up its own independent monetary authority when it joined the eurozone. Instead, the ECB has used the Greek financial crisis as a tool to drive down Greek wages and living standards.

Binding southern Europe with Germany has allowed Germany to run extraordinary trade surpluses with these other countries. For seven years after 2001, capital flows from Germany balanced German trade surpluses. However, Germany's trade surplus soared with the establishment of the euro in 2002. Most of this surplus was with its eurozone partners, who, without independent currencies, could not adjust to balance their trade.

Greece had a trade deficit even before joining the eurozone, but its deficit soared after it adopted the euro. Germany's surplus and Greece's deficits were balanced with borrowing when Greek banks accepted large deposits from Germans and others.

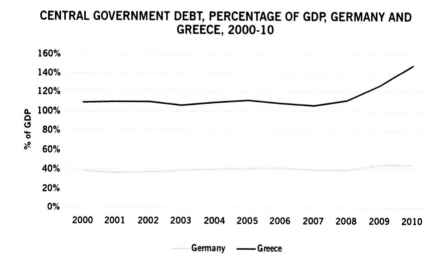

CENTRAL GOVERNMENT DEBT, PERCENTAGE OF GDP, GERMANY AND GREECE, 2000-10

Throughout the 2000s, the Greek government had a relatively high debt burden but remained stable before the economic crisis. Due to falling tax revenues and increased need for government services during the crisis, Greece experienced a sharp rise in its government deficit. Forcing austerity on Greece to stabilize its financial system has led to soaring unemployment. This has led to falling tax revenues and rising expenditures for unemployment relief, which have actually increased the government deficit.

AVERAGE USUAL HOURS WORKED (WEEKLY), EU MEMBERS, 2011

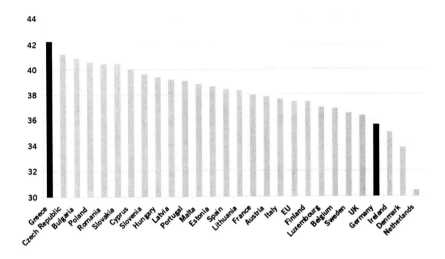

Greece's recent economic troubles come despite the country's work ethic. Relatively poor compared with others in the European Union, Greeks work more hours per week than workers in any other EU member country. By contrast, the relatively affluent Germans work about six hours a week less than the Greeks, and have many more vacation days. ❏

Sources: OECD.stat data base for gross domestic product, government deficits, and unemployment. Eurostat data base for hours worked. International Monetary Fund for trade data.

Article 10.6

WHY THE UNITED STATES IS *NOT* GREECE

BY JOHN MILLER AND KATHERINE SCIACCHITANO
January/February 2012

For almost two years, we've been hearing a new battle cry in the war against government spending: unless the United States slashes deficits we will become Greece, Europe's poster child for fiscal insolvency and economic crisis. The debt crisis in the eurozone, the 17 European countries that share the euro as their common currency, is held up as proof positive of the perils that await the United States if it continues its supposedly fiscally irresponsible ways.

Take the Heritage Foundation, the Washington-based think tank that specializes in providing red meat for anti-government pro-market arguments. Heritage introduces its 2011 chart on the rising level of government debt (to GDP) with this dire warning: "Countries like Greece and Portugal have suffered or are anticipating financial crises as a result of mounting debt. If the U.S. continues federal deficit spending on its current trajectory, it will face similar economic woes."

Even for those who understand that cutting deficits right now will only weaken a still-fragile recovery, and that weakening the recovery will only increase deficits, getting past the argument that "a eurozone crisis is on its way" is no easy task.

What follows is a self-defense lesson on why the United States is not Greece—or Europe. The U.S. economy is far larger and more productive than Greece. The United States has many more tools in its macro-economic policy box than countries in the eurozone. And while calls for austerity have kept the United States from undertaking government spending and investment large enough to support a robust economic recovery, at least thus far, the United States hasn't undertaken the same self-defeating austerity measures Europe has. If we learn the right lessons from what is happening in the eurozone now, we never will.

Central Banks and Deficit Spending

When economic activity plummeted during 2008 and 2009 in the United States, Europe, and throughout the world, coordinated stimulus spending of nations across the globe prevented the collapse of world output from becoming another Great Depression. Today, deficit spending remains critical as working people continue to struggle through an economic recovery that has done little to create jobs or to lift wages, but much to restore profits.

Governments finance deficit spending by borrowing. Governments sell bonds—promissory notes—to domestic and foreign investors as well as other government agencies, and then use the proceeds to pay for spending in excess of their tax revenues. In the United States, domestic investors, foreign investors, and government agencies hold near equal shares of government bonds issued by the Treasury and receive the interest paid on those bonds.

The Federal Reserve ("the Fed"), the U.S. central bank, can buy U.S. government bonds as well. The Fed can also create money (sometimes metaphorically called "printing money") simply by entering an appropriate credit on its balance sheet and spending it. When the Fed uses this newly created money to purchase bonds directly from the government, it is financing the government deficit. Economists call the Fed's direct purchase of government bonds "monetizing the deficit." By such direct purchases of bonds that finance the deficit, the Fed can fund government spending in an emergency, should it choose to do so. Monetizing the deficit also significantly expands the money supply, which pushes down interest rates, which can also help stimulate the economy.

In the current crisis, the Fed did precisely that. By purchasing government bonds, the Fed financed public-sector spending, and by pushing down interest rates, it encouraged private-sector borrowing. In doing so, the Fed supported a market recovery, but also helped to keep unemployment from rising even higher than it did.

In seeking to lower unemployment, the Fed was exercising what is known as its "dual mandate" under the law to promote both low inflation and low unemployment.

Nevertheless, the Fed's decision to inject more money into the economy has come under heavy fire from those who worry more about inflation than unemployment, and who think that "printing money" is always inflationary. Neither continued low inflation rates nor persistently high unemployment were enough to change the thinking of these inflation-phobes. Back in August, Rick Perry, the Texas governor and candidate for president in the Republican primary, went so far as to insist that if the Fed "prints more money between now and the election" (in November 2012) it would be "almost treasonous."

The central banks of most other countries have much the same abilities as the Fed has to inject money into their economies and to buy government debt. As with the Fed, they may or may not choose to use this power. But the power is unquestionably there.

Europe's Central Bank Is Different

The 17 countries in the eurozone, however, relinquished their ability to print money, expand their money supplies, and lower interest rates when they adopted the euro as their common currency. Only the European Central Bank—known as the ECB—can authorize the "printing of euros," and the ECB maintains control over the money supply of the eurozone.

Unlike the Fed, the ECB does not have a dual mandate to pursue low employment as well as low inflation. The ECB's authority is limited to maintaining low inflation, known as "price stability," which the ECB defines as an inflation rate below 2%.

And the ECB is prohibited from directly buying government bonds. The ECB is authorized to buy government bonds only on the "secondary" bond market, when original purchasers resell them.

The result of these policies is that eurozone countries must sell their bonds on the open market. That leaves them entirely dependent on private bond buyers (i.e., lenders), whether from their own country or other countries, to finance their government deficits. Governments must offer their bonds for sale with rates of returns (or interest rates) that will attract those bonds buyers. Each uptick in the interest rate adds to the debt burden of these countries, and makes deficit spending to stimulate the economy that much more expensive.

Another way a country can stimulate its economy is by increasing exports. Typically, individual countries' currencies (when not fixed to the value of a dominant currency such as the U.S. dollar) lose value, or "depreciate," when an economy falls into a crisis, such as the crisis Greece is in now. As the value of its currency depreciates, a country's exports become cheaper, and that boosts export sales and domestic production and aids recovery. While currency fluctuations can open the door to speculative excesses, the falling value of a country's currency is yet another way to help turn around a flagging economy not available to the eurozone economies. The problem is that all countries in the eurozone have the same currency. So individual countries can't let their currencies depreciate. Nor can they take steps countries outside the eurozone can take to intentionally lower their exchange rates to become more competitive, known as devaluing.

Similarly, central banks outside the eurozone routinely stimulate economies by pushing down key interest rates at which banks lend to each other. This helps lower other interest rates in the economy, such as rates for business and consumer loans, and can lead to the expansion of borrowing and spending. But the ECB targets one interest rate for lending between banks for the whole eurozone. It is not possible to set one interest rate for Germany to fight inflation, and a second, lower, rate in Greece or Italy to stimulate growth.

Without the ability to use separate exchange rates or interest rates to stimulate lagging economies, the crisis-ridden eurozone had but one public policy left to get their economies going again: expansionary fiscal policy. But even that remaining policy option was constrained. The ECB was not about to ease the burden of increased government spending (or the cost of tax cuts) by directly buying government bonds. Eurozone guidelines prohibit budget deficits that exceed 3% of GDP, or national debt in excess of 60% of their GDP. And there is no central fiscal authority with deep pockets to turn to. Contrast this with the United States, where states also share the same currency and the Fed targets one interest rate, but where states can turn to the federal government for assistance in times of economic stress.

In effect, the eurozone countries were left to confront the global downturn and the sovereign debt crisis with one policy hand tied behind their back, and a couple of digits lopped off the other. Market pressure on interest rates made it yet more difficult for eurozone countries to get out of trouble by undertaking countercyclical, or stimulus, spending when economies slowed.

In the few cases where eurozone authorities have provided loans to indebted countries, they have insisted on austerity measures ranging from slashing government spending to public- and private-sector wage cuts as the pre-condition for providing relief. But since cutting government spending in a downturn leads to both a fall in demand and rise in unemployment, this emergency lending is making it even harder for eurozone countries to recover.

No wonder the global downturn hit the most vulnerable eurozone countries so hard, turning their sovereign (or government) debt as toxic as the mortgage-based securities that sparked the initial global downturn. This is what we're seeing played out with the Greek debt crisis.

Greek Austerity

When the 2008-2009 global collapse pushed down GDP and trade, and pushed up budget deficits around the world, Greece already had a large trade deficit and high government debt. Greece had consistently run government deficits greater than 5% of its GDP, and had carried government debt that just about matched its GDP for nearly a decade, both clear violations of eurozone guidelines. Nonetheless, Greek banks, and then banks elsewhere in Europe (including Germany and France), readily lent money to the Greek government, buying their bonds, which regularly yielded a handsome 5% rate of return (the rate of interest on a ten-year government note), and which presumably carried limited risk as the sovereign debt of a developed country unlikely to default.

But as the Greek economy tumbled downward, Greece had to raise its interest rates to above 12% to sell the additional debt it needed to stay afloat. By the summer of 2010, Greece was pushed to the point of default—not being able to pay its lenders.

The European Union and the IMF gave Greece a $140 billion loan so debt payments to the banks could continue. But both the IMF and the European Union insisted on austerity to reduce deficits and ensure repayment. Greece was forced to agree to sharp cuts in government spending, public employment, and wages and benefits of public employees; to tax increases; and to privatization of government assets. The banks that had happily lent Greece money well beyond the allowable eurozone limits escaped without having to write down the value of their loans to the Greek government.

The Greek economy, on the other hand, dropped like a stone. In the year that followed, Greece lost more output than the United States had during the Great Recession. Unemployment rates reached 18.4%, over one-third of young people were unemployed, and more than one-fifth of the population was poverty stricken. The austerity measures did trim the Greek budget deficit. Nonetheless the ratio of public debt to GDP continued to rise as Greek output plummeted.

One year later, Greece was on the brink of default again. The interest rate on Greek government bonds had skyrocketed to above 20% on ten-year government bonds, only adding to Greece's already unsustainable debt burden.

In October 2011 the IMF and the European Union granted an additional $173 billion loan to Greece in return for a new round of austerity measures. More public-sector workers lost their jobs, public pensions were cut further, and the privatization program expanded. The austerity measures were "equivalent to about 14 percent of average Greek take-home income," according to the *Financial Times*, the authoritative British newspaper, or an impact about "double that brought about by austerity measures in the other two eurozone countries subject to international bail-out programmes, Portugal and Ireland."

Also as part of the price for its debt reduction, Greece would have to accept monitoring of its fiscal affairs by the European Union. Greek Prime Minister George Papandreou, forced to cancel a referendum on the second round of austerity cuts, resigned in favor of a "government of national unity" headed by Lucas Papademos, a former banker sure to listen to the markets.

This time, banks and other holders of Greek government bonds seemed not to have escaped unharmed. The value of their bonds were to be written down to 50% of their face value, meaning they could still insist on repayment of half the amount lent, although the market value of those bonds was surely far less than that. In addition, the agreement was "voluntary," and it is yet to be seen if the agreement will be enforced.

As 2011 came to a close with this second round of austerity measures and the near collapse of the Greek economy, the Greek government was paying out a crippling 35% interest rate to attract buyers for their ten-year bonds.

Vortex Europe

European banks are the main buyers of European debt. French and German banks hold large quantities of Greek bonds.

So does the ECB, which began buying Greek bonds and other sovereign debt on the secondary (or resale) market in 2010. It resumed the practice in late 2011 to ease pressures on interest rates. Ordinarily, this bond-buying would also stimulate the economy by increasing the money supply, since the ECB creates the money it uses to buy the bonds. But the ECB also "sterilizes" its bond buying by contracting the money supply in the same amount as its purchases. This eliminates any possibility of inflation, but also negates the stimulus effect.

The bottom line is that because of the extensive holdings of Greek and other government debt within the European banking system, a Greek default would cause substantial losses in the European banking system and destabilize it.

In the last weeks of 2011, the ECB did extend a financial lifeline to banks – exactly what it had refused to give to the Greek government. To help buffer them against sudden losses, the ECB offered the banks $638 billion in three-year loans with the bargain basement interest rate of 1%. The majority of eurozone banks, some 523 of them, took out loans. The ECB's backdoor bailout, as a *Wall Street Journal* editorial called it, was twice the combined size of the two rescue packages for Greece. The banks, unlike governments, would not have to turn to the bond markets for funding if a Greek default occurred. And like banks bailed out in the United States, no requirements were placed on them to continue lending—in Europe's case, to continue lending to governments.

While the ECB move shored up the banks for now, it won't protect them from the large losses that will come with an outright default by Greece or another of the crisis-ridden southern eurozone countries. Such large losses would in turn force countries to bail out banks again, as they did in 2008, to avoid the prospect of cascading banking failures. Because the ECB is prohibited from directly buying European government debt, a new round of bailouts would raise the specter of increasing government deficits, of rising interest rates, and of additional countries defaulting, a sequence that could induce a depression-like downturn.

As a result, private lenders are now insisting on higher interest rates on government bonds not just in Greece, but throughout much of Europe. These interest rate rises began in weaker economies with higher debt levels, including the Italian and Spanish economies, both of which are far larger than the Greek economy. Interest-rate hikes have even spread to France and (very briefly) to Germany, the eurozone's two largest economies. The spikes in rates not only increase the likelihood of default, they put real roadblocks in the way of the spending and investment needed for recovery and long-term growth.

The danger is not only to Europe. The European Union is the largest economy in the world, accounting for nearly 20% of global economic activity. Every region of the world that trades with Europe will be affected by a slowdown there. The eurozone is the largest export market for both the United States and China. The default of any European country would cause losses and instability throughout the global economy. The U.S. financial system would also be sharply affected, for European global banks provide much of the credit for the U.S. economy.

To stem the bleeding, many in Europe and beyond have urged and continue to urge the ECB to step up and find a way to act as most normal central banks would in the situation: inject money into these economies by buying government debt in unlimited quantities. That in turn would lower interest rates, and give countries time to rebuild and restart growth. Germany, the largest and the dominant economy in Europe, continues to block this option on the grounds that printing money is not only inflationary but a "moral hazard" and makes borrowing too easy. At the last European summit, Germany successfully insisted instead on a "fiscal stability union" that will require balanced budgets (before taking interest payments into account). In other words, austerity for workers.

Rejecting Austerity

Austerity won't work for Europe: Europe needs growth, and austerity can't produce growth. Austerity also can't work because the proposed cure—budget cuts—assumes the disease is government spending. But excessive social spending by its government did not cause Greece's debt problems. In 2007, the year before the crisis hit, Greece's social expenditures relative to the size of its economy stood at 21.3% of GDP, lower than the social expenditures in France (28.3% of GDP) and Germany (25.2% of GDP), the two countries most responsible for orchestrating the austerity measures that have slashed social spending in Greece.

Europe didn't have a government debt crisis before the subprime collapse of 2008. It had countries like Germany in the north with large permanent trade surpluses, and countries in the south like Greece with large permanent trade deficits. Fixing these trade deficits and imbalances can't be done by pushing down wages. In fact, repressive wage and labor policies, especially as practiced in Germany, are what lie at the heart of those imbalances that made the weaker southern eurozone countries so vulnerable to the crisis that followed.

Rather, what's needed is government investment and coordination throughout Europe. A public investment program could modernize the infrastructure of the southern eurozone economies and boost the productivity of their workforce by improving workers' health and education.

A recession—or worse—in Europe will slow down growth and raise budget deficits in the United States as well. It will create political pressure for austerity exactly when we need more investment and more stimulus spending.

If this happens, it will be more important than ever to remember that Europe is in the position it is in, first, because it insisted on austerity for Greece and, second, because Europe has a central bank that is prohibited from financing government deficits and whose sole policy mandate is to limit inflation. Without the insistence on austerity, and without having relinquished these basic tools of economic policy—both of which the United States retains—the mess in Europe could never have happened. The United States is not and will never be Greece.

Yet like the crisis in Europe, the crisis in the United States isn't temporary or fleeting. The outcome will determine what kind of jobs and economic security people will have for a long time to come. It will have a huge effect on public-sector unions. And it will affect democracy itself, especially if we stay silent. Austerity in Europe is being imposed from above. There's no reason to let it be imposed here. ❑

Sources: C. Lapavitsas, et al., "Breaking Up? A Route Out of the Eurozone Crisis," Research on Money and Finance, RMF Occasional Report, November 2011; Heiner Flassbeck and Friederike Spiecker, "The Euro—A Story of Misunderstanding," Intereconomics, 2011; "The ECB's Backdoor Bailout," *Wall Street Journal*, December 24, 2011; George Irvin and Alex Izurieta, "Fundamental Flaws in the European Project," Economic & Political Weekly, August 6, 2011; C.P. Chandrasekhar, "The Crisis in Europe," *The Frontline*, Jul. 30-Aug. 12, 2011; Robert Skidelsky, "The Euro in a Shrinking Zone," Project Syndicate, December 12, 2011; David Enrich, "European Banks Rush to Grasp Lifeline," *Wall Street Journal*, December 22, 2011; Paul Krugman, "Bernanke's Perry Problem," New York Times, August 25, 2011; Paul Krugman, "Currency Warnings that Europe Ignored," Krugman & Co., November 22, 2011; Andre Leonard, "The Republican plot to turn the U.S. into Greece," Salon.com, July 18, 2011; Sally Giansbury et al.," Greek austerity plans threaten growth," *Financial Times*, October 17, 2011; James Bullard, "The Fed's Dual Mandate: Lessons of the 1970s," *The 2010 Annual Report of the Federal Reserve Bank of St. Louis, April 2011.*

Article 10.7

THE FORMERLY ADVANCED ECONOMIES
Ruling elites' folly may doom Europe, the United States, and Canada.

BY ROBIN HAHNEL
January/February 2013

Just as the European settler economies in North America grew to eclipse the economic power of "old" Europe during the twentieth century, at least some of the BRICS—Brazil, Russia, India, China, and South Africa—were already on a trajectory to rise relative to both North America and Europe in economic power during the twenty-first century. However, a natural process that would have taken five decades or more may now be shortened to only a decade or two as the elites in charge of economic policy in the North Atlantic region seem hell-bent on committing economic suicide.

During the twentieth century it was common to distinguish between the "advanced" or "more-developed" economies, and the "under-" or "lesser-developed" economies. Soon it may become commonplace to refer to Europe, the United States, and Canada as the formerly advanced economies. What follows is a brief anatomy of econo-cide being committed by ruling elites in a region which long dominated the global economy but soon no longer will.

Escalating Inequality

What most distinguishes more-advanced from less-advanced economies is the size of the middle class. During the middle third of the twentieth century, political victories by progressive movements raised a significant portion of the workforce to middle-class status in Europe, the United States, and Canada as productivity gains from new technologies and expansion of education were more widely shared than ever before. Unfortunately, this trend came screeching to a halt at the end of the 1970s, and ever since we have experienced the most dramatic increase in economic inequality in world history. Not only is this terribly unfair, it has also proved to be destabilizing.

When wages rise along with increases in productivity, demand for goods and services and for the labor to make them tends to keep pace with productive capabilities. But when the top 1% appropriate the lion's share of productivity gains, as they have now for over thirty years, more and more income goes into purchasing assets rather than more production, creating two problems: Unemployment—which further aggravates the lack of demand for production—and asset bubbles—which eventually burst, destroying illusions of wealth.

Financial Deregulation

Whatever one may think about the pros and cons of markets in general, there should be no doubt that free-market finance is an accident waiting to happen! Theory predicts it, and history has proven it time and time again. Whenever the financial industry is allowed to do as it pleases it will engage in activities that increase their leverage and are highly profitable for them, but create ever-greater "systemic" risk for the rest of us. Only when the financial industry is subject to competent regulation can the risk of financial crises be reduced to socially acceptable levels.

In the aftermath of the financial crisis of 1929 that triggered the Great Depression, governments in the North Atlantic region imposed competent regulations on their financial industries which produced decades free from major financial crises in our advanced economies. But the financial industry predictably chafes under regulation, since restrictions prevent them from engaging in activities they know to be highly profitable. So the financial industry constantly searches for ways around existing regulations and lobbies politicians relentlessly to remove restrictions. And the more successful they are, the more profits they have to ply the political system to further deregulate their activities. As a result, eighty years after the crash of 1929, the financial system in the North Atlantic region was once again an accident waiting to happen.

However, this time there was one big difference. Instead of a massive financial crisis giving rise to successful political efforts to erect a competent regulatory system to prevent recurrence, Wall Street's influence with both major political parties was so great that it easily forestalled meaningful regulatory reform. The Dodd-Frank "Wall Street Reform and Consumer Protection Act" was neither. Instead it was a fig leaf providing cover for politicians but no real protections. More than four years after the crash of 2008, systemic risk in the financial system is just as great as it was before, consumers of financial services are still without effective protection, and taxpayers are still "on the hook," as former Treasury Secretary Hank Paulson put it when explaining to Congress in November 2008 that the big Wall Street Banks were too big for the rest of us to allow them to fail.

Ignoring Keynes at Our Peril

Paul Krugman summed it up well in a *New York Times* column:

> Slashing government spending in a depressed economy depresses the economy further; austerity should wait until a strong recovery is well under way. Unfortunately, in late 2010 and early 2011, politicians and policy makers in much of the Western world believed that they knew better, that we should focus on deficits, not jobs, even though our economies had barely begun to recover from the slump that followed the financial crisis. And by acting on that anti-Keynesian belief, they ended up proving Keynes right all over again.

In futile attempts to reduce deficits, the Tory government in the UK and the Conservative government in Canada have subjected their own middle and lower classes to crushing fiscal austerity. Hard-line fiscal conservatives in power at the European Commission and European Central Bank have visited even more draconian austerity policies on the citizens of the so-called PIIGS—Portugal, Ireland, Italy, Greece, and Spain—in exchange for financial bailouts that have proven time and time again to be too little, too late. Germany, sheltered from unemployment by favorable trade surpluses with the rest of the eurozone, steadfastly refuses to engage in fiscal stimulus. And when Obama aided his mortal Republican enemies by pivoting from an inadequate fiscal stimulus in 2009 to deficit reduction in 2010, the entire North Atlantic economic region was united in fiscal austerity. Unfortunately, what was, and still is desperately needed is exactly the opposite—fiscal stimulus!

When consumers are tapped out, when businesses have little reason to invest in new plant and capacity since they can't find customers to buy what they are already producing, government needs to step up to the plate and provide the necessary demand for goods and services to get the economy going again. That was Keynes' great truth. Instead, ruling elites in the North Atlantic region have united to reject the advice of Keynes and instead repeat Herbert Hoover's mistake. Instead of fiscal stimulus they are giving us ever more draconian fiscal austerity. This, more than any policy failure, has the North Atlantic region on the road to recession and mass unemployment without end.

As a result, for the first time in many generations, citizens of the formerly advanced economies are left to ask ourselves: "How does it feel / To be on your own/ With no direction home / Like a complete unknown / Like a rolling stone?" ❑

Chapter 11

RESISTANCE AND ALTERNATIVES

Article 11.1

GREECE AND THE CRISIS OF EUROPE: WHICH WAY OUT?

BY MARJOLEIN VAN DER VEEN
May/June 2013

The Greek economy has crashed, and now lies broken on the ground. The causes of the crisis are pretty well understood, but there hasn't been enough attention to the different possible ways out. Our flight crew has shown us only one emergency exit—one that is broken and just making things worse. But there is more than one way out of the crisis, not just the austerity being pushed by the so-called "Troika" (International Monetary Fund (IMF), European Commission, and European Central Bank (ECB)). We need to look around a bit more, since—as they say on every flight—the nearest exit may not be right in front of us. Can an alternative catch hold? And, if so, will it be Keynesian or socialist?

The origins of the crisis are manifold: trade imbalances between Germany and Greece, the previous Greek government's secret debts (hidden with the connivance of Wall Street banks), the 2007 global economic crisis, and the flawed construction of the eurozone (see sidebar). As Greece's economic crisis has continued to deepen, it has created a social disaster: Drastic declines in public health, a rise in suicides, surging child hunger, a massive exodus of young adults, an intensification of exploitation (longer work hours and more work days per week), and the rise of the far right and its attacks on immigrants and the LGBT community. Each new austerity package brokered between the Greek government and the Troika stipulates still more government spending cuts, tax increases, or "economic reforms"—privatization, increases in the retirement age, layoffs of public-sector workers, and wage cuts for those who remain.

Causes of Greece's Deepening Crisis

Trade imbalances. Germany's wage restraint policies and high productivity made German exports more competitive (cheaper), resulting in trade surpluses for Germany and deficits for Greece. Germany then used its surplus funds to invest in Greece and other southern European countries. As German banks shoveled out loans, Greek real estate boomed, inflation rose, their exports became less competitive, and the wealthy siphoned money abroad.

Hidden debt. To enter the eurozone in 2001, Greece's budget deficit was supposed to be below the threshold (3% of GDP) set by the Maastricht Treaty. In 2009 the newly elected Panhellenic Socialist Movement (PASOK) government discovered that the outgoing government had been hiding its deficits from the European authorities, with the help of credit default swaps sold to it by Goldman Sachs during 2002-06. The country was actually facing a deficit of 12% of GDP, thanks to extravagant military spending and tax cuts for (and tax evasion by) the rich.

Global crisis. When the 2007 global economic crisis struck, Greece was perhaps the hardest-hit country. Investments soured, banks collapsed, and loans could not be repaid. Debt-financed household consumption could no longer be sustained. Firms cut back on investment spending, closed factories, and laid off workers. Output has fallen 20% since 2007, the unemployment rate is now above 25%, (for youth, 58%), household incomes have fallen by more than a third in the last three years, and government debt has surpassed 175% of GDP.

The eurozone trap. Greece's government could do little on its own to rescue its economy. With eurozone countries all using the same currency, individual countries could no longer use monetary policy to stimulate their economies (e.g., by devaluing the currency to boost exports or stimulating moderate inflation to reduce the real debt burden). Fiscal policy was also weakened by the Maastricht limits on deficits and debt, resulting in tight constraints on fiscal stimulus.

While there are numerous possible paths out of the crisis, the neoliberal orthodoxy has maintained that Greece had no choice but to accept austerity. The country was broke, argued the Troika officials, economists, and commentators, and this tough medicine would ultimately help the Greek economy to grow again. As Mark Weisbrot of the Center for Economic and Policy Research (CEPR) put it, "[T]he EU authorities have opted to punish Greece—for various reasons, including the creditors' own interests in punishment, their ideology, imaginary fears of inflation, and to prevent other countries from also demanding a 'growth option.'" By focusing on neoliberal solutions, the mainstream press controls the contours of the debate. Keynesian remedies that break with the punishment paradigm are rarely discussed, let alone socialist proposals. These may well gain more attention, however, as the crisis drags on without end.

Neoliberal Solutions

Despite the fact that 30 years of neoliberalism resulted in the worst economic crisis since the Great Depression, neoliberals are undaunted and have remained intent on dishing out more of the same medicine. What they offered Greece were bailouts and haircuts (write-downs of the debt). While the country—really, the country's banks—got bailouts, the money flowed right back to repay lenders in Germany, France, and other countries. Very little actually went to Greek workers who fell into severe poverty. The bailouts invariably came with conditions in the form of austerity, privatization (e.g., water systems, ports, etc.), mass public-sector layoffs, labor-market "flexibilization" (making it easier to fire workers), cutbacks in unemployment insurance, and tax reforms (lowering corporate taxes and raising personal income and sales taxes). In sum, the neoliberal structural adjustment program for Greece shifted the pain onto ordinary people, rather than those most responsible for causing the crisis in the first place.

Austerity and internal devaluation

With steep cuts in government spending, neoliberal policy has been contracting the economy just when it needed to be expanded. Pro-austerity policy makers, however, professed their faith in "expansionary austerity." Harvard economists Alberto Alesina and Silvia Ardagna claimed that austerity (especially spending cuts) could lead to the expectation of increased profits and so stimulate investment. The neoliberals also hoped to boost exports through "internal devaluation" (wage cuts, resulting in lower costs and therefore cheaper exports). An economist with Capital Economics in London claimed that Greece needed a 30–40% decline in real wages to restore competitiveness. A fall in real wages, along with the out-migration of workers, the neoliberals suggested, would allow labor markets to "clear" at a new equilibrium. Of course, they neglected to say how long this would take and how many workers would fall into poverty, get sick, or die in the process.

Meanwhile, international financial capitalists (hedge funds and private equity firms) have been using the crisis as an opportunity to buy up state assets. The European Commission initially expected to raise €50 billion by 2015 from the privatization of state assets (now being revised downward to just over €25 billion through 2020). The magnitude of the fire sale in Greece is still five to ten times larger than that expected for Spain, Portugal, and Ireland. Domestic private companies on the

---

The Role of Goldman Sachs

Greece was able to "hide" its deficits thanks to Goldman Sachs, which had sold financial derivatives called credit-default swaps to Greece between 2002 and 2006. The credit-default swaps operated a bit like subprime loans, enabling Greece to lower its debts on its balance sheets, but at very high borrowing rates. Goldman Sachs had sales teams selling these complicated financial instruments not just to Greece, but to many gullible municipalities and institutions throughout Europe (and the United States), who were told that these deals could lower their borrowing costs. For Greece, the loans blew up in 2008-2009, when interest rates rose and stock markets collapsed. Among those involved in these deals included Mario Draghi (now President of the ECB), who was working at the Greece desk at Goldman Sachs at the time. While these sales generated huge profits for Goldman Sachs, the costs are now being borne by ordinary Greek people in the form of punishing austerity programs. (For more on Goldman Sachs's role, see part four of the PBS documentary "Money, Power, Wall Street.")

brink of bankruptcy are also vulnerable. As the crisis drags on, private-equity and hedge-fund "vulture capitalists" are swooping in for cheap deals. The other neoliberal reforms—labor and pension reforms, dismantling of the welfare state, and tax reforms—will also boost private profits at the expense of workers.

Default and exit from the euro

Another possible solution was for Greece to default on its debt, and some individuals and companies actively prepared for such a scenario. A default would lift the onerous burden of debt repayment, and would relieve Greece of complying with all the conditions placed on it by the Troika. However, it would likely make future borrowing by both the public and private sectors more difficult and expensive, and so force the government to engage in some sort of austerity of its own.

Some economists on the left have been supportive of a default, and the exit from the euro and return to the drachma that would likely follow. One such advocate is Mark Weisbrot, who has argued that "a threat by Greece to jettison the euro is long overdue, and it should be prepared to carry it out." He acknowledges there would be costs in the short term, but argues they would be less onerous "than many years of recession, stagnation, and high unemployment that the European authorities are offering." A return to the drachma could restore one of the tools to boost export competitiveness: allowing Greece to use currency depreciation to lower the prices of its exports. In this sense, this scenario remains a neoliberal one. (Many IMF "shock therapy" have included currency devaluations as part of the strategy for countries to export their way out of debt.)

The process of exit, however, could be quite painful, with capital flight, bank runs, black markets, significant inflation as the cost of imports rises, and the destruction of savings. There had already been some capital flight—an estimated €72 billion left Greek banks between 2009 and 2012. Furthermore, the threat of a Greek exit created fear of contagion, with the possibility of more countries leaving the euro and even the collapse of the eurozone altogether.

Keynesian Solutions

By late 2012, Keynesian proposals were finally being heard and having some impact on policymakers. Contrary to the neoliberal austerity doctrine, Keynesian solutions typically emphasize running countercyclical policies—especially expansionary fiscal policy (or fiscal "stimulus"), with deficit-spending to counter the collapse in private demand. However, the Greek government is already strapped with high deficits and the interest rates demanded by international creditors have spiked to extremely high levels. Additional deficit spending would require that the ECB (or the newly established European Stability Mechanism (ESM)) intervene by directly buying Greek government bonds to bring down rates. (The ECB has been lending to private banks at low rates, to enable the banks to buy public bonds.) In any case, a Keynesian approach ideally would waive the EU's deficit and debt limits to allow the Greek government more scope for rescuing the economy.

Alternatively, the EU could come forward with more grants and loans, in order to create employment, fund social-welfare spending, and boost demand. This kind of bailout would not go to the banks, but to the people who are suffering from unemployment, cuts in wages and pensions, and poverty. Nor would it come with all the other conditions the neoliberals have demanded (privatization, layoffs, labor-market reforms, etc). The European Investment Bank could also help stimulate new industries, such as alternative energy, and help revive old ones, such as tourism, shipping, and agriculture. In a European Union based on solidarity, the richer regions of Europe would help out poorer ones in a crisis (much as richer states in the United States make transfers to poorer ones, mostly without controversy).

Even some IMF officials finally recognized that austerity was not working. An October 2012 IMF report admitted that the organization had underestimated the fiscal policy multiplier—a measure of how much changes in government spending and taxes will affect economic growth—and therefore the negative impact of austerity policies. By April 2013, economists at UMass-Amherst found serious mistakes in research by Harvard economists Carmen Reinhart and Kenneth Rogoff, alleging that debt-to-GDP ratios of 90% or more seriously undermine future economic growth. Reinhart and Rogoff's claims had been widely cited by supporters of austerity for highly indebted countries. So yet another crack emerged in the pillar supporting austerity policies.

Keynesians have argued, contrary to the "internal devaluation" advocates, that the reduction in real wages just depressed aggregate demand, and made the recession deeper. Economists such as Nobel laureate Paul Krugman proposed that, instead, wages and prices be allowed to rise in the trade-surplus countries of northern Europe (Germany and the Netherlands). This would presumably make these countries' exports less competitive, at some expense to producers of internationally traded goods, though possibly boosting domestic demand thanks to increased wages. Meanwhile, it would help level the playing field for exporters in the southern countries in crisis, and would be done without the punishing reductions in real wages demanded by the Troika. The Keynesian solution thus emphasized stimulating domestic demand through fiscal expansion in both the northern and southern European countries, as well as allowing wages and prices to rise in the northern countries.

Signs pointing in this direction began to emerge in spring 2013, when some Dutch and German trade unions won significant wage increases. In addition, the Dutch government agreed to scrap its demands for wage restraint in some sectors (such as the public sector and education) and to hold off (at least until August) on its demands for more austerity. (Another €4.5 billion cuts had been scheduled for 2014, after the government spent €3.7 billion in January to rescue (through nationalization) one of the country's largest banks.)

Socialist Solutions

For most of the socialist parties in Greece and elsewhere in Europe, the neoliberal solution was clearly wrong-headed, as it worsened the recession to the detriment of workers while industrial and finance capitalists made out like bandits. Greece's Panhellenic Socialist Movement (PASOK) was an exception, going along with austerity, structural reforms, and privatization. (Its acceptance of austerity lost it significant support in the 2012 elections.) Other socialists supported anything that alleviated the recession, including Keynesian prescriptions for more deficit spending, higher wages, and other policies to boost aggregate demand and improve the position of workers. Greece's SYRIZA (a coalition of 16 left-wing parties and whose support surged in the 2012 elections) called for stopping austerity, renegotiating loan agreements, halting wage and pension cuts, restoring the minimum wage, and implementing a type of Marshall Plan-like investment drive. In many ways, these proposale resemble standard Keynesian policies—which have historically served to rescue the capitalist system, without challenging its inherent exploitative structure or vulnerability to recurrent crisis.

While Keynesian deficit-spending could alleviate the crisis in the short-term, who would ultimately bear the costs—ordinary taxpayers? Workers could end up paying for the corruption of the Greek capitalist class, who pushed through tax cuts, spent government funds in ways that mainly benefited themselves, and hid money abroad. Many socialists argued that the Greek capitalists should pay for the crisis, through increased taxes on wealth, corporate profits, and financial transactions, and the abolition of tax loopholes and havens. As SYRIZA leader Alexis Tsipras put it, "It is common knowledge among progressive politicians and activists, but also among the Troika and the Greek government, that the burden of the crisis has been carried exclusively by public and private sector workers and pensioners. This has to stop. It is time for the rich to contribute their share... ."

Slowly, the right-wing government began making gestures in this direction. In 2010, French finance minister Christine Lagarde had given a list of more than 2,000 Greeks with money in Swiss bank accounts to her Greek counterpart George Papaconstantinou, of the PASOK government, but Papaconstantiou sat on it and did nothing. But in the fall of 2012 the so-called "Lagarde list" was published by the magazine Hot Doc, leading to fury among ordinary Greeks against establishment political leaders (including the PASOK "socialists") who had failed to go after the tax dodgers. Another list of about 400 Greeks who had bought and sold property in London since 2009 was compiled by British financial authorities at the request of the current Greek government. In total, the economist Friedrich Schneider has estimated that about €120 billion of Greek assets (about 65% of GDP) were outside the country, mostly in Switzerland and Britain, but also in the United States, Singapore, and the Cayman Islands. The government also started a clamp down on corruption in past government expenditures. In the Spring of 2013, two politicians (a former defense minister and a former mayor of Thessaloniki, the country's second-largest city) were convicted on corruption charges.

Socialists have also opposed dismantling the public sector, selling off state assets, and selling Greek firms to international private equity firms. Instead of bailouts, many socialists have called for nationalization of the banking sector. "The banking system we envision," SYRIZA leader Alexis Tsipras announced, "will support environmentally viable public investment and cooperative initiatives.... What we need is a banking system devoted to the public interest—not one bowing to capitalist profit. A banking system at the service of society, a banking system that serves as a pillar for growth." While SYRIZA called for renegotiating the Greece's public debt, it favored staying in the euro.

Other socialist parties have put forth their own programs that go beyond Keynesian fiscal expansion, a more equitable tax system, and even beyond nationalizing the banks. For instance, the Alliance of the Anti-Capitalist Left (ANTARSYA) called for nationalizing banks and corporations, worker takeovers of closed factories, and canceling the debt and exiting the euro. The Communist Party of Greece (KKE) proposed a fairly traditional Marxist-Leninist program, with socialization of all the means of production and central planning for the satisfaction of social needs, but also called for disengagement from the EU and abandoning the euro. The Trotskyist Xekinima party called for nationalizing not just the largest banks, but also the largest corporations, and putting them under democratic worker control.

Those within the Marxist and libertarian left, meanwhile, have focused on turning firms, especially those facing bankruptcy, into cooperatives or worker self-directed enterprises. Firms whose boards of directors are composed of worker-representatives and whose workers participate in democratic decision-making would be less likely to distribute surpluses to overpaid CEOs or corrupt politicians and lobbyists, or to pick up and relocate to other places with lower labor costs. While worker self-directed enterprises could decide to forego wage increases or to boost productivity, in order to promote exports, such decisions would be made democratically by the workers themselves, not by capitalist employers or their representatives in government. And it would be the workers themselves who would democratically decide what to do with any increased profits that might arise from those decisions.

One Greek company that is trying to survive as a transformed worker cooperative is Vio.Me, a building materials factory in Thessaloniki. In May 2011 when the owners could no longer pay their bills and walked away, the workers decided to occupy the factory. By February 2013, after raising enough funds and community support, the workers started democratically running the company on their own. (They do not intend to buy out the owners, since the company owed the workers a significant amount of money when it abandoned the factory.) They established a worker-board, controlled by workers' general assemblies and subject to recall, to manage the factory. They also changed the business model, shifting to different suppliers, improving environmental practices, and finding new markets. Greek law currently does not allow factory occupations, so the workers are seeking the creation of a legal framework for the recuperated factory, which may enable more such efforts in the future. Vio.Me has received support from SYRIZA and the Greek Green party, from workers at recuperated factories in Argentina (see sidebar), as well as from academics and political activists worldwide.

Whither Europe and the Euro?

As Europe faces this ongoing crisis, it is also grappling with its identity. On the right are the neoliberal attempts to dismantle the welfare state and create a Europe that works for corporations and the wealthy—a capitalist Europe more like the United States. In the center are Keynesian calls to keep the EU intact, with stronger Europe-wide governance and institutions. These involve greater fiscal integration, with a European Treasury, eurobonds (rather than separate bonds for each country), European-wide banking regulations, etc. Keynesians also call for softening the austerity policies on Greece and other countries.

Proposals for European consolidation have inspired criticism and apprehension on both the far right and far left. Some on the far right are calling for exiting the euro, trumpeting nationalism and a return to the nation state. The left, meanwhile, voices concern about the emerging power of the European parliament in Brussels, with its highly paid politicians, bureaucrats, lobbyists, etc. who are able to pass legislation favoring corporations at the expense of workers. Unlike the far right however, the left has proposed a vision for another possible united Europe—one based on social cohesion and inclusion, cooperation and solidarity, rather than on competition and corporate dominance. In particular, socialists call for replacing the capitalist structure of Europe with one that is democratic, participatory, and embodies a socialist economy, with worker protections and participation at all levels of economic and political decision-making. This may very well be the best hope for Europe to escape its current death spiral, which has it living in terror of what the next stage may bring. ❏

Sources: Amitabh Pal, "Austerity is Killing Europe," Common Dreams, April 27, 2012 (commondreams.org); Niki Kitsantonis, "Greece Resumes Talks With Creditors," *New York Times*, April 4, 2013 (nytimes.com); Mark Weisbrot, "Where I Part from Paul Krugman on Greece and the Euro," *The Guardian*, May 13, 2011 (guardian.co.uk); Alberto F. Alesina and Silvia Ardagna, "Large Changes in Fiscal Policy: Taxes Versus Spending," National Bureau of Economic Research (NBER), October 2009 (nber.org); Geert Reuten, "From a false to a 'genuine' EMU," Globalinfo, Oct. 22, 2012 (globalinfo.nl); David Jolly, "Greek Economy Shrank 6.2% in Second Quarter," *New York Times*, Aug. 13, 2012; Joseph Zacune, "Privatizing Europe: Using the Crisis to Entrench Neoliberalism," Transnational Institute, March 2013 (tni.org); Mark Weisbrot, "Why Greece Should Reject the Euro," *New York Times*, May 9, 2011; Ronald Jannsen, "Blame It on the Multiplier," *Social Europe Journal*, Oct. 16, 2012 (social-europe.eu); Landon Thomas, Jr., and David Jolly, "Despite Push for Austerity, European Debt Has Soared," *New York Times*, Oct. 22, 2012; "German Public sector workers win above-inflation pay rise," Reuters, March 9, 2013 (reuters.nl); Liz Alderman, "Greek Businesses Fear Possible Return to Drachma," *New York Times*, May 22, 2012; Landon Thomas, Jr., "In Greece, Taking Aim at Wealthy Tax Dodgers," *New York Times*, Nov. 11, 2012; Rachel Donadio and Liz Alderman, "List of Swiss Accounts Turns Up the Heat in Greece," *New York Times*, Oct. 27, 2012; Landon Thomas, Jr., "Greece Seeks Taxes From Wealthy With Cash Havens in London," *New York Times*, Sept. 27, 2012; Niki Kitsantonis, "Ex-Mayor in Greece Gets Life in Prison for Embezzlement," *New York Times*, Feb. 27, 2013; Sam Bollier, "A guide to Greece's political parties," Al Jazeera, May 1, 2012 (aljazeera.com); Alexis Tsipras, "Syriza London: Public talk," March 16, 2013 (left.gr); Amalia Loizidou, "What way out for Greece and the working class in Europe," Committee for a Workers' International (CWI), March 19, 2013 (socialistworld.net); Richard Wolff, "Yes, there is an alternative to capitalism: Mondragón shows the way," *The Guardian*, June 24, 2012 (guardian.co.uk); Peter Ranis, "Occupy Wall Street: An Opening to Worker-Occupation of Factories and Enterprises in the U.S.," MRzine, Sept. 11, 2011 (mrzine.monthlyreview.org); viome.org.

Article 11.2

THE RETURN OF CAPITAL CONTROLS

BY ARMAGAN GEZICI
January/February 2013

In the wake of the global financial crisis, low interest rates and slow growth in advanced economies have led to a massive influx of capital into so-called emerging markets, where interest rates and growth have been higher. International investors, seeking higher returns, have moved their funds away from advanced economies into emerging-market securities like stocks, bonds, and mutual funds. The governments of many developing countries, as a result, have become increasingly concerned about the effects of these capital inflows—including stronger currencies, asset-price bubbles, and even inflation. In March 2012, Brazil's president Dilma Rousseff accused developed nations of unleashing a "monetary tsunami," which is undermining the competitiveness of emerging economies like her own. These concerns have motivated many countries to introduce measures to cope with cross-border capital flows.

Starting in late 2009, for example, Brazil began to implement "capital controls"—including a tax on capital inflows and other measures—to keep its currency (the real) from growing stronger against the dollar. Several Asian countries, including South Korea, Taiwan, and Thailand, have also implemented controls of various kinds on capital inflows. Suddenly, it appears, capital controls are back.

What Ever Happened to Capital Controls?

The debate about controls on international capital flows goes back to the World War II era. During the Bretton Woods negotiations (1944) establishing the international monetary order for the postwar period, Britain's chief negotiator, John Maynard Keynes, and his U.S. counterpart, Harry Dexter White, agreed that a distinction should be made between "speculative" capital and "productive" capital. Both believed that speculative (or "hot money") capital flows should be subject to controls. Keynes went further, arguing that "control of capital movements, both inward and outward, should be a permanent feature of the post-war system." For much of the postwar period, controls such as restrictions on the types of assets banks could hold and limits on capital outflows (used even by the United States between 1963 and 1973) were, indeed, implemented by many capitalist countries. Beginning in the 1980s, however, international financial institutions like the International Monetary Fund (IMF), many Western governments, and private high finance began to oppose capital controls. The U. S. government and the IMF became staunch advocates of "capital-account liberalization" (that is, the deregulation of international capital flows) during this period.

The recent crisis resulted in widespread recognition, around the world, that deregulated financial activity can result in major economic disruptions. In most of the world's largest economies, possible measures to re-regulate finance on the national level came back on the political agenda. Cross-border finance, however, was largely left out of the discussion, as if it did not require any regulation. Conventional discussions of this issue have also involved a peculiar twist in terminology: financial regulations are typically called "regulations" when purely domestic, yet when they involve cross-border flows, they carry the more ominous-sounding label of "controls"—as if to emphasize the undesirable nature of these regulations from a free-market perspective.

Why Capital Controls?

The essential problem with international capital flows is that they are "pro-cyclical"— that is, they amplify the patterns of the business cycle. Capital tends to flow in when economies are expanding, promoting "overheating" and inflation, and tends to flow out during downturns, exacerbating the decline in output and rise in unemployment. They also narrow the ability of governments to respond to cyclical economic problems. The economic literature on capital flows cites five fears that drive countries to adopt capital controls:

Fear of appreciation: Massive and rapid capital inflows may cause the country's currency to become stronger (increase in value relative to other currencies), making its exports more expensive and damaging its international competitiveness.

Fear of "hot money": Short-term speculative capital inflows may cause financial instability and increase the fragility of the domestic financial system. The short-term nature of these flows leads to a "maturity mismatch" between domestic financial institutions' assets and liabilities. In effect, they have borrowed short-term while lending long-term. As the sudden reversal of hot money occurs at the whim of international investor sentiments, a domestic banking crisis is likely to follow.

Fear of large inflows that can disrupt the financial system, even if they are not all "hot money": Large inflows of foreign capital may feed asset bubbles, such as unsustainable increases in stock or real-estate prices or unsustainable booms in consumer credit.

Fear of loss of monetary autonomy: It is not possible for a country to achieve (simultaneously) full international capital mobility, monetary-policy autonomy, and exchange-rate stability. (This is known as the "trilemma" of international macroeconomics.) If a country does not control international capital flows, inflows can cause exchange-rate appreciation. The government can counteract this by increasing the money supply, but then its monetary policy is not independent. To avoid exchange-rate appreciation and sustain an independent monetary policy, a country should give up full capital mobility.

Fear of capital flight: In the event of a crisis, "herding" behavior by international investors may expose a country to the risk of sharp reversals in capital flows (with capital leaving just as quickly as it came).

What Happened During the Crisis?

Between 2002 and 2007, there were massive flows of capital into emerging markets with high growth rates and relatively developed financial systems. This surge in capital inflows was interrupted after the collapse of the U.S. investment house Lehman Brothers in September 2008, which led global capital to flee to the "safety" of the U.S. market, wreaking havoc in emerging markets. (See figure.) While there was no comparable financial crisis in these economies, more than half of them experienced negative growth in 2009. Countries with already-large trade deficits were among the hardest hit, as they were highly dependent on capital inflows.

Between 2008 and 2011, however, the governments of the industrialized countries lowered interest rates in an attempt to stimulate production and employment. Capital again began to flow into emerging markets, attracted by higher interest rates and growth. The "carry trade" was a key mechanism that triggered these flows. In the carry trade, investors borrow money in one country at a low interest rate and invest it in another country at a higher rate. This strategy allows investors not only to exploit the differences in interest rates, but also take advantage of exchange-rate movements. If the currency of the country with higher interest rates becomes stronger, over time, relative to the currency of the country with lower interest rates, investors stand to make even larger profits.

By late 2008, government policymakers in emerging economies had become alarmed about the problems these inflows could cause—currency appreciation, asset bubbles, inflation, and the sudden turn toward large outflows. From March 2009 to March 2010, Brazil saw the value of the real go up by 30% against the dollar, due at least in part to the carry trade. Under normal circumstances, the conventional macroeconomic tool to stem asset bubbles or inflation would have been an increase in interest rates. By increasing interest rates, monetary authorities would have curbed the appetite to borrow and reduced the amount of money available for spending in the economy. With less spending, the economy would slow down and inflation would decline. However, because of the carry trade, such a policy could actually fuel further inflows and therefore exacerbate these problems. For example, in 2009, interest rates were around 12% in Brazil and less than 1% in the United States; if Brazil had raised interest rates in an attempt to curb asset bubbles and inflation, it could actually have attracted even higher capital inflows.

**NET PORTFOLIO INVESTMENT—EQUITY,
THREE DEVELOPING REGIONS**

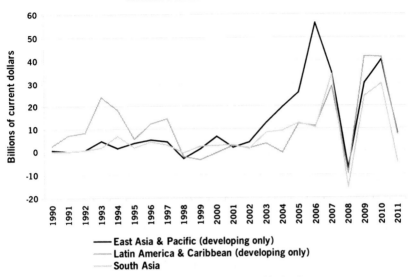

—— East Asia & Pacific (developing only)
········· Latin America & Caribbean (developing only)
········· South Asia

Source: World Bank, Data, Portfolio equity, net inflows (BoP, current US$), (data.worldbank.org)

The Brazilian government was the most vocal critic of these capital flows at the G-20's 2010 summit in Seoul. The Brazilian finance minister declared the surge in capital flows, the subsequent exchange-rate appreciations, and the various policy responses by emerging countries to be the beginning of a "currency war." In late 2009, the Brazilian government imposed a 2% tax on various forms of capital inflows. In October 2010, it twice increased the tax rate, first to 4% and then to 6%. In January 2011, Brazil introduced new reserve requirements on capital inflows (see sidebar) to curb the appreciation of the real against the dollar.

In 2009, nations across Asia also began to deploy controls, having seen large appreciations of their currencies. Between the end of 2008 and early 2010, South Korea's currency (the won) appreciated by over 30% against the dollar. Starting in July 2010, South Korean banks faced new restrictions on their international currency holdings. The South Korean government also tried to steer investment away from speculation by permitting bank loans in foreign currencies only for the purchase of raw materials, for foreign direct investment, and for repayment of debts. Meanwhile, in November 2009, the government of Taiwan banned foreign investment funds from investing in certificates of deposit with domestic banks, a move aimed at preventing foreign investors from betting on currency appreciation. At the end of 2010, it also placed restrictions on banks' holdings of foreign currencies. In 2010, Thailand introduced a 15% tax on interest income and capital gains earned by foreign investors. Meanwhile, Indonesia placed limits on short-term external borrowing and introduced a one-month minimum holding period for foreign investors purchasing some types of government-issued securities.

It is still too early to draw final conclusions about the effectiveness of these controls. A study by Kevin Gallagher of the Global Development and Environment Institute (GDAE) provides a preliminary assessment for the cases of Brazil, Taiwan, and South Korea. All three were trying to create a space for independent monetary policy and stem the appreciation of their currencies by placing restrictions on capital mobility. Interest rates between the United States and each of these nations have become less correlated. (A strong correlation between interest rates may indicate that, when the U.S. Fed lowers interest rates, causing capital flows to these other countries, the latter are forced to respond with lower interest rates of their own to stem the appreciation of the currency.

How to Impose Capital Controls?

The particular form of capital controls that a government imposes depends on its policy goals. If its main goal is to slow down capital inflows, the types of regulations that it can choose from include:

- Unremunerated reserve requirements: A certain percentage of new capital inflows must be kept on reserve in the country's central bank. "Unremunerated" in this context refers to the fact that no interest would be earned on these funds.
- Taxes on new inflows.
- Limits or taxes on how much domestic banks and other financial institutions can owe in foreign currencies.
- Restrictions on currency mismatches: Borrowing and lending activities of domestic banks or firms should be denominated in the same currency. For example, only firms with foreign-exchange revenues from exports can borrow in foreign currencies.
- Limitations on borrowing abroad: For example, such borrowing may be allowed only for foreign investment and trade activities, or only for firms with positive net revenues in a foreign currency (as from exports).
- Mandatory government approvals for some or all international capital transactions.
- Minimum stay requirements: Foreign investors might be required to stay in the domestic economy for at least a certain length of time.

On the other hand, different measures are available to a country that wants to focus on preventing or slowing down outflows of capital, including:

- Mandatory government approval for domestic residents to invest abroad or hold bank accounts in a foreign currency.
- Requirements for domestic residents to report on foreign investments and transactions done with foreign bank accounts.
- Limits on sectors in which foreign individuals and companies can invest.
- Restrictions on amounts of principal or capital income that foreign investors can send abroad.
- Limits on how much non-residents can borrow in the domestic market.
- Taxes on capital outflows.

In addition to the distinction between controls imposed on outflows or inflows, measures are usually categorized as "price-based" or "quantity-based," depending on the mechanism through which they impact capital flows. Minimum stay requirements, for example, are one kind of quantity-based control. Taxes on inflows or on outflows are one kind of price-based control.

That is, they lack monetary independence.) So these findings suggest that the controls have, to some extent, allowed a more autonomous monetary policy.

In the cases of Brazil and Taiwan, there is some evidence that controls have been associated with a slower rate of currency appreciation. But in the case of South Korea, currency appreciation has continued and the rate of appreciation has actually increased since controls were initiated. This difference can be explained by the structural differences across these countries, as well as the different types of controls used. South Korea's strong export performance is an important factor putting upward pressure on the value of its currency. (Demand for a country's exports is one factor determining the demand for its currency, since that country's companies usually require payment in the national currency.) Moreover, unlike Brazil and Taiwan, South Korean authorities did not use any of the "price-based controls" (see sidebar) that would have automatically placed additional costs on international investors seeking to enter Korean markets. These differences in effectiveness can shed some light on what kinds of capital controls might work in different countries, given their unique conditions.

The IMF and Capital Controls

Not long after developing-country governments began implementing capital controls, official views about controls began to shift. Since 2010, the IMF has produced a series of official papers on capital-account liberalization, on capital inflows and outflows, and on the multilateral aspects of regulating international capital flows. In November 2012, it released a comprehensive "institutional view" on when and how nations should deploy capital-account regulations. The same institution that pushed for the global deregulation of cross-border finance in the 1990s now says that capital-account liberalization is more of a long-run goal, and is not for every country at all times. The IMF now accepts that capital controls—which it has renamed "capital-flow management measures"—are permissible for inflows, on a temporary basis, en route to liberalization; regulations on capital outflows, meanwhile, are permissible only during or just after financial crises.

While more flexible than its previous stances, the new IMF position still insists on the eventual deregulation of global financial flows and emphasizes that controls should only be temporary. Behind this insistence lies the institution's ideological commitment to free markets, as well as the influence of finance capital and Wall Street interests on the institution's decision making. As the experience of developing economies in the recent crisis bears out, rather than being treated as temporary measures, capital controls should be adopted as permanent tools that can be used counter-cyclically—to smooth out economic booms and busts. As described earlier, international capital flows are strongly pro-cyclical. By regulating inflows during a boom, a government can manage booms better, while avoiding exchange-rate problems or additional inflationary pressures. By restricting outflows during a downturn, it can mitigate capital flight, which has the potential of triggering financial crisis, and create some room for expansionary monetary policy.

The IMF guidelines, in addition, give scant attention to policy-design issues related to capital controls. A great deal of international experience shows that controls can lose their effectiveness over time, as foreign investors learn to evade regulation through the use of financial derivatives and other securities. Nations such as Brazil and South Korea have increasingly "fine-tuned" their regulations in an attempt to keep ahead of investors' ability to circumvent them.

The IMF also fails to acknowledge that capital flows should be regulated at "both ends." The industrialized nations are usually the source of international capital flows, but generally ignore the negative spillover effects on other countries. So far, the entire burden of regulation has fallen on the recipients of inflows, mostly developing countries.

Where to Now?

As industrialized nations aim to recover from the crisis, they hope that credit and capital will stay "at home." Meanwhile, the developing world has little interest in having to receive capital inflows. This creates an obvious alignment of interests. Industrialized nations could adjust their tax codes and deploy other types of regulation to keep capital in their countries, as emerging markets deploy capital controls to reduce the level and change the composition of capital flows that may destabilize their economies.

One important obstacle to such coordination is the prohibition, in many trade and investment treaties, on regulation of cross-border finance. For example, in Asia, where capital controls are most prevalent, the Association of South East Asian Nations (ASEAN) requires member countries to eliminate most controls by 2015, with relatively narrow exceptions. Trade and investment agreements with the United States, such as the North American Free Trade Agreement (NAFTA) and the Dominican Republic-Central America Free Trade Agreement (CAFTA-DR), provide the least flexibility. Since the 2003 U.S.-Chile Free Trade Agreement, every U.S. trade or investment agreement has required the free flow of capital (in both directions) between the United States and its trading partners, without exception.

In January 2011, some 250 economists from across the globe called on the United States to recognize that the consensus on capital controls has shifted and to permit nations the flexibility to deploy controls to prevent and mitigate crises. The appeal was rebuffed by prominent U.S. business associations and the U.S. government. Treasury Secretary Timothy Geithner declared that U.S. policy would remain unchanged: "In general, we believe that those risks are best managed through a mix of fiscal and monetary policy measures, exchange rate adjustment, and carefully designed non-discriminatory prudential measures, such as bank reserve or capital requirements and limitations on exposure to exchange rate risk." In other words, he suggested the use of mainly conventional domestic macroeconomic policies and some domestic financial regulation, but excluded controls on international flows.

With the exception of speculators who profit from volatility in the markets, all nations and actors within them would benefit from the financial stability that an international system of financial regulation could help provide. After the opening of capital markets in developing economies, in varying degrees, we have seen extreme volatility of international capital flows. This volatility has been exacerbated by the monetary policies of advanced economies: over the past 30 years expansionary monetary policy in advanced economies has led to capital flows to emerging-market economies, while contractionary policies have produced the reversal of capital flows and, in turn, helped set off the crises of the 1980s and 1990s. The stability provided by an international system of capital controls would not only allow emerging economies to preserve their own growth and stability but also improve the effectiveness of policies in advanced economies.

Some financial interests, however, would have to bear the costs. Capital controls would either make financial transactions more costly, reducing profit margins, or not allow financial companies to take advantage of certain investment opportunities, again reducing potential profits to investors. These "losers" from a capital-controls regime are highly concentrated and very powerful politically. The "winners," in terms of the general public, are comparatively scattered and weaker politically. Despite the optimism that briefly emerged, especially in policy circles, about a future with more effective regulation of international capital flows, these political realities may be the biggest obstacles for 21st-century capital controls. ❏

Sources: Kevin Gallagher, "Regaining Control? Capital Controls and the Global Financial Crisis," Political Economy Research Institute, Working Paper 250, 2011; Stephany Griffith-Jones and Kevin P. Gallagher, "Curbing Hot Money Flows to Protect the Real Economy," *Economic and Political Weekly,* Jan. 15, 2011, Vol. XLVI, No 3; Ilene Grabel, "Not Your Grandfather's IMF: Global Crisis, Productive Incoherence, and Developmental Policy Space," Political Economy Research Institute, Working Paper 214, 2010; International Monetary Fund, The Liberalization And Management Of Capital Flows: An Institutional View, Washington, D.C., 2011.

Article 11.3

EQUAL TREATMENT FOR IMMIGRANTS

BY ALEJANDRO REUSS

July 2013; Washington Spectator

In this age of mass migration, U.S. immigration policy has mixed relative openness to immigration (since 1965) with nativist hostility toward immigrants. On the state level, we have seen a wave of anti-immigrant legislation (like the Arizona "papers, please" law); on the federal level, the militarization of the U.S.-Mexico border coupled with spasms of workplace immigration raids. Recent reform proposals, including the bill passed by the Senate, have coupled "guest worker" provisions with still more military-police-prisons immigration enforcement. Nativist fantasies of walling off the United States, it is clear, are doomed to fail. Given the harm that such measures cause in both economic and human terms, moreover, it would be bad if they succeeded.

Immigration today is inextricably bound up with globalization. In fact, immigration *is* globalization. Just as surely as international trade, investment, and finance, the international movement of people connects different countries economically. The corporate-driven globalization under which we are living has helped drive mass immigration. First, the flood of agricultural imports from high-income countries has accelerated the decimation of small-farmer agriculture in low-income countries, and with it the exodus from rural areas. Second, imports of manufactured goods have also increased the allure of "first-world" lifestyles, and so created an additional spur to immigration from low-income to high-income countries.

Globalization in its current form, however, has been shaped by the wealthy and powerful to their own advantage. This is obvious when we compare the treatment of the international movement of capital to the international movement of people.

Under the guise of "equal treatment of investors in similar circumstances"—as put by the World Bank's *Guidelines on the Treatment of Foreign Direct Investment*—international trade-and-investment agreements have guaranteed corporations' ability to invest abroad without fear of unfavorable government intervention. A NAFTA tribunal, for example, notoriously decided against Mexico in a case where the Mexican government had blocked foreign investment in the form of a toxic-waste dump.

International agreements, in contrast, have varied dramatically in their treatment of international migration—the movement of people as opposed to the movement of capital. The European Union, for all its shortcomings, allows nearly unencumbered migration between member countries. NAFTA, on the other hand, has created a three-country zone where goods and capital can move with little restriction, but people face harsh barriers to migration.

The U.S.-Mexico border is one of the most militarized in the world—lined with razor-wire, armed patrols, and even drone aircraft—and undocumented immigrants live in constant peril of arrest and deportation. A recent article in *The Economist* paraphrases UC San Diego economist Gordon Hanson on the results of U.S. immigration policy: "inflicting economic self-harm by spending so much to keep workers out." The self-harm hardly compares to that inflicted on undocumented migrants themselves.

We can see the operation of unequal power here in three ways.

First, undocumented immigrants lack political power. In addition to being denied formal political rights, like the vote, their insecure status poses an additional obstacle to legal social protest. On the other hand, the increasing significance of Latinos as an electoral constituency is a political counterweight. Many Latinos rightly see attacks on "illegal immigration" as thinly veiled attacks on them, so immigrant-bashing politicians risk an electoral backlash. That's why some Republicans are talking immigration reform now.

Second, labor wields far less political influence than capital. It is employers, not labor, who have gotten what they wanted from trade-and-investment agreements (mainly the ability to locate operations where labor costs are low and government regulation lax). While organized labor has not always championed immigrants' rights, U.S. unions have turned more pro-immigrant in recent years, especially as they have come to see immigrant workers as crucial to their own futures.

Third, global corporations have powerful governments on their side. The U.S. government fights for agreements protecting the interests of U.S.-based companies. The governments of many lower-income countries advocate in favor of their nationals abroad, but they have less muscle on the international political scene. Unsurprisingly, their efforts have been less successful.

Today, discrimination on the basis of national origin is a central principle of immigration law. Even though U.S. labor laws, on their face, cover all workers regardless of immigration status, everyone knows this is a fiction because undocumented immigrants' precarious status keeps them from reporting violations to the authorities.

Imagine, instead, that the contours of political power were reversed. Instead of untrammeled freedom for globetrotting corporations, we would have guarantees for people of the right to move, live, and work where they wish. Instead of the "equal treatment" for global investors under trade-and-investment agreements, we would have equal treatment for workers, regardless of nationality, wherever they worked. That would be good not only for immigrants, but also for workers in general, by reducing labor-market competition and strengthening workers' overall bargaining power. As the late legal scholar Anna Christensen put it, in the context of Europe, "Equal treatment of foreign and domestic workers ... is no threat to the position of domestic labor. If anything, the reverse is true."

That is a far cry from the current situation. Indeed, it is a far cry from the Senate bill, which includes still more money for coercive enforcement measures, plus guest-worker provisions that would leave immigrant workers largely at the mercy of their employers.

Equal treatment, however, is the immigration reform we need. ❏

Article 11.4

ON STRIKE IN CHINA
A Chinese New Deal in the Making?

BY CHRIS TILLY AND MARIE KENNEDY
September/October 2010

> "[There will] never be a strike [at the Hyundai plant in Beijing]. Strikes in China would jeopardize the company's reputation."
> —*Zhang Zhixiong, deputy chairman of the union at that plant, 2003*

> "About 1,000 workers at Hyundai's auto parts factory [in Beijing] staged a two-day strike and demanded wage increases."
> —*China Daily/Asia News Network, June 4, 2010*

Workers in China are on the move. The media initially fixed on the downward trajectory of desperate workers jumping from the roofs of Foxconn, the enormous electronics manufacturer that assembles the iPhone and numerous other familiar gadgets, but soon shifted to the upward arc of strike activity concentrated in the supply chains of Honda and Toyota.

But the auto-sector strikes in China's industrialized Southeast, as well as in the northeastern city of Tianjin, are just the tip of the iceberg. June strikes also pulled out thousands of workers at Brother sewing machine factories and a Carlsberg brewery in the central part of the country; machinery, LCD, and rubber parts plants in the east-central Shanghai area; a shoe manufacturer further inland in Jiujiang; and apparel and electronics workers outside the auto sector in the Southeast and Tianjin. "There are fifteen factories launching strikes now," Qiao Jian of the Chinese Institute of Industrial Relations (CIIR) told us in mid-June. Since that time, still more strikes have been reported, and many others are likely going unreported by Chinese media, which despite their growing independence remain sensitive to government pressure. None of the strikes had approval by the All China Federation of Trade Unions (ACFTU), the only labor movement authorized by Chinese law.

This explosion of wildcat walkouts prompts several questions. Why did it happen? What do the strikes mean for China's low-wage, low-cost manufacturing model? Equally important, what do they imply for China's party- and state-dominated labor relations? China's labor relations scholars—an outspoken bunch—are animatedly discussing that last question in public and in private.

What Happened and Why

The spark for the recent strike wave was the May 17th walkout of hundreds of workers from a Honda transmission plant in Nanhai, near Guangzhou in the Southeast.

According to research by Wang Kan of CIIR, the strike was an accident: two employees embroiled in a dispute with Honda consulted a lawyer who advised them to threaten a strike as a bluff and even drew up a set of demands for them. They apparently were as shocked as anyone when workers spontaneously walked out. Accident or not, the workers demanded a 67% raise. Two weeks later, they agreed to return to work with a 42% wage increase. By that time, copycat strikes had erupted at other Honda suppliers in the Southeast and at Hyundai; workers at Toyota suppliers soon followed suit, as did employees from other sectors and regions. Most of these actions won wage settlements in the twenty-percent range.

Why did this strike wave happen now? The first thing to understand is that strikes in China did not begin in 2010. As Berkeley doctoral student Eli Friedman points out, "the number of strikes and officially mediated labor disputes in China [has] been increasing rapidly for at least fifteen years." So-called "mass incidents," of which experts estimate about a third to be strikes, numbered 87,000 in 2005, and were unofficially pegged at 120,000 in 2008. Mediated labor disputes, many of which only involve an individual, have grown even faster, rising in round figures from 19,000 in 1994 to 135,000 in 2000, 350,000 in 2007, and 700,000 in 2008. The huge increase in 2008 is due at least in part to new laws on labor contracts and labor mediation passed that year that bolster workers' ability to bring complaints.

Still, "the Honda strike marks a turning point," in the words of law professor Liu Cheng of Shanghai Normal University. "Previous strikes were mainly about enforcing labor law. This is the first successful strike about collective bargaining." Anita Chan, a labor researcher at the University of Technology in Sydney, agrees, saying the current strikers "are negotiating for their interests and not for their rights—it's a very different set of stakes." The Nanhai Honda action was also a breakthrough in that for the first time strikers demanded the right to elect their own union representatives—a demand to which the provincial union federation has agreed, though the election has not yet taken place. Many subsequent strikes reiterated this demand, although they have focused more on economic issues. Even the economic demands extend beyond wages: at Honda Lock, strikers demanded noise reduction measures to improve the work environment.

The long-term growth in strike activity owes much to demographic changes. Predominantly women, China's industrial workers hail overwhelmingly from the ranks of rural migrants, 140 million of whom live and work in the cities but lack long-term permission to stay there or receive social benefits there. When Deng Xiaoping's market liberalization first spurred rapid industrial growth in the 1980s, migrants were willing to "eat bitterness," enduring hardships and low wages to send remittances home to families who were worse off than they. This stoic attitude and decades of policies aimed at growth at almost any cost are reflected in the decline of labor's share of total national income from 57% in 1983 to 37% in 2005. Unpaid or underpaid overtime and only one or two days off a month—violations of Chinese law—became common in China's manufacturing sector.

But the new generation of migrants, reared in a time of relative prosperity and comparing themselves to their peers in the cities, expect more. "Our demands are higher because we have higher material and spiritual needs," a young Honda striker who identified himself only as Chen told Agence France-Presse. "Our strike demands are based on our need to maintain our living standards." With urban housing costs soaring, this has become a pressing issue. "I dream of one day buying a car or apartment," said Zhang, a 22-year-old man working at the same plant, "but with the salary I'm making now, I will never succeed."

Another long-run factor is the government's new willingness to tolerate strikes as long as they stay within bounds, in contrast to the harsh repression meted out in the 1980s and early 1990s.

Still the "Workshop of the World"?

The current wave of strikes owes its energy, too, to the lopsided policies China's government adopted in response to the global economic crunch. "With the global financial crisis, the income gap and social disparities worsened," commented Qiao of the CIIR. Panicking at the fall-off in demand for Chinese exports, authorities froze the minimum wage in 2009 even as the cost of living continued its upward march. They also put hundreds of billions of dollars into loans to help exporters and allowed employers to defer their tax payments and social insurance contributions.

Perhaps most important for workers' quality of life, provincial and local governments relaxed their enforcement of labor regulations—at a time when examples of hard-pressed businesses closing down and cheating workers out of months of back pay were becoming increasingly common. In Foshan, a government official declared in 2009 that employers violating the Labor Contract Law protecting basic worker rights would "not be fined, and will not have their operating licenses revoked." A year later, Honda workers in the city walked off the job.

But the business-friendly, worker-unfriendly government response to the crisis does not explain why autoworkers went out. "I don't know why the Honda workers went on strike, because their salaries and conditions are better than ours," Chen Jian, a 24-year-old worker at Yontai Plastics, not far from the Nanhai Honda plant, said to the Guardian newspaper. "We are not satisfied, but we will not go on strike. Some workers tried that last year and they were all fired. That is normal."

Despite Chen's puzzlement, his comments touch on the reason autoworkers led the way: power rooted in the specifics of the auto production process. Autoworkers wield a degree of skill that makes them more difficult to replace. Assembly line technology within the plant, and a division of labor that often locates fabrication of a particular part in a single plant, make it possible for a small number of strategically located workers to shut down the whole production process, a fact exploited by autoworkers around the world going back to the Flint sit-down strike in 1937. And Japanese-initiated just-in-time techniques have cut down inventories, speeding up the impact of strikes. Friedman reports that by the fourth day of the Nanhai strike, work at all four Honda assembly plants in China had ground to a halt due to lack of transmissions.

Pundits have speculated on whether the Chinese workforce's new demands will upend China's export machine. Andy Xie, a Hong Kong-based economist and business analyst formerly with Morgan Stanley, remarks, "To put it bluntly, the key competence of a successful [manufacturer] in China is to squeeze labor to the maximum extent possible." But in fact, Chinese manufacturing wages had already begun rising significantly in the years before the crisis—in part because of earlier strikes and protests. Some companies had already begun relocating work to Vietnam or Bangladesh. Most observers, including Xie, expect incremental adjustment by businesses, not a stampede. Limited worker demands could even play into the Chinese government's goal of increasing productivity and shifting into higher value-added manufacturing, as well as expanding the buying power of Chinese consumers. But as James Pomfret and Kelvin Soh of Reuters write, China's Communist Party "has faced a policy tightrope. It must also ensure that strikes don't proliferate and scare investors or ignite broader confrontation that erodes Party rule."

"Taking the Same Boat Together to Protect Growth"

Where was the All China Federation of Trade Unions as the working class rose up? Friedman points out that though ACFTU leaders were concerned about defending worker interests in the crisis, they were equally concerned with defending employers' interests. The result was what the ACFTU called "mutually agreed upon actions," which combined promises to desist from job actions with what Friedman describes as "weakly worded requests for employers." "Taking the same boat together to protect growth," a joint March 2009 release by government, unions, and the employer association in Guangdong, was typical, imploring businesses to "work hard" to avoid layoffs and wage cuts—an appeal that seems to have had little real impact on employers.

This ACFTU stance grows directly out of the federation's longstanding focus on "harmonious enterprises," which is rooted in the unions' historic role in state enterprises. "Each trade union is under the control of the local Party branch," Lin Yanling of the CIIR told us. "So, Party, company, and union leadership are often the same." Indeed, the ACFTU typically invites companies to name their union officials; as a result, middle managers often hold those posts. Along the same lines, Shanghai Normal's Liu Cheng stated, "These company unions don't work. They have nothing to do but entertainment. In the summer, they buy watermelon for the workers to celebrate the festivals." Lin Yanling concluded, "Now is the time to change trade unions in China!"

Recommendations for change circulating within China vary widely. "Some local trade union leaders say to reform the trade union, you must sever the relation between the trade union and the local Party branch," said Lin. "If the local union would only listen to upper trade union officials, the problem could be solved." Local state and Party representatives are particularly closely tied to the local businesses, whereas the national officialdom has more often advocated for workers' interests, for example through the new 2008 labor laws. He Zengke, executive director of the Center for Comparative Politics and Economics, expressed support for shifting control to the national level: "Local government has historically supported business, but the [Party Secretary] Hu government is now asking them to pursue a balanced policy—also pro-people, pro-poor."

But Lin is skeptical of this limited fix, arguing that "if you want the unions to change, you need the workers to elect the trade union chairperson." Liu Cheng agrees, but also advocates for unions to have the right to litigate on behalf of workers. Liu argues it is premature to push for the right to strike, whereas Zheng Qiao of CIIR holds that this is a good opportunity to define that right. Qiao Jian of CIIR advocates democratizing unions within a revitalized tripartite (union federation/employer association/government) system, but his colleague Lin insists, "That system will not function," because the unions don't yet have enough independence within the triad to adequately represent workers. The disagreements are passionate, if good-humored, since these scholars see the future of their country at stake.

Western observers, and some Hong Kong-based worker-rights groups, have gone farther to call for the right for workers to form their own independent unions— what the International Labor Organization calls "freedom of association." But labor relations experts within mainland China, and the strikers themselves, have so far steered clear of such radical proposals. Liu Cheng commented, "Without reform of the unions, I think freedom of association would result in disorder, and destroy the process of evolution. I don't like revolution—with most revolutions, there is no real progress, just a change of emperors." However, he did express the view that as the Chinese labor movement matures, it will reach a point when freedom of association will be possible and desirable.

"If People Are Oppressed, They Must Rebel"

But will the unions change—and will the Party and state let them? The question is complicated by the conflicting currents within the union federation itself and within China's official ideology. The same Party that promotes "harmonious enterprises" also enshrines Mao Zedong's dictum, "It's right to rebel." So perhaps it's not surprising that Li, a young striker at Honda's exhaust plant, told Agence France-Presse, "Safeguarding your own rights is always legitimate … . If people are oppressed they must rebel. This is only natural."

ACFTU responses to date, reported by Friedman and labor activist and blogger Paul Garver, reflect this mixed consciousness. At the Nanhai Honda strike that inaugurated the current wave, the local ACFTU leadership sent a group of 100 people with union hats and armbands to persuade the strikers to stand down. Whether by design or not, the conversation degenerated into a physical confrontation in which some strikers were injured, none severely. On the other hand, provincial-level union leaders then agreed to the strikers' demands to elect their own representatives. The top two Guangdong ACFTU officials, Deng Weilong and Kong Xianghong, subsequently spoke out in favor of the right to strike and pledged to replace current management-appointed officials with worker-elected ones.

When workers at the Denso (Nansha) car-parts factory in Guangzhou (also in Guangdong province) later went on strike, the local union response was different from that in Nanhai. The municipal union federation publicly supported the strikers, refusing to mediate between labor and management. There have even been signs of life from unions in other sectors: about a month after the Nanhai strike, the municipal union federation in Shenyang, in the far northeast of the country, hammered out the nation's first collective bargaining contract with KFC (whose fast-food restaurants blanket China), including a wage increase of nearly 30%.

On the government side, authorities in many provinces have responded to the strike wave with a wave of minimum-wage hikes. Premier Wen Jiabao declared in a June address to migrant workers, "Your work is a glorious thing, and it should be respected by society," and in August told the Japanese government that its companies operating in China should raise wages. Acknowledging that "a wide range of social conflicts have occurred recently," Zhou Yongkang, another top Party official, stated, "Improving people's livelihoods should be the starting and end point of all our work." In August, BusinessWeek reported that Guangdong's state legislature was discussing a law formalizing collective bargaining, empowering workers to elect local representatives, and even recognizing the right to strike—particularly noteworthy since Guangdong is China's industrial heartland. Still, pro-worker rhetoric is nothing new, the Guangdong provincial union federation is more progressive and powerful than most, and right around the time of Wen's June speech the Chinese government shut down a website calling for ACFTU democratization.

Amidst these cross-currents, China's labor relations scholars, aware that their own role is "marginal," as one of them put it, remain cautiously optimistic. "I think the situation will lead to union reform," said the CIIR's Zheng Qiao. When asked how activists in the United States can support the Chinese workers, her colleague Lin suggested, "Ask the big American brands to give a larger percentage back to the workers at their suppliers!" At Shanghai Normal, Liu Cheng reasoned through the prospects for change. "If the ACFTU does not do more, there will be more and more independent strikes, and in the end some kind of independent union. So the ACFTU will be scared, and the party will be angry with the ACFTU."

"So," Liu Cheng concluded, "the strike wave is a very good thing." ❑

Sources: Eli Friedman, "Getting through hard times together? Worker insurgency and Chinese unions' response to the economic crisis," paper presented at the International Sociological Association annual conference, Gothenburg, Sweden, July 2010; LabourStart page on China labor news, www.labourstart.org; James Pomfret and Kelvin Soh, "Special Report: China's new migrant workers pushing the line," Reuters, July 5, 2010; "The right to strike may be coming to China," *Bloomberg Businessweek*, August 5, 2010; ITUC/GUF Hong Kong Liaison Office, "A political economic analysis of the strike in Honda and the auto parts industry in China," July 2010.

Article 11.5

KEEP IT IN THE GROUND

An alternative vision for petroleum emerges in Ecuador. But will Big Oil win the day?

BY ELISSA DENNIS
July/August 2010; Updated October 2013

In the far eastern reaches of Ecuador, in the Amazon basin rain forest, lies a land of incredible beauty and biological diversity. More than 2,200 varieties of trees reach for the sky, providing a habitat for more species of birds, bats, insects, frogs, and fish than can be found almost anywhere else in the world. Indigenous Waorani people have made the land their home for millennia, including the last two tribes living in voluntary isolation in the country. The land was established as Yasuní National Park in 1979, and recognized as a UNESCO World Biosphere Reserve in 1989.

Underneath this landscape lies a different type of natural resource: petroleum. Since 1972, oil has been Ecuador's primary export, representing 57% of the country's exports in 2008; oil revenues comprised on average 26% of the government's revenue between 2000 and 2007. More than 1.1 billion barrels of heavy crude oil have been extracted from Yasuní, about one quarter of the nation's production to date.

At this economic, environmental, and political intersection lie two distinct visions for Yasuní's, and Ecuador's, next 25 years. Petroecuador, the state-owned oil company, has concluded that 846 million barrels of oil could be extracted from proven reserves at the Ishpingo, Tambococha, and Tiputini (ITT) wells in an approximately 200,000-hectare area covering about 20% of the parkland. Extracting this petroleum, either alone or in partnership with interested oil companies in Brazil, Venezuela, or China, would generate approximately $7 billion, primarily in the first 13 years of extraction and continuing with declining productivity for another 12 years.

The alternative vision is the simple but profound choice to leave the oil in the ground. Environmentalists and indigenous communities have been organizing for years to restrict drilling in Yasuní. But the vision became much more real when President Rafael Correa presented a challenge to the world community at a September 24, 2007 meeting of the United Nations General Assembly: If governments, companies, international organizations, and individuals pledge a total of $350 million per year for 10 years, equal to half of the forgone revenues from ITT, then Ecuador will chip in the other half and keep the oil underground indefinitely, as this nation's contribution to halting global climate change.

The Yasuní-ITT Initiative would preserve the fragile environment, leave the voluntarily isolated tribes in peace, and prevent the emission of an estimated 407 million metric tons of carbon dioxide into the atmosphere. This "big idea from a small country" has even broader implications, as Alberto Acosta, former Energy Minister and one of the architects of the proposal, notes in his new book, *La Maldición de la Abundancia (The Curse of Abundance)*. The Initiative is a "punto de ruptura," he writes, a turning point in environmental history which "questions the logic of extractive (exporter of raw material) development," while introducing the possibility of global *"sumak kawsay,"* the indigenous Kichwa concept of "good living" in harmony with nature.

Sumak kawsay is the underlying tenet of the country's 2008 Constitution, which guarantees rights for indigenous tribes and for "Mother Earth." The Constitution was overwhelmingly supported in a national referendum, but putting the document's principles into action has been a bigger challenge. While Correa draws praise for his progressive social programs, for example in education and health care, the University of Illinois-trained economist is criticized for not yet having wrested control of the nation's economy from a deep-rooted powerful elite bearing different ideas about the meaning of "good living." Within this political and economic discord lies the fate of the Yasuni Initiative.

An Abundance of Oil

Ecuador, like much of Latin America, has long been an exporter of raw materials: cacao in the 19th century, bananas in the 20th century, and now petroleum. Shell discovered the heavy, viscous oil of Ecuador's Amazon basin in 1948. In the 1950s, a series of controversial encounters began between the native Waorani people and U.S. missionaries from the Summer Institute of Linguistics (SIL). With SIL assistance, Waorani were corralled into a 16,000-hectare "protectorate" in the late 1960s, and many went to work for the oil companies who were furiously drilling through much of the tribe's homeland.

The nation dove into the oil boom of the 1970s, investing in infrastructure and building up external debt. When oil prices plummeted in the 1980s while interest rates on that debt ballooned, Ecuador was trapped in the debt crisis that affected much of the region. Thus began what Correa calls "the long night of neoliberalism": IMF-mandated privatizations of utilities and mining sectors, with a concomitant decline of revenues from the nation's natural resources to the Ecuadorian people. By 1986, all of the nation's petroleum revenues were going to pay external debt.

After another decade of IMF-driven privatizations, oil price drops, earthquakes, and other natural disasters, the Ecuadorian economy fell into total collapse, leading to the 2000 dollarization. Since then, more than one million Ecuadorians have left the country, mostly for the United States and Spain, and remittances from 2.5 million Ecuadorians living in the exterior, estimated at $4 billion in 2008, have become the nation's second highest source of income.

Close to 40 years of oil production has failed to improve the living standards of the majority of Ecuadorians. "Petroleum has not helped this country," notes Ana Cecilia Salazar, director of the Department of Social Sciences in the College of Economics of the University of Cuenca. "It has been corrupt. It has not diminished poverty. It has not industrialized this country. It has just made a few people rich."

Currently 38% of the population lives in poverty, with 13% in extreme poverty. The nation's per capita income growth between 1982 and 2007 was only 0.7% per year. And although the unemployment rate of 10% may seem moderate, an estimated 53% of the population is considered "underemployed."

Petroleum extraction has brought significant environmental damage. Each year 198,000 hectares of land in the Amazon are deforested for oil production. A verdict is expected this year in an Ecuadorian court in the 17-year-old class action suit brought by 30,000 victims of Texaco/Chevron's drilling operations in the area northwest of Yasuní between 1964 and 1990. The unprecedented $27 billion lawsuit alleges that thousands of cancers and other health problems were caused by Texaco's use of outdated and dangerous practices, including the dumping of 18 billion gallons of toxic wastewater into local water supplies.

Regardless of its economic or environmental impacts, the oil is running out. With 4.16 billion barrels in proven reserves nationwide, and another half billion "probable" barrels, best-case projections, including the discovery of new reserves, indicate the nation will stop exporting oil within 28 years, and stop producing oil within 35 years.

"At this moment we have an opportunity to rethink the extractive economy that for many years has constrained the economy and politics in the country," says Esperanza Martinez, a biologist, environmental activist, and author of the book *Yasuní: El tortuoso camino de Kioto a Quito (Yasuní: The Tortuous Road from Kyoto to Quito)*. "This proposal intends to change the terms of the North-South relationship in climate change negotiations."

Collecting on Ecological Debt

The Initiative fits into the emerging idea of "climate debt." The North's voracious energy consumption in the past has destroyed natural resources in the South; the South is currently bearing the brunt of global warming effects like floods and drought; and the South needs to adapt expensive new energy technology for the future instead of industrializing with the cheap fossil fuels that built the North. Bolivian president Evo Morales proposed at the Copenhagen climate talks last December that developed nations pay 1% of GDP, totaling $700 billion/year, into a compensation fund that poor nations could use to adapt their energy systems.

"Clearly in the future, it will not be possible to extract all the petroleum in the world because that would create a very serious world problem, so we need to create measures of compensation to pay the ecological debt to the countries," says Malki Sáenz, formerly Coordinator of the Yasuní-ITT Initiative within the Ministry of Foreign Relations. The Initiative "is a way to show the international community that real compensation mechanisms exist for not extracting petroleum."

Indigenous and environmental movements in Latin America and Africa are raising possibilities of leaving oil in the ground elsewhere. But the Yasuní-ITT proposal is the furthest along in detail, government sponsorship, and ongoing negotiations. The Initiative proposes that governments, international institutions, civil associations, companies, and individuals contribute to a fund administered through an international organization such as the United Nations Development Program (UNDP). Contributions could include swaps of Ecuador's external debt, as well as resources generated from emissions auctions in the European Union and carbon emission taxes such as those implemented in Sweden and Slovakia.

Contributors of at least $10,000 would receive a Yasuní Guarantee Certificate (CGY), redeemable only in the event that a future government decides to extract the oil. The total dollar value of the CGYs issued would equal the calculated value of the 407 million metric tons of non-emitted carbon dioxide.

The money would be invested in fixed income shares of renewable energy projects with a guaranteed yield, such as hydroelectric, geothermal, wind, and solar power, thus helping to reduce the country's dependence on fossil fuels. The interest payments generated by these investments would be designated for: 1) conservation projects, preventing deforestation of almost 10 million hectares in 40 protected areas covering 38% of Ecuador's territory; 2) reforestation and natural regeneration projects on another one million hectares of forest land; 3) national energy efficiency improvements; and 4) education, health, employment, and training programs in sustainable activities like ecotourism and agro forestry in the affected areas. The first three activities could prevent an additional 820 million metric tons of carbon dioxide emissions, tripling the Initiative's effectiveness.

Government Waffling

These nationwide conservation efforts, as well as the proposal's mention of "monitoring" throughout Yasuní and possibly shutting down existing oil production, are particularly disconcerting to Ecuadorian and international oil and wood interests. Many speculate that political pressure from these economic powerhouses was behind a major blow to the Initiative this past January, when Correa, in one of his regular Saturday radio broadcasts, suddenly blasted the negotiations as "shameful," and a threat to the nation's "sovereignty" and "dignity." He threatened that if the full package of international commitments is not in place by this June, he would begin extracting oil from ITT.

Correa's comments spurred the resignations of four critical members of the negotiating commission, including Chancellor Fander Falconí, a longtime ally in Correa's PAIS party, and Roque Sevilla, an ecologist, businessman, and ex-Mayor of Quito whom Correa had picked to lead the commission. Ecuador's Ambassador to the UN Francisco Carrion also resigned from the commission, as did World Wildlife Fund president Yolanda Kakabadse.

Correa has been clear from the outset that the government has a Plan B, to extract the oil, and that the non-extraction "first option" is contingent on the mandated monetary commitments. But oddly his outburst came as the negotiating team's efforts were bearing fruit. Sevilla told the press in January of commitments in various stages of approval from Germany, Spain, Belgium, France, and Switzerland, totaling at least $1.5 billion. The team was poised to sign an agreement with UNDP last December in Copenhagen to administer the fund. Correa called off the signing at the last minute, questioning the breadth of the Initiative's conservation efforts and UNDP's proposed six-person administrative body, three appointed by Ecuador, two by contributing nations, and one by UNDP. This joint control structure apparently sparked Correa's tirade about shame and dignity.

Correa's impulsivity and poor word choice have gotten him into trouble before. Acosta, another former key PAIS ally, resigned as president of the Constituent Assembly in June 2008, in the final stages of drafting the nation's new Constitution, when Correa set a vote deadline Acosta felt hindered the democratic process for this major undertaking. The President has had frequent tussles with indigenous and environmental organizations over mining issues, on several occasions crossing the line from staking out an economically pragmatic political position to name-calling of "childish ecologists."

Within a couple of weeks of the blowup, the government had backpedaled, withdrawing the June deadline, appointing a new negotiating team, and reasserting the position that the government's "first option" is to leave the oil in the ground. At the same time, Petroecuador began work on a new pipeline near Yasuní, part of the infrastructure needed for ITT production, pursuant to a 2007 Memorandum of Understanding with several foreign oil companies.

If the People Lead...

Amid the doubts and mixed messages, proponents are fighting to save the Initiative as a cornerstone in the creation of a post-petroleum Ecuador and ultimately a post-petroleum world. In media interviews after his resignation, Sevilla stressed that he would keep working to ensure that the Initiative would not fail. The Constitution provides for a public referendum prior to extracting oil from protected areas like Yasuní, he noted. "If the president doesn't want to assume his responsibility as leader...let's pass the responsibility to the public." In fact, 75% of respondents in a January poll in Quito and Guayaquil, the country's two largest cities, indicated that they would vote to not extract the ITT oil.

Martinez and Sáenz concur that just as the Initiative emerged from widespread organizing efforts, its success will come from the people. "This is the moment to define ourselves and develop an economic model not based on petroleum," Salazar says. "We have other knowledge, we have minerals, water. We need to change our consciousness and end the economic dependence on one resource." ❑

Resources: Live Yasuni, Finding Species, Inc. (liveyasuni.org); "S.O.S. Yasuni" (sosyasuni.org); "Yasuni-ITT: An Initiative to Change History," Government of Ecuador, (yasuni-itt.gov.ec).

Update

Declaring "the world has failed us," Ecuador's President Rafael Correa signaled the termination of the Yasuni ITT Initiative this past August. Citing a meager $116 million in pledges, he announced the decision to move forward with the Plan B that was always in the background: extraction of oil from the Ishpingo, Tambococha, and Tiputini fields in the eastern section of Yasuni National Park. The drilling will only impact 0.1% of the parklands, Correa contends, noting that the estimated value of oil in the targeted area has increased from $7 billion to $18 billion. Despite street demonstrations in Quito and Cuenca and calls for a national referendum, the National Assembly ratified Correa's action in October with legislation protecting indigenous communities and prohibiting drilling in an "untouchable zone" to be preserved as a wildlife sanctuary.

Correa, a U.S. trained economist, has consistently ridiculed "infantile" environmentalists, and is clearly most comfortable with a pragmatic economic development model of extractivism with equitable distribution of resources. Like his Bolivian counterpart Evo Morales, Correa has run afoul of indigenous communities and the environmental Left through efforts to transform the nation from exploited exporter of raw materials into savvy user of natural resources to fuel economic growth and social programs. Correa's critics say his government never wholeheartedly supported the Yasuni effort, and point to a growing Chinese political and economic influence. Since Correa's 2008 move to default on the nation's IMF debt, China has provided billions of dollars to Ecuador, with oil production pledged as repayment of some of that debt. China is also a key investor in Ecuador's oil industry, including links to ITT. —*Elissa Dennis*

CONTRIBUTORS

Frank Ackerman, a founder of *Dollars & Sense*, is a senior economist at Synapse Energy Economics in Cambridge, Mass. His extensive publications on economics and the environment are available at frankackerman.com.

David Bacon is a journalist and photographer covering labor, immigration, and the impact of the global economy on workers.

Dean Baker is an economist and co-director of the Center for Economic and Policy Research (www.cepr.net) in Washington, D.C.

Cornel Ban is an Assistant Professor of International Relations at Boston University.

Drucilla K. Barker is the Director of the Women's and Gender Studies Program at the University of South Carolina. She is co-author of *Liberating Economics: Feminist Perspectives on Families, Work, and Globalization.*

Tom Barry is a senior policy analyst and director of the TransBorder Project at the Center for International Policy in Washington, D.C.

Sarah Blaskey is a student at the University of Wisconsin-Madison and a member of the Student Labor Action Coalition.

Sasha Breger Bush is a lecturer at the Josef Korbel School of International Studies at the University of Denver and author of *Derivatives and Development* (Palgrave Macmillan, 2012).

Robin Broad is a Professor of International Development at the School of International Service, American University.

Roger Bybee is the former editor of the union weekly *Racine Labor* and is now a consultant and freelance writer whose work has appeared in *Z Magazine*, *The*

Progressive, Extra!, The Progressive Populist, In These Times, and other national publications and websites.

John Cavanagh is the Director of the Institute for Policy Studies in Washington, D.C.

James M. Cypher is a research professor in the doctoral program in development studies, Universidad Autónoma de Zacatecas (Mexico).

Elisa Dennis is a consultant to nonprofit affordable housing developers with Community Economics, Inc., in Oakland, Calif.

Maurice Dufour teaches political science at Marianopolis College in Montreal, Quebec.

Gerald Epstein is a professor of economics and a founding co-director of the Political Economy Research Institute (PERI) at the University of Massachusetts, Amherst.

Susan F. Feiner is professor of economics and women's studies at the University of Southern Maine. She is co-author of *Liberating Economics: Feminist Perspectives on Families, Work, and Globalization.*

Max Fraad Wolff teaches economics at the New School University graduate program in International Affairs.

Ellen Frank teaches economics at the University of Massachusetts-Boston and is a *Dollars & Sense* collective member. She is the author of *The Raw Deal: How Myths and Misinformation about Deficits, Inflation, and Wealth Impoverish America.*

Gerald Friedman is a professor of economics at the Univeristy of Massachusetts-Amherst.

Kevin Gallagher is an associate professor of International Relations at Boston University.

Heidi Garrett-Peltier is an assistant research professor at the Political Economy Research Institute at the University of Massachusetts, Amherst.

Phil Gasper teaches at Madison College and writes a column for *International Socialist Review.*

Armagan Gezici, co-editor of this volume, is an assistant professor of economics at Keene State College, Keene, N.H.

Robin Hahnel is a professor of economics at Portland State University in Portland, Ore.

Jim Hightower is a national radio commentator, writer, public speaker, and author of *Swim Against The Current: Even A Dead Fish Can Go With The Flow* (Wiley, 2008). He was twice elected Texas Agriculture Commissioner.

Sara Hsu is an assistant professor of economics at the State University of New York at New Paltz.

Marie Kennedy is professor emerita of Community Planning at the University of Massachusetts-Boston and visiting professor in Urban Planning at UCLA. She is a member of the board of directors of Grassroots International.

Arthur MacEwan, a founder of *Dollars & Sense*, is professor emeritus of economics at the University of Massachusetts-Boston and is a *D&S* Associate.

John Miller is a member of the *Dollars & Sense* collective and teaches economics at Wheaton College.

Anuradha Mittal is founder and director of the Oakland Institute in Oakland, Calif. She is an internationally renowned expert on trade, development, human rights, and agriculture issues.

William G. Moseley is a professor of geography at Macalester College in Saint Paul, Minn.

Immanuel Ness is a professor of political science at Brooklyn College-City University of New York. He is author of *Immigrants, Unions, and the New U.S. Labor Market* and editor of *WorkingUSA: The Journal of Labor and Society*.

Thomas Palley is an economist and the author of *Financialization: The Economics of Finance Capital Domination* (Palgrave Macmillan, 2013).

Robert Pollin teaches economics and is co-director of the Political Economy Research Institute at the University of Massachusetts-Amherst. He is also a *Dollars & Sense* Associate.

Smriti Rao teaches economics at Assumption College in Worcester, Mass., and is a member of the *Dollars & Sense* collective.

Alejandro Reuss is co-editor of *Dollars & Sense* and author of *Labor and the Global Economy* (Dollars & Sense, 2013).

Patricia M. Rodriguez is an assistant professor of politics at Ithaca College.

Peter Rosset is is a researcher at the Centro de Estudios para el Cambio en el Campo Mexicano (Center of Studies for Rural Change in Mexico), and co-coordinator of the Land Research Action Network. He is based in Oaxaca, Mexico.

Katherine Sciacchitano is a former labor lawyer and organizer. She teaches at the National Labor College in Silver Spring, Maryland, and as a freelance labor educator.

Dariush Sokolov has writen about and taught economics in Latin America. He now lives in London and is part of the Kaput anarchist economics collective (network23.org/kaput).

Chris Sturr is co-editor of *Dollars & Sense*.

Chris Tilly is director of the Institute for Research on Labor and Employment and professor of urban planning at UCLA and a *Dollars & Sense* Associate.

Marie Trigona is an independent journalist based in Buenos Aires. She is also a member of Grupo Alavío, a direct action and video collective.

Marjolein van der Veen is an economist. She has taught economics in Massachusetts, the Seattle area, and the Netherlands.

Ramaa Vasudevan is an assistant professor of economics at Colorado State University.

Mark Weisbrot is an economist and co-director of the Center for Economic and Policy Research (www.cepr.net) in Washington, D.C.